the hamlyn herb book

the hamlyn herb book

Arabella Boxer

photography by Sandra Lane
and Roger Stowell

Publishing Director: Laura Bamford

Senior Editor: Sasha Judelson

Editor: Barbara Horn

Art Director: Keith Martin

Senior Designer: Louise Leffler

Recipe Photographer: Sandra Lane
and pages 55 and 61

Herb Directory Photographer: Roger Stowell

Home Economist: Louise Pickford

Stylist: Wei Tang

*Illustrations: page 1, Rocket and
Watermelon Salad with Feta Cheese and
Mint, recipe page 208, page 2, Potato Pot
Potatoes, recipe page 163*

First published in Great Britain in 1996 by
Hamlyn, a division of Octopus Publishing Group Ltd

This edition published in 2008 by Bounty Books,
a division of Octopus Publishing Group Ltd
2–4 Heron Quays, London E14 4JP
www.octopusbooks.co.uk

An Hachette Livre UK Company
www.hachettelivre.co.uk

Design & illustrations copyright © Octopus Publishing Group Ltd 1996
Text copyright © Arabella Boxer 1996

ISBN: 978-0-753717-76-9

A CIP catalogue record for this book is available from the British Library

Printed and bound in China

contents

introduction

The word 'herb' no longer has any clearly defined meaning in the English language. According to the *Shorter Oxford English Dictionary*, it can be 'applied to all plants of which the leaves, or stems and leaves, are used for food or medicine, or for their scent or flavour.' In earlier times, however, the terminology was more precise. Herbs were divided into pot herbs, which were those plants that were actually cooked and eaten for their own sake, as opposed to sweet herbs, which were aromatic plants used to flavour cooked dishes. (Those that were eaten raw, in salads, were called salad plants.)

For the purposes of this book I have chosen to concentrate on the classic aromatic, herbs such as rosemary, sage and dill, while including a few salad leaves that may be eaten raw or used as garnishes, like rocket and mâche. I have also featured a few flowers that have for centuries been grown in herb gardens, and which have some specific use in the kitchen, like damask roses and violets, nasturtiums and marigolds. Then there are the exotic flavourings, like ginger and lemon grass, which are becoming increasingly popular. Lastly, I have chosen to include the flowers and/or berries of two trees: the lime, or linden, and the elder, for both have an important role to play in this context.

When I first started writing about herbs in 1980, fresh herbs were hard to find unless you had your own garden, as I did in those days. In the country the village shop might have a bunch of curly parsley or mint when new potatoes and green peas were on sale, but little else. Dried herbs were considered a perfectly good substitute for the real thing, and every kitchen had a shelf jammed full of small glass jars, way past their sell-by date — only those did not exist then. In the city you fared better, but only just. A few speciality food shops sold three or four varieties of fresh herbs during their short season, after which you were reduced to using dried herbs or going without.

Yet however frustrating this might have been, at least it was based on reality and the changing seasons. Now we can buy herbs all year round, and in variety, in most of the big supermarkets. But are they really fresh herbs in the true sense? Fresh yes, herbs no. For these fragile green fronds, neatly packaged in plastic containers, are like *fin de race* descendants of their predecessors. While their appearance is charming, delicate and ethereal, with no trace of earthly substance clinging to their frilly leaves, their flavour has been eroded until is is only a faint echo of its former self.

At first I could not understand why I was using three and four tablespoonfuls of chopped herbs in a recipe, whereas I used to find one teaspoon sufficient. Then I learnt that these supermarket herbs have been grown hydroponically, in a salt-water solution, without ever coming into contact with the soil. Now I understand why their depth of flavour has literally been watered down, and why their therapeutic qualities have been reduced to next to nothing, since it is the trace elements in the soil that supply both flavour and goodness. Readers who grow their own herbs, or are able to get them from someone who does, will probably find that they can cut down the amounts of herbs in my recipes by about one-third.

The current popularity of certain plants, like mâche and rocket, that were once considered exotic, forms part of an ever-changing cycle. As each new star becomes generally available, both chefs and the public tire of it and move on to look for something new. Not many adopted dishes last for ever in an alien country, although a few, like pesto, and tomato and mozzarella salad, last longer than most. Perhaps rocket and Parmesan will also stay the course; I certainly hope so.

People's reactions to herbs, both in general and specific terms, can be quite extreme and totally unpredictable. I find my own tastes have changed radically over the years. Sometimes I find my initial dislike sprang from a failure to understand the herb in question and how it should be used. Trying to eat savory raw was a case in point. Both sage and rosemary were anathema to me for

years, just as they were to Elizabeth David, as she recounts in *Spices, Salts and Aromatics in the English Kitchen* (Penguin 1970). Now, however, I have changed my mind, largely because I have learnt to use them in ways that give me pleasure: sprigs of rosemary used with garlic in dishes of fried and roast potatoes, and whole leaves of sage fried and scattered over pasta or grilled vegetables. One herb that seems to me strangely under-used is dill, despite the growing popularity of gravadlax. But few people cure their own salmon, and perhaps they can see no other use for dill. Yet anyone who has eaten it in Scandinavia, with plainly boiled potatoes or mixed with soured cream in a sauce for fresh shrimps, could not fail to be converted. Another neglected herb is chervil, which has long been one of my favourites.

With the growing emphasis on salads in our diet, salad leaves have once again acquired huge importance. I say 'once again', as we must not forget that in the seventeenth century salads were considered vital. John Evelyn's 'Salad Calendar', published in 1699 in his *Acetaria*, lists no less than thirty-eight different salad leaves and herbs. These include rocket, purslane, sorrel, corn salad, chicory, endive, mustard and cress, and six kinds of lettuce, as well as fennel, chives, sage, balm, tarragon, chervil and mint. How strange it seems that only twenty years ago the eminent food writer Jane Grigson was bemoaning the fact that so many of these excellent plants had been all but forgotten. Now many of them seem to have made a speedy and unexpected comeback. Yet with such extremes of fashion there is always the danger that the food in question may be overused and fall out of favour again. Already sorrel seems to have suffered this fate, for it is no longer as popular as it was in 1970, while basil and rocket may well follow suit, having been over-promoted by misguided chefs.

The first time I ever ate a salad as a first course was in the house of a Greek friend, who was himself an exceptional cook. Having invited ten friends to lunch on a Sunday, he simply went into his garden an hour or two before they arrived and picked the youngest and best of all his salad leaves and herbs. These were served in a huge bowl, simply dressed, as a first course. This must have been twenty years ago, and the effect was quite startling, for we had become conditioned to expect a salad with or after the main course, never before.

Despite the encouraging number of herb plants that have been brought back to use in the kitchen, there are still others that seem to have been truly forgotten. What has become of the curly-leafed dandelion, the oak-leafed plantain and the strangely named ice plant?

spring onions *Allium cepa*

Spring onions are also called salad onions and green onions. In Ireland and in the United States they are called scallions, just as they were in Elizabethan England.

Spring onions are not a species in their own right; they are simply the immature form of any number of varieties. This explains why they differ so widely in shape; some are like the Kate Moss of the vegetable world, while others resemble Dolly Parton. Certain varieties, like White Lisbon, are more suited to eating at an early stage than others. The Welsh onion, *Allium fistulosum*, with hollow leaves, is widely cultivated for sale as a spring onion, while in California the immature form of a red onion is used in this fashion, which makes a delightful garnish for a dish of grilled vegetables.

Until quite recently, spring onions were only eaten raw in many Western countries. They are still served raw with many dishes, but with the growing fondness for Eastern food they are now being cooked as well. Many people find them too potent to eat raw, like Irma Rombauer who wrote of the spring onion in her classic American cookbook *The Joy of Cooking*: 'The leaf is good as a soup flavouring, the white flesh is often braised, and they are eaten raw by self-assertive people...'

Spring onions form an inseparable part of the small group of flavourings we associate with stir-frying; the others being garlic, ginger, chillies and fresh coriander. They are also delicious steamed whole, or grilled.

Cultivation

Spring onions are grown from seed, never from sets. The seed should be sown in spring, in fine well-drained garden soil, in partial shade. Welsh onions are especially easy to grow, and can be propagated by dividing the clumps in spring, and replanting 30 cm (12 inches) apart. Some may be lifted and used as spring onions while the rest are left to mature. In this way they may be dug as needed all through the year.

Medicinal

Onions were used for medicinal purposes in ancient times by the Egyptians and Persians, Greeks and Romans, and they are still widely used in this way today. They act as a natural antiseptic, antiscorbutic, diuretic, and a stimulant to the digestive system. They are often eaten on a regular daily basis to ward off colds and flu. Spring onions have the same therapeutic properties as fully grown onions.

garlic *Allium sativum*

Garlic grew first in Central Asia and has been used both as a flavouring agent for food and as a medicament since ancient times, most notably in ancient Egypt. It is now grown throughout the world, but most prolifically in Asia, California and in the Mediterranean countries, especially in southwest France and Provence, where special garlic fairs and markets are held during the summer. Although garlic was known in Britain in Elizabethan times, it fell into disuse until after World War II, when the writings of Elizabeth David brought it back into favour. There are many different varieties: the two types most popular in France are the white garlic, which is harvested there in June, and the pink, which is lifted in July.

Garlic is a perennial bulb, a member of the onion family. The edible part is the bulb, which grows underground and can be divided into cloves. These are usually peeled before use, then crushed or chopped and fried in oil. Unpeeled cloves may be roasted whole, around a bird for instance, then squashed into a purée. Raw garlic is fairly pungent, but effective when used in moderation, as in the Tuscan *bruschetta*. Here a thick slice of country bread is grilled, then rubbed with a cut clove of garlic and drizzled with olive oil.

Dried garlic is available throughout the year. The freshest garlic, which is delicious, with large, mild, juicy cloves, is best bought in early summer, directly after its harvest.

Cultivation

Garlic is easy to grow at home. The cloves should be planted 3 cm (1 ¼ inches) deep and 10 cm (4 inches) apart in light well-drained soil, in late winter or early spring. When the leaves die back in summer, the garlic can be lifted and hung up in a cool, airy place to dry.

Medicinal

Garlic has a multitude of beneficial effects on health: it is a natural antiseptic and antibiotic, it stimulates the digestive system, it lowers the blood pressure, and it is believed to regulate the level of cholesterol in the bloodstream.

Chives are perennial and may be grown from seed sown in spring, then thinned out to a distance of 30 cm (12 inches). Germination is slow, however, and once a bed is established it is easier to increase it by lifting plants in spring or autumn and dividing them into small clumps. These are then replanted about 23 cm (9 inches) apart. Old plants should be lifted and divided every three to four years.

Chives are hardy, and will grow in any good soil. They are extremely decorative when used as an edging, or in drifts. The pinky blue flower heads add greatly to their charm. Strictly speaking, these should be cut off as soon as they form, in order to retain as much energy as possible in the leaves. I find, however, that by the time a herb flowers it is in any case past its best from the point of view of flavour, and I therefore prefer to let it bloom unchecked.

chives *Allium schoenoprasum*

Chives are a member of the onion family, and grow wild in Britain, Europe, Asia and the United States. They are easily grown in the garden, or even in pots on the windowsill. The flavour of chives is a fugitive and elusive one, for their essential oil is highly volatile. For this reason they are best used in cold dishes, like vichyssoise, *salsa verde* and potato salad. When used in hot dishes, like chive sauce for boiled beef, or consommé, they should be added only after the cooking is terminated. They contribute a delicious sharp, fresh, green flavour that makes a marvellous foil to pale, bland, creamy dishes.

Medicinal

Chives have important medicinal qualities, although their efficacy is less than that of the other, stronger-smelling members of the *Allium* family. None the less, they stimulate the appetite and aid the digestion, act as a gentle laxative and a mild sedative, and contain some iron and vitamin C.

Above: Common chives
Right: from left, Garlic chives and Common chives,

lemon verbena

Aloysia triphylla, Lippia citriodora

Cultivation

This is a tender plant, and is best grown in a sheltered sunny corner, possibly between two walls. Even so it will need protection through the winter. Like many herbs, it does best in a poor soil and should not be fertilized. It can be propagated by stem cuttings, which can be taken at any time during the spring, summer or early autumn.

Medicinal

The leaves of lemon verbena are often used to make an infusion, which is believed to have a calming effect. It has also been used to treat conditions such as nausea, indigestion, spasms and flatulence.

Lemon verbena, or lemon-scented verbena as it is sometimes called, grew first in South America. It is a handsome plant growing up to 1.5 m (5 feet) tall, with feathery fern-like leaves and panicles of mauve or white flowers in late summer. It warrants a place in any herb garden, especially a scented garden, for its leaves are deliciously aromatic. Their flavour is too perfumed for my taste, although they can be used, with caution, as a substitute for lemon grass. (I prefer to use lemon balm or lemon rind.)

dill

Anethum graveolens

Cultivation

Dill is easily grown from seed sown in spring in drills some 25 cm (10 inches) apart, later thinned to 20 cm (8 inches). It likes a well-drained loam and plenty of water. It should not be transplanted, as this causes the plant to burst into flower. Once it has flowered, it is of no more use as a herb, for all its strength now goes into making woody stems. A few plants may be left to self-seed for the following year, and the others dug up and discarded (unless, of course, you plan to harvest the seeds). If you grow dill solely for the leaves, sow in batches, ten days apart.

Medicinal

Dill has been used since ancient times for both its magical powers and its medicinal properties. It combines the virtues of a stimulant and a sedative, and is both aromatic and carminative. Like aniseed, caraway and fennel, dill seed aids the digestion by stimulating the digestive juices. Yet its effects are so mild that it may safely be used to treat babies, and dill (or gripe) water has long been used to calm wind, hiccups and lack of sleep in infants. It is also rich in minerals.

Dill is an annual, a native of continental Europe, which grows up to 60 cm (2 feet) high, with hollow stems, very thin, thread-like leaves and umbels of yellow flowers. The seeds look very like caraway seeds, while the whole plant is so similar to fennel as to be almost indistinguishable from it.

Dill has become one of my favourite herbs in recent years. It was not until I had been to Denmark twice that I learnt to appreciate it, for the Scandinavians use it constantly, and to great effect. For example, they use vast quantities of dill to preserve salmon as Gravadlax (see page 105), which is served with a Mustard and Dill Sauce (see page 176) and they serve whole stems of dill wreathed around plain boiled or steamed potatoes to accompany fish. Dill is also very popular mixed with soured cream, served with crayfish, prawns and shrimps. In Poland and other parts of Central Europe dill is much used, often with soured cream, and in soups, sauces, salads, vegetable dishes and pickles. Dill pickles are small cucumbers preserved in vinegar and flavoured with dill; these are the traditional accompaniment to salt beef sandwiches. In the United States the terms dill seed and dill weed (the leaves) are used to distinguish between the two useful parts of the herb.

angelica *Angelica archangelica*

Angelica tends to dominate the herb garden, for it grows up to 2 m (6 feet) high, thus confounding the widely held belief that all herbs are small plants, suitable for growing in a window box.

Angelica grew first in the far north, in Greenland, Russia and Scandinavia, but later became naturalized in much of Europe; a wild form with purplish stems also grows in Britain. Its main uses have always been in a candied or crystallized form for decorating cakes and trifles, and as an ingredient in liqueurs. For crystallizing, the leaf stalks and young stems are used, picked while still very young. These are traditionally used in the Russian Easter dish called *Pascha*, made with drained curd cheese and crystallized fruit. The young stems are also used as a sweetening agent, for adding to sour dishes like gooseberries and rhubarb. In some parts of Europe the leaves are cooked and eaten as a vegetable.

Cultivation

This is a robust biennial, easily grown from seed, with hollow woody stems, large indented leaves, and round umbels of greenish-white or lime-green flowers, which appear in its second year. The seed may be sown as soon as it has ripened in late summer, and the seedlings then planted out to a distance of 50 cm (20 inches). The edible parts should be picked in early summer of the plant's first year, while they are still tender. In its second year the plant is of no further use, apart from its flowers bearing seed, and may therefore be deemed a waste of space and dug up.

Medicinal

Both the roots and the seeds of the angelica plant are used as a carminative, an expectorant and to stimulate the appetite.

camomile

Anthemis nobilis, Chamaemelum nobile

Camomile, or chamomile, is a low-growing perennial that has been used for centuries for making paths or small lawns in herb gardens. Its name derives from the Greek *khamaimelon*, meaning 'earth-apple', a reference to the aroma of the leaves and flowers, which is released at the slightest touch. Camomile seems to grow best when walked on.

Cultivation

Camomile may be grown from seed sown in spring, or propagated by dividing the roots into small clumps and replanting some 20 cm (8 inches) apart. It needs a light dry soil and plenty of sunlight. If grown in the shade, the plants grow leggy as they reach for the light. The small white daisy-like flowers are borne in early summer, and should be picked when fully open and then dried in the shade.

Medicinal

The flowers are used mainly for making infusions and have various medicinal properties: digestive, febrifugal and calming. They are also used in cosmetics as a rinse for fair hair.

chervil

Anthriscus cerefolium

I believe that this is currently the most underrated of herbs, yet I cannot help wishing that it might remain so, thus escaping the fate of the over-exposed basil and rocket.

Chervil first grew in the Middle East and southern Russia, and was probably introduced to many European countries by the Romans. It is a biennial, growing about 40 cm (16 inches) tall, with feathery fern-like leaves, small white flowers, and strange little black seed pods. There is also a curly-leafed form, which is especially pretty for using as a garnish, but I think that all chervil is as decorative as it is delicious.

The essential oil of chervil is one of the most fugitive, and it should never be subjected to extreme heat. The leaf is best treated as a garnish, and in the case of hot dishes it should be added after the cooking is over, shortly before serving. It is utterly delicious in delicate consommés, with poached chicken or fish, in a cream sauce, with rice, potatoes and most cooked vegetables, and in lettuce salads. It also forms part of the classic *fines herbes* mixture, along with tarragon, parsley and chives. The *omelette fines herbes* made with this combination, is one of the great egg dishes of all time.

Cultivation

Chervil should be grown from seed, scattered or sown in drills, any time between spring and the end of summer. It can later be thinned out to 20 cm (8 inches) apart. The plants need plenty of water but not too much sun; a cool northern bed kept moist with frequent watering is ideal. The best time to use chervil is before flowering. Like most herbs, chervil loses much of its flavour after it has flowered, even if the flower heads are removed before the seeds have formed.

Medicinal

Chervil is rich in vitamin C, iron, magnesium and carotene. When drunk in the form of raw juice (somewhat unpalatable, alas) or as an infusion, it cleanses the blood, acts as a diuretic and benefits the liver. It is also good for treating gout, rheumatism, and eye troubles.

celery leaf

Apium graveolens

Although celery may not be generally thought of as a herb, it deserves a place in the herb garden, if only for the sake of its leaves. In some countries a variety of celery is grown specially for its leaves, while in many others celery is sold with all its leaves on, rather than trimmed. The Belgian dish of *anguilles au vert* (eels in green sauce) depends almost entirely for its flavour on large handfuls of celery leaves. Some time ago, on the Greek island of Lesbos, I bought bunches of celery leaves under the impression that they were flat-feaf parsley; they were the only fresh herb to be found on the island at that time.

Celery leaves have a fresh sappy flavour, similar to lovage but less coarse. Like lovage, they can be cooked for long periods with no loss of flavour. A celery stalk forms part of the traditional bouquet garni, with bay leaf, thyme and parsley stalks tucked within it. The crushed seeds are mixed with sea salt to make celery salt for serving with gulls' eggs during their short season.

In medieval times celery grew wild in Britain in damp ditches, water meadows and near the sea, and still does so today in parts of North and South America. A cultivated form was developed by French and Italian gardeners in the seventeenth century, and was imported into England. Smallage was the old-fashioned name for wild celery, which was much used in the past as a pot herb, like parsley.

There are two basic forms of cultivated celery – blanched, or white, and unblanched, or green. The white variety is often preferred for eating raw, since it is less bitter than the green. It used to be hard to grow, but now there is a self-blanching variety that is much simpler.

Cultivation

Celery is a biennial. During its second year it produces flowers and seeds, but is of no further use as a vegetable or herb. It is a winter vegetable, in season from autumn to spring. It is best sown under glass, then planted out when the seedlings are a few centimetres high. The turnip-rooted variety, called celeriac, also produces leaves that can be used as a herb, although in less abundance than true celery.

Medicinal

Celery leaf is a good food for slimmers: since it is composed mainly of cellulose and water, it has few calories while supplying valuable fibre and vitamin C. It is a general tonic for the system, particularly for the nerves and for nervous stomachs. It also acts as a diuretic, laxative and carminative.

horseradish

Armoracia rusticana

Cultivation

Horseradish needs a fine moist soil that has been deeply dug and well manured before planting to enable its roots to reach the correct depth. Buy, beg or borrow a plant from a friend, then take root cuttings the following spring. These should be about 5 cm (2 inches) long, and must be planted horizontally, lying 5 cm (2 inches) below the surface, in rows 1 m (3 feet) apart. The bed should be kept well watered.

Do not expect more than a small crop the first year. However, horseradish is all too easy to grow, and tends to take over the garden unless the roots are contained within an old bucket, or some other similar vessel, with the bottom cut out. Roots may be dug and used as required, or some may be dug up at the onset of winter and stored in sand in a cool shed.

Medicinal

Horseradish contains considerable amounts of vitamin C. It also acts as a diuretic, an antiscorbutic, and a tonic for the system.

This is a perennial herb, which probably grew first on the borders of Europe and Asia. It forms a thick, buff-coloured tap root, which spreads laterally. Large wavy-edged leaves and small flowers reach a height of 60 cm (2 feet).

In many countries the root of the horseradish plant is grated and mixed with soured cream, whipped cream or vinegar to serve as a condiment with hot or cold roast beef, or smoked fish. In Scandinavia, however, it is used more imaginatively and more simply. Small heaps of grated horseradish are laid on slices of rare roast beef; horseradish sauce is served with fried and poached flat fish; and grated horseradish is mixed with stewed apple to make a sauce for duck and goose.

tarragon
Artemisia dracunculus

French tarragon comes from southern Europe, and likes to grow in a warm, dry climate. It is semi-hardy, and may need some protection from frost. A bushy perennial shrub, it grows 75–90 cm (2½–3 feet) high, with narrow tapering leaves and small white flowers in summer. The flavour varies from plant to plant, as with mint.

An understandable confusion exists between French tarragon (*Artemisia dracunculus*) and Russian tarragon (*A. dracunculoides*). Although they are almost identical in appearance, the difference can soon be ascertained by tasting a leaf: whereas the true French tarragon has a strong, clear scent and flavour, the inferior Russian variety has virtually no taste at all, just a faint muddy hint of flavour.

Tarragon has been part of the classic French cuisine for hundreds of years, and is one of the few herbs that has never fallen out of favour. It has a special affinity with chicken, eggs, salads and cream sauces, and makes one of the best of all flavoured vinegars. Much of its appeal derives from its delicacy, and it is easy to see that its essential oil is a volatile one. Yet it will withstand short periods of cooking, although all its flavour is lost on drying.

Cultivation

French tarragon can rarely be grown from seed, and the best way of starting your own supply is by begging a friend with a good plant to give you a few cuttings or a root. (Russian tarragon, on the other hand, is easily grown from seed, but does not deserve space in the herb garden.) Plant the cuttings 30 cm (12 inches) apart in good garden soil, in a sunny spot. Feed them during the growing period, then cut them down to ground level in autumn, and cover them with straw or bracken. Because tarragon uses up all the trace elements in the soil, it should be lifted every year and replanted in a fresh spot; otherwise the flavour will deteriorate.

Medicinal

Like many other herbs, tarragon acts as a stimulant and a calming agent at the same time, for while it stimulates the appetite, the kidneys and the bladder, it calms down attacks of indigestion, flatulence and hiccups. It acts on the system as a general tonic as well as a diuretic, laxative and vermifuge.

orache *Atriplex hortensis*

Also known as summer spinach, or mountain spinach, this edible plant is believed to have grown first in Russia. It is an annual that grows about 2 m (6 feet) tall, with arrow-shaped leaves, which may be red, or pale or dark green, depending on the variety. It was well known in England in medieval times. It is now rarely seen, but still grows wild in parts of England, and in Ireland, where it is known as Fat Hen. (In England, this amusing name is given to Good King Henry, which is another member of the large Goosefoot family.) Orache is widely cultivated in France, where it is cooked like spinach or sorrel.

Cultivation

Orache grows best in a fairly rich soil. It is best grown from seed sown in early spring in drills 60 cm (2 feet) apart. Successive sowings are advisable, since it tends to run to seed. For the same reason, the flowers should be picked off as soon as they have formed.

Medicinal

Since orache belongs to the same family as spinach, it possesses some of the same benefits, although to a lesser degree. It contains some iron and other minerals, and vitamin C. It acts as a calming agent for indigestion, hysteria and other nervous troubles, and is a mild aperient. It is effective when taken in the form of an infusion, although the taste is unpleasant.

borage *Borago officinalis*

Cultivation

Borage is easily grown from seed, which may be sown either in autumn or spring. Autumn-sown crops will flower in late spring, while those sown in spring should bloom in summer. (This is preferable, for its uses are related to midsummer.) Borage may also be propagated by taking cuttings.

Medicinal

Although it is rarely seen nowadays except in summer drinks, in the Middle Ages borage was believed to be an effective aid to good health. It was thought to dispel melancholy and promote courage and good spirits, and to possess restorative powers. It is rich in mineral salts, calcium and potassium, and acts as a diuretic by helping to stimulate sluggish kidneys. The leaves may be made into an infusion, to be drunk hot to relieve catarrh, or at any temperature to combat stress.

Borage is a showy plant, which adds interest and appeal to the herb garden. It is a hardy annual, very easy to grow, reaching about 50 cm (18 inches) high. It has large pale green hairy leaves and small bright blue star-shaped flowers.

Its most common use is as a garnish for Pimms and other wine- or fruit-based cups. Whole sprigs, complete with leaves and flowers, are immersed in the cup, which is served in a large glass jug. Both leaves and flowers give a faint cucumber-like flavour. The flowers are sometimes crystallized for decorating iced cakes, and the leaves and flowers may be eaten raw in salads.

mizuna *Brassica rapa* var. *japonica*

According to Joy Larkcom in *Oriental Vegetables* (John Murray, 1991), her classic book on the subject, mizuna is a plant of Chinese origin that has been cultivated for centuries in Japan. I first encountered it in California in 1987, where it was as popular as rocket is today. Now it is gradually starting to make its appearance elsewhere. Although it may not yet be widely available in shops or supermarkets, it is being cultivated by enterprising growers for avant-garde restaurants and for particular ethnic communities.

Cultivation

Mizuna is easy to grow, being remarkably hardy and slow to bolt. It may be sown out of doors, *in situ*, from late spring to early autumn. (Its season may be extended from early spring to late autumn by the use of cloches.) Some two to three weeks after sowing, the seedlings will be ready for transplanting; this should be done so that they are 10–25 cm (4–10 inches) apart, depending on whether you want small or large plants. Mizuna can also be grown throughout the winter in an unheated greenhouse, and provides an extremely valuable winter salad.

marigold
Calendula officinalis

The marigold originated in southern Europe, and has been cultivated in Britain for hundreds of years; it was always included in medieval herb gardens. Cultivated throughout the world, the marigold is a hardy annual growing about 30 cm (12 inches) high, which closes up its petals at dusk and opens them again at sunrise. It is mentioned in *The Winter's Tale* accordingly: 'The marigold that goes to bed wi' the sun, and with him rises weeping.'

The marigold has been popular as a pot herb, as a cheap substitute for saffron, and as a way of introducing colour into what were often dull-looking dishes. In the past it was used not just for sweet dishes, but also for meat and fish. The petals, usually dried, were strewn over a soup or a beef stew, or a salad. They were also used with fish and rice, and in sweets like egg custard, and in cakes and biscuits.

Cultivation

Marigolds are best grown from seed sown in spring. The plants should be thinned out to 30 cm (12 inches) apart, enabling them to spread. They thrive in a light rich soil, in a sunny position. If some of the flower heads are left on the plants after flowering, they will seed themselves the following year.

To dry marigolds, simply lay the flower heads on sheets of paper and dry quickly in an airy place out of the sun. Once they have dried, rub off the petals and store them in airtight jars.

Medicinal

The marigold was formerly used for for treating bronchial problems and for bathing the eyes. It is now used in lotions for chapped skin.

curry leaves

Chalcas koenigii, Murraya koenigii

Cultivation

The tree that bears the curry leaf we are concerned with is easy to grow and small enough to include in the garden, but it is not often found in nurseries outside Asia.

Medicinal

In India the bark, leaves and root are used as a tonic.

There is much confusion between curry leaves (*Chalcas koenigii*), the curry plant (*Helichrysum italicum*), and daun salaam (*Eugenia polyantha*). Curry leaves are small, glossy evergreen leaves, much like small bay leaves in appearance. They are borne on a decorative tree, a native of southeast Asia, and they give off a delicious Eastern fragrance in the breeze. The leaves are best used fresh, though it is hard to buy them in this state in the West; the dried leaves have less flavour. Curry leaves are one of the ingredients of commercially made curry powders, and are also used in the home to make curries and similar dishes. They may be chopped or crumbled, then fried in oil at the start of a dish, before adding the spices, or added at the end of cooking, after frying with spices, as in a tarka dhal. Dried leaves may also be ground to a powder or made into a paste for flavouring curries and other dishes. Their flavour combines well with garlic, ginger, chillies and fresh coriander.

The curry plant is entirely different: a low-growing herbaceous plant with silvery-green spiky leaves and yellow flowers. Although it is a pretty plant to include in the herb garden, space permitting, it is of no use in the kitchen, despite the fact that its leaves emit a pleasant smell of curry when crushed.

Daun salaam is a highly aromatic evergreen leaf much used in Indonesian cooking. It is very similar to the curry leaf both in appearance and in flavour. Like the curry leaf, it is best used fresh, as the dried leaf has little flavour.

Good King Henry

Chenopodium Bonus-Henricus

Also called Mercury, Goosefoot or Fat Hen, Good King Henry is one of the old English plants that has been largely forgotten, although it still grows wild in parts of England. It used to be widely cultivated in Lincolnshire, where its shoots were esteemed as a substitute for asparagus. It was also much grown for the sake of its young leaves, which may be cooked and served like spinach.

A perennial, Good King Henry grows some 60 cm (2 feet) high and has dark green, triangular, arrow-shaped leaves. It is a hardy plant, and one that is easy to cultivate. When grown in a sunny corner of the garden, in a bed that has been thoroughly dug and well manured, it will be productive for several years.

Cultivation

Seed should be sown in early spring, in drills 23 cm (9 inches) apart, while plants should be dug in, also 23 cm (9 inches) apart, slightly later. If you plan to use the shoots, blanch them by earthing up, but since only a few shoots should be cut the first year, this is probably not worth the trouble. Some of the young leaves, but not too many, may be cut the first year; the following year picking and cutting may start in earnest. The shoots are ready to cut when they are almost as thick as your little finger; the season should last for about three months in spring and early summer. The young leaves may be picked at any time.

Medicinal

Since Good King Henry is a member of the Goosefoot (*Chenopodiaceae*) family, it shares many of the virtues of spinach and related plants. It is highly nutritious, with generous amounts of vitamins A and C. It is also rich in iron and calcium, although these minerals are rendered largely inactive by the plant's high oxalic acid content.

The leaves of Good King Henry are a natural antiseptic, and may be used as a poultice to treat sores, wounds and skin problems. An infusion made of the leaves is mildly laxative while the seeds can be used to treat diarrhoea. The flowers can also be made into an infusion to lower fevers.

feverfew

Chrysanthemum parthenium, Matricaria eximia

Feverfew is a hardy perennial, related to the chrysanthemum. It grows about 60 cm (2 feet) tall, with bright green leaves shaped like those of the oak tree. In midsummer it bears daisy-like flowers, with yellow centres surrounded by stumpy white petals. There is a single and a double variety, as well as a dwarf form, which is useful for edging beds.

Feverfew is a medicinal herb with no culinary virtues at all. In fact, its taste is vile, and most people find it unpalatable. For centuries it has been renowned as a cure for migraine, and recent tests have proved its efficacy in this respect. I was once prescribed a sandwich of feverfew leaves in brown bread, to be eaten daily, as a cure for migraine. The taste was so bitter and hard to stomach that I am ashamed to say I gave up halfway through.

Feverfew is a pretty plant so it is worth finding space for it in your garden. It looks equally well grown in a bed or pot.

Cultivation

Feverfew is easy to grow, and will thrive in well-drained soil in a sunny spot. Allow to self-seed, or propogate by one of the following methods:

1 Seed sown under glass in early spring, then thinned out to 5–7 cm (2–3 inches). Transplant outside in summer.

2 Cuttings taken in summer from the strong new shoots, taking a 'heel' with each cutting. Shorten to 7 cm (3 inches) and plant outside in light sandy soil, well-watered.

3 Root division in autumn or spring.

Medicinal

Feverfew leaves are taken as an infusion to relax muscles, thus relieving most forms of headache. It is also a stimulant, aperient and carminative, and acts as a tonic. The leaves may be used externally to relieve insect bites and stings.

tansy

Chrysanthemum vulgare, Tanacetum vulgare

Cultivation

Tansy is very undemanding to grow, and at least one plant should be included in every herb garden. It will grow well in any soil, and can be increased by root division in autumn or spring. The rootlets should be planted out at least 30 cm (1 foot) apart, and the growing plants should be kept under control, as they tend to spread rapidly. If you wish to increase leaf production, cut off the flower heads as they form.

Medicinal

Tansy was highly esteemed in former times for its many medicinal properties. Infusions of the leaves were drunk during Lent to symbolize the bitter herbs of the Passover, and were also taken as tonics for the system as a whole and for the nerves in particular, to stimulate sluggish kidneys, to relieve flatulence and as a vermifuge. Cloths soaked in a hot infusion were used to reduce swellings and strains; the bruised leaves were also put to this purpose. The root was also used, preserved in honey, as a cure for gout.

This is a charming plant with a very pretty name, but its flavour is definitely unpleasant, at least to modern palates. Yet it was very popular throughout the sixteenth, seventeenth and eighteenth centuries, when it was mixed with eggs, breadcrumbs, cream and spices to make cakes, tarts, pancakes and puddings. A 'tansy' was a pastry case filled with the juice of spinach and tansy, eggs and cream, and was traditionally eaten at Easter. The leaves were also eaten, chopped, with roast lamb, much as we eat mint today.

Although it is rarely seen in the herb garden nowadays, tansy grows wild throughout marshy areas and by the roadside. This perennial grows up to 1 m (3 feet) high, and has feathery fern-like leaves smelling of camphor. The bright yellow flowers, which look like small buttons, are borne in late summer. The wild tansy is even prettier than the garden variety, and smells more pleasant.

coriander

Coriandrum sativum

A native of the eastern Mediterranean, coriander is mentioned in the Bible, and seeds have been found in ancient Egyptian tombs. It was brought to northern Europe by the Romans, who used it as a flavouring, a preservative and a medicament. In 1492 it was taken by Columbus to the Caribbean, and from there it reached the Latin American countries.

Coriander is a member of the carrot family, almost indistinguishable from flat parsley, growing about 120 cm (2 feet) tall. It is a pretty plant, with feathery leaves, small white flowers in early summer, and light brown ridged seeds. All parts of the plant are edible, and today it is used throughout the world.

Both individuals and countries react to coriander in quite extreme ways. Few people are dispassionate about it: they either love it or hate it. It is much loved, for example, in all the Latin American countries, the Caribbean, India and China, but not in Japan. It is widely used in North Africa and the Middle East, but not at all on the northern shore of the Mediterranean. It is not known in Spain, yet it is much liked in Portugal. It is probably in Southeast Asia that it is most appreciated. In Indonesia the seeds alone are used, while in neighbouring Thailand both leaves and root are used as flavouring.

Ever since coriander was first brought to Britain the seeds have remained fairly constantly in use, usually as a pickling spice, but the leaves fell into disuse, and were rarely seen until recently. In her *Vegetable Book*, published in 1978, Jane Grigson makes no mention of coriander. In my first book on herbs, published in 1980, I appear never to have heard of it, but in 1984 it features for the first time in one of my other books.

The fresh coriander leaf goes marvellously well with garlic, chillies, ginger, spring onions and fresh tomatoes. It lends its own special character to fresh, hot, vibrant dishes, and complements chicken, fish and vegetables equally well. Mexican dishes like guacamole and salsa could not be made without it. It should not be dried, but freezes reasonably well. The white flowers look pretty scattered over a green salad.

Cultivation

Coriander is easy to grow, given certain conditions. It needs a light well-drained soil, plenty of moisture and sun. It should be sown in early spring, once all danger of frost is past. When it has flowered, the leaves alter their character and their flavour deteriorates. Unless you wish it to self-seed, this is the time to dig it up.

Medicinal

Coriander was used as a medicament by the ancient Greeks and Romans. It combines the effects of a sedative and a stimulant, and can become addictive if abused. The seeds may be chewed as a digestive or diuretic, while both the leaves and seeds can be used to make an infusion.

lemon grass

Cymbopogon citratus

Lemon grass is a native of southeast Asia, where it is highly valued, since lemons do not grow in tropical climates. Like coriander, lemon grass is one of those exotic herbs that only recently became widely available. In a previous book on herbs that I wrote in 1980 I seem to have been unaware of its existence. Now, however, it is to be found in every supermarket.

Lemon grass is a curious plant, like a cross between a root vegetable and a grass. The part that we use as a flavouring is the bottom section of the swollen leaf stem, just above the root. It is very hard indeed, and should be crushed before use. In most cases it is removed before the dish is eaten, having served its purpose, but in some cases, as in a stir-fry, it needs to be eaten in the dish. In this case only the very tender inner parts should be used, and finely sliced, chopped or grated beforehand. When fresh lemon grass is not available, a dried form called *sereh* can be bought in shops stocking Indonesian foods.

Like lemon balm and lemon verbena, lemon grass contains one of the components of the lemon, oil of lemon, without the other, citric lemon acid. So it possesses the fragrant lemony quality of the lemon without its tart, zingy character. Therefore, as a fresh substitute, use lemon balm, lemon verbena or lemon zest.

Lemon grass is usually used in conjunction with garlic, ginger, chillies and coriander, to enhance spiced dishes of fish, chicken and noodles, soups and salads. In her book *Indonesian Regional Food and Cookery* (Doubleday, 1994), Sumatra-born Sri Owen suggests using lemon grass as a little brush with which to baste foods with sauces while grilling or barbecuing. She cuts off and discards the extreme end of the lemon grass, then crushes the cut end until the edges fray to make a brush.

Cultivation

A fresh root of lemon grass may be potted up and grown under glass or as a houseplant. Alternatively, it may be grown in a pot out of doors during the summer, then moved inside for the colder months.

Medicinal

The crushed stalk is sometimes used in an infusion as a sedative and to relieve colic. It can be used with lovage and geranium leaves to make a cleansing bath for oily skin.

rocket *Eruca sativa*

Rocket originated in southern Europe. It has always been popular in France, where it is called *roquette*, and in Italy, where it is known as *rucola*, as well as in Turkey, the Middle East, and the United States, where it is called arugula. It was introduced to Britain in the sixteenth century, and was a popular kitchen herb in Elizabethan and Stuart times, eaten raw in salads, like land cress, watercress, and mustard. Although naturalized by the mid-seventeenth century – after the Great Fire of London in 1666 rocket spread rapidly through the ruins – it was later forgotten and did not regain its culinary position until the early 1980s. It is expensive to buy in supermarkets, since they tend to sell it in small packets.

Cultivation

Rocket is easily grown at home by sowing seed in the open in spring. It must be watered regularly or it will become rank and sour. Frequent picking encourages new growth. The leaves have a delicious peppery flavour, and can be eaten alone or mixed with other green leaves. The wild leaf has a much stronger flavour; the cultivated leaf is larger, milder and less bitter.

Medicinal

Rocket is a recognized antiscorbutic, and was formerly used for this purpose and as a tonic and a mild stimulant. For medicinal purposes, the plant is at its most effective when gathered while it is still in flower.

fennel

Foeniculum vulgare, F. officinale, F. dulce

Fennel grew wild in southern Europe, around the shores of the Mediterranean, and later became naturalized around the coastline of Britain. There are three main varieties: wild fennel, *Foeniculum vulgare*, common garden fennel, *Foeniculum officinale*, and Florence fennel, *Foeniculum dulce*. The first is grown mainly for the sake of its seeds and its leaves, while the others are cultivated for use as a vegetable.

Fennel is very similar to dill and angelica, in both its appearance and its pattern of growth, with hollow, woody stems, umbels of yellow flowers, small, finely divided leaves and tiny oval seeds.

Fennel can be treated as a herb, as it traditionally was in England – the leaves chopped and added to a sauce for fish – or as a vegetable, as it is in France and Italy, for example: eaten raw, thinly sliced, as a salad, or braised and served as a hot vegetable. In Provence dried fennel stalks are thrown on the fire before grilling fish over the open flames. In Italy raw fennel stalks used to be eaten at the end of a meal, like celery – but without the cheese – as a digestive.

Cultivation

Fennel is easily grown, requiring little more than some well-drained soil and a sunny position. It also needs plenty of room if it is not to swamp the other plants, for it grows about 1.5 m (5 feet) tall. It can be propagated either by seed or by root division. If sown, the seeds should be placed in drills 40 cm (15 inches) apart, and later transplanted. Once cut, the leaves are almost indistinguishable from dill; the two plants should not be grown in close proximity or they will cross-pollinate.

Medicinal

Fennel has been much valued for its therapeutic properties for hundreds of years as a spring cure, an antidote to wind, a diuretic, tonic, sedative, and a cure for failing eyesight. The roots, leaves and seeds have generally been used in the form of poultices, infusions, and baths for eyes, hands and feet.

hops *Humulus lupulus*

Before they were cultivated, hops grew wild in Britain, most of Europe and North America. The young shoots are much prized in Belgium, Germany and parts of northern France, and the wild hop shoots are considered a delicacy in Venice, as Elizabeth David recounts so entertainingly in *An Omelette and a Glass of Wine* (Jill Norman, 1984). They may be cooked like asparagus, in lightly salted boiling water, then served on toast with melted butter, or with poached or scrambled eggs. The first time I ate them was in Brussels, where they are called *jets d'houblon*, and I thought them quite wonderful. They also make an excellent risotto, as is done in Venice with the wild hop shoots (called *bruscandoli*) in early May.

It is almost impossible to get hold of hop shoots that have not been sprayed, which is all the more reason for growing one's own. Hops are extraordinarily decorative plants, and they come in two forms: green and golden. They are climbers, very similar to vines, with pretty pale yellowish-green cones. These are the female flowers, and contain the resin that gives the hop its distinctive smell and flavour. At Hardwick Hall, the romantic Elizabethan mansion in Derbyshire built by Bess of Hardwick, one of the most striking decorative features of the herb garden is the alternating pillars of green and golden hops, trained over tripods of tall poles, rising out of herb beds. The building of Hardwick was only some 50 years after the first imports of hops from the Continent, in the first half of the sixteenth century, and the introduction of 'hopped' ale.

Cultivation

Hops are perennials and are easy to grow so long as they are given some support. Although they die down to ground level each winter, the new shoots will grow roughly 6–7.5 m (18–25 feet) each year. Hops can be grown from seed sown out of doors in early spring, then thinned out to 15–30 cm (6–12 inches) apart. The plants can be increased by root division, also in spring. Whether you plan to cook them or not, the young shoots should always be thinned out in the spring.

Medicinal

Hops were viewed with mistrust for centuries, believed to induce melancholy. Yet they have accepted powers, especially as a tonic for the nerves, being both sedative and soporific. They also act as a diuretic and can calm pain. For medicinal purposes, only the female flowers are used, both fresh and dried.

hyssop
Hyssopus officinalis

Hyssop is a pretty plant with a pleasant, aromatic smell. This low-growing, bushy evergreen, with spikes of deep pink, blue or white flowers, originated in southern Europe, and was grown in Britain in medieval times for use as a strewing herb. It is used to flavour liqueurs like Chartreuse.

Hyssop attracts bees, and therefore deserves a place in the herb garden, although its uses in the kitchen are not very numerous. It has a pleasant minty taste with undertones of bitterness. A sprig may be added to stews or sauces of meat or game, while a few leaves can be thrown over a green salad.

Cultivation

Hyssop can be grown from seed sown out of doors in spring, then thinned to 30 cm (1 foot). Once established, hyssop will seed itself. It can be increased by taking stem cuttings in the spring, or by root division in early spring or autumn. Hyssop is often used as an edging for beds of other herbs.

Medicinal

The medicinal virtues of hyssop easily outweigh its culinary potential. Both leaves and flowers have their uses. While the flowers, both fresh and dried, can be made into an infusion to be drunk warm as a treatment for asthma, catarrh and other ailments of the throat, chest, lungs and stomach, the leaves may be used as poultices to heal wounds and bruises, and to alleviate rheumatic pains.

bay *Laurus nobilis*

The bay tree has been growing wild around the shores of the Mediterranean since ancient times. It was believed to possess magical powers against witchcraft and disease, and came to symbolize excellence. For this reason it was chosen by the Greeks and Romans to weave into wreaths with which to crown their victors.

Bay leaves are not true herbs, since the bay tree grows up to 18 m (60 feet) high, yet, being highly aromatic, they have always been treated as such. They form part of the classic bouquet garni along with parsley and thyme, and are used to flavour fish stocks and court-bouillons, meat stocks and soups, terrines and casseroles. They require long, slow cooking to bring out their flavour, and may be used equally well plucked fresh off the tree or dried. They are very potent and should be used with caution. The dried leaves are quite tough, so it is best to use them whole in cooking and to remove them before serving.

The bay tree is rarely allowed to grow to its full height; it is more frequently seen as a bushy shrub or a small tree grown in a pot or tub and trimmed into a decorative shape. It is a handsome plant, with its glossy, dark evergreen leaves, its yellowish flowers, and the small black berries that follow.

Cultivation

The bay tree is simple to cultivate, for it grows well in any garden soil and likes the sun. It does equally well in tubs or large pots and in open ground. It can be increased by cuttings taken in spring or autumn.

Medicinal

Bay leaves have some medicinal uses – an infusion helps to stimulate appetite and aids digestion, while rubbing with bay oil eases muscular aches and pains – but it is in the kitchen that they are most valuable.

lavender

Lavandula angustifolia

Lavender is an evergreen perennial shrub, low-growing and bushy in shape, with silvery-grey leaves and spikes of flowers in mauve, light blue, purple or white. *Lavandula angustifolia*, commonly known as English lavender, grows about 1 m (3 feet) high, with light blue flowers, making a handsome hedge; there is also a dwarf variety, which is useful for edging beds of herbs or flowers.

In medieval times lavender was much used as a strewing herb, and was almost always included in herb gardens. I have seen it still used for strewing today, when spending Easter on the Greek isle of Patmos some years ago. Here wild lavender is spread thickly over the streets before the holy procession is due to pass, and in the square where the Easter ceremonies are held.

In Tudor times, lavender was used for scenting linen, for medicinal purposes and, to a lesser degree, in food, to flavour honey, creams and jellies, while little twigs of peeled lavender were employed to spear sweetmeats. Today lavender is used mainly in making lavender water and essential oil, and in scented pillows, sachets and pot-pourri. It can also be put to good use in the kitchen: to flavour custards and ice creams, and to add its inimitable flavour to jams and jellies.

Cultivation

Lavender can be grown from seed or from cuttings. Cuttings should be about 7 cm (3 inches) long, and planted in a sandy compost. If this is done in late summer or early autumn, in a cold frame or under a cloche, the cuttings will be ready for planting out the following spring. Lavender needs a well-drained sandy soil in an open sunny position.

Medicinal

Lavender has myriad medicinal uses, as a diuretic, for calming nervous disorders of the stomach, and as an inhalant for asthma.

lovage *Levisticum officinale*

Lovage is a native of the Mediterranean region, and, like so many plants, was probably spread through Europe by the Romans. It now grows wild near the sea in northeast England and in the northeastern United States, and a related variety, Scottish Lovage (*Levisticum scoticum*), can be found growing on rocky coasts in Scotland. It is a very vigorous plant which can grow over 180 cm (6 feet) high. The leaves are deeply indented, similar to those of celery, which they also resemble in flavour. It has yellow flowers borne in umbels. If you have room for it in your garden, preferably in a corner near the back, it is worth including, for it is a handsome plant.

In former times all parts of the plant were eaten: the stems and roots were boiled and eaten as a vegetable, the leaves used as a pot herb, and the seeds used in baking, like caraway seeds. The young stems and shoots were candied, like angelica. Now lovage is rarely seen and hard to buy, perhaps because it takes up too much room in the herb garden, or perhaps because its flavour is too strong for modern tastes. I must admit to preferring celery leaves, which give a similar flavour but in a gentler, subtler way, and can be used as a replacement for lovage. Lovage is useful as a pot herb, however: athough only the very young leaves are tender enough to eat; the older ones may be used as part of a bouquet garni for flavouring stocks when you have no celery to hand.

Cultivation

Lovage is a hardy perennial, easy to grow so long as you give it plenty of room. It does best in a fairly rich soil, in full sun or partial shade. It dies down to ground level each winter, when it may be increased, if desired, by root division. Then it sends out new shoots in the spring.

Medicinal

All parts of lovage possess medicinal qualities, although their use is not advised for pregnant women. An infusion made from the seeds, leaves or roots may be taken for rheumatism, while one made from the leaves is good for treating urinary troubles and jaundice.

lemon balm *Melissa officinalis*

Lemon balm originated in the Mediterranean region. It is a pretty plant with white or yellowish flowers and a very vigorous growth. The aromatic leaves give off a lemon scent when crushed, so lemon balm was once widely used as a strewing herb. Lemon balm should always be included in a scented garden or a bee garden, for it is very attractive to bees and gives a good flavour to the honey.

In the kitchen its uses are various. The leaves have a slightly scented lemon flavour, like a cross between lemon rind and lemon grass. They may be used as a substitute for either of them, or chopped and added to stuffings and salads, or used whole in fruit cups. They also make an excellent infusion.

Cultivation

Lemon balm is a perennial plant, growing 45–75 cm (1½–2½ feet) high, bearing small white flowers in early summer. It is best grown on poor soil, and should never be dressed with manure or fertilizer, or the growth will become too vigorous. It should be propagated by root division, either in the spring or in the early autumn.

Medicinal

Lemon balm has many medicinal uses, notably as a cure for nervous afflictions, insomnia, depression and palpitations. A liqueur, *eau de mélisse*, was made by French monks in the seventeenth century to cure headaches. Dried leaves can be used in a poultice to treat insect bites.

mint *Mentha sp.*

Mint is part of the vast family of herbs called *Labiatae*, which also includes sage, thyme, marjoram, oregano, rosemary, basil, savory and lemon balm, among others. All except basil originated in the Mediterranean region, and many have been in use since ancient times.

There are 25 varieties, ranging in size from the giant Bowles' mint to the tiny pennyroyal, but their tendency to cross-fertilize has resulted in a wide number of hybrids. From a culinary point of view, only two or three are of interest. Culinary mint is a hybrid of two wild mints: horsemint and spearmint. It may adopt the characteristics of its parents in varying proportions, which is why everybody's mint plants taste different. Nor will its seed run true to form, so a much-loved plant must always be propagated by cuttings, rather than seed.

Spearmint, the common or garden mint, is one of the most popular for use in the kitchen. It grows about 60 cm (2 feet) tall, has smooth bright green leaves and bears small white flowers in summer. Bowles' mint, a hybrid of spearmint and apple mint, grows up to 150 cm (5 feet) high, with blue flowers and soft, downy leaves. These have an excellent flavour, but the texture may prove unappealing in food. The prettiest mint is apple mint, with variegated white-and-green leaves and a good flavour. Eau-de-Cologne mint, basil mint, pineapple mint, black peppermint and ginger mint are all appealing plants, but too scented for use in the kitchen.

Whereas mint was once used mainly as a digestive, an antidote to rich, fatty food, like the mint sauce served with roast lamb, its potential has now been reassessed, and its fresh, cool, juicy character recognized. It blends harmoniously with tomatoes, cucumbers, coriander, and yogurt in cold soups and salads. In India it is made into a fresh chutney, as a cool contrast to curries.

Mint is one of the few herbs that dry well – particularly spearmint – and in the Middle East every family dries their own, and uses it in preference to fresh.

Cultivation

Mint is a perennial, and all too easy to grow. Since it has a creeping rootstock, it tends to take over the garden unless its roots are contained within a large flower pot or metal bucket. Because of its tendency to cross-hybridize, each variety should be kept apart from other mints. In many ways it is best grown above ground, in a stone urn or old porcelain sink. On the other hand, pennyroyal and Corsican mint, both creeping varieties under 5 cm (2 inches) high, can be used to create a carpet in a corner of the garden, or it can be sown between paving stones.

Mint may be propagated by planting cuttings or small pieces of root 5 cm (2 inches) deep and 5 cm (2 inches) apart, in rows 20–25 cm (8–10 inches) distant. This should be done in late winter or early spring, in moist soil and partial shade.

Medicinal

Spearmint and peppermint are the varieties of mint that are most often used medicinally, primarily as antispasmodics and carminatives, and in conjunction with other remedies for colds.

Above: from left, Lime mint, Black pepper-mint and Pineapple mint
Right: from left, Ginger mint, Spearmint, Bowles Apple mint and Eau de Cologne mint

bergamot

Monarda didyma

The name bergamot is confusing because it can be used to refer to three unrelated plants. One is a form of orange called *Citrus bergamia*, whose peel is candied and whose oil is used in scent. Another is a mint called *Mentha citrata* or *M. odorata*. The third is a herbaceous plant called *Monarda didyma*, named after Nicholas de Monardes, a Spanish botanist and physician of the sixteenth century. It is the third that interests us, for it is one of those charming old-fashioned plants that has for centuries been included in the herb garden.

Its uses in food are not numerous, and since they are mainly visual, it is probably most useful when blooming, in midsummer. The chopped leaves can be added to salads, as can the whole petals. Both flowers and leaves may be added to fruit or wine cups, while sprigs look pretty in a bouquet of mixed herbs for a table decoration.

Cultivation

Bergamot is a pretty perennial growing about 40 cm (16 inches) high. It is easy to grow, likes full sun, and looks wonderful grown in great clumps or scattered individually through other herbs. It has dark reddish-green leaves rather like dark opal basil, and scarlet flowers like small dahlias.

Medicinal

The therapeutic properties of bergamot are few, but its red petals, which keep their colour even after drying, make a pretty herbal tea. Both the leaves and the flowers, fresh or dried, make an infusion which can be used for relieving menstrual pains, dispelling flatulence, and treating insomnia.

sweet cicely

Myrrhis odorata

Cultivation

Sweet cicely can be grown from seed in spring or autumn; it will also seed itself freely, and can later be transplanted. Alternatively, it may be propagated by root division. Like a more delicate form of cow parsley, it grows 60–90 cm (2–3 feet) tall, with lacy leaves and clusters of small white flowers. It is one of the loveliest herbs for cutting to decorate the table on a balmy summer night.

Medicinal

The ripe black seeds of sweet cicely used to be chewed as a digestive. The roots are antiseptic and can be made into an infusion for treating flatulence and coughs.

Sweet cicely is a member of the celery family, and grows wild in wooded regions of western Europe. It is one of the many herbs that were much loved in former times, being used predominantly in sweet dishes, but are rarely used today. Yet I would include this one in any herb garden if I had room, simply because it is such a pretty plant.

The roots used to be boiled and eaten cold as a salad, while the leaves were used as a flavouring herb, and as an infusion. The seeds were pounded in oil and used to polish and scent furniture.

watercress

Nasturtium officinale

Watercress grows wild, in streams, ditches and water meadows. Although it is easily found, it must be treated with caution, for it can be a dangerous carrier of diseases, including typhoid. Unless the water in which it grows is known to be clean for several kilometres upstream, free from sewage or cattle drinking, it is best avoided. If some doubt lingers, then the watercress should always be cooked, never eaten raw.

The cultivation of watercress began almost 200 years ago, and is now done on a huge scale. The commercially grown product has much larger leaves than the wild plant, but the flavour varies widely.

Watercress is an extremely valuable food, just as delicious in its way as more fashionable leaves like rocket, mâche and mizuna. Very adaptable, it can be used equally well raw or cooked. Its depth of flavour makes it a perfect foil for bland foods, and enables it to stand up to generous amounts of cream, in cold soups for instance, without being overwhelmed. It is so full of flavour that it needs no extra seasoning, and is therefore very useful for people on salt-free diets.

Cultivation

Watercress is not easy to grow yourself, since it involves grubbing about in muddy streams and all the frustrations that ensue with underwater planting. If you still want to try, you must first locate a suitable source of clean water. Watercress likes to grow with its roots underwater, in mud, and its tips in the open air. Therefore the water should be no more than 7–10 cm (3–4 inches) deep. The seed may be sown in seedboxes in early summer or autumn, then planted out *in situ* some 15 cm (6 inches) apart. It is probably simpler to divide a plant into pieces, each one with a piece of root attached, then to replant the pieces in the stream bed.

There are other cresses worth trying too, if you can find the seeds. One is English land cress, which has a broad-leafed variety called Mega. Another is a wild cress, with small leaves, which enjoys the name of hairy bitter cress.

Medicinal

Watercress is rich in iron and other minerals, and in vitamin C. In the sixteenth century it was used as an antiscorbutic. It is also effective in combating bronchial problems and stimulating the circulation.

basil

Ocimum basilicum, O. minimum

Basil is an annual, a low-growing plant with bright lettuce-green leaves and small white flowers. It is one of the most tender and fragile of summer herbs, with a unique flavour, both delicate and intense. Basil grew first in India, where it has always been considered a holy plant, and is to be found growing around Hindu temples. Being considered holy, it is not eaten. In Greece the small-leafed bush basil is often seen planted in old petrol cans near a cottage door, for it is believed to bring good luck. Like the Indians, the Greeks do not eat basil.

It is probably most appreciated for its culinary virtues in Liguria, in and around Genoa, where pesto was invented. This marvellous sauce for pasta and gnocchi is made with large quantities of basil, pine nuts, and two cheeses – Sardo and Grana – pounded to a fragrant paste with olive oil. The Genoese sailors claim they can smell the scent of basil wafting out on the breeze as they return home to port.

There are many different varieties of basil; each one is esteemed in different countries, for different reasons. The large lettuce-leafed variety from Naples is a handsome plant and easy to use in the kitchen. The Genoese favour a smaller-leafed variety with an excellent flavour. The very small-leafed bush basil, as seen in Greece, makes a very pretty plant, but is less remarkable for cooking, while the beautiful dark opal basil deserves a place in the herb garden on looks alone, although its flavour is less intense than that of the green-leafed varieties.

The essential oil of basil is one of the most volatile and evaporates quickly when subjected to heat, so the herb is best added to dishes after cooking, almost as a garnish, or to cold food. It has a great affinity with tomatoes, and with bland cheeses like mozzarella, as in the ubiquitous but delicious tomato and mozzarella salad.

Cultivation

Basil must be sown from seed each year in spring, then planted out in light, rich soil some 20 cm (8 inches) apart. The little plants should be kept well watered until they are firmly rooted. Basil needs the maximum of warmth to bring out its true flavour, so choose a sunny, sheltered spot or grow it under glass until midsummer. Do not plant it near rue, as the two herbs will not grow in proximity.

Medicinal

The fresh or dried leaves or flowers may be made into an infusion for treating migraine, nervous tension, constipation and insomnia. An infusion or gargle can be helpful for treating coughs and sore throats.

Basil is a natural disinfectant; a poultice made from the crushed leaves or a cloth soaked in a strong infusion can be used to dress snake bites and the stings of wasps, bees and hornets.

marjoram *Origanum majorana, O. onites*

There are two main types of marjoram: sweet marjoram (*Origanum majorana*) and pot marjoram (*O. onites*). (For a third, closely related variety, see Oregano (*O. vulgare*), page 49.) Both come from the Mediterranean region: sweet marjoram from North Africa, pot marjoram from southern Europe. In their native habitat they are grown as perennials, but in harsher climates they are best treated as annuals, for they rarely survive the winter. Pot marjoram is the more robust, and may be grown as a perennial in milder climates.

Sweet marjoram, which is also known as knotted marjoram, grows about 60 cm (2 feet) high, with small, pale green leaves and light mauve and white flowers. This is the variety most often used for cooking, for it has a delicate, warm, sweet flavour. Pot marjoram is stronger, indeed almost too strong, and is best kept for robust dishes. All varieties of marjoram go well with tomatoes, pasta, chicken, veal and most vegetable dishes. Pot marjoram may be added to dishes during the cooking, but the more delicate sweet marjoram is best added when the cooking is virtually finished.

Cultivation

Sweet marjoram may be grown from seed sown in early spring. The seed is sometimes mixed with sand, then sown in drills 23 cm (9 inches) apart or simply scattered in a warm sunny spot in light rich soil. Do not expect sweet marjoram to survive the winter unless it is grown in pots and brought indoors.

Pot marjoram may be propagated by root cuttings or root division in spring or early autumn, then planted out 30 cm (1 foot) apart.

Both varieties dry remarkably well, and some whole plants should be cut during flowering and dried for winter use.

Medicinal

Sweet marjoram is a carminative and an excellent digestive aid, but pot marjoram has no known medicinal uses.

oregano *Origanum vulgare*

Cultivation

Oregano is propagated by root cuttings or root division in the spring or early autumn. Plant out the little plants about 30 cm (1 foot) apart. Despite its robust character, oregano is a tender plant and will not survive a cold winter unless it is brought indoors.

Medicinal

Oregano is the most powerful of the marjoram tribe for medicinal purposes, and it has long been recognized for its therapeutic properties as a sedative and calming agent, and as a diuretic, tonic and gargle.

This is wild marjoram, familiar to many people as the *rigani* of Greece. Closely related to marjoram (*O. majorana*), it originated in southern Europe. Although a perennial in origin, oregano is best grown as an annual in northern climates. It is stronger and spicier than marjoram, and is the herb used by Italians in pizzas and pizza-style tomato sauces.

Oregano is a robust herb with an unusually stable essential oil; this means that it can be dried very successfully. For the same reason it can withstand fairly long periods of heat, so may be added to dishes early in the cooking process.

sweet-scented geranium

Pelargonium fragrans, P. tomentosum,

The sweet-scented geranium, or pelargonium as it should be called, has traditionally been included in the herb garden for the sake of its leaves, while its decorative flowers add enormously to the aesthetic appeal of the garden. There are a number of different varieties, with leaves smelling of nutmeg, peppermint, lemon and apples. Although its uses are limited, this is a charming plant and it would be a pity to leave it out of any herb garden. The scented leaves can be used to flavour syrups and sorbets, or as a base for making ice cream, and the flowers may be crystallized for use in decorating iced cakes.

Cultivation

The cultivation of pelargoniums is relatively easy. They can be grown from seed, but I would recommend buying one or two plants with different scented leaves, then propagating them by taking stem cuttings. in spring or in late summer. The cuttings should be about 15 cm (6 inches) long, dusted with rooting powder, then planted in pots, filled with potting compost. These should be kept moist, without over-watering.

Medicinal

Some of the scented varieties of geranium have essential oils with various therapeutic powers, which are used in aromatherapy. Many have leaves with astringent properties, which can be used to treat stomach troubles such as dysentery and duodenal ulcers.

parsley

Petroselinum crispum, P. crispum neapolitanum

Parsley, a native of southern Europe, has been growing wild for at least 400 years, The earliest form of cultivated parsley had flat leaves, but the curly-leafed form, *Petroselinum crispum*, later became more popular in Britain and the United States. Flat-leaf parsley, *P. crispum neapolitanum*, has always been preferred in continental Europe.

For the past fifty-odd years, parsley has been grievously misused in most cuisines. All too often treated merely as a decorative garnish by restaurant chefs, and left uneaten on the plate, its many strengths were ignored. Now, however, thanks to a growing interest in healthy eating and an enthusiasm for Middle Eastern dishes, it is coming back in force. Quite apart from its many therapeutic uses, parsley has much to offer. I much prefer flat-leaf parsley, both for flavour and texture, and use it almost always, except in a few traditional English dishes where the curly-leafed variety seems more appropriate.

Parsley mixes well with other herbs, as in the classic herb combinations bouquet garni and *fines herbes*. It is also good with basil, and with mint, as in the Lebanese salad called *fattoush*. It goes splendidly with bland foods like noodles and grain. And it makes a great sandwich, thickly layered between slices of buttered wholegrain bread.

It is unwise to pick wild parsley for use in the kitchen, as it is hard to distinguish from the poisonous hemlock.

Cultivation

Parsley is a biennial, but is best treated as an annual and dug after its first year, for during the second year it concentrates on producing stalks and flowers, while the leaves are almost nonexistent and unsatisfactory in flavour. It is easily grown, but slow; it may take as long as six weeks to germinate. It should be sown 3 mm (⅛ inch) deep, in drills some 25 cm (10 inches) apart, and later thinned out to 15 cm (6 inches). Alternatively, the seed may be scattered over the ground, with a layer of finely sieved compost sprinkled over it. It is best sown after the soil has warmed up, in late spring or early summer, or under plastic. Some gardeners believe in pouring a kettle full of boiling water over the seeds after sowing.

Medicinal

Rich in vitamins A, B and C, parsley is also a storehouse of iron and calcium. It is a natural antiseptic, a diuretic, and an effective treatment for hepatitis, rheumatic disorders and gout.

Above: from left, Flat-leaf Parsley and Curly Parsley

purslane *Portulaca oleracea, Claytonia perfoliata*

There are many different varieties of purslane, but the most common one is *Portulaca oleracea*, the green purslane which is sometimes called 'continental watercress'. It is quite unusual, and easy to recognize once you know it, with round fleshy stalks bearing a rosette of leaves at the top. It grew first in India, but was being widely grown – and flourishing as a weed – in Elizabethan England. Purslane is a popular salad plant in Greece, Turkey and the Middle East. It is a vital part of the Lebanese salad called *fattoush*, in which it is used in conjunction with large quantities of flat parsley and mint. Although they can be cooked, the young leaves are most often used raw in salads, while the older stalks are used for making pickles.

Winter purslane (*Claytonia perfoliata*) bears little resemblance to green purslane. It is a low-growing plant, very pretty, with small trumpet-shaped leaves. Grown in an unheated greenhouse, or in a plastic tunnel, it makes a good leaf for winter salads.

Cultivation

Green purslane is an annual, best sown in spring in drills 30 cm (12 inches) apart. The seedlings should later be thinned to 23 cm (9 inches) apart. They thrive in a sunny open position, in well-drained soil. Like the other purslanes, winter purslane is also an annual, and easy to grow from seed.

Medicinal

Purslane is a valuable medicament and may be used in a number of ways for different purposes. The juice may be drunk freshly pressed to treat coughs, or used to soak dressings for applying to sores and inflamed areas, and to painful gums. The whole leaves, fresh and lightly crushed, can be used like a poultice to treat headaches, eye strain and gout. The seeds were formerly used as a vermifuge.

salad burnet *Poterium sanguisorba*

Salad burnet is a perennial which grows wild all over France. It is a pretty plant, like a round cushion of leaf stems bearing small toothed leaves. The red and green flowers are borne in midsummer on tall stalks. A variety of burnet was grown in Britain in Tudor times, and was later taken to America by the early settlers.

The young leaves have a delicious flavour, mild and subtle, redolent of cucumbers. They have one of the least robust of flavours, however, and it is best to use them raw, scattered over salads or chilled soups, in cucumber sandwiches or over scrambled eggs. Salad burnet also makes an excellent flavoured vinegar (see page 244) for use in salad dressings.

Cultivation

Salad burnet must be grown from seed, and this should be done every year, for the young leaves of new plants are the most tender. Sow the seed in spring, in well-drained garden soil, and thin out later to 30 cm (12 inches) apart. While the flower heads should really be picked off as they form to encourage leaf growth, if some are left, they will self-seed naturally.

Medicinal

Salad burnet is a nutritious plant, rich in vitamin C. The leaves may be used, fresh or dried, to make infusions for the prevention of infectious diseases. They are also effective against gout and rheumatism, and help to encourage perspiration in cases of fever. Infusions also act as an aid to digestion, a tonic and a mild diuretic. The fresh leaves may be used whole as a poultice to promote the healing of wounds.

rose *Rosa damascena, R. gallica officinalis*

Roses were widely grown in herb gardens in England in Elizabethan and Stuart times. The flowers were valued for their beauty, both for their visual appeal and their scent, and for their many applications. As well as their obvious use in pot pourri for scenting linen presses and rooms, roses were used to make rose water, rose-flavoured honey, and syrups for flavouring ices and other sweet dishes. Rose petals and buds were also gathered and crystallized for decorating cakes, and used fresh in sandwiches. Crystallized rose petals can still be bought in Paris today, in glass jars, for decorating cakes, as can a deep pink jelly subtly flavoured with rose petals.

The most popular roses for use in the kitchen and still room have always been the old varieties, in particular the damask rose (*Rosa damascena*) and the apothecary's rose (*R. gallica officinalis*), which have never been improved upon for depth of flavour or of scent. In Turkey roses have been an important part of the cuisine for centuries. The sweet tooth for which the Turks are famous, combined with their love of perfumed flavours, accounts for the high esteem in which such things as rose water and rose syrup are held. A delicious scented syrup called shrub is made with roses, using both flowers and leaves.

Rose water is also very popular in the countries of the Mahgreb, on the southern shores of the Mediterranean. In Tunisia, Algeria and Morocco it is used to flavour sweet pastry dishes filled with pistachios. The dried buds of a variety of damask rose, called *coeurs de rose*, are widely used in Morocco in complex spice blends, like the famous *ras el-hanout*, which combines more than thirty different spices and is mixed to order and to your individual taste in the spice shops.

Medicinal

Roses have many therapeutic properties, and as a small child growing up during World War II I remember picking rose hips in the hedgerows to make rose-hip syrup, a valuable source of vitamin C. According to the famed herbalist Maurice Mességué, an infusion of roses has valuable properties that help in curing inflammation of the bronchial tubes and of the digestive passages. The same infusion can be used with effect to counteract the destructive effect of antibiotics on the internal bacteria.

rosemary

Rosmarinus officinalis

Cultivation

Growing rosemary from seed is a lengthy business; better to buy a plant or get cuttings from a friend. These should be about 15 cm (6 inches) long. Plant in sand, then transplant the following spring. Root division may also be carried out in autumn or early spring.

Rosemary grows slowly, but needs plenty of space, for it can grow up to 18 m (6 feet) high. It needs some protection from frost, so it is best grown in a sunny, sheltered spot, or in a large pot, which can be brought indoors in winter.

Medicinal

Rosemary is valued for its medical properties as a diuretic, a stimulant and a gargle.

This attractive evergreen grew first in the eastern Mediterranean region. In its chosen surroundings it is a perennial, but in northern climes it often fails to survive the winter. It is a pretty plant, a bushy shrub with spiky leaves like needles, dark green on top and silvery grey underneath. In early summer the branches are decked with pale blue flowers, which attract the bees.

Rosemary is much used as a seasoning in France, particularly in Provence, and in Italy. It has a powerful flavour, and should be used with caution if its camphor overtones are not to become too dominant. It is best used alone, although it is mixed with thyme and other Mediterranean herbs in the mixture of dried herbs called Herbes de Provence (see page 70). A sprig of rosemary inserted into a bottle of wine vinegar makes a splendid flavouring for adding to pan juices when roasting lamb or chicken. Rosemary leaves go marvellously well with roast, grilled or fried potatoes.

Rosemary is one of the few herbs that dries well, preserving all its flavour, although, as it is an evergreen, the leaves can equally well be left on the shrub and picked as needed throughout the year. If picking them for drying, the best time is in autumn, when the plant produces marvellous shoots 20–23 cm (8–9 inches) long. But don't ever cut it back to the old wood; always leave the last whorl of leaves on the new shoots intact. Rosemary was intended to be nibbled by goats, who would never eat beyond the tender tips.

Cultivation

Sorrel is a perennial, growing in a sturdy clump some 45–60 cm (18 inches–2 feet) high. It is easily grown from seed, and successive sowings are advised, since only the young leaves should be used. Seed should be sown in spring or autumn, in drills 35 cm (14 inches) apart. Alternatively, sorrel may be propagated by root division in spring. Later, the seedlings should be thinned out to a distance of 30 cm (12 inches). In order to retain the best possible flavour, the plants should be lifted every two to three years, then divided, and replanted in a different spot. Failure to do this will result in a coarseness of flavour. Sorrel does best in a medium rich soil, in a sunny spot.

Medicinal

Like spinach, to which it is related, sorrel is rich in potassium and in vitamins A, B and C. Also like spinach, unfortunately, it has a high oxalic acid content and should therefore be avoided by people suffering from gout, rheumatism or arthritis. For others, it has a number of helpful properties.

The roots and seeds are efficacious infused and drunk as a treatment for urinary troubles, colic, dysentery, diarrhoea and stomach aches. An infusion of fresh or dried leaves may be used as a diuretic, antiscorbutic, tonic or mild laxative. It also makes an effective gargle for treating mouth ulcers. An infusion made with wild sorrel helps to cleanse the blood and purify the system. A cloth soaked in the fresh juice of sorrel can be used to treat wounds and swellings.

sorrel

Rumex acetosa, R. scutatus

Various forms of sorrel grow wild in Europe, while still others are found throughout the United States. The British and American cultivated form derives from *Rumex acetosa*, while the French one comes from *R. scutatus*. The latter is superior in terms of flavour, being more acidic, and these plants should be acquired whenever possible.

Sorrel was popular in Britain in medieval times, but was later more or less forgotten, while in France it retained its popularity. It is one of those oddly placed plants halfway between a leaf vegetable and a herb. It has merit in both roles. When cooked as a vegetable, it resembles spinach, but with an added tang that gives a lift to soups and sauces alike. Again like spinach, its water content is very high, so it shrinks dramatically on cooking, and at least 250 g (8 oz) must be allowed for each person. Its other disadvantages are that it loses its colour on cooking, turning a dull sludgy brown, and its texture becomes slimy. When it is combined with spinach in purées, sauces and soups, these less attractive qualities are not apparent. When treated as a herb, its value is as a garnish, used raw, when its tart acidic quality adds enormously to bland, creamy dishes.

sage *Salvia officinalis*

Sage originated on the northern shores of the Mediterranean. It is a perennial, a low-growing shrub about 30–45 cm (12–18 inches) high, with soft, velvety leaves of pale grey-green. Its flowers are pink or mauve. All the varieties of sage are pretty plants, some – like the purple, red, golden or variegated sage – especially so. But the common or garden sage is best for use in the kitchen. Unlike most herbs, sage can withstand long cooking without loss of flavour, for its essential oil is a stable one. For the same reason it dries well.

I have only recently become converted to sage, having been put off for years by the musty taste of dried sage used to excess in sausages. Now, however, I have learned to love it, and use it constantly. Whole leaves can be fried crisp and scattered over pasta, gnocchi or grilled vegetables. Freshly picked leaves may be chopped and stirred into an onion purée or apple sauce for serving with goose, duck, pork or sausages. Sage is a powerful herb, rather like rosemary, and must be treated with caution. Again like rosemary, it is best used alone, for its slightly camphorous flavour does not mix well with other herbs.

Cultivation

Sage is easy to grow, given a sheltered spot in partial shade, but it may need some protection from frost, as it is only semi-hardy. It grows well in a container, which may be moved indoors in very cold weather. It is not hard to grow from seed, but this is a slow process, and it will not be ready to pick until its second year. The seed may be sown in early spring under glass, then transplanted into the open a couple of months later.

It is quicker to grow sage from cuttings taken from a mature plant in late spring and planted out of doors, 40–45 cm (16–18 inches) apart. In order to prevent them becoming leggy, the plants will need to have their growing tips pinched out at some stage. Sage tends to become straggly after flowering, and may need clipping back to create a compact bushy shape. With judicious clipping, it can be made into a low hedge to enclose beds in the herb garden.

Medicinal

Sage has many therapeutic properties, and has been used by physicians for centuries. It is a natural antiseptic, a tonic and stimulant. It is also antispasmodic and an antidote to fatigue. It aids the digestion of rich and fatty foods, which is why it has always been used in sauces and stuffings for dishes like roast pork and sausages, goose and duck. Fresh sage leaves make an excellent herb tea, which acts as an effective digestive.

Above: from left, Sage purple, Sage golden, Sage tricolour, Sage green

elder *Sambucus nigra*

This variety of elder makes a bushy shrub or tree growing up to 10 m (30 feet) tall, bearing heads of creamy-white flowers in early summer, followed by small, purplish-black berries a couple of months later.

Since earliest times the elder has been credited with magical powers. In Eleanour Sinclair Rohde's fascinating book *A Garden of Herbs*, published in 1920, we learn that every herb garden in Britain used to include an elder tree, for its spirit was believed to act as protection for the other herbs. On the last day of April country folk used to gather elder leaves, which they fixed to their windows and doors to keep away witches. Were you to stand under an elder tree at midnight on Midsummer Eve you might see the King of Elves and all his train pass by. In Scandinavian countries the elder is believed to possess supernatural powers and to act as a good-luck charm when used in the correct way. But its wood should never be used for making furniture or floors, or – worst of all – a baby's cradle, or dire misfortune will follow.

Quite apart from its mystical virtues, the elder has many uses in the kitchen. The flowers have a subtle and aromatic taste, redolent of muscat grapes, which they readily impart to syrups, fools and jams. They must be picked at the precise moment when they have just opened, for otherwise their scent, and their flavour, may be sickly and unpleasant. When picked at their prime, they can be used to make a delicious cordial for flavouring sorbets, soft drinks and cocktails. (This is now made commercially, but is even better when made at home.) In Austria the flower heads are dipped in a light batter and deep fried, either for serving as a vegetable or, sprinkled with caster sugar, as a dessert.

The berries have a completely different taste from the flowers: lighter, less remarkable, but good none the less. They are most commonly used for making elderberry wine; they can also be made into mousses and fools.

Cultivation

Elder is not ideal for growing in a small herb garden and cannot be grown in a container. It is a robust plant, needing plenty of space, a sunny, open situation, and moist garden soil. It should be pruned in early spring or late autumn, and can be propagated by cuttings or by root division.

Medicinal

All the elder's parts – leaves, bark, flowers and berries – have medicinal properties, and have been used for centuries to treat colds, fevers and rheumatism, and as a laxative and diuretic.

summer & winter savory

Satureja hortensis

Savory is a pretty plant, growing 15–45 cm (6–18 inches) high, with narrow tapering leaves and small pink flowers. There are two varieties: summer or garden savory, *Satureja hortensis*, which is an annual, and winter or mountain savory, *S. montana*, which is biennial. Summer savory is a native of the Mediterranean, while winter savory grew first in the mountainous regions of southern Europe and North Africa. Both varieties were brought to Britain and northern Europe by the Romans, and were taken to North America by the early colonists.

Well known in Elizabethan England, when bitter herbs were well liked, savory is rarely seen in Britain now, although both varieties are popular in France. There they are used as a flavouring for bean dishes, especially broad beans, and in Provence a wild savory called *poivre d'âne* is used to coat a ewes'-milk cheese called *banon*. Savory is also popular in the countries of Central Europe, for it goes well with the somewhat heavy dishes that are enjoyed there.

I have an aversion to winter savory, which is a truly bitter herb and cannot be eaten raw. But summer savory is milder, with much to be said for it. Its very specific use is as a flavour enhancer, to strengthen the effect of other herbs, or alone to enhance the flavour of the food itself. Even a jar of commercially made tomato and basil sauce warmed through slowly with ½ teaspoonful of dried savory will take on a new character, as the herb mellows it and smooths it out.

Both winter and summer savory are best used in conjunction with other herbs and, ideally, in dishes that are cooked for long periods. Effective in stuffings, forcemeats, sausages, stews and bean dishes, they are very potent and should be used in carefully judged amounts.

Cultivation

Savory likes a rich soil. It can be grown from seed sown in spring, preferably *in situ*, for it does not like being moved. (Both varieties can be grown from seed, but in my opinion only summer savory is worth the trouble.) Thin out plants to 20 cm (8 inches). Pick most of the plants to ground level just before they flower, and dry them. Savory dries exceptionally well. Plants left to flower will seed themselves.

Medicinal

Savory is best used as an infusion, which can be made with fresh or dried leaves and flowers. This is primarily a digestive. It is also a diuretic, and beneficial to people suffering from gout, rheumatism or breathing disorders.

Above: from top, Winter savory and Summer savory

mustard

Sinapis alba, Brassica nigra, B. juncea

There are many different varieties of mustard; two – white (*Sinapis alba*) and brown (*Brassica juncea*) – are grown mainly for their seeds, which are used in making mustard powder. Black mustard (*Brassica nigra*) is no longer grown commercially, having been superseded by brown varieties. Black and white mustard grew first around the Mediterranean, while brown mustard comes from the Himalayas.

Until recently the main use of white mustard seedlings was in sandwiches, mixed with cress. Only the first pair of leaves, or cotyledons, are used for this purpose, although the plants can, of course, be left in the ground to produce larger leaves for use in salads or for cooking.

Now, however, in their never-ending search for new salad leaves to please their customers, chefs and their suppliers are experimenting with a range of mustards imported from the East. These are the mustard greens, or red and black mustards. These peppery little leaves are delicious when used like rocket or mizuna in salads of mixed leaves. Alternatively, they may be allowed to grow a stage larger and then braised or stir-fried. The danger with all the mustards is that once they are past the seedling stage, the leaves have a tendency to become hairy.

In California various sorts of mustard greens are easily available all year round. In her book *The Savoury Way* (Bantam, 1990), chef Deborah Madison uses three different forms of mustard in a dish of haricots verts and spring onions: mustard oil, yellow mustard flowers and sautéd brown or black mustard seeds. (The young seeds of any mustard may be quickly fried and scattered over a salad.)

Cultivation

All the mustards are easily grown, although it may be hard to find seeds of black or brown mustard or mustard greens.

Mustard may be grown in virtually any soil and, although it prefers humidity and warmth, it is remarkably tolerant of frost. It can be grown from spring onwards and picked at any time: as seedlings for sandwiches, as young leaves for salads, or as larger leaves for cooking. Mustard is also effective as 'green manure' and in crop rotation.

Medicinal

Only the seeds are ever used in this context, usually in the form of a poultice, bath or infusion.

The poultice is made with the crushed seeds stuck on sheets of brown paper. It is very effective for treating muscular aches and pains, such as lumbago, arthritis, rheumatism and neuralgia, for chilblains, and for pneumonia, bronchitis and congestion of the chest and lungs. Foot and hand baths containing mustard seeds are often given, while whole baths are are generally considered to be too powerful for most people.

alexanders

Smyrnium olusatrum

Cultivation

Supplies of seed are hard to come by, but if you do succeed in getting hold of some, they should be sown in ordinary garden soil in the autumn, then transplanted the following spring. Alexanders needs plenty of space, like angelica, for it grows up to 1.5 m (5 feet) high. It may be blanched like celery if you wish, but I wouldn't bother.

Medicinal

The leaves, flowers, stem and root may all be used medicinally, either fresh or dried. Infusions can be taken as a diuretic, carminative, laxative, stimulant or nerve tonic. They have proved helpful for sluggish kidneys, gout and rheumatism. In past times the dried leaves were taken on sea voyages as an antiscorbutic.

An umbelliferous plant, sometimes called black lovage or horse parsley, alexanders belongs to the celery family, and looks like a cross between angelica and lovage. It was much used both as a food and medicament before the introduction of cultivated celery, but is rarely seen today.

It is sad to see that alexanders has been forgotten, for it has much to recommend it. The young shoots have a delicate celery taste, and may be used raw in salads, while the older stems, with a flavour halfway between celery and parsley, make excellent pot herbs for adding to soups and stews. The seeds are borne in pairs: oval, brownish-black and ridged, with a warm peppery taste. All in all, I find alexanders infinitely superior to lovage.

comfrey

Symphitum officinale

Comfrey is a perennial, growing some 60–75 cm (2–3 feet) high, with large, oval, hairy leaves and spikes of purple, mauve or white flowers which are borne all through the summer. It grew first in western Europe, spreading across from Britain and Spain to the Asian border.

Although rarely seen nowadays, comfrey was once a popular plant in medieval herb gardens, valued as much for its medicinal qualities as for its culinary ones. The young leaves may be cooked like spinach, or mixed with other leaves in a green salad. They may also be made into fritters by dipping in a light batter and frying in deep oil.

Cultivation

Comfrey is easily grown from seed sown in early spring, then thinned to 30 cm (12 inches). It will seed itself and can also be propagated by root division in the spring. It needs plenty of space, for the roots tend to spread, and it also demands copious watering. The whole plant is valuable for its use in breaking down compost, and as a mulch.

Medicinal

Comfrey, especially the wild variety, is an important natural medicament with many valuable properties. Above all, it has the power to soothe, whether it be stomach troubles like ulcers, dysentery and diarrhoea, or inflammation of any sort. The fresh or dried leaves or the root may be made into infusions for treating the conditions mentioned above, as well as for coughs and sore throats. The fresh leaves can be made into poultices for laying on cuts, bruises, boils, sprains and swellings; they can also help heal broken bones.

dandelion

Taraxacum officinale

The dandelion is a native of Europe, a wild meadow plant with deeply indented leaves and bright yellow flowers, which become transformed into balls of downy fluff. It is one of the most valuable wild plants, both as food and for its medicinal properties. The young leaves may be eaten raw in salads, and form part of the Provençal salad of tiny bitter leaves called *mesclun* – which also includes some of the following: chicory, rocket, mâche and baby lettuces, dressed with garlic-flavoured croûtons. The older leaves can be cooked like spinach and served warm with olive oil and lemon juice. In the past the root was often dried, roasted and ground for use as a substitute for coffee, and all parts of the plant have been used in wines and beers.

Leaves to be eaten raw should be gathered in the spring before the flowers have formed, for after that point they become too bitter to be palatable. This can be offset by blanching: simply invert a large flower-pot over the plant for seven to ten days before picking, with a piece of slate over the hole so that the dandelion grows in total darkness. This renders the leaves pale and reduces the bitterness.

The cultivated form of dandelion is infinitely superior from the culinary point of view, although not from the medicinal one. The leaves are larger, with a much milder flavour, and they do not need to be blanched. These are ideal for making that excellent dish of wilted dandelion salad with diced bacon, dressed with the warm bacon fat and white wine vinegar.

Cultivation

Dandelions are all too easy to grow from seed. The main problem is to stop them seeding themselves everywhere in the garden. With this in mind, be sure to pick off all the flower heads before the seeds start to fly.

Medicinal

The flowers, and the large tough leaves of dandelions may be used to make tea, while the roots can be infused in white wine for three days to make a powerful tonic. Both the wine and the tea may be taken – without much pleasure, it must be said – as an effective diuretic, digestive or liver stimulant.

thyme *Thymus vulgaris*

Cultivation

Thyme may be grown from seed sown *in situ* in spring, then later thinned out to 30 cm (12 inches) apart. If growing more than one variety, be careful to keep them separate, as they hybridize easily. Thyme may also be raised from cuttings taken in early summer. The creeping forms can be increased by division in late summer. These low-growing varieties are the most hardy; the others need some protection from frost. Alternatively, they may be grown in large pots and moved indoors during the worst of the winter.

Medicinal

Thyme was highly valued by the Romans, who used it as a cure for melancholy and an aid to failing memory. It is also a natural antiseptic because of its high thymol content, a diuretic, digestive and antispasmodic.

Above: from left, English winter thyme, Broad-leaf thyme and Lemon thyme

Thyme originated in southern Europe, probably on the northern shore of the Mediterranean. There are about 100 different varieties, but the one most used in the kitchen is the common or garden thyme, *Thymus vulgaris*. The thymes are aromatic bushy shrubs, growing 7–30 cm (3–12 inches) high, with tiny oval grey-green leaves and tiny flowers in shades of pink, mauve, red and white. The low-growing prostrate forms are useful for carpeting small patches of the garden, or for paths.

Thyme likes to grow in a sunny sheltered spot in rocky, arid soil. It is one of the most useful culinary herbs, as its essential oil is remarkably robust, so it can withstand long cooking, and it is equally effective used fresh, semi-dried or dried. There is not often much point in drying it since you can pick it all through the year, except for the two months when it is flowering and the leaves lose their flavour. If picking thyme in bulk for drying, you can cut it twice: once just before flowering, then remove the flower heads and allow the plant to grow again before making your second cut.

Thyme marries well with other herbs, as in the classic bouquet garni, where it is combined with parsley and bay, and in Herbes de Provence (see page 70). Thyme goes well with most Provençal dishes and can be substituted for marjoram or oregano in many others, like pizzaiola sauce and terrines. I like to use it in fish soups and in almost all dishes containing tomatoes.

Wild thyme, *T. serpyllum*, grows in the United States and most of northern Europe, including Britain. It is a low-growing variety, generally considered inferior in flavour to the common thyme, except in France, where it is called *serpolet*. It is also very popular in Lebanon, where it is called *zaatar* and is mixed in equal parts with toasted sesame seeds to coat small soft cheeses called *labneh*, which are eaten for breakfast. Lemon thyme, *T. citriodorus*, is a useful herb for cooking, having the usual thyme flavour overlaid with lemon.

linden

Tilia europaea, T. americana

Medicinal

The linden flower makes one of the best herb teas, good for treating colds, flu and sore throats, and for calming the nerves and sedating the system. It is sometimes combined with mint, which is both delicious and therapeutic, for mint has digestive qualities that complement the soporific powers of the linden flower. Linden flowers are also diuretic, and the leaves and flowers may be used in the form of a compress to treat skin irritations and burns. Be careful to pick flowers and leaves from trees deep in the countryside. Those near a busy road or in a town will be polluted.

The linden flower is the blossom of the lime tree, or linden, as it is called in German. *Tilia europaea*, a hybrid of *T. platyphyllos* and *T. cordata*, grows in Britain and northern continental Europe, while the related *T. americana* grows in the eastern United States and Canada. Growing up to 36 m (120 feet) high, *Tilia europaea* has heart-shaped leaves and greenish-yellow flowers, while the flowers of *T. americana* are white or yellow. In both cases the flowers are deliciously scented and filled with nectar, and much loved by bees: the resulting honey is quite delicious.

nasturtium

Tropaeolum majus, T. minus

The nasturtium grew first in the Peruvian forests, and is believed to have been brought to Europe by the Spaniards in the sixteenth century. A decorative plant, the nasturtium has long been included in herb gardens, and with good reason, for every part of it is edible and rich in minerals and vitamins. The common nasturtium (*Tropaeolum majus*) is a climbing plant and may grow as much as 3 m (10 feet) high if given adequate support. Alternatively, it may be left to sprawl along the ground. There is also a dwarf form (*Tropaeolum minus*), which flowers even more profusely, and is probably more suitable for small gardens.

The nasturtium has pretty, light green leaves, which are blunt-edged, almost round, in shape. The trumpet-shaped flowers are orange, red or yellow, with small purple blotches. The leaves have a warm peppery flavour, not unlike watercress. (The Latin name of watercress is *Nasturtium officinale*, which is often confusing.) The flowers have a similar, milder flavour and look very effective scattered over a green salad. Both seeds and flower buds may be pickled in vinegar and used in the same way as capers.

Cultivation

Nasturtiums are annuals, easily grown from seed sown *in situ* in spring. They grow quickly, and will flower two to three months after sowing. They prefer a moist soil free from lime, but it should not be too rich, for this will encourage leafy growth at the expense of flowers. Be careful not to overpick the leaves; at least a third should be left on the plant if it is to thrive. The flowers should be picked as soon as they have opened, or even before, while the seeds are ready once they have filled out. Some of the seeds may be kept back to sow the following spring, or left on the plant to self-seed.

Medicinal

In the past nasturtiums were used to combat scurvy, for they are rich in sulphur. They also contain valuable amounts of iron and vitamin C, and have been used for centuries as a tonic, stimulant and aphrodisiac.

violet *Viola odorata*

The sweet violet, one of the loveliest wild flowers, grows on banks and in hedgerows. It is a bushy little plant growing 15 cm (6 inches) high, with dark green heart-shaped leaves and scented purple flowers. Unlike the pansy, which has four petals on the uppermost side and one below, the violet has three above and two below. It is a perennial, and spreads naturally by a system of creeping rootstock. Whenever possible, it should be included in the herb garden, for it has been used for flavouring and decorating food and as a medicament for centuries.

In the seventeenth century violets were much appreciated in the kitchen, for highly scented flowers were very popular at that time. They were made into pastes, syrups and conserves, and crystallized for decorating cakes and sweetmeats. Although the flowers are still used today, albeit in a more limited way, for decorating iced cakes, I find the scented taste overpowering and prefer to enjoy them visually, growing in the herb garden. The violet cream used to fill chocolates was one of the banes of my childhood, and I spent many indecisive hours hovering over the chocolate box trying to avoid it.

Cultivation

Violets can be grown from seed sown in seedboxes in autumn, and kept under glass through the winter before planting out the following spring. They may also be propagated by dividing each plant into three soon after flowering, then replanting them 30 cm (12 inches) apart. Or they can be grown from cuttings taken in early spring and planted in a cold frame, then planted out in the late spring or early summer.

Violets will grow in almost any soil, although they prefer one on the heavy side that has been well manured. They do best in a cool spot, in partial shade. They make a charming low hedge for edging beds, and look pretty grown in pots.

Medicinal

Violets were much used in ancient Greece and Rome for their therapeutic properties, and are still used by herbalists today. They are effective when used as a purgative, a laxative, and as a treatment for bronchial troubles.

ginger *Zingiber officinale*

Cultivation

Ginger is a tropical or subtropical plant, and requires both heat and humidity to do well. In colder climates it can be grown in a heated greenhouse or warm room. Pieces of the rhizome 5 cm (2 inches) long, complete with buds, should be planted 5 cm (2 inches) deep in pots of rich compost, then moved into larger pots as they grow.

Medicinal

Slices of fresh root ginger make a delicious infusion. Drink hot to cleanse the blood and purify the system, or to treat a cold.

Ginger originated in the jungles of southern Asia, and it has since been cultivated for centuries in China, India, Southeast Asia and Japan. Today it is widely grown for export in West Africa and the West Indies. It is a perennial plant, with leafy stems growing 1 m (3 feet) tall from swollen rhizomes lying just below the surface of the soil. The rhizomes are the edible part of the plant, although the young shoots are also eaten in Japan.

Ginger can be bought in a number of different forms: the whole root in its fresh state; the same root dried; the most tender part, called stem ginger, preserved in syrup; pickled ginger; and ground ginger. The latter has been popular since medieval times as a flavouring in ginger-nuts, gingerbread and other biscuits and cakes, and in steamed puddings. In recent years, with the growing popularity of Asian foods, the fresh root has become readily available. This is usually grated or finely chopped after peeling, or crushed to extract the juice. It may also be sliced and used in infusions. Ginger blends remarkably well with garlic, spring onions and chillies – a combination that crops up again and again in Asian dishes.

herb mixtures

bouquet garni

This is the customary combination of herbs for flavouring liquid dishes, such as soups and stews, in the French classical tradition. Usually consisting of 1 bay leaf, 1 sprig thyme and 3 stalks parsley, it is often enclosed in a piece of celery stalk or a piece of leek, tied with string. Alternatively, it is sometimes wrapped in a small square of muslin, tied with thin string.

fines herbes

A subtle and carefully balanced mixture of delicate summer herbs, this combination cannot be improved upon for flavouring omelettes and other egg dishes, salads of soft, mild lettuce leaves, and cream sauces. The classic combination usually consists of equal parts of chervil, chives, parsley and tarragon.

herbes de Provence

Unlike the fines herbes *combination described above, this is a mixture of dried Provençal herbs, which contributes its own inimitable flavour to dishes of that region. Always included are the two main ingredients, rosemary and thyme, while the others usually consist of marjoram and basil, and sometimes also savory and/or tarragon.*

Right: Bouquet garni

soups

red pepper soup
with yellow pepper garnish

1 Stick the red peppers and the yellow peppers for the garnish on long skewers, 2 at a time, and grill, turning at regular intervals, until they have blackened evenly all over. Leave to cool. Repeat the same process, very briefly, with the chillies for the garnish. Once the peppers are cool enough to handle, scrape off the skins and discard the stalks and seeds. Chop the red peppers coarsely; set the yellow ones aside, with the chillies.

2 Cook the chopped leeks slowly in the oil for about 5 minutes, adding the chopped garlic towards the end. Then add the chopped red peppers and the potato, and continue to cook gently for 3–4 minutes. Pour on the heated stock, add salt and pepper, and bring slowly to the boil. Simmer for 25 minutes, then leave to cool. Purée in a liquidizer or food processor, or push through a medium food mill, then return to a clean pan.

3 To make the garnish, chop the grilled and skinned yellow peppers roughly and purée them in a liquidizer or food processor. Skin, seed and finely chop the chillies and add to the puréed yellow peppers, together with the olive oil, chopped mint or coriander, and salt and pepper to taste. Process until reduced to a hash. Alternatively, chop the peppers, chillies and mint or coriander very finely indeed by hand, using a mezzaluna or long knife, then stir in the olive oil and salt and pepper.

4 To serve, reheat the soup and serve in bowls, with a heaped teaspoonful of the cold garnish in the centre of each one.

Note: If the chillies are too small to thread on skewers, just omit the grilling and chop them finely, discarding the seeds.

Serves 4 to 6

6 large red peppers
2 leeks, chopped
2 tablespoons sunflower oil
1 large garlic clove, finely chopped
1 potato, peeled and thickly sliced
900 ml (1½ pints) chicken stock, heated
salt and black pepper

Yellow Pepper Garnish:

2 yellow peppers
2 green chillies
1 tablespoon extra virgin olive oil
2 tablespoons chopped mint or coriander

Previous pages: Red Pepper Soup with Yellow Pepper Garnish

black bean soup
with coriander

This delicious soup is based on one of Frances Bissell's recipes, with my variations and her consent. It can be made with red kidney beans if black ones are hard to find.

1 Start 1 day in advance. Soak the dried beans generously covered in cold water for 8 hours or overnight. Then drain them and cover with fresh cold water. Do not add salt at this stage. Bring to the boil and boil hard for 10 minutes, then reduce the heat and simmer gently for 50 minutes or until the beans are soft. Leave to cool for about 1 hour, then drain the beans in a colander standing over a large bowl. Reserve about 500 g (1 lb) of the cooked beans, and purée the rest in a food processor with 600 ml (1 pint) of their cooking liquid. Alternatively, push the cooked beans through a coarse food mill, together with the same volume of cooking liquid. Reserve the rest of the bean stock in case it is required later.

2 Fry the chopped onion gently in the oil for 5–6 minutes, then add the garlic and chillies and cook for another 2–3 minutes, stirring often to make sure they do not stick. Then add the tomato purée and cook for a further 4–5 minutes, stirring as before. Now add the heated stock, bring to the boil and simmer for 30 minutes. Stir in the puréed beans, the reserved whole beans, cayenne, and salt and pepper to taste. If the soup is too thick, add a little of the reserved cooking bean stock to thin it. Stir in the lime juice. If possible, let stand for a few hours and reheat before serving.

3 To serve, spoon the soup into individual bowls, adding a dash of Bourbon for those who like it, and a dollop of crème fraîche or soured cream, sprinkled with coriander. Alternatively, serve the soup quite plain, adding Bourbon for those who wish, and hand around the cream and coriander at the table.

Serves 6 to 8

500 g (1 lb) dried black (or red) kidney beans
1 large red onion, finely chopped
3 tablespoons light olive oil
3 large garlic cloves, finely chopped
3 red chillies, deseeded and finely chopped
2 tablespoons tomato purée
600 ml (1 pint) chicken or vegetable stock, heated
a pinch of cayenne
1½ tablespoons lime juice
salt and black pepper

To garnish:

6–8 tablespoons Bourbon whisky (optional)
150 ml (¼ pint) crème fraîche or soured cream
3–4 tablespoons chopped coriander

game consommé
with pasta and basil

**I litre (1¾ pints) game stock, free
from fat
40 g (1½ oz) pasta
¼ teaspoon soy sauce
2–3 tablespoons chopped basil
salt and black pepper**

The addition of pasta makes this a more sustaining dish than the usual consommé, but it is still elegant enough for a smart occasion. I like to use a very simple form of soup pasta: either flat noodle squares or flat noodles broken up by hand into short lengths.

1 Heat the stock. When it reaches boiling point, drop in the pasta and boil for about 4 minutes or until it is soft. Add salt and pepper. Once the pasta is cooked, turn off the heat and add the soy sauce. Then stir in the chopped basil and let stand for a few minutes before serving.

Serves 4

Right: Game Consommé with Pasta and Basil

chicken soup
with lettuce and pasta

Although this soup evolved from the remains of a lunch party, it is so good that I find it more than worth making from scratch. Its smooth texture and delicate flavour make it quite unusual.

1 Put 900 ml (1½ pints) of the chicken stock in a pan and add the sliced carrots. Bring to the boil and cook gently for 5 minutes, then add the leeks and the chicken breast. Bring back to the boil, lower the heat and simmer gently for 5 minutes, then add the spring onions. Bring back to the boil and cook gently for 5 minutes more, then add the noodles and cook for 3–4 minutes, until tender. Set the soup aside.
2 Melt the butter in a small pan and add the whole lettuce. Turn it around in the butter for 5 minutes, then heat and add the remaining chicken stock. Add salt and pepper and cook gently for 25 minutes, turning the lettuce over from time to time.
3 Remove the chicken breast from the soup, discard skin and any bone, and cut into neat squares. Chop the braised lettuce into squares, and add the braising liquid to the soup. Reheat the soup, adding salt and pepper and the cream. When it is hot, stir in the chopped chicken and lettuce and mix well. Lastly, stir in the chopped herbs.

Serves 5 to 6

I litre (1¾ pints) chicken stock

2 small carrots, cut in 5 mm (¼ inch) slices

2 small leeks, cut into I cm (½ inch) chunks

I chicken breast

I bunch spring onions, cut into I cm (½ inch) slices

40 g (1½ oz) flat noodles, broken into small squares

15 g (½ oz) butter

I Little Gem lettuce

200 ml (7 fl oz) single cream

2 tablespoons chopped chervil

2 tablespoons chopped tarragon

2 tablespoons chopped dill

salt and black pepper

courgette & tomato
soup with basil

½ medium onion

500 g (1 lb) courgettes

300 g (10 oz) tomatoes, skinned

3 tablespoons light olive oil

900 ml (1½ pints) light chicken
stock, heated

3 tablespoons chopped basil or flat-
leaf parsley

salt and black pepper

1 Cut the onion in slices 5 mm (¼ inch) thick, then across into 5 mm (¼ inch) squares. Cut the courgettes into 7 mm (⅓ inch) slices. Cut the skinned tomatoes in quarters, then scoop out the insides, leaving only the outside wall. Cut this into 1 cm (½ inch) strips.

2 Cook the onion slowly in the oil for 5–6 minutes, until softened, without allowing it to brown. Then add the courgettes and cook for a further 6 minutes, stirring now and then. Pour on the heated stock and bring to the boil, then simmer for 20 minutes, adding salt and pepper. Add the tomatoes and remove from the heat. Stir in the chopped basil or parsley, and let stand for 5–10 minutes before serving. If making in advance, add the herb only after reheating.

Note: To make a slightly more substantial soup, add 25 g (1 oz) thin noodles, vermicelli or Chinese egg noodles before adding the tomatoes. Cook them for 3 minutes, then add the tomatoes and proceed as above in the main recipe.

Serves 4 to 5

crème sénégale
with coriander

This old-fashioned New York soup is brought up to date by the addition of fresh coriander, which goes perfectly with the flavourings of saffron and curry powder.

1 Heat the stock and drop in the chicken breast. Simmer gently for 10 minutes, then remove the breast. Place the saffron in a small bowl and pour a few spoonfuls of the hot stock over it. Set aside.

2 Melt the butter in a heavy saucepan and add the curry powder. Stir for 1 minute over gentle heat, then add the flour and cook for another 2–3 minutes, stirring. Pour on the hot stock, little by little, stirring all the time. Stir till smooth, and simmer gently for 3 minutes. Add the saffron infusion, the lemon juice, cream, and salt and pepper to taste. Stand the pan in a sink half full of cold water to cool quickly, stirring often to prevent a skin forming. Once the soup has cooled to room temperature, pour into a bowl and chill for several hours or overnight.

3 Cut the chicken breast into neat dice. Ladle the chilled soup into bowls, and divide the chicken breast between them. Sprinkle each serving generously with chopped coriander.

Serves 6

900 ml (1½ pints) good chicken
  stock
1 chicken breast
¼ teaspoon saffron
40 g (1½ oz) butter
1½ teaspoons light curry powder
2 tablespoons flour
1½ tablespoons lemon juice
150 ml (¼ pint) single cream
salt and black pepper
1½ tablespoons chopped coriander,
  to garnish

Elsbeth's cold green soup

An unusual cold soup in that it is both refreshing and sustaining at the same time.

1 Poach the whole courgettes in a little of the chicken stock until they are just tender; allow 6–8 minutes depending on size. Cool them in the stock, then cut into smallish pieces and place in a liquidizer or food processor with their juice, the avocados, garlic, yogurt, remaining chicken stock, salt and pepper to taste and mint. Process until you have a fairly thick purée; it does not need to be absolutely smooth. Chill for several hours or overnight before serving.

Serves 8 to 10

625 g (1¼ lb) courgettes
900 ml (1½ pints) chicken stock
2 large avocados, peeled, stoned and
  cut in pieces
1 large garlic clove, crushed
150 ml (¼ pint) Greek yogurt
2 tablespoons chopped mint
salt and black pepper

ginger consommé

A light and elegant first course for a dinner party.

1 Start 1 day in advance. Put the carcass in a deep pan with the vegetables, bay leaf, salt and peppercorns. Cover with the water and bring slowly to the boil, skimming frequently. When the surface is clear, cover the pot and simmer for 2½ hours. When the time is up, strain the soup and measure it. You should have about 900 ml (1½ pints). If there is much more, boil up again for a little while to reduce. Leave to cool, then chill overnight.

2 Next day take all the fat off the surface. Reheat the soup gently, adding salt and pepper as required. Just before serving, bring to the boil and add the chopped ginger. Simmer for 30 seconds, then spoon into individual bowls, floating a small sprig of watercress in each one.

Serves 4

1 duck, pheasant or chicken carcass
1 onion, unpeeled, cut in quarters
1 large leek, halved
1 large carrot, halved
1 celery stick, halved
1 bay leaf
1 teaspoon sea salt
6 black peppercorns
1.5 litres (2½ pints) cold water
1½ tablespoons finely chopped fresh
  root ginger
4 small sprigs watercress, to garnish

corn soup
with coriander salsa

4 ears sweetcorn, or 375 g (12 oz)
   frozen sweetcorn kernels
2 leeks, white parts only, chopped
40 g (1½ oz) butter
900 ml (1½ pints) chicken stock,
   heated
salt and black pepper
Coriander Salsa (see page 169),
   minus lime or lemon juice,
   to serve

1 Scrape the sweetcorn kernels off the cobs and set aside. Sauté the chopped leeks in the butter for 5 minutes, then add the sweetcorn. Using the back of a small knife, scrape any remaining juice out of the cobs into the saucepan. Stir around for 1–2 minutes, then pour on the heated stock and bring to the boil. Add salt and pepper and simmer for 15 minutes, then allow to cool a little. Tip into a food processor or a liquidizer and purée, then return to a clean pan.
2 Make the coriander salsa, omitting the lime or lemon juice, and set aside. To serve, simply reheat the soup and spoon into bowls, with 1 tablespoon of the salsa in each one. Alternatively, serve the salsa separately in a small bowl.

Serves 6

watercress soup

200 g (7 oz) watercress in bunches,
   or 150 g (5 oz) trimmed
40 g (1½ oz) butter
1 tablespoon light olive oil
1 potato, peeled and diced
900 ml (1½ pints) chicken stock,
   heated
150 ml (¼ pint) double cream
salt and black pepper

1 Reserve 6 perfect sprigs of watercress and chop the rest roughly. Stew the chopped watercress gently in the butter and oil for 5 minutes, then add the diced potato and cook for another 5 minutes, stirring often. Add the heated stock, bring to the boil, and add salt and pepper to taste. Simmer for 25 minutes, then remove from the heat and cool slightly. Purée the mixture in a liquidizer or food processor, adding the cream, then reheat gently in a clean pan. Serve in bowls, with a sprig of watercress in each one.

Note: A simple variation on this classic soup may be made by substituting 100 g (3½ oz) rocket for half the watercress.

Serves 6

Previous pages: from left, Coriander Salsa, recipe page 169 and Corn Soup with Coriander Salsa, recipe above

fish soup with herbs

1 Heat the oil and butter in a deep pan and brown the chopped onion, leek, carrot and celery. After 3 minutes, add the garlic and tomatoes, then the crumbled bay leaf, dried herbs, salt and pepper. After another 3 minutes, put in the pieces of fish, stirring well to mix them with the vegetables and dried herbs. Pour on the pernod, ouzo or vodka, and continue to cook gently for another 2–3 minutes, stirring. Add the very hot water and bring slowly to the boil. Cover the pan and simmer slowly for 1 hour.

2 Towards the end of the cooking time, tip the saffron into a small bowl and pour a couple of spoonfuls of the hot fish stock over it, then leave to infuse. When the cooking time is up, leave the soup to cool for a little while, then pick out the big, bony pieces of fish and discard. Save some of the best pieces of fish for later, and push the rest of the soup through a coarse sieve or food mill, mashing the pieces of fish and the vegetables against the sides.

3 Tip into a clean pan and reheat, adding the saffron infusion and more salt and pepper to taste. Then stir in the reserved fish, which you have flaked, free from skin and bone, and the marjoram, thyme and crushed red peppercorns.

4 To serve, spoon into bowls, and garnish each one with a slice of dried French bread.

Serves 6

1½ **tablespoons olive oil**
25 g (1 oz) **butter**
1 **small onion, chopped**
1 **leek, chopped**
1 **carrot, chopped**
1 **celery stick, chopped**
1 **garlic clove, chopped**
2 **tomatoes, chopped (unskinned)**
1 **small bay leaf, crumbled**
½ **tablespoon dried Herbes de Provence**
1–1.25 kg (2–2½ lb) **mixed white fish: grey mullet, monkfish, conger eel, cut into bite-sized pieces**
4 **tablespoons pernod, ouzo or vodka**
1 litre (1¾ pints) **very hot water**
⅛ **teaspoon saffron**
1 **tablespoon chopped marjoram**
1 **tablespoon chopped thyme**
½ **teaspoon crushed red peppercorns**
salt and black pepper
6 **slices French bread, dried in the oven, to garnish**

celery soup
with lovage and chives

1 Chop the celery, reserving the leaves. Cook the chopped celery in the butter for 5 minutes, then add the potatoes and lovage or alexanders and stir around for a further 3–4 minutes. Pour on the heated stock, add salt and pepper, and bring to the boil. Simmer the soup gently for 35 minutes, then leave to cool. Purée the soup in a liquidizer or food processor, or push through a medium food mill, then return to a clean pan.

2 To serve, chop the reserved celery leaves finely and reheat the soup. When it is ready, pour into bowls and garnish each one with a swirl of cream and 1 teaspoon each of chopped celery leaves and chives.

Serves 6

I large head celery, inner parts and
  leaves only
40 g (1½ oz) butter
500 g (1 lb) potatoes, peeled and
  thickly sliced
1½ tablespoons roughly chopped
  lovage or alexanders
1.2 litres (2 pints) chicken stock,
  heated
salt and black pepper

To garnish:

150 ml (¼ pint) single cream
1½ tablespoons chopped chives

Right: Celery Soup with Lovage and Chives

lentil soup
with mint

1 Heat the butter and oil. Add the sliced onion, leek, carrot and celery, and cook for 5 minutes, stirring often. Then add the lentils and stir around for about 3 minutes, while you heat the stock in a separate pan. Pour on the hot stock and bring slowly to the boil, add salt and pepper, half cover the pan and simmer gently for about 35 minutes or until the lentils are tender.

2 Leave to cool for a little while, then lift out about half the cooked lentils and put in a liquidizer or food processor with some of their stock. Process to a purée, then return to the pan and mix with the whole lentils. Adjust seasoning to taste. The soup can now be left until almost ready to serve. Then reheat gently, stirring, and add the chopped mint.

Serves 4

Note: In hot weather this soup is good served cold. But in this instance 'cold' means cool, at room temperature, never chilled. Reserve the mint till last. Stir the yogurt into the soup, then spoon the soup into bowls and scatter the chopped mint over each one.

Serves 4 to 5, with the addition of natural yogurt.

25 g (1 oz) butter
1 tablespoon olive oil
1 onion, halved and thinly sliced
1 leek, thinly sliced
1 carrot, thinly sliced
1 celery stick, thinly sliced
175 g (6 oz) lentilles de Puy, washed
**1.2 litres (2 pints) game, duck or
  chicken stock**
salt and black pepper
**2 tablespoons chopped mint,
  to garnish**

For a cold soup only:

300 ml (½ pint) natural yogurt

mixed mushroom

soup with herbs

This soup is best when made with a generous proportion of wild, or culti-vated exotic, mushrooms.

1 small red onion, finely chopped

3 tablespoons olive oil

1 large garlic clove, finely chopped

1 red chilli, finely chopped

750 g (1½ lb) mixed mushrooms,
  coarsely chopped

900 ml (1½ pints) chicken stock,
  heated

2 teaspoons plain flour

150 ml (¼ pint) soured cream

4 tablespoons chopped coriander

4 tablespoons chopped flat-leaf
  parsley

6 tablespoons natural yogurt

salt and black pepper

3 tablespoons chopped chives,
  to garnish

1 Soften the onion in the oil for 3 minutes, then add the garlic and chilli. Cook gently for another 3 minutes, stirring often. Then add the chopped mushrooms and stir well to mix. After a couple of minutes, add the hot stock, with plenty of salt and pepper. Bring to the boil, lower the heat and simmer for 25 minutes or until the mushrooms are soft. Then remove from the heat and leave to cool for 10–15 minutes.

2 Process the mushroom mixture in a liquidizer or food processor until fairly smooth, then tip back into a clean pan and reheat gently. Stir the flour into the soured cream, then drop this mixture by degrees into the soup as it nears boiling point. Stir well until each addition has been amalgamated, then adjust the seasoning and stir in the chopped coriander and parsley.

3 To serve, pour into bowls and add a spoonful of yogurt to each one, then scatter ½ tablespoon of chopped chives on top.

Serves 6

grilled tomato soup
with croûtons and basil

1 Stick the tomatoes on skewers and grill them, turning frequently, just until the skins have blistered. Remove from the grill and leave to cool, then remove the skins and chop the flesh coarsely, retaining seeds and juice. Cook the spring onions gently in the oil for 3 minutes, then add the garlic and ginger and cook for another minute. Tip the chopped tomatoes into the pan and stir for 3 minutes, then pour on the heated stock. Add salt and pepper, bring to the boil, and simmer gently for 10 minutes, half covered. Remove from the heat and cool for a little while. Purée the soup in a liquidizer or food processor, then tip back into a clean pan.

2 Make the garnish. Cut the bread in slices about 1 cm (½ inch) thick. Grill them until light golden, then rub each side with the scored garlic clove.

3 To serve, reheat the soup gently and pour into individual bowls. Lay a grilled bread slice in each bowl and dribble a little extra virgin olive oil over the surface. Scatter torn basil over the soup in each bowl and serve immediately.

Note: To serve cold, omit the grilled bread and olive oil. Simply chill the soup well for a few hours after processing or overnight. Then pour into chilled bowls and sprinkle the basil on top.

Serves 6

750 g (1½ lb) beefsteak tomatoes
1 large bunch spring onions, sliced
2 tablespoons olive oil
1 large garlic clove, finely chopped
**1 cm (½ inch) square fresh root
ginger, peeled and finely chopped**
**600 ml (1 pint) light chicken stock,
heated**
salt and black pepper

To garnish:

4 slices Italian country bread
**1 large garlic clove, cut in half
and scored**
1½ tablespoons extra virgin olive oil
1½ tablespoons torn basil

cabbage soup
with oregano

½ medium green cabbage, about
  375 g (12 oz)
40 g (1½ oz) butter or beef dripping
2 leeks, chopped
1 potato, peeled and sliced
900 ml (1½ pints) chicken or beef
  stock, heated
300 ml (½ pint) milk
1½ tablespoons chopped oregano
salt and black pepper

1 Cut the half cabbage in 2, remove the core, and cut across in thick slices. Bring 5 cm (2 inches) lightly salted water to the boil in a heavy saucepan, add the cabbage and cook, covered, for 10 minutes, then set the pan aside until later.

2 Melt the butter or dripping in a heavy pan and cook the chopped leeks gently for 6–8 minutes, until soft. Then add the sliced potato and cook for a further 2 minutes. Pour on the heated stock and bring to the boil, then simmer for 30 minutes.

3 Drain the cabbage, reserving the liquid, and chop it by hand. Add it with its liquid to the pan of potato and leeks, and cook for a further 5 minutes, adding salt and pepper. Remove from the heat and add the milk and the chopped oregano. Cover and leave for 15 minutes or so, then blend half the soup in a liquidizer or food processor. Return it to the rest of the soup in its pan and reheat thoroughly, adjusting the seasoning to taste.

Serves 6 with thick slices of rye bread.

eggs

Danish egg cake
with chives

1 tablespoon plain flour
75 ml (3 fl oz) milk
4 eggs, beaten
15 g (½ oz) butter
4 tablespoons chopped chives
salt and black pepper
6–8 bacon rashers, grilled,
  to garnish

1 Using a wire whisk, beat the flour into the milk, then add the beaten eggs gradually, continuing to beat. Add salt and black pepper to taste while beating. Then heat the butter in a frying pan. When it is hot, pour in the beaten eggs and cook quickly until set, as for an omelette, tilting the pan from side to side and lifting the edge of the omelette to allow the liquid egg to run underneath. When it is set, slide it on to a flat dish and scatter the chopped chives thickly over the top. Garnish with grilled bacon rashers.

Serves 2 with a green salad; grilled tomatoes also go well with this simple dish.

eggs on spinach
with watercress sauce

Watercress Sauce (see page 167)
1 kg (2 lb) spinach
4 eggs

1 Have the watercress sauce already made and keeping warm over hot water. Drop the spinach into some lightly salted boiling water and cook for 4–5 minutes, depending on whether it is summer or winter spinach. Drain it well in a colander, pressing out the water with the back of a wooden spoon. Then divide it equally between 4 bowls. Lower the eggs into boiling water and cook for exactly 5 minutes. Cool for a few moments in a bowl of cold water, then shell them and lay one egg in each bowl of spinach. Pour the watercress sauce on top and serve as soon as possible.

Serves 4 as a first course or light main dish.

Previous pages: from left, Grilled Tomatoes, recipe page 196, Danish Egg Cake with Chives, recipe above

eggs in coriander mayonnaise

1 Drop the eggs into lightly salted boiling water and cook for 8 minutes. Transfer them to a bowl of cold water, then shell them carefully. Separate the lettuces into leaves, and lay them on a shallow dish. Lay the whole eggs over them, then scatter the prawns or flaked crabmeat over and among them. Mix the soured cream with the mayonnaise, then stir in the chopped coriander, keeping back a little for the garnish. Spread the mayonnaise mixture over the dish and scatter the reserved coriander over all. Chill for 1–2 hours before serving.

Serves 4 as a first course.

8 eggs
2 Little Gem lettuces
500 g (1 lb) cooked peeled prawns
   or 250 g (8 oz) white crabmeat,
   flaked
300 ml (½ pint) soured cream
300 ml (½ pint) Mayonnaise
   (see page 168)
2 tablespoons finely chopped
   coriander

herb omelette

1 Have the lightly beaten eggs in a bowl. Add salt and pepper, then stir in the chopped herbs. Heat an omelette pan, drop in the butter and swirl around once. Tip in the eggs before the butter has time to burn, and leave them to set for a moment. Then use a small spatula to lift the edge of the omelette, tilting the pan at the same time to allow the uncooked eggs to flow underneath. When almost all the eggs have set, fold the omelette in two, using the spatula, and slide it on to a hot dish. Serve immediately.

Serves 2 as a light main course with a green salad.

5 eggs, lightly beaten
1½ tablespoons chopped chervil
1½ tablespoons chopped chives
5 g (¼ oz) butter
salt and black pepper

eggs on green peas with chervil

1 Cook the peas in the chicken stock until soft, then drain them, reserving the stock. Put the peas in a liquidizer or food processor with 300 ml (½ pint) of the stock and process to a purée. Put the purée into a clean pan and stir in the butter over a gentle heat. Add the cream, and salt and pepper to taste.

2 Cook the eggs in lightly salted boiling water for 5 minutes exactly, then cool them in cold water and shell.

3 To make the sauce, melt the butter, add the flour and cook for 1 minute, stirring. Measure 150 ml (¼ pint) of the chicken stock reserved from cooking the peas, reheat, and add to the sauce, stirring until smooth. Add the cream and cook gently for 3 minutes. Stir in most of the chopped chervil, keeping back a little for a garnish, and season to taste with salt and pepper.

4 Place an egg in each of 4 shallow bowls. Spoon the pea purée over the eggs, and spoon the chervil sauce on top. Scatter the remaining chervil over each bowl, and serve.

Serves 4 as a first course.

**375 g (12 oz) peas, fresh or frozen,
  weighed after shelling
  or defrosting**
450 ml (¾ pint) chicken stock
25 g (1 oz) butter, cut in small bits
2 tablespoons single cream
4 eggs
salt and black pepper

Sauce:

15 g (½ oz) butter
1 tablespoon plain flour
150 ml (¼ pint) single cream
2 tablespoons chopped chervil

eggs in pastry with herbs

1 Make the pastry. Sift the flour and salt into a food processor, add the butter and process until the mixture resembles fine breadcrumbs. Then add the iced water gradually through the lid while processing, until the dough has formed into a ball. Alternatively, sift the flour and salt into a large bowl, rub in the butter with your fingertips until the mixture resembles fine breadcrumbs, then stir in the iced water gradually, mixing with the blade of a knife, and stopping as soon as the dough starts to cling together. Turn the dough out on to a lightly floured surface. Knead briefly, then wrap in clingfilm and chill in the refrigerator for 20 minutes.

2 Roll out the pastry thinly and use to line 6 small round tins, about 7 cm (3 inches) in diameter. Line the pastry cases loosely with foil and weigh down with a few dried beans. Bake blind in a preheated oven, 200°C (400°F), Gas Mark 6, for 6 minutes. Remove the beans and foil, brush the pastry with the egg yolk beaten with the milk, and put back in the oven for a further 6–8 minutes, till light golden brown.

3 To make the sauce, melt the butter, then add the flour and cook for 1 minute, stirring. Then add the heated stock gradually, stirring, and simmer for 3 minutes. Shake in the grated Parmesan, stirring till melted, and add the cream. Season with sea salt and black pepper, and stir in 2 tablespoons of the chopped dill, reserving the remainder for the garnish. Set aside.

4 Divide the cooked rice for the filling equally between the pastry cases and warm through in a preheated oven, 150°C (300°F), Gas Mark 2, for 5 minutes. Bring a broad shallow pan of water to simmering point, carefully crack open and drop in 3 of the eggs and poach gently for 2 minutes or until the whites have just set. Lift them out with a slotted spoon and drain briefly on a folded cloth, then lay each one in a pastry case. Repeat the process with the remaining eggs. Reheat the herb and cheese sauce and pour over the eggs. Sprinkle the reserved dill over them and serve immediately.

Serves 6 as a first course.

Pastry:

250 g (8 oz) plain flour, sifted
a pinch of salt
125 g (4 oz) butter, chilled and cut in small bits
3–4 tablespoons iced water

Glaze:

1 egg yolk
1 tablespoon milk

Filling:

6 tablespoons freshly cooked white long-grain rice
6 small eggs, size 1 or 2

Herb and Cheese Sauce:

25 g (1 oz) butter
½ tablespoon plain flour
175 ml (6 fl oz) chicken stock, heated
75 g (3 oz) freshly grated Parmesan cheese
4 tablespoons double cream
3 tablespoons chopped dill
sea salt and black pepper

egg custard with leeks and garlic

25 g (1 oz) butter

1 tablespoon sunflower oil

1 leek, very finely chopped

2 garlic cloves, very finely chopped

6 eggs

600 ml (1 pint) chicken stock

2½ tablespoons chopped chervil

salt and black pepper

75 g (3 oz) mâche or rocket, to garnish

1 Heat the butter and oil in a frying pan and cook the chopped leek for 3 minutes, then add the garlic and cook for another minute. Set the pan aside.

2 Break the eggs into a bowl, adding salt and pepper to taste. Stir in the leek and garlic mixture, and then the chicken stock. Lastly, add 1½ tablespoons of the chopped chervil and mix well. Pour into 6 small soufflé or *oeuf en cocotte* dishes that have been well buttered. Stand them in a broad casserole with enough water to come halfway up their sides. Bring to the boil and cook gently for 12–14 minutes, covered, being very careful that the water does not boil up over the sides of the dishes.

3 When the custards are set, take the dishes out of the casserole and leave them to stand for 5 minutes, covered. Have small plates arranged with a bed of mâche or rocket. Run a small knife round the edge of the custards and turn them out on to the green leaves. Sprinkle the rest of the chopped chervil over them and serve immediately. These custards are also good served cold.

Serves 6

Right: Egg custard with Leeks and Garlic, recipe above

stuffed eggs
with curry and chives

1 Cook the spring onions in the oil for 3 minutes, then add the curry powder and cook for another 2 minutes. Remove from the heat and leave to cool. Shell the eggs and cut them in half lengthways. Ease out the yolks and mash them with a fork. Stir the egg yolks into the onions, adding salt and pepper. Blend in the chutney, cream and chopped chives, then pile back into the halved egg whites. Lay on a flat dish to serve, garnished with cress, shredded lettuce or other herbs.

Serves 4 as a first course, or 3 as a light main dish.

1 bunch spring onions, chopped
2 tablespoons sunflower oil
1 teaspoon mild curry powder
6 eggs, hard-boiled
1 tablespoon mango chutney, chopped
4 tablespoons single cream
2 tablespoons chopped chives
salt and black pepper
1 punnet cress or a few lettuce leaves, shredded, or some rocket or mâche, or tender sprigs of watercress, to garnish

tomato jelly
with scrambled eggs

This summery jelly is especially good when made with freshly squeezed tomato juice; this can be bought in some supermarkets or made at home if you have a juice extractor.

Jelly:

600 ml (1 pint) tomato juice, freshly squeezed if possible
celery salt to taste
paprika to taste
1 teaspoon sugar
1 tablespoon lemon juice
½ teaspoon Tabasco
6 sprigs dill
1 tablespoon powdered gelatine
sea salt and black pepper

Filling:

6 eggs, beaten
15 g (½ oz) butter
sea salt and black pepper
2 tablespoons chopped chives or dill, to garnish

1 Pour the tomato juice into a saucepan. Add the celery salt and paprika, sugar, lemon juice, Tabasco, and salt and pepper. Heat the mixture slowly. Just before it reaches boiling point, add the sprigs of dill and remove from the heat. Stand, covered, for 20 minutes, then remove the dill sprigs from the pan. Reheat the tomato juice until almost boiling, then remove from the heat and shake in the gelatine. When it has dissolved, strain the tomato juice into a jug and leave to cool. When cooled, pour into a ring mould and chill in the refrigerator for a few hours or until set.

2 Shortly before serving, unmould the jelly on to a flat dish. To make the filling, season the beaten eggs with salt and pepper, then heat the butter in a shallow pan and scramble the eggs, removing them from the heat while they are still slightly runny. Let them cool almost to room temperature, about 20 minutes, then spoon them into the centre of the tomato jelly ring and scatter the chopped chives or dill thickly over the top. Serve immediately, with thinly sliced rye bread.

Serves 4 as a first course, or 3 as a light main dish accompanied by a green salad.

fish

moules à la crème
au safran

1 Clean the mussels thoroughly in cold water. Discard any mussels that do not close tightly when tapped.

2 Warm the cream in a small pan. Shake in the saffron and heat almost to boiling point, then remove from the heat and cover the pan.

3 Melt the butter in a deep pot, then add the shallot, parsley and celery leaves, and cook gently for 4 minutes. Tip the mussels into the pot, add the wine and bring to the boil quickly. Then cover the pan and cook for 3–5 minutes, until the mussels have opened. Lift out the mussels and keep warm in a large bowl or soup tureen. Discard any mussels that have not opened. Strain the liquid into a clean pan and reheat. Pour the saffron infusion through a small strainer into the mussel stock. Boil all together for a moment, then pour over the mussels and sprinkle with chopped coriander or parsley.

Serves 4

- 2 kg (4 lb) mussels
- 150 ml (¼ pint) double cream
- ¼ teaspoon saffron
- 15 g (½ oz) butter
- 1 shallot, chopped
- 3 stalks parsley, chopped
- 6 large celery leaves, chopped
- 300 ml (½ pint) dry white wine
- 2 tablespoons chopped coriander or flat-leaf parsley, to garnish

Previous pages: Moules à la Crème, recipe above

gravadlax

This is the Scandinavian equivalent of smoked salmon. Unlike smoked salmon, however, it is easily made at home, and well worth the effort. Try to get a nice middle cut of salmon, and choose a wild one when in season. But be sure of a plentiful supply of fresh dill before even starting; small supermarket packets of dill will go nowhere and cost the earth.

1.5 kg (3 lb) middle cut of salmon

175 g (6 oz) dill, stalks and leaves, coarsely chopped

2 tablespoons white peppercorns, coarsely crushed

50 g (2 oz) sea salt

50 g (2 oz) granulated sugar

4 tablespoons finely chopped dill, to garnish

1 Start 2–3 days in advance. Ask your fishmonger to split the fish in half horizontally, and to remove the backbone. When you get it home, use tweezers to pull out all the small bones. Make small jabs in the skin sides with the point of a small knife. Spread one-third of the dill in a wide shallow dish and lay half the salmon on this, skin side down.

2 Pound the peppercorns with the sea salt and sugar until you have a coarse mixture, evenly ground. Spread half of this over the cut surface of the salmon in the dish. Lay another one-third of the dill over this.

3 Spread the remaining pepper mixture over the cut side of the second piece of fish and lay it, skin side up, over the first half, as if reconstructing the fish. Spread the remaining dill over the top and cover with a piece of foil. Lay a board on top and weigh down with 3 x 500 g (1 lb) weights. Place low down in the refrigerator for 2–3 days, turning the pieces of fish over each day.

4 To serve, scrape off all the dill and pepper, and lay the pieces of fish, skin side down, on a board. Sprinkle the dill over the surface of both pieces, and cut downwards, slightly on the diagonal, in slices about 5 mm (¼ inch) thick. Gravadlax is best served with Mustard and Dill Sauce (see page 176).

Note: This useful dish can be kept for up to 1 week in the refrigerator or frozen for up to 4 weeks.

Serves 8

grilled squid with coriander

Buy the squid already cleaned if possible.

16 small squid, cleaned
2 tablespoons sunflower oil
1 egg white, lightly beaten
4 tablespoons sesame seeds
salt and black pepper

To garnish:

1 tablespoon sunflower oil
12 sprigs coriander
2 lemons, cut in quarters
Watercress Sauce (see page 167)
** (optional)**

1 If the squid have not already been cleaned, proceed as follows. Pull the head, with tentacles attached, out of the body sac. Cut across the head just above the eyes, discarding everything that falls below that line. Open out the tentacles, squeeze out the central polyp and discard it. Wash the body sac under cold running water; pull out the central transparent 'quill' or 'pen' and discard, together with any odd bits and pieces within the sac. If there is an ink sac, discard this also, as ink is not required for this recipe. Wash the body well, inside and out, and pull off the outer skin. Cut off the triangular fins and discard. Chop the tentacles and set aside.

2 Slit each body sac in half and score the outer sides in a diagonal criss-cross pattern, using the point of a sharp knife. Rub them on both sides with sunflower oil. Thread the clumps of tentacles on skewers, then rub them with sunflower oil. Sprinkle all the squid parts with salt and pepper, then lay them on the grill pan. Brush the top surfaces with the lightly beaten egg white, then scatter the sesame seeds on top. Grill the squid for 1½ minutes under a fierce heat, then turn them over and grill the second side for 1½ minutes.

3 While the squid are grilling, prepare the garnish. Heat the sunflower oil in a small frying pan. When it is very hot, throw in the coriander and fry for 30 seconds, turning over and over, then lift out on to kitchen paper to drain.

4 To serve, lay the squid sacs on a flat dish, take the tentacles off the skewers and add them to the dish, then lay the fried coriander sprigs over and around them. Serve the lemon quarters and watercress sauce, if using, separately.

Serves 4 as a first course.

Right: Grilled Squid with Coriander, recipe above

smoked haddock salad
with herbs

1 Put the fish in a wide pan and cover with cold water. Bring slowly to the boil, then cover the pan, remove from the heat, and leave for 30 minutes. Take out the fish and allow it to cool for a little while. Once it is cool enough to handle, remove the skin and bones, and flake the fish. Tip into a large bowl and season with salt and pepper. Stir in the sliced spring onions, olive oil and lemon juice. Mix gently, trying not to break up the fish, then fold in most of the chopped herbs, keeping back 1 tablespoon for a garnish.

2 Turn the fish mixture on to a flat dish to serve, and sprinkle with the rest of the herbs. Serve within 2 hours of making and, if possible, at room temperature.

Note: Try to get whole smoked haddock for this dish; boned fillets are not as good.

Serves 4 as a first course.

**875 g (1¾ lb) whole smoked
  haddock**
1 bunch spring onions, sliced
3 tablespoons extra virgin olive oil
2 tablespoons lemon juice
**2 tablespoons chopped flat-leaf
  parsley**
2 tablespoons chopped chives
salt and black pepper

lobster salad

This simple and delicious dish is rarely seen these days, alas.

**1 large lobster, weighing about
1.25 kg (2½ lb), cooked**

**3–4 ripe tomatoes, skinned and cut
in pieces**

**300 ml (½ pint) Mayonnaise (see
page 168)**

3 shakes Tabasco

1½ tablespoons chopped chervil

1½ tablespoons chopped chives

salt and black pepper

**small salad leaves (rocket, mâche,
watercress), to garnish**

1 Take the lobster flesh out of its shell and cut into chunks. Pulp the tomatoes in a liquidizer or food processor, then measure 6 tablespoons of the tomato pulp and stir it into the mayonnaise, adding the Tabasco, salt and pepper, and most of the chopped herbs, keeping back a little for a garnish.

2 Fold the lobster into this sauce, and tip on to a flat dish to serve. Sprinkle the remaining herbs over the top, and arrange some small salad leaves around the edges of the dish. Serve at room temperature soon after making.

Note: If making in advance, chill the lobster in its sauce in a bowl covered with clingfilm before arranging on its dish. Take it out of the refrigerator 1 hour before serving, then turn out and garnish as above.

Serves 2 as a main dish, needing no accompaniment.

salmon pasties with dill

I buy puff pastry to use for this dish, but you can make your own if you prefer.

1 Choose a pan just large enough to hold the fish. Bring some lightly salted water to the boil, lower in the fish, bring back to the boil and simmer gently for 15 minutes. Remove the fish, drain well and leave to cool. Later, flake the fish, discarding all the skin and bones.

2 Boil the rice according to the packet instructions until tender, then drain well. Mix it with the flaked fish, adding the chopped spring onions, chopped dill, and salt and pepper. Finally stir in the melted butter and set aside.

3 Roll out the pastry quite thinly and cut it in circles about 7 cm (3 inches) across. Lay these on a floured surface and roll them out again, separately, until you have very thin circles about 10 cm (4 inches) in diameter. Lay 1½ tablespoons of the salmon and rice filling on one half of each circle. Damp the edges of the pastry with water, all round the circle, and fold one half over on top of the other, pressing the edges together to seal. Trim the edges if necessary, using a small knife, and make a small slit in the centre of each. Beat the egg yolk with the milk and brush all over the pasties. Lay them on a greased baking sheet and bake in a preheated oven, 180°C (350°F), Gas Mark 4, for about 15–20 minutes until they are glazed golden brown.

4 Serve soon after baking, alone or with watercress sauce as a light main dish with a green salad, or as a substantial first course or snack.

Makes about 12; serves 4 to 6.

375 g (12 oz) salmon
125 g (4 oz) white long-grain rice
2 tablespoons chopped spring onions
3 tablespoons chopped dill
40 g (1½ oz) butter, melted
375 g (12 oz) puff pastry
salt and black pepper
Watercress Sauce (see page 167) (optional)

To glaze:

1 egg yolk
1 tablespoon milk

smoked salmon
with new potatoes and dill

This is a useful way of transforming smoked salmon into a light main course. Gravadlax (see page 105) may be substituted for smoked salmon, or chives for dill, if preferred. It is important to get a really good waxy new potato; the best varieties for this are Jersey Royal, Belle de Fontenay and La Ratte.

750 g (1½ lb) new potatoes
3 tablespoons virgin olive oil
1 tablespoon white wine vinegar
4 tablespoons chopped dill
500 g (1 lb) smoked salmon,
  thinly sliced
black pepper

1 Boil the potatoes in their skins, then drain in a colander. As soon as they are cool enough to handle, peel them and cut into thick slices. Put them in a bowl and add the olive oil, vinegar and black pepper, mixing very gently so as not to break up the potatoes. Lastly, stir in half of the chopped dill. Shortly before serving (the potatoes should still be warm), arrange the smoked salmon on 4 large plates, covering one half of each plate. Lay the potato salad on the other half of each plate and scatter the reserved dill over all.

Serves 4 as a light main course, with buttered rye bread and a green salad to follow.

steamed prawns
with ginger and lemon grass

This dish should be made with large uncooked prawns. The freshwater king prawns are probably the best, but the stripy saltwater tiger prawns also work well. I always shell them, leaving only the tails, before cooking, as it is a messy business trying to shell them on the plate in a sauce. But some of my friends do not mind doing that, and prefer to leave the shells on until the last moment. If you want to serve them in the shells, allow 1 extra minute steaming.

1 Cut 4 pieces of foil about 15 cm (6 inches) square, and rub each with a few drops of sesame oil. Divide the prawns evenly between them, and sprinkle with the sliced spring onions, chopped garlic and ginger. Lay a piece of lemon grass, or some of the chopped lemon balm, in the centre of each pile, sprinkle with salt and pepper and a dash of soy sauce. Wrap up the foil parcels and seal the edges by pinching together. Steam them for 4–6 minutes over boiling water. (This timing is based on the assumption that the foil packages are not too crowded and there is plenty of room for the steam to circulate. If this is not the case, allow an extra 1–2 minutes steaming.)

2 To serve, unwrap each package and slide the contents on to a warm plate, discarding the lemon grass. Serve immediately, garnished with chopped coriander.

Note: The little packages may be prepared in advance and kept in the refrigerator for 2–3 hours. Since the actual cooking time is so brief, this is a useful dish for suppers after the cinema.

Serves 4 as a first course or a light main dish. If serving as a main dish, accompany with a bowl of plain boiled basmati rice.

1 tablespoon sesame oil

approx. 500 g (1 lb) large uncooked prawns, or 4–6 per person, depending on size, shells removed except for tails

8 spring onions, sliced

1 garlic clove, finely chopped

25 g (1 oz) fresh root ginger, finely chopped

1 stalk lemon grass, cut in 4 and lightly crushed, or 1 tablespoon chopped lemon balm

2 teaspoons soy sauce

sea salt and black pepper

1½ tablespoons finely chopped coriander, to garnish

Previous pages: Steamed Prawns with Ginger and Lemon Grass, recipe above

scallop salad
with mint

This is a dish to make in summertime, when young, tender leaves of spinach and mint are readily available.

150 ml (¼ pint) dry white wine

150 ml (¼ pint) water

6 large scallops

175 g (6 oz) young spinach, stalks removed

125 g (4 oz) button mushrooms, caps only, sliced

4 tablespoons sunflower oil

4 tablespoons lemon juice

3 tablespoons mint, cut in strips

salt and black pepper

1 Bring the wine and water to the boil. Add the scallops and poach for 4 minutes. Drain and cool the scallops while you prepare the rest of the salad.

2 Wash and drain the spinach, then shake and pat dry with a cloth. Pile loosely in a salad bowl. Scatter the sliced mushrooms over the spinach. Cut the scallops into 2–3 round slices; if they are still warm, so much the better. Lay them over the mushrooms. Mix the oil and lemon juice and pour over the salad. Add salt and pepper, and the sliced mint. Mix gently and serve as soon as possible.

Serves 4 as a first course.

fish cakes

with parsley and chilli sauce

500 g (1 lb) cod fillet

500 g (1 lb) floury potatoes

1 egg, beaten

4 tablespoons milk

4 tablespoons chopped parsley

a little flour

25 g (1 oz) butter

2 tablespoons sunflower oil

Chilli Sauce (see page 170)

salt and black pepper

1 Make the chilli sauce and start the fish cakes a day in advance. Cook the fish in lightly salted boiling water until tender, then drain. Once it is cool enough to handle, discard the skin and flake the flesh. Boil the potatoes in their skins; drain and skin them as soon as you can touch them. Push through a medium food mill into a large bowl, then stir in the flaked fish. Mix well, beating with a wooden spoon. Beat the egg with the milk, salt, pepper and chopped parsley, then stir into the fish and potato mixture. Beat till smooth, then cover the bowl with clingfilm and chill for several hours or overnight.

2 Next day, form the fish mixture into round flat cakes and sprinkle them with flour. Heat the butter and oil in a broad frying pan and fry the fish cakes until golden, turning once. Drain on kitchen paper, then transfer to a heated dish. Reheat the chilli sauce gently – it does not want to be very hot – and serve separately.

Serves 4 to 5

Right: from left, Chilli Sauce, recipe page 170 and Fish Cakes with Parsley and Chilli Sauce, recipe above

stir-fried scallops
with coriander

1 If using large scallops, cut them in quarters and discard the orange tongues. Heat a wok or deep pan. Add the oil and heat, then throw in the sliced spring onions and toss for 30 seconds. Add the lemon grass and ginger and toss for another 30 seconds. Put in the scallops and stir-fry for 2 minutes, then drain off the liquid and add the fruit juice and soy sauce. Heat through very quickly, then continue to toss for 1 minute. Remove from the heat and stir in the chopped coriander.

Serves 3 with boiled rice.

500 g (1 lb) queen scallops or
　12 large scallops
2 tablespoons sunflower oil
1 bunch spring onions, sliced
5 cm (2 inch) piece lemon grass,
　finely chopped
1½ tablespoons finely chopped
　fresh root ginger
4 tablespoons Seville orange juice,
　or 3 tablespoons orange juice and
　1½ tablespoons lime juice
1 tablespoon soy sauce
3 tablespoons chopped coriander,
　to garnish

Dover sole Colbert

Sadly overlooked in recent years, this is a simple and delicious dish.

1 Make the parsley butter in advance and keep it chilled in the refrigerator until ready to use.

2 Using a small knife, make an incision down the centre of the fish on the top side between the two fillets. Cut through the backbone twice, freeing a section about 5 cm (2 inches) long but leaving it in place. Dip the fish in the seasoned flour, then in the beaten egg and finally in the breadcrumbs. Heat 5 cm (2 inches) sunflower oil in a wide pan. When it is very hot, about 180°C (350°F), lower in the fish and fry till golden brown, then drain. Part the fillets where they have been cut, and remove the section of bone. Put a lump of parsley butter in the opening, fold the flaps of fish back over it and serve immediately.

25 g (1 oz) Parsley Butter (see page 240) per fish
1 x 425 g (14 oz) Dover sole per person, skinned, without head
seasoned flour
1 egg, beaten
dry white breadcrumbs
sunflower oil

marinated sole
with Seville oranges and coriander

In Latin America raw fish or shellfish is marinated in lime juice and called seviche. Loosely based on the original idea, this version is quite delicious, but can be made only when Seville oranges are available.

1 Cut the fillets of Dover sole diagonally into strips about 1 x 5 cm (½ x 2 inches). Put them in a bowl and pour the fruit juices over them. Cover the bowl with clingfilm and stand it in the refrigerator for 6–8 hours or overnight. Shortly before serving, drain off the fruit juices and stir in the sunflower oil, chopped onion, chilli and coriander. Spoon into small dishes or large shells to serve.

Serves 4 as a first course.

500 g (1 lb) fillets of Dover sole
150 ml (¼ pint) juice of
  Seville oranges
150 ml (¼ pint) lime juice
1 tablespoon sunflower oil
1 tablespoon finely chopped onion
1 green chilli, deseeded and finely
  chopped
2 tablespoons finely chopped
  coriander

lobster & dill sandwich

This sandwich makes the best ever pre-theatre snack, accompanied by a glass of chilled Sauvignon Blanc.

1 Take the lobster meat out of its shell and chop coarsely. Mix with the chopped celery, mayonnaise, salt and pepper. Spread the bread thinly with the butter and divide the lobster filling evenly between 2 of the slices. Sprinkle them quite thickly with dill, then cover with the remaining bread slices. Press together lightly, cut off the crusts, and cut each sandwich into 4.

Serves 2

500 g (1 lb) lobster
25 g (1 oz) celery, tender sticks
  only, chopped
2 tablespoons mayonnaise
4 large thin slices brown bread
25 g (1 oz) butter, at room
  temperature
1½ tablespoons chopped dill
sea salt and black pepper

squid stuffed
with herbs and breadcrumbs

1 If the squid have not already been cleaned, proceed as follows. Pull the head, with tentacles attached, out of the body sac. Cut across the head just above the eyes, discarding everything that falls below that line. Open out the tentacles, squeeze out the central polyp and discard it. Wash the body sac under cold running water; pull out the central transparent 'quill' or 'pen' and discard, together with any odd bits and pieces within the sac. If there is an ink sac, discard this also, as ink is not required for this recipe. Wash the body well, inside and out, and pull off the outer skin. Cut off the triangular fins and discard. Chop the tentacles and set aside.

2 For the stuffing, put the onions, carrots and celery sticks in a blender or food processor and chop to a fine hash, or do the same thing by hand. Brown the hashed vegetables in the olive oil and butter in a sauté pan, adding the finely chopped garlic after a few minutes. Then add the chopped bacon and tentacles and continue to cook gently for 4–5 minutes, stirring often. When the cooking is completed, stir in the chopped fresh herbs and remove from the heat.

3 Soak the bread in the hot milk for 10 minutes, then squeeze dry and add to the pan. Mix well, mashing the bread into the rest of the stuffing with the back of a wooden spoon. Beat in the egg yolk and season with salt and pepper. Stuff the bodies of the squid with this mixture, using a coffee spoon to avoid tearing the opening. Do not fill the squid more than three-quarters full, then secure with wooden toothpicks.

4 Heat the oil and butter for the sauce in a clean pan, add the onion, and cook until it starts to colour. Add the stuffed squid and cover with the chopped tomatoes. Pour on the wine, add salt and pepper to taste, and cover the pan. Simmer gently for 35 minutes, shaking the pan from time to time. Transfer to a dish to serve, and sprinkle with the basil.

Serves 4 as a first course or as a light main dish.

8 small squid, with bodies about
  10 cm (4 inches) long, bought
  already cleaned if possible

Stuffing:

2 onions
2 carrots
2 celery sticks
2 tablespoons olive oil
40 g (1½ oz) butter
1 garlic clove, finely chopped
4 rashers of rindless bacon,
  finely chopped
2 tablespoons chopped basil
2 tablespoons chopped flat-leaf
  parsley
25 g (1 oz) dry white bread,
  crusts removed
150 ml (¼ pint) hot milk
1 egg yolk
salt and black pepper

Sauce:

1 tablespoon olive oil
15 g (½ oz) butter
1 onion, finely chopped
250 g (8 oz) tomatoes, skinned
  and chopped
175 ml (6 fl oz) dry white wine
1½ tablespoons basil, torn in strips,
  to garnish

poultry
and
game

grilled chicken wings
with herbs

This simple dish may be served alone, as a first course, or as part of a number of other dishes. It is good at any temperature and makes a useful snack to have on hand over a holiday. When served alone, it may be accompanied by Cucumber and Yogurt Sauce (see page 171). Chicken wings can be bought very cheaply in packets at most supermarkets; they can also be frozen successfully.

1 Prepare the chicken wings 2 hours ahead. Line the grill pan with foil and rub it with a little of the oil. Lay the chicken wings on it. Mix the remaining oil with the lemon juice and pour it over the chicken wings, rubbing it over them thoroughly. Spread the crushed garlic, dried herbs, salt and pepper over the joints, and leave for a couple of hours.

2 Heat the grill and cook the little joints for 8–10 minutes on each side. They should be nicely browned on the outside without being burnt, and just cooked, still juicy, within. Divide each one in half before serving; this makes them easier to eat in the fingers, but is not essential. They may be served hot, warm or after cooling.

Serves 4 on its own as a first course or snack, or 6 with other dishes.

1 kg (2 lb) chicken wings (joints only, without breast)
4 tablespoons olive oil
2½ tablespoons lemon juice
1–2 garlic cloves, crushed
1 tablespoon dried Herbes de Provence
sea salt and black pepper

Previous pages: from left, Grilled Chicken Wings with Herbs, recipe above and Cucumber and Yogurt Sauce, recipe page 171

tarragon chicken mould

2 kg (4 lb) chicken
I onion, halved
I carrot, halved
I celery stick, halved
I bay leaf
10 black peppercorns
salt
½ bottle dry white wine

To garnish:

I bunch tarragon
I tablespoon powdered gelatine
300 ml (½ pint) single cream
4 medium carrots
I tablespoon chopped tarragon

1 Start 1–2 days in advance. Put the chicken in a pressure cooker or casserole with the flavouring vegetables, bay leaf and seasonings. Add the wine and enough water to cover the thighs of the bird. Bring to the boil, cover and cook under pressure for 25 minutes or simmer gently in a casserole for 1¼ hours or until the bird is tender. If you can spare the time, leave it to cool in the stock, then remove it and strain the stock. Either way, chill the strained stock in the refrigerator overnight.

2 Next day, remove all fat from the surface of the stock and put the stock back in the pressure cooker or casserole. Cut the chicken off the bones, discard the skin and fat, and wrap the meat in clingfilm. Put the bones back into the stock, bring to the boil and cook for 20 minutes under pressure or 1 hour in a casserole. Now strain the stock again, and boil to reduce by about half: you will need only 600 ml (1 pint). Put the tarragon sprigs in a bowl and then pour the reduced chicken stock over them while still very hot. Leave for 20 minutes, then strain again and reheat. Remove from the heat, shake in the gelatine and leave to dissolve, then stir in the cream.

3 Make 4–5 incisions down the sides of the carrots using a canelle knife, then cut them in 5 mm (¼ inch) slices. Cook in slightly salted boiling water for 4 minutes, then rinse under cold running water. Tear the chicken into fillets. Make a layer of carrot slices in the bottom of a shallow bowl holding about 1.2 litres (2 pints). Pour a little of the cool, creamy chicken stock on top, then fill up the dish with layers of chicken fillets and sliced carrots. Pour the rest of the creamy stock over all, and chill for several hours or overnight.

4 Turn out on to a flat dish to serve; this is best done by running a small knife round the edges of the dish, then standing it in about 5 cm (2 inches) warm water for 1–2 minutes, just long enough to loosen the base of the jelly. Scatter the chopped tarragon over all, and serve with boiled new potatoes, dressed with olive oil and chopped chervil.

Serves 6

sliced chicken on noodles

1 Put the carrot, leek, celery, bay leaf, salt and peppercorns in a wide lidded pan large enough to hold the half chicken. Add the cold water and the chicken neck and wing tips. Bring slowly to the boil, cover the pan, and cook for 30 minutes. Then lay the half chicken over the vegetables, add the wine, and bring back to the boil. Cover the pan and cook gently for 45 minutes, or until the chicken is cooked through. Lift out the bird and keep warm while you strain the stock and remove the fat from the surface. Then reheat the stock in a small pan and add the chopped herbs. Set aside.

2 To serve, cook the noodles according to the packet instructions or until tender, drain well and divide between 4 soup plates. Cut the chicken into broad wedges, discarding the bones, and lay over the noodles. Pour the broth with the herbs over the pieces of chicken and serve immediately.

Serves 4 as a combined first and main course.

I large carrot, cut in quarters

I large leek, cut in quarters

I celery stick, cut in half

I small bay leaf

½ tablespoon sea salt

8 black peppercorns

900 ml (1½ pints) cold water

½ chicken, weighing about 875 g
  (1¾ lb), plus neck and wing tips

175 ml (6 fl oz) dry white wine

2 tablespoons chopped chervil

2 tablespoons chopped tarragon

2 tablespoons chopped chives

250 g (8 oz) noodles

poached chicken

in herb sauce

4 chicken breasts

2 large spring onions, sliced

2 x 5 mm (¼ inch) slices fresh
  root ginger

10 black peppercorns,
  lightly crushed

½ teaspoon sea salt

Herb Sauce:

25 g (1 oz) butter

1½ tablespoons plain flour

300 ml (½ pint) chicken stock (see
  recipe)

150 ml (¼ pint) single cream

½ tablespoon chopped chervil

½ tablespoon chopped dill

½ tablespoon chopped
  tarragon

salt and black pepper

1 Put the chicken breasts into a saucepan and add enough water to cover them. Remove the chicken and put the spring onions, ginger, peppercorns and salt into the pan. Bring to the boil, replace the chicken breasts, bring back to the boil, and simmer gently for 10 minutes. Then lift out the chicken breasts and strain the stock. Measure 300 ml (½ pint) and set aside. Put the breasts back in the remaining stock to keep warm while you make the sauce.

2 Melt the butter, add the flour and cook for 1 minute, stirring. Then add the 300 ml (½ pint) chicken stock and bring to the boil, stirring. Simmer gently for 3 minutes, stirring from time to time. Add the cream, and salt and pepper to taste. Finally, stir in the chopped herbs and remove from the heat.

3 To serve, lay the chicken breasts on a flat dish and pour some of the sauce over them. Serve the rest separately in a small jug.

Serves 4 with rice, noodles or new potatoes, and a green salad.

braised pheasant
with lovage

1 Heat the oil in a casserole and brown the bird, turning frequently. Remove the bird and put the sliced vegetables in the pan. Cook gently, stirring now and then, for 5 minutes, then make them into an even layer in the bottom of the pan and lay the bird on it. Sprinkle the oregano or marjoram over the contents of the pan, and tuck the lovage or alexanders leaves around the bird. Heat the stock and wine together and pour over the bird. Add salt and pepper, cover the pot, and cook in a preheated oven, 160°C (325°F), Gas Mark 3, for 1¼ hours. (Allow an extra 5 minutes for a cock bird; longer still for old birds.) Test to see when it is done by piercing a leg with a thin skewer; the juices should run faintly pink.

2 Shortly before the bird has finished cooking, stir the flour into the butter to make a smooth paste. Take the casserole out of the oven, lift out the bird and keep warm. Discard the lovage or alexanders leaves. Set the casserole over a low heat and drop in the flour-and-butter paste by degrees, stirring constantly until smoothly blended. Simmer for 3 minutes, then set aside.

3 Cut the bird into quarters. (If serving more than 2, it will be better to carve it into smaller pieces, so that each person gets a mixture of light and dark meat.) Lay them on a shallow dish and spoon the vegetables in their sauce over and around the bird. Scatter the chopped parsley over all and serve, with a purée of potatoes or Rice and Noodle Pilaf (see page 159) and a green vegetable. Sage and Onion Sauce (see page 170) may also be served if desired.

Note: If you choose to braise two birds, to serve 4–6, the same amount of vegetables and other ingredients will suffice, but remember to allow longer cooking time for cock pheasants and older birds.

Serves 2 to 3

4 tablespoons olive oil

1 young pheasant, preferably a hen

1 small onion, sliced

2 leeks, sliced

2 carrots, sliced

1½ tablespoons chopped oregano or marjoram

15 g (½ oz) lovage leaves or 25 g (1 oz) alexanders, leaves only

125 ml (4 fl oz) chicken stock

125 ml (4 fl oz) red wine

1 teaspoon flour

5 g (¼ oz) butter, at room temperature

salt and black pepper

1½ tablespoons roughly chopped flat-leaf parsley, to garnish

Right: Braised Pheasant with Lovage, recipe above

grouse salad

Cold game salads are as delicious as they are unusual, and simpler by far to execute than the exact timing and tricky accompaniments demanded by roast birds. The grouse should be left to cool to room temperature after roasting is completed.

1 Lay the grouse upside down on a rack in a roasting tin. Cook them in a preheated oven, 200°C (400°F), Gas Mark 6, for 25 minutes, then leave to cool.

2 After about 2 hours cut the grouse in halves or quarters. Lay the rocket on a flat dish and place the sliced beetroot over it. Mix all the ingredients for the dressing together and pour over the salad. Toss the salad lightly, then lay the grouse on top. Serve at room temperature.

Serves 4 as a light main dish after a substantial first course.

2 young grouse, barded with fat bacon
125 g (4 oz) rocket
4 small beetroot, freshly cooked and thickly sliced

Dressing:

4 tablespoons extra virgin olive oil
1 tablespoon white wine vinegar
1 tablespoon lemon juice
¼ teaspoon Dijon mustard
a pinch of sugar
sea salt and black pepper

wood pigeons with grapes

8 thin rashers unsmoked bacon

4 wood pigeons

25 g (1 oz) butter

2 tablespoons olive oil

4 shallots, chopped

750 g (1½ lb) grapes

24 sage leaves

salt and black pepper

1 Lay the bacon rashers over the breasts of the pigeons and tie with string to hold in place. Heat the butter and oil in a casserole, add the shallots and cook until they start to colour. Add the birds and brown them all over, then take them out of the pan. Put two-thirds of the grapes in the casserole and stir around for a few minutes, then bury the birds among them. Scatter the sage leaves in among the grapes, and add salt and pepper to taste. Squeeze the remaining grapes and pour their juices into the pan. Cover closely, with a layer of kitchen foil under the lid, and cook in a preheated oven, 160°C (325°F), Gas Mark 3, for 1¾ hours.

2 To serve, lift the birds out of the casserole, cut the string, and remove and discard the bacon. Lay the grapes on a serving dish, place the birds on them and pour the juices over all.

Serves 4 with French bread and a green salad.

poussins with thyme and garlic

*When made with squabs (farmed pigeons) instead of poussins, this is
even more delicious, but much more expensive.*

1 Put the butter in a casserole with 2 tablespoons of the oil. Heat the
fat, then add the birds and brown them all over. Take out the birds and
put the garlic cloves into the casserole. Cook very gently for
1–2 minutes, then add the wine, thyme, salt and pepper. Bring to the
boil, lay the birds on the garlic and cover the casserole. Cook in a preheated oven, 190°C (375°F), Gas Mark 5, for 30–35 minutes .

2 Meanwhile, heat the remaining tablespoon of oil in a frying pan, add
the chopped shallot and cook gently for 1–2 minutes. Then add the
chicken livers and continue to cook briefly, just until they are cooked
through. Set aside in a warm place.

3 When the birds are cooked, transfer them to a plate and keep warm.
Discard the thyme and push the garlic cloves through a medium food
mill into a bowl. Then purée the livers and the chopped shallots and
pour on to the garlic. Put the casserole over a low heat and add the liver
purée to the juices, stirring to blend well. Add the crème fraîche or
double cream, and salt and pepper to taste. Bubble up for a moment or
two, then pour into a bowl and sprinkle with chopped parsley.

4 Make a bed of mâche on a flat dish. Cut the birds in half and lay
them on it. Serve the sauce separately.

Serves 4 with boiled rice, noodles or new potatoes, and a salad.

25 g (I oz) butter
3 tablespoons sunflower oil
2 poussins
12 garlic cloves, unpeeled
150 ml (¼ pint) dry white wine
4 sprigs thyme
I shallot, chopped
**50 g (2 oz) chicken livers, cut in
   pieces**
**2 tablespoons crème fraîche or
   double cream**
salt and black pepper

To garnish:

¼ tablespoon finely chopped parsley
75 g (3 oz) mâche

quail with Calvados

If you don't have any Calvados, you can use brandy instead.

25 g (1 oz) butter
1½ tablespoons olive oil
1 small onion, finely chopped
4 quail
4 tablespoons Calvados
4 tablespoons chicken stock, heated
2 sprigs hyssop, if available
1½ tablespoons chopped thyme
salt and black pepper

1 Heat the butter and oil in a sauté pan, and cook the chopped onion until it starts to soften. Add the quail, turning them over and over to brown, and sprinkle with salt and pepper. Pour the Calvados into a ladle and warm over a low heat, then set light to it and pour it, flaming, over the quail. Tilt the pan from side to side, and spoon the spirit over the birds. When the flames have died down, add the heated stock and the hyssop, if using, and sprinkle with chopped thyme. Cover the pan and cook gently for 20 minutes, by which time the quail should be ready. Lift them on to a serving dish, and pour the juices over and around them.

Serves 4 with a dish of rice, noodles, or a potato purée and another vegetable, or serves 2 with just a green salad.

meat

pork sausages
with fresh herbs

Anyone with a sausage-making attachment for their mixer, and/or a friendly butcher who will supply the skins, may like to try making their own sausages. The casings are made from the small intestines of the pig or sheep, and your butcher may be prepared to supply these if he makes his own sausages. He may even be prepared to fill them for you with your own filling. But do not consider making your own sausages without a food processor. The flavouring of the filling is a very personal thing, which you can adjust to your own taste, while the use of fresh herbs as opposed to the musty aroma of dried sage can only be welcome.

1 Cut the lean pork from the leg in cubes and put in the food processor. Separate the lean meat from the fat of the belly meat and add it, also cut in cubes, to the pork already in the processor. Process both together to give a nice coarse texture. Cut the fat from the belly by hand into neat cubes about 5 mm (¼ inch). Mix all the meat together in a large bowl.

2 Soak the bread in the milk for 10 minutes, then squeeze it dry and add to the meat, mixing thoroughly. Put the chopped garlic in a mortar with the sea salt, peppercorns and juniper berries. Crush roughly, just until most of the peppercorns are broken, then mix with the ground spices and stir into the meat. Lastly, stir in the chopped fresh herbs and mix again. Try out a small ball by frying in a drop of oil, and adjust the seasonings to your taste.

3 Fill your casings according to the directions that came with your machine, or give them to your butcher. Some recipes tell you to hang your sausages for 2–3 days before using, but I like to cook them as soon as possible after making. These sausages are best cooked slowly: either fried or grilled, or in a preheated oven, 180°C (350°F), Gas Mark 4, for 30–35 minutes.

Note: If casings are hard to come by, the same mixture can be used like sausagemeat and cooked as croquettes or meat loaf, or used as a stuffing for vegetables like cabbage and marrow.

Makes about 750 g (1½ lb).

300 g (10 oz) lean, boneless pork,
  from the leg
300 g (10 oz) belly of pork
75 g (3 oz) soft white breadcrumbs
  (use coarse country bread)
6 tablespoons milk
2 garlic cloves, chopped
2 teaspoons sea salt
1 teaspoon black peppercorns
12 juniper berries
¼ teaspoon ground mace
¼ teaspoon ground allspice
2 tablespoons coarsely chopped
  flat-leaf parsley
2 tablespoons coarsely chopped
  basil

Previous pages: Pork Sausages with Fresh Herbs, recipe above

braised beef with horseradish

1.5 kg (3 lb) rolled rump, top rump
or topside of beef
I large onion, sliced
2 large carrots, quartered
2 celery sticks, halved
2 garlic cloves, peeled
2 bay leaves
2 sprigs thyme
I bottle red wine
40 g (1½ oz) butter
I tablespoon olive oil
125 g (4 oz) mushrooms,
coarsely chopped
I calf's foot or I pig's trotter,
split in 4
salt and black pepper

To garnish:

I bunch small carrots
Horseradish Sauce with Chives
(see page 177)

1 Start 1 day in advance. Put the beef in a deep bowl and smother it with all the sliced vegetables (except the mushrooms) and the herbs. Pour the red wine on top and leave overnight in a cool place, basting once or twice.

2 Next day, lift the beef out of the marinade and pat dry with kitchen paper. Strain the wine, reserving the vegetables and herbs. Heat the butter and oil in an oval casserole and brown the meat on all sides, then remove it and put in the vegetables. Add the chopped mushrooms and cook gently, stirring, for 4 minutes. Return the meat to the casserole and tuck the calf's foot or pig's trotter in beside it. Heat the strained marinade and pour it over, adding salt and pepper. Cover closely with a layer of foil under the lid and bake in a preheated oven, 160°C (325°F), Gas Mark 3, for 2½ hours.

3 When the meat is cooked, lift it out and strain the marinade. Discard the vegetables and herbs, and boil the marinade to reduce it a little. Carve the beef in fairly thick slices, about 5 mm (¼ inch) thick, and lay them in a shallow dish. Pour over a little of the marinade, just enough to moisten the meat, and garnish with the small whole carrots, plainly boiled and laid around the edge of the dish. Serve the rest of the marinade in a heated sauceboat, and the horseradish sauce with chives in a small bowl.

Serves 6 with plain boiled potatoes and a green vegetable, or with noodles and a green salad.

braised breast of lamb

with celery leaves

1 First make the stuffing. Soak the bread in the milk for 10 minutes, then squeeze dry. Drop the spinach into lightly salted boiling water and cook briskly for 4–5 minutes, depending on the time of year. (Tender summer spinach needs only 4 minutes.) Drain in a colander, rinse under cold running water and drain again. When it is cool enough to handle, squeeze out the excess moisture and chop coarsely by hand. Mix with the bread, adding the chopped herb, mace, egg yolk, and salt and pepper to taste. Mix well, then lay out the breast of lamb and spread the stuffing evenly over it, leaving 5 mm (¼ inch) clear around the edges. Roll up firmly and tie securely round the middle with 3–4 pieces of string.

2 Braise the lamb. Heat the butter in an oval casserole, put in the sliced vegetables, and stew them gently for 5 minutes, stirring now and then. Lift most of the vegetables out with a slotted spoon to make room for the lamb. Put the lamb in the pan and brown gently all over, turning often. Pack the sliced vegetables back around the meat, adding the bay leaf. Heat the stock and wine together and pour over the meat. Bring to the boil, then cover and cook in a preheated oven, 150°C (300°F), Gas Mark 2, for 2 hours.

3 To serve, lift out the meat and carve in thick slices. Using a slotted spoon, transfer the sliced vegetables to a serving dish. Discard the bay leaf. Lay the sliced meat over the vegetables and keep warm. Strain the stock and remove excess fat. Use a few spoonfuls of the stock to moisten the meat, and serve the rest in a small jug. Sprinkle the torn parsley over the dish and serve with a purée of potatoes and a green salad.

Serves 3 to 4

I breast of lamb, boned

2 tablespoons flat-leaf parsley, torn in bits, to garnish

Stuffing:

50 g (2 oz) dry white bread, crusts removed

125 ml (4 fl oz) milk

250 g (8 oz) spinach

2 tablespoons roughly chopped celery leaves or lovage

¼ teaspoon mace

I egg yolk

salt and black pepper

Braising:

40 g (1½ oz) butter

2 onions, sliced

2 leeks, sliced

2 carrots, sliced

2 celery sticks, sliced

I bay leaf

125 ml (4 fl oz) chicken stock

125 ml (4 fl oz) dry white wine

Moroccan lamb

750 g (1½ lb) boneless lamb *or* half
  a small boned leg or shoulder
seasoned flour
3 tablespoons olive oil
2 onions, sliced
2 green peppers, cut in strips
1 fennel, sliced
½ teaspoon ground ginger
600 ml (1 pint) chicken or veal
  stock, heated
⅛ teaspoon saffron
125 g (4 oz) dried apricots, chopped
1–2 tablespoons lemon juice
3 tablespoons chopped coriander
salt and black pepper

1 Cut the lamb into cubes and toss in the seasoned flour. Heat the oil in a sauté pan and brown the lamb, turning frequently. Remove it from the pan and put in the prepared vegetables. Cook them gently for 4–5 minutes, stirring often, until they are lightly coloured. Add the ginger towards the end, then replace the meat and pour on the heated stock, with the saffron, salt and pepper. Cover the pan and simmer gently for 1 hour, then add the chopped apricots and cook for a further 15 minutes, until all is tender. Finally, stir in some lemon juice, to taste, and mix in half the chopped coriander. Turn into a serving dish and sprinkle the remaining coriander thickly over the top.

Serves 4 with boiled basmati rice and a green salad.

roast loin of pork
with stuffing

If you buy your pork from a butcher, ask him to leave the loin unrolled and to score the outside for you. He will probably even stuff it for you as well if you give him the stuffing a few hours in advance, but it is not hard to do this yourself.

1.25 kg (2½ lb) boned loin of pork
Savory (or Sage) and Onion Stuffing
  (see pages 172)
150 ml (¼ pint) red or white wine

1 If the meat has not been prepared for you, lay it out flat, skin side up, and use the point of a small sharp knife to make parallel cuts about 1 cm (½ inch) apart diagonally, making a crisscross pattern. You should aim to cut through the surface of the skin but no farther.

2 Turn the meat over, lay the stuffing on it and roll up from the narrow end. Tie securely with several rounds of thin string. Weigh the meat to calculate the cooking time, then lay it on a rack in a roasting tin. Roast in a preheated oven, 200°C (400°F), Gas Mark 6, for about 2¼ hours or 35–40 minutes per 500 g (1 lb). There is no need to baste.

3 When the time is up, take the meat out of the oven and lay it on a carving platter. Cover it loosely with foil and a thick towel, and let stand for about 25 minutes while you make the gravy.

4 To make a thin gravy, simply pour off most of the fatty juices in the roasting tin, leaving the residue. Stand the tin over a moderate heat and pour in the wine. Let it bubble for 2–3 minutes, scraping all the crusty bits into the gravy as it cooks. Then pour through a strainer into a sauceboat and keep warm.

5 When ready to serve, carve the meat in medium thick slices and lay directly on to plates with some of the crackling and stuffing on each plate. Serve with Sage and Apple Sauce (see page 172) and Purée of Potatoes with Garlic and Olive Oil (see page 162). A green salad or a simple boiled or steamed vegetable is all that is needed to complete a delicious dish.

Note: Sage may be substituted for savory in the stuffing if more convenient, but it will make a less unusual dish.

Serves 6

Right: Roast Loin of Pork with Stuffing, recipe above

pancakes with Mexican beans

Batter:

75 g (3 oz) flour
75 g (3 oz) potato flour
¼ teaspoon salt
1 egg, beaten
100 ml (3½ fl oz) milk
100 ml (3½ fl oz) water
butter, for frying

Filling:

**2 x 300 g (10 oz) cans red kidney
  beans**
1 small onion, finely chopped
2 tablespoons sunflower oil
2 garlic cloves, finely chopped
**1 green chilli, deseeded and finely
  chopped**
salt and black pepper

To garnish:

200 g (7 oz) fromage frais
**4 tablespoons roughly chopped
  coriander**

1 Make the batter shortly before using. Sift the flours into a food processor with the salt. Beat the egg roughly with the milk and water. Start to process, adding the egg mixture through the lid. The batter should be like fairly thick cream. Alternatively, put the flour and salt in a large bowl and make a well in the centre. Tip the beaten egg into the centre and beat with a wire whisk, pouring in the milk and water while continuing to beat.

2 Drain the canned kidney beans and rinse them under cold running water. Fry the chopped onion in the oil for 5 minutes, then add the garlic and chilli and cook for another 1–2 minutes. Add the drained beans and stir around for a few moments, until well mixed and heated through. Add salt and pepper to taste, then cover and keep warm while you make the pancakes.

3 Heat a small frying pan and grease with a tiny piece of butter smeared on a piece of foil. Beat the batter once more, then, when the pan is good and hot, pour in about 1¾ tablespoons of the batter and tilt the pan to spread it around evenly. Cook for about 1 minute on each side, until set and speckled with golden brown. The batter should make about 12 x 12 cm (5 inch) pancakes, but you may need to discard the first one, as it does not always come up to scratch, at least in my experience.

4 Fill each pancake with 2 tablespoons of kidney beans, then add a dollop of fromage frais and a generous sprinkling of coriander. Roll them up loosely and lay on a flat dish. Alternatively, the pancakes may be piled on a platter and set on the table with bowls of beans, fromage frais and chopped coriander so that each person may roll his or her own.

Serves 4 to 6 as a first course, or as part of a vegetarian meal with other dishes.

Previous pages: Pancakes with Mexican Bean, recipe above

wild mushroom koulibiac

500 g (1 lb) wild mushrooms, such
   as *pieds de mouton*, shiitake, oyster
50 g (2 oz) wild rice
125 g (4 oz) white basmati rice
75 g (3 oz) butter
2 tablespoons sunflower oil
a dash of light soy sauce
4 tablespoons chopped chervil
4 tablespoons chopped chives
salt and black pepper
Watercress Sauce (see page 167)

Pastry:

500 g (1 lb) plain flour, sifted
½ teaspoon salt
250 g (8 oz) butter, cut into cubes
2–4 tablespoons iced water

Glaze:

1 egg yolk
2 tablespoons milk

1 Wipe the mushrooms carefully, trim the stalks and divide the larger mushrooms into 2–3 pieces.

2 Put 750 ml (1¼ pints) water in a saucepan, add salt and bring to the boil. Shake in the wild rice, bring back to the boil and cook uncovered for 40–45 minutes until it is tender. Drain well.

3 Rinse the basmati rice thoroughly, then shake into a saucepan containing 1.5 litres (2½ pints) lightly salted boiling water. Bring back to the boil and cook uncovered for 10 minutes. Drain well. Mix together with the wild rice, stirring in 50 g (2 oz) of the butter, melted, and salt and pepper to taste.

4 Make the pastry. Place the flour and salt in a bowl, add the butter and rub in with your fingertips until the mixture resembles fine breadcrumbs. Add enough iced water to hold the dough together. Wrap in clingfilm, chill for 30 minutes, then divide into 2 equal pieces. Roll each piece out thinly on a lightly floured surface to make a rectangle roughly 20 x 25 cm (8 x 10 inches). Lay one on a greased baking sheet and spread half the buttered rice over it, being careful to leave 1 cm (½ inch) free all round the edge.

5 Heat the remaining butter with the oil in a wide pan. Add the mushrooms and cook briskly, stirring often, until they soften and wilt. This will probably take about 10 minutes. Add a generous dash of light soy sauce, salt and pepper. Mix the herbs together and scatter half of them over the rice on the pastry, then spread the mushrooms over the herbs. Sprinkle the remaining herbs over the mushrooms, and place the remaining rice on top. Dampen the edges of the pastry, then lay the second piece over it and seal by pressing the edges together. Trim with a small knife and make a tiny slit in the centre to allow the steam to escape. Make a diagonal crisscross pattern on the top surface, then brush with the egg yolk and milk beaten together. Bake in a preheated oven, 200°C (400°F), Gas Mark 6, for 25 minutes or until golden brown. Cut into thick slices and serve with watercress sauce.

Serves 6 with a green salad.

potato & lentil patties

with cucumber and yogurt sauce

1 Put the mashed potato in a large bowl and stand a coarse food mill over it. Push the cooked lentils through the mill and mix well with the potato, beating with a wooden spoon. Heat 2 tablespoons of the sunflower oil in a frying pan and cook the chopped spring onions, adding the chillies after 1–2 minutes. Then add the cumin and coriander and cook gently for 2–3 minutes, stirring constantly. Tip the contents of the frying pan on to the potato–lentil purée and mix well, adding plenty of salt and pepper. Stir in the chopped mint. Form the mixture into 8 round patties and chill for several hours or overnight.

2 To cook the patties, dip them in the beaten egg, then in sifted flour. Heat the butter with the remaining tablespoon of sunflower oil in a large frying pan. When it is good and hot, put in half the patties and cook quite quickly, turning once, until browned on both sides and well heated through. Drain on kitchen paper, then keep warm while you fry the rest. Serve as soon as possible, with the chilled cucumber and yogurt sauce in a separate bowl.

Serves 4 as a first course or light main dish, or with other vegetarian dishes.

250 g (8 oz) freshly mashed potato
375 g (12 oz) cooked green lentils
3 tablespoons sunflower oil
½ bunch spring onions, chopped
1–2 green chillies, deseeded and finely chopped
1 teaspoon ground cumin
1 teaspoon ground coriander
2 tablespoons chopped mint
1 egg, beaten
a little plain flour, sifted
25 g (1 oz) butter
salt and black pepper
Cucumber and Yogurt Sauce (see page 171)

potato gnocchi
with rocket pesto

Gnocchi can be made successfully only with floury old potatoes, and these can be found only during the winter months. Large 'new' potatoes, which are sold as 'suitable for mashing' during the summer months, just will not do.

750 g (1½ lb) floury old potatoes
125 g (4 oz) plain flour, sifted
25 g (1 oz) butter, cut in bits
1 egg yolk, beaten
Rocket Pesto (see page 174)
salt and black pepper

Garnish:

15 g (½ oz) butter (optional)
50 g (2 oz) freshly grated
  Parmesan cheese

1 Boil the potatoes in their skins, then drain well. Once they are cool enough to handle, peel them, and push through a medium food mill into the same pan. Dry out by stirring for a few moments over gentle heat, then turn into a bowl and beat in the sifted flour, butter, egg yolk, and salt and pepper to taste. Turn out the dough on to a floured surface and knead lightly once or twice, then cut in quarters. Form each quarter into a roll about 2.5 cm (1 inch) thick. Rest the dough while you make the pesto.

2 Shortly before serving, bring a wide pan of lightly salted water to the boil. Cut the rolls of potato dough into slices about 1 cm (½ inch) thick, and press each one gently into the palm of your hand, using the prongs of a fork to give a lightly ridged effect. When all are done, drop them, a few at a time, into the gently simmering water. Cook for about 3 minutes after the water comes back to the boil. Shortly after the gnocchi rise to the surface, lift them out with a slotted spoon and drain briefly, while you cook the second lot. Then transfer the first batch to a heated serving dish and keep warm. When all are done, add just enough pesto to give a generous coating – don't drown them – folding it in lightly, then dot with butter, if using, and sprinkle with a little freshly grated Parmesan. Serve immediately, with the remaining Parmesan in a small bowl.

Note: There will be lots of pesto left over; it can be frozen or refrigerated for serving with other pasta dishes.

Serves 4 as a first course, or 3 to 4 as a light main dish.

steamed rice
in a bowl with herbs

1 Put the rice in a saucepan, add 600 ml (1 pint) lightly salted water and bring to the boil. Lower the heat as much as possible, cover the pan and cook for 20 minutes or until the water has been absorbed.

2 Heat 4 tablespoons of the oil gently and cook the sliced spring onions for 2–3 minutes. Then throw in the chopped herbs and stir around for 1 minute over, a low heat, just long enough to warm and soften them. Have ready 4 small bowls rubbed with oil; ones holding 300 ml (½ pint) are ideal. Divide the spring onion and herb mixture between them, and sprinkle with a little light soy sauce. Pile the brown rice on to the herbs, adding a dribble of oil and a shake of soy as you do so. Cover each little bowl with a foil lid.

3 If serving immediately, simply stand the bowls in a steamer, covered, over boiling water for about 8 minutes. Alternatively, they may be kept for up to 1 week in the refrigerator, and steamed for 15 minutes (from room temperature) before serving. To serve, turn them out on to flat plates and accompany with 2–3 simply cooked vegetables.

Note: Other grains may be used instead of brown basmati rice: white basmati rice; a mixture of wild and brown or white rice; buckwheat; couscous. Simply cook the grain according to the packet instructions, then proceed as above. If you don't have any small bowls, one large bowl holding about 1.2 litres (2 pints) may be used instead. In this case, steam it for 20 minutes if freshly made, or 45 minutes if reheating from room temperature.

Serves 4

250 g (8 oz) brown basmati rice
6 tablespoons sunflower oil
1 bunch spring onions, sliced
6 tablespoons chopped mixed herbs,
    such as flat-leaf parsley, tarragon,
    oregano, chervil
a few shakes of light soy sauce

lentils with orache

When orache is not available, use Good King Henry or the larger leaves of red or black mustard.

375 g (12 oz) Puy lentils
125 g (4 oz) orache, or other green
  leaf, stalks removed
3 tablespoons olive oil
1 red onion, thinly sliced
1 large garlic clove, chopped
2½ tablespoons lemon juice
sea salt and black pepper

1 Wash the lentils well, then put them in a pan and cover generously with cold water. Bring to the boil and cook steadily for just about 25 minutes or until they are tender, adding some salt towards the end of cooking. Drain them, reserving the liquid.

2 Wash the green leaves, removing all stalks and even the central ribs of the leaves if necessary. Throw the leaves into a pan of lightly salted boiling water and cook for 2–4 minutes or until tender. Drain in a colander and reserve.

3 Heat the oil in a heavy pan and cook the sliced red onion gently for 6–8 minutes, until it starts to soften. Then add the garlic and cook for another 1–2 minutes before adding the lentils. Stir the lentils around to coat them with the oil, then leave to simmer gently for 5 minutes, adding lots of salt and pepper. Separate the orache leaves and stir them gently into the lentils with the lemon juice. Add 6 tablespoons of the reserved lentil stock and simmer, covered, for another 5 minutes.

Serves 4 with other dishes, or 3 on its own.

pasta salad with coriander

The pasta used may be Chinese egg noodles or Italian taglierini, or, indeed, any very thin noodle roughly 1 mm (¹⁄₁₆ inch) wide.

1 Place the aubergine on the bars of the oven shelf and bake in a pre-heated oven, 180°C (350°F), Gas Mark 4, for 50 minutes, turning it over from time to time. Then take it out of the oven and leave it to cool. Grill the pepper slowly, turning often, until the skin is charred and blackened evenly all over. Leave to cool.

2 When the aubergine is cool enough to handle, cut it in half length-ways and scoop out the interior. Chop it coarsely by hand, then mash it roughly with a fork. Skin the pepper and cut it into small dice. Cut large thin slices from the outside of the tomato; discard the interior with seeds and juice. Cut the slices into dice, like the pepper. Mix the vegetables together, adding olive oil and lemon juice.

3 Bring a large pan of lightly salted water to the boil, drop in the pasta and cook for 2–3 minutes, until just tender. Drain well, then turn into a large bowl and add the vegetables. Mix gently, adding salt and pepper and chopped coriander. Serve warm, or at room temperature.

Serves 4

1 aubergine
1 yellow pepper
1 beefsteak tomato, skinned
4 tablespoons extra virgin olive oil
2 tablespoons lemon juice
375 g (12 oz) thin egg noodles
4 tablespoons roughly chopped
  coriander
salt and black pepper

grilled potatoes with rosemary

This is an excellent dish to serve with roast game or grilled beef or lamb.

1 Boil the potatoes in their skins. Drain well, and peel as soon as the potatoes are cool enough to handle. Cut the potatoes in slices about 5 mm (¼ inch) thick and lay on a baking sheet. Pour over the oil, adding the sliced onion and the sprigs of rosemary. Leave for 1 hour, then pour off most of the oil. Sprinkle the potatoes with salt and pepper and cook them under a hot grill for 8–10 minutes. Remove most of the rosemary before serving.

Serves 4

750 g (1½ lb) waxy potatoes
6 tablespoons olive oil
1 small red onion, thinly sliced
3–4 sprigs rosemary
salt and black pepper

Previous pages: Pasta Salad with Coriander, recipe above

millet croquettes
with coriander

I like to serve these with Cucumber and Yogurt Sauce (see page 171) and a tomato salad.

300 ml (½ pint) water,
  lightly salted
150 g (5 oz) millet
4 tablespoons sunflower oil
1 bunch spring onions, sliced
3 tablespoons chopped coriander
1 egg, beaten
2 tablespoons fromage frais
salt and black pepper

1 Bring the water to the boil. Shake in the millet, bring back to the boil, and cover the pan. Simmer for 25 minutes, or until all the water has been absorbed. Then turn the millet into a bowl.

2 Heat half the oil in a frying pan and cook the sliced spring onions for 2–3 minutes, then mix them with the millet. Add the chopped coriander and mix again. Beat the egg and fromage frais together, then stir into the millet, adding salt and pepper. Form the mixture into 8 round patties.

3 Heat the remaining oil in a large nonstick frying pan and cook the croquettes until golden on both sides. Drain briefly on kitchen paper, then serve on a flat dish.

Serves 4

potato pasties with dill

500 g (1 lb) potatoes
50 ml (2 fl oz) milk
125 g (4 oz) butter
4 tablespoons chopped dill
75 g (3 oz) filo pastry
salt and black pepper

1 Boil the potatoes; drain and peel as soon as they are cool enough to handle. Push them through a medium food mill. Warm the milk with half the butter. When the butter has melted, pour on to the mashed potatoes. Stir in the dill, and salt and pepper to taste. Leave to cool.

2 Cut the sheets of filo into rectangles measuring roughly 12 x 25 cm (5 x 10 inches). Melt the remaining butter and brush it all over the filo rectangles. Divide the potato purée into 8 parts. Form each one into a fat roll and lay it on the end of a piece of filo. Fold over the side edges to enclose the filling, then roll up. Brush the pasties all over with melted butter, thus sealing the ends. Lay them on a baking sheet and bake in a preheated oven, 180°C (350°F), Gas Mark 4, for 20–25 minutes or until golden brown. Serve at once.

Serves 4 as a first course or as part of a vegetarian meal.

couscous with herbs

1 Soak the couscous in the cold water for a minimum of 10 minutes or as long as it is convenient. Then stir in 3 tablespoons of the extra virgin olive oil, the lemon juice, and salt and pepper to taste. Stir in the sliced spring onions and tomatoes, and the chopped herbs. Set aside for 1–2 hours, then add a little more olive oil before serving.
Note: 1 small head fennel, chopped, may be substituted for the tomatoes, if you like.

Serves 2 to 3 on its own, or 3 to 4 with other dishes

250 g (8 oz) couscous
250 ml (8 fl oz) cold water
5–6 tablespoons extra virgin olive oil
1 tablespoon lemon juice
1 bunch spring onions, sliced
6 cherry tomatoes (unskinned), sliced
1½ tablespoons chopped mint
1½ tablespoons chopped flat-leaf parsley
salt and black pepper

green risotto

1 Cook the chopped shallots slowly in the oil for 3 minutes, then add the garlic and cook for another minute. Put the rice in the pan, stir around in the oil for 1 minute, then add half the heated stock and the robust herbs. Pour 2–3 tablespoonfuls of the remaining hot stock over the saffron in a small bowl and set aside. Simmer the rice slowly in the stock, stirring often, for about 8 minutes, or until the stock has almost all been absorbed. Then add the saffron and half the remaining stock. When that also has been absorbed, the rice will probably be tender. If not, add the rest of the stock and cook a few minutes longer. Shortly before serving, stir in the tender herbs, turn on to a serving dish, and sprinkle with the grated Parmesan. The risotto must be served immediately or the grains of rice will stick together.

Serves 3 to 4

2 shallots, finely chopped
3 tablespoons olive oil
1 garlic clove, finely chopped
250 g (8 oz) risotto rice, washed and drained
750 ml (1¼ pints) chicken stock, heated
1½ tablespoons chopped robust herbs, such as lovage, oregano, thyme
a pinch of saffron
1½ tablespoons chopped tender herbs, such as dill, chervil, tarragon
40 g (1½ oz) freshly grated Parmesan cheese

Right: Green risotto, recipe above

potato salad with rocket

When made with a really good potato like Jersey Royal, Ratte or Belle de Fontenay, this dish is sublime.

1 Boil the potatoes in their skins. Once they are done, drain them well, and leave to cool for a few minutes. When they are cool enough to handle, peel and cut the potatoes into thick slices. Put them in a shallow bowl and pour over the olive oil and vinegar, mixing gently so as not to break the potatoes. Stir in the chopped shallots, salt and pepper. Lastly, fold in the chopped herbs.

2 To serve, make a bed of rocket on a flat dish and turn out the potato salad on to it. Serve soon after making.

Serves 4 as a course on its own.

750 g (1½ lb) waxy new potatoes
6 tablespoons extra virgin olive oil
3 tablespoons white wine vinegar
4 shallots, finely chopped
3 tablespoons chopped chives
3 tablespoons chopped flat-leaf parsley
sea salt and black pepper
125 g (4 oz) rocket, to garnish

sautéd potatoes
with curry leaves

1 Boil the potatoes in their skins and drain well. When they are cool enough to handle, peel and cut the potatoes into thick slices.

2 Heat the oil in a wide pan and fry the sliced onion gently for 3–4 minutes. Add the garlic, then the curry leaves and continue to fry, stirring gently, for 4–5 minutes. Add the potatoes, with plenty of salt and pepper, and stir around, trying not to break up the potatoes, for a further 4–5 minutes. Finally, tip into a serving dish and scatter the toasted sesame seeds over the top.

Serves 4 as an accompaniment, but for a simple meal I like to eat this as a delicious main dish with a green salad.

750 g (1½ lb) waxy potatoes
3 tablespoons sunflower oil
1 red onion, halved and sliced
2 garlic cloves, finely chopped
4 heaped tablespoons curry leaves
3 tablespoons sesame seeds, lightly toasted
sea salt and black pepper

ring mould with wild mushrooms

1 Cook the wild rice in 750 ml (1¼ pints) lightly salted boiling water for 40–45 minutes. Cook the basmati rice in 750 ml (1¼ pints) lightly salted boiling water for 10 minutes. Cook the buckwheat in 175 ml (6 fl oz) lightly salted boiling water, covered, for about 14 minutes or until all the water has been absorbed. Mix the 3 types of grain together thoroughly and pack into an oiled ring mould holding roughly 1.2 litres (2 pints). Cover loosely with foil and keep warm in a low oven.

2 Fry the shallots in the olive oil, adding the garlic after 2 minutes. Cook for 1 minute more, then add the mushrooms. Sauté gently, tossing frequently, for about 8 minutes or until the mushrooms have softened. Then add the parsley, and salt and pepper to taste.

3 To make the sauce simply mix the soured cream and yogurt together, beating until smooth. Serve at room temperature in a sauceboat.

4 To serve, turn out the mould on to a flat dish and spoon some of the mushrooms into the centre. Serve the rest in a separate bowl and accompany with the yogurt sauce.

Serves 3 to 4 as a light main dish.

50 g (2 oz) wild rice

50 g (2 oz) basmati rice, rinsed

50 g (2 oz) roasted buckwheat

Filling:

4 shallots, chopped

4 tablespoons olive oil

2 garlic cloves, finely chopped

375 g (12 oz) mixed wild mushrooms, cut in large pieces

125 ml (4 fl oz) coarsely chopped flat-leaf parsley

salt and black pepper

Sauce:

150 ml (¼ pint) soured cream

150 ml (¼ pint) natural yogurt

rice & noodle pilaf

This is based on a Turkish recipe, and I find it goes well with simple game dishes like Quail with Calvados (see page 133).

1 Heat the butter and cook the chopped onion in it for 3 minutes. Add the noodle pieces and continue to cook for another 2–3 minutes, stirring almost constantly. Add the rice and cook for a further 3 minutes, stirring frequently. Pour on the heated stock, add salt and pepper, and boil for 1 minute. Then lower the heat, cover the pan and cook gently for about 10 minutes until the stock is absorbed and the rice is cooked. Turn off the heat, place a cloth under the pan lid and let stand for 10 minutes. Before serving, fold in the chopped parsley and turn into a serving dish.

Serves 4 to 5

50 g (2 oz) butter

1 small onion, finely chopped

50 g (2 oz) extra thin noodles, such as tagliolini or vermicelli, broken into short lengths

175 g (6 oz) basmati rice, washed

600 ml (1 pint) light chicken stock, heated

4 tablespoons coarsely chopped flat-leaf parsley

salt and black pepper

roast potatoes
with rosemary

1 The potatoes may be peeled or not, as you prefer. Cut them almost through, in slices about 7 mm (⅓ inch) thick, stopping just before you reach the bottom. Lay them in an oiled baking dish and spoon over the olive oil. Pull the needles off the rosemary sprigs and scatter them over the potatoes, pushing them down between the cut slices. Add sea salt and pepper to taste, and bake in a preheated oven, 190°C (375°F), Gas Mark 5, or whatever temperature the oven may already be at if roasting with a chicken or joint of meat, for about 1 hour. The timing is very flexible.

Serves 4

750 g (1½ lb) potatoes
6 tablespoons olive oil
6 sprigs rosemary
sea salt and black pepper

purée of potatoes
with garlic and olive oil

I like to use a firm, slightly waxy potato for this dish rather than the floury potato that is usually deemed essential for mashing. A firm, yellow potato like Wilja or Belle de Fontenay is my favourite.

1 Boil the potatoes in their skins, then drain well. Peel them as soon as they are cool enough to handle, then allow them to dry out in a clean pan, stirring for a few moments, over a gentle heat. Push the potatoes through a medium food mill back into the cleaned pan, and stir over a very low heat to dry out still further.
2 Warm the oil and milk together in a small pan, then stir in the crushed garlic. Beat into the potato purée, adding plenty of salt and pepper. Finally, when all is smooth and well-seasoned, stir in the chopped parsley and turn into a serving dish.

Serves 4

1 kg (2 lb) potatoes
4 tablespoons extra virgin olive oil
4 tablespoons milk
3 large garlic cloves, crushed in a garlic press
4 tablespoons chopped flat-leaf parsley
sea salt and black pepper

Previous pages: from left, Purée of Potatoes with Garlic and Olive Oil, recipe above, Potato Pot Potatoes with Extra Virgin Olive Oil and Herbs, recipe right and Roast Potatoes with Rosemary, recipe above

potato pot potatoes
with extra virgin olive oil and herbs

Potato pots – the unglazed earthenware lidded pots for cooking unpeeled potatoes on top of the heat without any liquid or fat – have been popular for many years. Ignoring the instructions, which insist that nothing should be added to potatoes in the potato pot, I have taken to adding a few spoonfuls of good olive oil and a handful of herbs. Either sage or rosemary seems the obvious choice: not only do both these herbs complement potatoes, but their robust character can withstand the long cooking that is required.

750 g (1½ lb) large new potatoes (egg-sized)

4 tablespoons extra virgin olive oil

5 sprigs sage or rosemary

1 Scrub the potatoes, leaving the skins on, and pack them into the potato pot or other large ceramic pot with a lid. Dribble over the olive oil, shaking the pot about to distribute it evenly, then throw in the sprigs of herbs. Do not bother with salt and pepper; they are best added on the plate. Cover the potato pot, place over a very low heat, and cook for 1 hour, shaking around briskly from time to time.

Serves 4

sauces, stuffings and garnishes

fresh tomato sauce

1 Cook the chopped shallots in the oil and butter until they start to colour. Add the garlic and cook for 1 minute more. Then add the chilli and the yellow pepper and cook for another 2 minutes. Put half the tomatoes in the pan, adding salt and pepper, and simmer for 15 minutes. Now add the rest of the tomatoes, spring onions and basil. Remove from the heat immediately and stir in the olive oil. Serve warm over freshly cooked pasta.

Serves 6

2 shallots, chopped

2 tablespoons olive oil

15 g (½ oz) butter

1–2 garlic cloves, flnely chopped

1 green chilli, deseeded and finely chopped

1 small yellow pepper, grilled, skinned and chopped

750 g (1½ lb) tomatoes, skinned deseeded and chopped

1 bunch spring onions, chopped

2 tablespoons basil, torn in bits

2 tablespoons extra virgin olive oil

salt and black pepper

couscous stuffing

Use this stuffing for poultry, fish and vegetables.

1 Pour the cold water over the couscous and leave for 10 minutes, by which time the water should have been absorbed. Cook the spring onions gently in the oil for 3 minutes, then add the couscous and cook for another 3 minutes, stirring. Pour on the stock and continue cooking very gently, stirring almost constantly, for another 5 minutes, adding salt and pepper. Remove from the heat and stir in the chopped herbs. Leave to cool before using.

Makes about 375 g (12 oz) stuffing, enough to fill a fairly large chicken.

125 ml (4 fl oz) cold water

125 g (4 oz) couscous

1 bunch spring onions, sliced

1 tablespoon sunflower oil

125 ml (4 fl oz) chicken or fish stock, heated

2 tablespoons chopped tarragon

2 tablespoons chopped dill

2 tablespoons chopped chervil

2 tablespoons chopped flat-leaf parsley

salt and black pepper

Previous pages: clockwise from left, Fresh Tomato Sauce, recipe above, Watercress Sauce, recipe right, Couscous Stuffing, recipe above, Fried Parsley, recipe top right

fried parsley

This garnish must be made at the very last moment so that it can be served immediately.

frying oil

12 large sprigs very fresh
    curly parsley

1 Have a deep pan or a wok three-quarters full with frying oil. Heat it until hot enough to brown a small cube of bread in 20 seconds (180°C/350°F), then drop in the parsley sprigs, six at a time. Lift them out again almost immediately, using a broad mesh-based skimmer; 20–30 seconds in the hot fat will be long enough to make the parsley bright emerald green, crisp and brittle. Lay the sprigs on kitchen paper to drain, then use immediately as a garnish for dishes of fried fish.

Serves 4

watercress sauce

Serve this sauce with poached fish, steamed or poached chicken, hard-boiled eggs or vegetables.

1 bunch watercress

450 ml (¾ pint) fish or chicken stock

40 g (1½ oz) butter

2 tablespoons plain flour

300 ml (½ pint) single cream

salt and black pepper

1 Pull the leaves off the watercress and set aside. Chop the stalks roughly and put in a pan with the stock. Bring to the boil slowly, cover and simmer for 20 minutes. Strain, then discard stalks and measure the stock. You should have about 300 ml (½ pint); if less, make up to this amount with extra stock or water.

2 Melt the butter, add the flour and cook for 1 minute, stirring. Add the hot watercress stock and bring back to the boil. Simmer the mixture for another 3 minutes. Combine the cream with the watercress leaves in a liquidizer or food processor and add to the sauce. Stir well, reheating gently, and adding salt and pepper to taste. Serve hot.

Serves 4

Note: For a cold sauce, make as above, then allow the sauce to cool. Process in a liquidizer or food processor once more, adding 125 ml (4 fl oz) natural yogurt.

Serves 4 to 5, with the addition of natural yogurt.

mayonnaise

Homemade mayonnaise is not only delicious in its own right, for serving with shellfish, hard-boiled eggs, cold fish and chicken, and warm vegetables, it also provides an admirable vehicle for using chopped fresh herbs and garlic. And it is adaptable: it can be mixed with natural yogurt, crème fraîche, fromage frais or lightly whipped fresh cream to make a variety of different sauces.

Do not use the best extra virgin olive oil for making mayonnaise, for it will be too rich, heavy and cloying. I prefer to use a light olive oil, pale, fairly thin and almost lacking in flavour, or a mixture of a good (but not the very best) olive oil and a light sunflower or nut oil. If desired, a couple of spoonfuls of extra virgin olive oil may be added at the end for flavour.

1 Place a large heavy bowl with a firm base on a damp cloth on a wooden surface so it will not slip. Have the oil(s) in a jug, and the vinegar and lemon juice to hand.

2 Place the egg yolks in the bowl, add the salt and beat for a little while with a wooden spoon. Now, using an electric handbeater or a balloon whisk, start to add the oil very slowly indeed, almost literally drop by drop to begin with, and beat without cease until an emulsion is formed. (This can be ascertained by the change in texture and appearance of the eggs as they start to absorb the oil and become transformed by it.) If making mayonnaise for the first time, it may be helpful to use a large spoon holding only a little oil at the very beginning of the process, letting the oil drip off the end of the spoon into the egg yolks.

3 Continue to add the oil slowly, beating constantly, until about half has been used; then you may start to add it more quickly, in a thin stream, stopping every now and then until it has been absorbed. If the mixture becomes too thick, thin it with half the vinegar or lemon juice. When all the oil has been used, add the remaining vinegar and lemon juice, also slowly, then taste, adding the extra virgin olive oil if desired. **Note:** The mayonnaise may be stored in the refrigerator, covered with clingfilm, for 3 days.

Makes about 325 ml (11 fl oz); serves 4 to 6.

2 egg yolks

a pinch of sea salt

300 ml (½ pint) light olive oil, *or* olive oil and sunflower oil mixed in equal parts

1½ tablespoons white wine vinegar

1½ tablespoons lemon juice

2 tablespoons extra virgin olive oil (optional)

coriander salsa

This fresh and tasty relish may be served with all manner of bland foods, such as grilled fish, chicken or lamb, vegetable soups and bean dishes.

1 Put the tomatoes into a food processor and reduce to a hash, or chop them very finely by hand. Tip into a bowl and stir in the sliced spring onions, chopped chillies, lime or lemon juice, coriander, and salt and pepper to taste.

Note: For a variation, use 2 beefsteak tomatoes and 1 red pepper instead of the 4 tomatoes. Grill the vegetables, stuck on skewers for easy turning, until the skins have blackened and charred evenly all over. Allow to cool, then remove the skins and proceed as above.

Serves 4 to 6
Illustrated on page 82

4 tomatoes (unskinned), cut into eighths
I bunch spring onions, sliced
2 green chillies, deseeded and fi\nely chopped
2 tablespoons lime or lemon juice
2 tablespoons chopped coriander
salt and black pepper

dill sauce
with mustard

1 Put the mustard in a bowl and stir in the oil, drop by drop, as if making mayonnaise. When they have amalgamated, stir in the yogurt. Add lemon juice, then stir in the chopped dill. Serve cold, with Grilled Chicken Wings (see page 124), giant prawns, or pork chops.

Serves 4

½ tablespoon Dijon mustard
½ tablespoon olive oil
4 tablespoons natural yogurt
1½ tablespoons lemon juice, or to taste
2 tablespoons chopped dill

chilli sauce

1 Heat the butter with half the oil in a frying pan and cook the onion gently until it starts to soften and colour. Add the tomatoes with their juice, and heat, stirring. Add the half bay leaf, sugar, and salt and pepper, and simmer, uncovered, for about 15 minutes or until thick.

2 Meanwhile, grill the red pepper until the skin has blackened, then scrape off the skin and cut the pepper into little strips. Heat the remaining oil in a small frying pan and cook the chopped chilli for 1 minute, then add the grilled pepper strips and cook for another minute, stirring constantly. Add to the tomatoes and mix well. Simmer together for a moment or two, then remove the bay leaf from the sauce and turn off the heat. Add a dash of Tabasco if you wish, then stir in the coriander and leave to cool. Purée briefly in a blender or food processor, or rub through a coarse food mill, then chill, covered, overnight.

3 Reheat gently to serve, but do not allow to boil.

Serves 4 to 5, with fish cakes, grilled chicken or hamburgers.
Illustrated on page 117

25 g (1 oz) butter
2 tablespoons sunflower oil
1 small onion, chopped
425 g (14 oz) canned tomatoes,
  roughly chopped
½ bay leaf
½ teaspoon sugar
1 red pepper
1 red chilli, deseeded and
  finely chopped
a dash of Tabasco (optional)
3 tablespoons chopped coriander
salt and black pepper

sage & onion sauce

Serve this sauce with roast or grilled pork, braised lamb, roast pheasant or hard-boiled eggs.

1 Put the onion pieces in a pan, cover with lightly salted water and bring to the boil. Cook gently for 15 minutes, then drain. Heat the butter, add the flour, and cook for 1 minute, stirring constantly. Then add the hot milk gradually, stirring till smooth. Cook the sauce gently for 3 minutes, then stir in the cooked onions.

2 Cook all together for 2–3 minutes, then remove from the heat and leave to cool for a few minutes. Purée in a liquidizer or food processor, or rub through a coarse sieve or food mill. Reheat in a clean pan, adding the sage, cream, and salt and pepper to taste.

Serves 6

1 Spanish onion, about 500 g (1 lb)
  in weight, cut into 1 cm (½ inch)
  chunks
40 g (1½ oz) butter
2 tablespoons plain flour
300 ml (½ pint) milk, heated
2 tablespoons coarsely
  chopped sage
5 tablespoons double cream
sea salt and black pepper

cracked wheat stuffing

This is an excellent stuffing, and adaptable for use in a wide range of dishes: roast poultry and game; stuffed cabbage, vegetable marrow and squash; peppers and beefsteak tomatoes.

1 Soak the cracked wheat in cold water to cover for 45 minutes, then drain and squeeze out the excess moisture. Cook the spring onions in the oil for 3 minutes, then stir into the cracked wheat, adding salt and pepper and chopped parsley. Leave to cool before using.

Makes about 375 g (12 oz) stuffing; enough to fill a good-sized chicken.

175 g (6 oz) cracked wheat
1 bunch spring onions, sliced
1½ tablespoons sunflower oil
6 tablespoons chopped parsley
salt and black pepper

cucumber & yogurt sauce

1 Put the yogurt in a liquidizer or food processor. Using your hands, squeeze out any excess liquid from the grated cucumber, then add the cucumber to the yogurt with the crushed garlic, salt and pepper. Process briefly, just until amalgamated. Alternatively, beat the yogurt by hand until smooth, then fold in the cucumber and garlic and mix well, adding salt and pepper to taste. Stir in most of the mint, reserving a little. Turn the sauce into a small bowl and scatter the rest of the mint over the top. Chill until ready to serve, with roast lamb, meatballs or Grilled Chicken Wings (see page 124).

Serves 3 to 4
Illustrated on page 123

150 ml (¼ pint) natural yogurt
½ cucumber, peeled and
   coarsely grated
1 garlic clove, crushed
1½ tablespoons chopped fresh mint
   or 1½ teaspoons dried mint
salt and white pepper

savory & onion stuffing

This is a particularly good stuffing, which may be used in the same way as a sage and onion stuffing, with Roast Loin of Pork (see page 140), goose and duck. When savory is not available, sage may be used instead.

1 Cook the chopped onion in water to cover for 10 minutes, then drain. When it is cool enough to handle, squeeze out as much moisture as possible. Mix the breadcrumbs with the shredded suet, adding the chopped or dried savory, salt and pepper. Then stir in the beaten egg and mix well. Use as a stuffing or roll the mixture into round balls and fry in 1 tablespoon of light oil, and serve with roast pork.
Note: If using sage instead of savory, use the same amounts. Fresh or dried sage may be used, just as with savory.

Makes enough to stuff a loin of pork, a goose or a duck.

125 g (4 oz) onion, chopped
50 g (2 oz) soft white breadcrumbs
50 g (2 oz) shredded suet
1½ tablespoons chopped savory
  or 1 tablespoon dried savory
1 egg, beaten
salt and black pepper

sage & apple sauce

This unusual sauce is good with roast pork, duck and goose.

1 Melt the butter in a small saucepan, add the chopped onion, cover and cook slowly until it has softened, without allowing it to brown. This will take about 10 minutes. Then add the chopped sage and cook for another 2 minutes, uncovered. Set aside.
2 Put the apples in a heavy pan with just enough water to cover the bottom. Add the sugar and bring slowly to the boil, then cover the pan and simmer slowly until the apples are soft. Cool for a few minutes, then push them through a medium food mill into a clean pan. Reheat gently, adding the sage and onion mixture, and a very little salt and black pepper. When the sauce is hot, remove it from the heat and let it stand, covered, for 10–15 minutes before serving; it is best warm.

Serves 6

15 g (½ oz) butter
125 g (4 oz) onion, finely chopped
1 tablespoon chopped sage
500 g (1 lb) Bramleys, peeled, cored
  and thickly sliced
a pinch of sugar
salt and black pepper

herb sauce

75 ml (3 fl oz) natural yogurt
75 ml (3 fl oz) fromage frais
3 tablespoons chopped chervil,
tarragon or dill
25 g (1 oz) butter
1 tablespoon plain flour
175 ml (6 fl oz) fish or chicken
  stock, heated
1 teaspoon Dijon mustard
salt and black pepper

1 Purée the yogurt and fromage frais in a liquidizer or food processor with the chopped herbs. Melt the butter in a saucepan over a low heat, add the flour and bring to the boil, stirring. Cook for 1 minute, continuing to stir, then pour on the heated fish or chicken stock. Add the mustard, salt and pepper, and bring back to the boil. Simmer for 3 minutes, stirring occasionally, then remove from the heat and stir in the herb mixture. Reheat very gently, keeping well below boiling point. Serve soon after making, with poached fish or chicken, hard-boiled eggs, or vegetables.

Serves 4

parsley & bread stuffing

The best stuffing for roast turkey: simple but excellent.

375 g (12 oz) shallots, chopped
125 g (4 oz) butter
375 g (12 oz) soft white
  breadcrumbs
40 g (1½ oz) chopped parsley
sea salt and black pepper

1 Cook the shallots slowly in the butter until they are pale golden, then add the breadcrumbs and mix well. Remove from the heat, stir in the chopped parsley, and add plenty of salt and pepper. Allow to cool before using.

Makes enough stuffing to fill a 6 kg (12 lb) turkey.

fresh mint sauce

3 tablespoons chopped mint
1 tablespoon caster sugar
3 tablespoons lemon juice
150 ml (¼ pint) boiling water

1 Put the chopped mint into a mortar and pound it. Add the sugar and pound again. Add the lemon juice, then the boiling water. Mix well, then leave to cool. Serve with roast lamb.

Serves 4 to 5

rocket pesto

The true pesto is, of course. made with basil, but alternative versions can be made with other herbs. Here rocket is used; you might also want to try coriander. This pesto is perfect for pasta and gnocchi (see page 149).

1 Put the rocket in a food processor with the garlic, pine nuts, Parmesan and salt. Process until blended, stopping to scrape down the sides once or twice. Then process again, while adding the olive oil slowly through the lid. Alternatively, chop the rocket and pine nuts finely, then pound in a mortar with the garlic, Parmesan and salt. Then add the oil gradually, beating it in with a wooden spoon.

2 Once made, turn the pesto into a small bowl, cover with clingfilm, and chill in the refrigerator until needed. It will keep for several days under refrigeration, or for weeks in the freezer. Serve over pasta, gnocchi, boiled potatoes and in minestrone-type soups.

Note: For a classic pesto, as made in Genoa, substitute basil (leaves only) for the rocket and reduce the pine nuts by half. If possible, use half Sardo (a hard cheese from Sardinia) and half Parmesan.

Makes enough for 2 to 3 meals.

125 g (4 oz) rocket leaves, minus stalks, torn in pieces
1 garlic clove, crushed
50 g (2 oz) pine nuts
50 g (2 oz) freshly grated Parmesan cheese
a pinch of sea salt
75 ml (3 fl oz) extra virgin olive oil

mushrooms
stuffed with aubergine and peppers

1 Lay the mushrooms, gills up, on an oiled baking sheet. Brush the gills with sunflower oil, allowing about 1 teaspoon of oil for each mushroom. Bake the the mushrooms in a preheated oven, 180°C (350°F), Gas Mark 4, for 15 minutes or until they have just softened. Do not allow them to collapse. Take out of the oven and leave to cool.
2 To make the stuffing, bake the aubergine in a preheated oven, 180°C (350°F), Gas Mark 4, for 1 hour, turning often. Set aside to cool. Cut the peppers in half, discard the stalks and seeds, and grill until the skin has blackened and blistered all over. Set them aside to cool.
3 Later, cut the aubergine in half and scoop out the inside. Chop the flesh roughly by hand, then mash it with a fork. Do not be tempted to put it in a food processor, as it does not want to be too smooth. Peel or scrape the skin off the grilled peppers and cut the flesh into neat dice. Stir the diced pepper into the aubergine purée, then add the sliced spring onions. Finally, stir in the olive oil and lemon juice, parsley, and salt and pepper to taste. Make mounds of the stuffing on the mushrooms and lay on a flat dish. Serve at room temperature.

Serves 4 as a first course

8 medium to large flat mushrooms
3 tablespoons sunflower oil
1 large aubergine
2 yellow peppers
6 large spring onions, sliced
3 tablespoons extra virgin olive oil
1½ tablespoons lemon juice
3 tablespoons roughly chopped
  flat-leaf parsley
salt and black pepper

Previous pages: Mushrooms Stuffed with Aubergines and Peppers, recipe above

aubergine & tomato
sandwiches with mint

300 ml (½ pint) Greek yogurt

**1 large aubergine, cut in 5 mm
(¼ inch) slices**

4 tablespoons olive oil

15 g (½ oz) butter

**250 ml (8 oz) tomatoes, cut in
5 mm (¼ inch) slices**

1–2 garlic cloves, crushed

1½ tablespoons chopped mint

salt

1 Start 2 hours ahead: tip the yogurt into a strainer lined with butter muslin and leave to drain.

2 About 1½ hours later, sprinkle the aubergine slices with salt and leave to drain in a colander for 30 minutes. Then rinse off the salt and pat dry in a cloth.

3 Heat the oil in a nonstick frying pan and put in just enough aubergine slices to fit in 1 layer. Cook until golden brown on each side. Drain them on kitchen paper while you fry the next batch. When all are done, put the butter into the same pan and fry the sliced tomatoes briefly, turning once, then remove from the heat.

4 Beat the drained yogurt until smooth, then stir in the garlic and mint. Lay half the aubergine slices on a large flat dish and spread each one with the yogurt. Cover with the remaining aubergine slices, and top each one with a tomato slice. Serve at room temperature.

Serves 4 as a first course

cauliflower & eggs
with chervil and chives

1 Drop the cauliflower florets into 600 ml (1 pint) lightly salted boiling water, cover and cook until they are just tender. Drain, reserving the water. Boil it, if necessary, to reduce to 300 ml (½ pint) and set aside. Shell the eggs and cut into chunks. Lay the cauliflower florets in a shallow dish and scatter the chopped eggs over and among them. Keep warm while you make the sauce.

2 Melt the butter, shake in the flour and bring to the boil, stirring. Cook for 1 minute, continuing to stir, then pour in the hot cauliflower stock. Bring to the boil, stirring till smooth, then simmer gently for 3 minutes. Add the cream, salt and pepper to taste, then stir in the chopped herbs. Remove from the heat immediately, and pour over the cauliflower and eggs. Serve as soon as possible.

Serves 2 to 3 as a light main dish, or serves 4 as a first course for a summer lunch, followed by a chicken or shellfish salad.

I **cauliflower, cut into florets**
3 **eggs, hard-boiled**

Sauce:

25 g (I oz) **butter**
2 **tablespoons plain flour**
300 ml (½ pint) **cauliflower stock**
  (see recipe)
75 ml (3 fl oz) **single cream**
I½ **tablespoons chopped chervil**
I½ **tablespoons chopped chives**
salt and black pepper

braised celery with lovage

3 heads celery, trimmed and halved

50 g (2 oz) butter

600 ml (I pint) game, chicken or
 vegetable stock

I tablespoon lemon juice

I½ tablespoons chopped lovage

salt and black pepper

Sauce (optional):

I teaspoon plain flour

I5 g (½oz) butter, at room
 temperature

75 ml (3 fl oz) soured cream

salt and black pepper

1 Blanch the halved celery for 5 minutes in fast boiling water, then drain in a colander. Rub a heavy casserole with some of the butter and lay the celery in it, in one layer if possible. Dot with the rest of the butter. Heat the stock and pour half of it over the celery, adding the lemon juice, chopped lovage, and salt and pepper.

2 Cover and cook gently over a very low heat for 1½–2 hours, until the celery is tender all the way through. Turn the pieces over every 30 minutes, adding more stock as required, and start testing them with a skewer after 1½ hours. When they are ready, transfer them to a serving dish and pour the juices over them. Alternatively, the juices can be made into a sauce in the following way.

3 Stir the flour into the butter to make a smooth paste. Drop this by degrees into the cooking juices left in the casserole, stirring until amalgamated and free from lumps. Cook gently for 3 minutes, then add the soured cream, and salt and pepper to taste. Finally, pour the cream sauce over the celery.

Note: I like this best with the juices left unthickened when serving with game, poultry and beef, but I like the cream sauce for serving with other vegetable dishes or a bowl of brown rice. Lovage is hard to find in shops, but easily grown in the garden. Failing all else, use celery leaves instead.

Serves 4, with roast game or chicken, or a beef stew.

braised onions
with sage

1 Put the peeled onions in a small pan with the cold stock. Bring to the boil, cover, and simmer gently until they are soft when pierced with a skewer. This will probably take 15–30 minutes, depending on size. Using a slotted spoon, lift the onions out of the pan and drain in a colander. In a clean pan melt the butter, and add the vinegar, sugar, and salt and pepper to taste. Then put in the onions and cook slowly, turning them constantly, until they are golden brown all over. Cover the pan and set aside.

2 Heat the sunflower oil in a small frying pan. When it is very hot, throw in the sage leaves and fry for about 30 seconds. Lift out and drain on kitchen paper while you transfer the onions to a serving dish. Scatter the fried sage leaves over them, and serve as soon as possible.

Serves 4

750 g (1½ lb) small onions, peeled
275 ml (9 fl oz) game or
  chicken stock
40 g (1½ oz) butter
1½ tablespoons white wine vinegar
1 teaspoon sugar
2 tablespoons sunflower oil
10–12 large sage leaves
salt and black pepper

Previous pages: from left, Braised Onions with Sage recipe above and Tomatoes Stuffed with Couscous, recipe right

tomatoes
stuffed with couscous

8 large tomatoes, or smallish
   beefsteak tomatoes

Stuffing:

175 g (6 oz) couscous
175 ml (6 fl oz) cold water
1 bunch spring onions, sliced
1½ tablespoons sunflower oil
400 ml (14 fl oz) chicken stock,
   heated
2 tablespoons chopped basil
25 g (1 oz) butter, cut in small bits
salt and black pepper

1 Cut a thin slice off the top of each tomato and set aside. Hollow out the tomatoes, using a curved grapefruit knife and teaspoon, and leave them upside down to drain while you make the stuffing.

2 Put the couscous in a bowl and pour the cold water over it. Leave to soak for 10 minutes, by which time the water will have been absorbed. Cook the spring onions slowly in the oil for 3 minutes, then add the couscous and cook for another 3 minutes, stirring. Add 175 ml (6 fl oz) of the chicken stock, and salt and pepper to taste, and simmer for another 5 minutes, stirring often. Remove from the heat, stir in the chopped basil, and leave to cool.

3 About 1 hour before serving, dry the tomatoes with kitchen paper and fill them with the stuffing. Stand them in a buttered baking dish, cover with their lids, and pour over the remaining stock. Dot with butter and bake in a preheated oven, 180°C (350°F), Gas Mark 4, for 25 minutes until the tomatoes are soft but not yet starting to collapse. These are best served hot or warm.

Serves 4 as a main course with a green salad.

grilled vegetables
with basil

While this appetizing dish may be prepared several hours beforehand, be sure to serve it at room temperature.

1 Stick each pepper firmly on a long skewer. Heat the grill and put the peppers under it, turning them at regular intervals, until the skins are blackened all over. Remove and set aside to cool.

2 Cut a thin slice off each side of the aubergine and discard. Cut the rest of the aubergine lengthways in slices 1 cm (½ inch) thick. Brush them on both sides with a little of the olive oil, then place under the grill and cook until nicely coloured and softened, turning once. Set aside to cool.

3 Cut the courgettes in diagonal slices about the same thickness as the aubergine. Brush with olive oil on both sides and grill until speckled golden brown and fairly soft. Set aside to cool.

4 Trim the leeks down to the white parts. If very small, leave them whole, otherwise split them in half lengthways. Drop them into lightly salted boiling water and cook for 5 minutes, then drain well and pat dry in a cloth. Brush with olive oil and grill until lightly coloured.

5 Cut the fennel lengthways in slices about 1 cm (½ inch) thick. Brush with olive oil and grill till coloured, turning once. Then set aside.

6 Cut the red onions in fairly thick horizontal slices, allowing 4 slices to each onion. Brush them with olive oil and grill till they are soft and slightly blackened.

7 Arrange the vegetables on a flat dish. Sprinkle with garlic, basil, salt and pepper. Mix the oil and vinegar together and pour it over all.

Serves 4 to 6, with crusty bread, as a first course.

I large red pepper

I large yellow pepper

I aubergine

4–6 tablespoons olive oil

2 courgettes

3 small leeks

2 heads fennel

3 small red onions

Dressing:

I large garlic clove, finely chopped

2 heaped tablespoons basil,
   torn in bits

4 tablespoons extra virgin olive oil

½ tablespoon white wine vinegar

sea salt and black pepper

Right: Grilled Vegetables with Basil, recipe above

herb fritters

This pretty dish may be served alone as a light first course, as a vegetable accompaniment or, when made in small quantities, as a garnish. It must be eaten as soon as it is made, which limits its uses, alas.

2–3 dozen sprigs salad burnet, curly parsley, chervil, tarragon, dill or other herbs
vegetable oil, for frying
2–3 lemons, cut in quarters, to garnish

Batter:

125 g (4 oz) plain flour, sifted
a pinch of salt
2 tablespoons sunflower oil
150 ml (¼ pint) warm water
1 egg white, beaten

1 Start by making the batter, 1–2 hours ahead of time, if possible. Sift the flour and salt into a food processor and gradually add the oil, then the water through the lid while processing. Alternatively, sift the flour and salt into a large bowl and beat in first the oil and then the water by hand, using a large balloon whisk. The batter should be the consistency of fairly thick cream. Set aside for about 1 hour to rest.

2 When ready to fry, process (or beat) the batter again thoroughly, then fold in the beaten egg white. Heat a pan three-quarters full of oil until it is hot enough to brown a small cube of bread in 20 seconds (180°C/350°F).

3 Dip each sprig of herb in the batter and scrape off the excess on the sides of the bowl, then drop them, a few at a time, into the hot oil. Fry them for about 2 minutes, turning over once, then lift out with a slotted spoon and drain on kitchen paper while you fry the next batch. Serve as soon as made, garnished with lemon quarters.

Serves 4 to 6 as a side dish, or use as a garnish.

savoury elderflower
fritters

In many Central European countries elderflower fritters are made in early June and served as a vegetable dish, either on their own or to accompany a cooked meat dish like escalopes of veal. They are made in the same way as the sweet Elderflower Fritters (see page 217), simply omitting the sugar in the batter and in the garnish.

comfrey fritters

Comfrey is one of those herbs with large hairy leaves which make excellent fritters. This batter, made with soda water or sparkling mineral water, is eminently suited to delicate foods like leaves.

1 A batter made with sparkling water should not be made in advance, but just before using. Prepare the comfrey leaves first: trim off the stalks, rinse the leaves carefully under cold running water, then shake and pat dry in a cloth.

2 Shortly before serving, heat a large pan full of clean vegetable oil – a wok is ideal for this – until hot enough to brown a small cube of bread in 20 seconds (180°C/350°F). While the oil is heating, make the batter. Sift the flour with the salt into a food processor or large bowl. Add the oil, processing or beating by hand, then start to add the sparkling water gradually, processing or beating constantly, stopping when the batter has reached the consistency of fairly thick cream. Lastly, fold in the stiffly beaten egg white.

3 When the oil has reached the right temperature, dip each leaf in the batter, scraping off the excess on the sides of the bowl, then drop them, a few at a time, into the hot oil. Cook them for about 3 minutes, then lift them out and drain on kitchen paper while you cook the next batch. As soon as they have drained, transfer them to a warm dish. Garnish with lemon quarters, and serve alone or with other dishes.

comfrey leaves
vegetable oil for frying
lemon quarters, to garnish

Batter:

125 g (4 oz) plain flour
a pinch of salt
2 tablespoons sunflower oil
150 ml (¼ pint) soda water or
  sparkling mineral water
1 egg white, stiffly beaten

to cook Good King Henry

Good King Henry is closely related to spinach, and its young leaves may be cooked in exactly the same way. Even better, however, are the young shoots, which may be steamed or boiled briefly, then drained and dressed with melted butter. These are also delicious served on rectangles of buttered toast, sprinkled with sea salt and some freshly ground black pepper.

braised chicory
with orange juice and basil

1 Melt the butter in a sauté pan with a lid, and put in the chicory. Add the orange juice and water, then cover the pan and cook gently for 20 minutes, shaking the pan from side to side occasionally. Remove the lid, add the basil, salt and pepper, and continue cooking uncovered for 12 minutes. Turn the chicory over frequently, using a spatula, to prevent it sticking. If the liquid has almost boiled away, add another 2 tablespoons water. At the end the chicory should be well browned, almost burnt, and the liquid nearly evaporated. This unusual dish goes well with roast or grilled chicken, roast game or grilled lamb, or, for a simple vegetarian meal, serve it with brown rice.

Serves 4

50 g (2 oz) butter
750 g (1½ lb) chicory, cut in eighths lengthways
6 tablespoons orange juice
2 tablespoons water
2 tablespoons basil, cut in strips
salt and black pepper

baked tomatoes
with ginger and coriander

1 Scoop out most of the seeds from each halved tomato, and lay the halves upside down to drain. Mix the chopped spring onions, garlic, ginger, lemon verbena and coriander in a bowl. Dab the cut surface of the tomatoes with kitchen paper, then spoon the herb mixture into them, pressing it lightly into the crevices, and doming it up slightly. Lay the tomatoes in a buttered baking dish and season with salt and pepper. Pour a little olive oil over each one, then some orange juice.
2 Bake in a preheated oven, 180°C (350°F), Gas Mark 4, for about 20 minutes or until the sides of the tomatoes are soft when pierced with a skewer. Serve hot.

Serves 4 as a main course with a rice dish, or as part of a vegetarian meal, or 6 as an accompaniment to fish, poultry or meat.

4 beefsteak tomatoes, cut in half
1 bunch large spring onions, chopped
1 large garlic clove, finely chopped
1 cm (½ inch) square fresh root ginger, finely chopped
2 tablespoons chopped lemon verbena
4 tablespoons chopped coriander
3 tablespoons olive oil
6 tablespoons orange juice
salt and black pepper

hop shoots with eggs

The young shoots are picked in spring, when the hops are pruned. But commercially grown hops cannot be used today because they will have been sprayed with chemicals. If you have space in your garden, try growing two or three hops trained roughly over a tall tripod made of bamboo canes. Hops are delicious for a short time and highly decorative for the rest of the year.

375 g (12 oz) young hop shoots
4 slices white country bread, 1 cm
  (½ inch) thick, crusts removed
50 g (2 oz) butter, melted
2 hard-boiled eggs, shelled and
  roughly chopped
sea salt and black pepper

1 Treat the hop shoots exactly like asparagus: trim to the same length, wash well, then tie in bundles. Bring a large pan of lightly salted water to the boil, drop in the bundles and cook for about 10 minutes or until tender when pierced with a skewer, testing often.

2 Drain the hop shoots in a colander while you toast the slices of bread. Lay 1 piece of bread on each of 4 plates. Arrange the hop shoots over the bread, pour the melted butter on top, scatter the chopped egg over all and sprinkle with sea salt and black pepper. Serve immediately.

Note: If hop shoots are in short supply, a few can be served on toast, as above, with a poached egg on top. Alternatively, they may be served without the toast, as a garnish to a dish of scrambled eggs with, or without, a few slices of prosciutto.

Serves 4 as a first course.

tartlets with asparagus
and spring onions

1 Make the pastry. Place the flour and salt in a bowl, add the butter and rub in with your fingertips until the mixture resembles fine breadcrumbs. Mix in the egg yolk and just enough iced water to hold the dough together. Wrap in clingfilm and chill for 20 minutes, then roll out thinly and use to line 4 well-buttered tartlet tins measuring about 10 cm (4 inches) in diameter and 1.5 cm (¾ inch) deep. Brush the pastry with the egg yolk beaten with the milk, and prick here and there with a fork. Bake in a preheated oven, 190°C (375°F), Gas Mark 5, for 10 minutes, then take out of the oven and leave to cool. (This can be done in advance.)

2 To make the filling, take the tender part of the asparagus, probably about two-thirds of the spear, cut diagonally in 1 cm (½ inch) chunks, reserving the tips. Bring 450 ml (¾ pint) lightly salted water to the boil in a small pan, drop in the asparagus chunks and cook for 8–10 minutes until they are just tender. Drain them, reserving the water, then bring it back to the boil. Throw in the spring onions and cook for 5 minutes, then drain. Strain the water and reserve 150 ml (¼ pint).

3 To make the sauce, melt the butter, add the flour and cook for 1 minute, stirring. Add the reserved asparagus water slowly, stirring till blended, and cook gently for 3 minutes. Add the cream, season with salt and pepper to taste, then fold in the asparagus chunks, spring onions and the chopped chervil and chives. Reheat the pastry cases in a preheated oven, 180°C (350°F), Gas Mark 4, for 5 minutes. Then fill them with the vegetables in sauce, and put back in the oven for another 5 minutes. While they are gently baking, cook the asparagus tips for 4 minutes in a steamer, or a colander set over boiling water. To serve, lay 1–2 asparagus tips in the centre of each case.

Note: If you prefer, include the tips with the asparagus chunks. After taking the filled tartlets out of the oven, lay a few shavings of Parmesan cheese over the top of each one. This is quicker, and very tasty, but not quite so pretty.

Serves 4 as a first course.

Pastry:

250 g (8 oz) plain flour, sifted
½ teaspoon salt
125 g (4 oz) chilled butter, cut in small bits
1 egg yolk
2–4 tablespoons iced water

Glaze:

1 egg yolk
1 tablespoon milk

Filling:

250 g (8 oz) medium green asparagus
2 bunches spring onions, bulbs only

Sauce:

25 g (1 oz) butter
1½ tablespoons plain flour
75 ml (3 fl oz) single cream
1 tablespoon chopped chervil
1 tablespoon chopped chives
salt and black pepper

Right: Tartlets with Asparagus and Spring Onions, recipe above

courgettes in tomato

and mint sauce

Here is a dish that is good only when made with fully ripe tomatoes. Those still on the vine are probably the best for this purpose.

500 g (1 lb) small courgettes
1 bunch spring onions, sliced
25 g (1 oz) butter
1 tablespoon sunflower oil
2.5 cm (1 inch) square fresh root ginger, finely chopped
375 g (12 oz) tomatoes, skinned and chopped
2 tablespoons chopped mint
salt and black pepper

1 Steam the whole courgettes until tender, some 6–8 minutes. Cook the spring onions for 3 minutes in the butter and oil, then add the ginger and cook for another 2 minutes. Add the chopped tomatoes and cook for 5 minutes. Process very briefly, using a hand-held blender if you have one; otherwise use the pulse setting or button on a liquidizer or food processor. Season to taste with salt and pepper, stir in the chopped mint and pour over the courgettes in their serving dish.

Serves 4

grilled tomatoes

with sage dressing

Serve alone as a first course, or with a simple meat or chicken dish. Grilled pork chops, lamb cutlets and chicken wings all go well with it.

6 medium tomatoes, cut in half
3 large garlic cloves, finely chopped
6 tablespoons chopped flat-leaf parsley
4 tablespoons olive oil
salt and black pepper

Sage Dressing:

sunflower oil
15 large sage leaves

1 Scoop out most of the seeds from the tomatoes. Mix the chopped garlic and parsley, and pile into the tomato halves. Add salt and pepper and 1 teaspoon olive oil to each. Lay them in a shallow oiled dish and grill for 10–15 minutes, until lightly browned. Keep warm.
2 Heat enough sunflower oil to cover the bottom of a heavy pan by 1 cm (½ inch). Throw in the sage leaves and fry for 30 seconds, lift out and drain on kitchen paper. Scatter over the tomatoes and serve at once.

Serves 4
Illustrated on page 94

leek & potato gratin
with thyme

This makes a useful vegetarian main course, accompanied by Grilled Tomatoes (see page 196) and a green salad.

1 Rub a gratin dish with a little of the oil and make alternate layers of sliced potatoes and leeks, starting and ending with potatoes. Season each layer with salt, pepper and thyme, reserving some of the thyme for the garnish. When all is done, pour the stock and then the remaining olive oil over the top layer of potatoes, then scatter the reserved thyme on top. Bake in a preheated oven, 180°C (350°F), Gas Mark 4, for 1¼ hours or until the potatoes are soft. Just before serving, drizzle the extra virgin olive oil over the top.

Serves 4 as a first course or light main dish.

4 tablespoons olive oil

3 medium waxy potatoes, peeled and thinly sliced

3 leeks, thinly sliced

2 tablespoons chopped thyme or 1 tablespoon dried thyme

300 ml (½ pint) chicken stock, heated

salt and black pepper

1½ tablespoons extra virgin olive oil, to garnish

braised lettuce
with chervil

When made with a good chicken stock, this is a delicate and unusual dish, perfect for light summer meals.

1 Choose a pan into which the lettuces just fit in one layer. Melt the butter in it, then add the lettuces. Cook gently for 5 minutes, turning them over once or twice. Pour on the heated stock, add salt and pepper, and bring to the boil. Cover the pan and simmer for 25 minutes. Transfer the lettuces to a serving dish. Add the chopped chervil to the stock, stir around to mix, then pour over the lettuces.

Serves 4 to 6 as a vegetable accompaniment, or 3 as a light meal with a bowl of rice

6 Little Gem lettuces

40 g (1½ oz) butter

300 ml (½ pint) chicken stock, heated

2 tablespoons chopped chervil

salt and black pepper

salads

green salad
with herbs and flowers

2 Little Gem lettuces

10 sorrel leaves, cut in thin strips

10 sprigs chervil

5 marigolds, petals only,
  or 10 nasturtiums

Dressing:

1 tablespoon lemon juice

1 tablespoon white wine vinegar

4 tablespoons light olive oil

a pinch of sugar

a pinch of mustard powder

sea salt and black pepper

1 Break the lettuces up into leaves, wash them and drain well. Pile them in a bowl and lay the sorrel and chervil over them. Mix together all the ingredients for the dressing and pour it over the salad; toss well, then scatter the marigold petals or the whole nasturtiums on top.

Serves 4 as a separate course.

Previous pages: Green Salad with Herbs and Flowers, recipe above

carrot, fennel & celery salad

This salad goes well with grilled meat and with other vegetable dishes.

1 Grate the three vegetables fairly coarsely. Mix them in a large bowl and stir in the oils and lemon juice. Add half the toasted sesame seeds, and half the chopped leaves of fennel and celery, depending on what is available. Pile into a salad bowl, and scatter the remaining sesame seeds and chopped leaves over the top.

Note: If fennel and celery leaves are unobtainable use 2 tablespoons of chopped alexanders, when available.

Serves 4 as the accompaniment to other dishes, or 3 on its own.

250 g (8 oz) carrots
125–150 g (4–5 oz) fennel, tender parts only, plus 2 tablespoons chopped leaves
125–150 g (4–5 oz) celery, tender stalks only, plus 2 tablespoons chopped leaves
2 tablespoons sunflower oil
1 tablespoon sesame oil
2 tablespoons lemon juice
2 tablespoons toasted sesame seeds

a Tuscan salad

1 Mix the broad beans with the rocket in a shallow bowl. Mix the olive oil and lemon juice together and dress the salad. Season with pepper to taste. (No salt is needed because of the Parmesan.) Scatter the shavings of Parmesan over and among the vegetables.

Serves 4 as a first course.

375 g (12 oz) shelled broad beans
40 g (1½ oz) rocket, weighed after removing stalks
65 ml (2½ fl oz) extra virgin olive oil
1½ tablespoons lemon juice
40 g (1½ oz) Parmesan cheese, thinly shaved
black pepper

Lebanese herb salad

This is one of those delicious Middle Eastern salads that are usually served as part of a mixed meze, or array of first course dishes, rather than as the accompaniment to a main dish. It is immensely nutritious, being made of fresh herbs, raw salad vegetables and grain. Often incorrectly made as a grain dish with herbs, it is, in fact, a herb dish with a little added grain. Getting the right grain is essential, for there are several different forms of cracked wheat. Crushed wheat is too fine, while kibbled wheat is too coarse. The one to use is bulgar (sometimes called burghul), which has been cracked and parboiled. You also need a large amount of parsley, although the exact quantity is not vital.

1 Soak the bulgar in a bowl of cold water for 30 minutes, then drain it and squeeze dry. Put it in a clean bowl and mix with the chopped spring onions, using your hands. Add the chopped tomatoes, chopped herbs, salt and pepper, and mix well. Lastly, stir in the olive oil and lemon juice. Pile the salad into a shallow bowl.

Note: The traditional way of serving this salad in Lebanon is on a huge platter, surrounded with the crisp inner leaves of cos lettuce, which are used as scoops to eat it with. This works especially well in a buffet as 'finger food'.

Serves 4 with other dishes.

50 g (2 oz) bulgar, washed
2 bunches spring onions, chopped
2 tomatoes, skinned, deseeded and chopped
50 g (2 oz) flat-leaf parsley, leaves only, chopped (weigh before washing)
4 tablespoons chopped mint
3 tablespoons extra virgin olive oil
3 tablespoons lemon juice
sea salt and black pepper
inner leaves of 1 cos lettuce, to garnish (optional, see note)

desserts

elderberry mousse

This recipe was given to a friend of mine by the wife of a lock-keeper on a canal in Burgundy, where elder grows in profusion. She used crème fraîche, but I prefer to use double cream, lightly whipped.

1 Plunge the elderberries, still on their stems, into a basin of cold water and swirl them about to wash well. Then strip them into a basin, using a fork. Press them gently against the sides of the basin, using the back of a wooden spoon, to release some of the juice.

2 Strain off the juice into a heavy pan and add the sugar. Bring to the boil and cook very gently for 2–3 minutes, until the sugar has melted. Then put the berries in the pan, cover it and cook gently for 10 minutes, stirring occasionally. When the time is up, turn the berries into a strainer lying over a bowl and press them with the back of a wooden spoon to release all their juice. Discard the berries and measure the juice; you should have about 600 ml (1 pint).

3 Take about 100 ml (3½ fl oz) of the juice and heat it. Remove from the heat just before it boils and shake in the gelatine, stirring until it has dissolved. Then mix this with the rest of the juice and pour through a fine strainer. Whip the cream lightly and fold into the juice. A few turns of an electric beater will facilitate this. Pour into a straight-sided soufflé dish and place in the refrigerator for several hours or overnight to set. This is quite a concentrated dish, and it is a good idea to serve small plain cakes or biscuits such as madeleines or *langues de chat* with it.

Serves 4 to 5

1.25 kg (2½ lb) elderberries, weighed after stripping
50 g (2 oz) sugar
20 g (¾ oz) powdered gelatine
300 ml (½ pint) double cream, lightly whipped

Previous pages: Elderberry Mousse, recipe above

gooseberry
and elderflower compote

4 tablespoons sugar, or to taste

750 g (1½ lb) gooseberries, trimmed
and washed

3 elderflowers, washed

1 Put enough water into a heavy pan to cover the bottom by about 5 mm (¼ inch). Add the sugar and bring slowly to the boil. Cook gently until the sugar has melted, then add the gooseberries and elderflowers. Cover the pan and simmer gently, shaking the pan from time to time, until the gooseberries start to soften and burst. Remove the pan from the heat and let stand until the contents have cooled to room temperature. Discard the elderflowers. Transfer the gooseberries to a serving dish, and strain the juice over them. Serve at room temperature or chilled with crème fraîche or vanilla ice cream.

Serves 4

apple sorbet with mint

This will be only as good as the apple juice you use. Best of all is your own freshly pressed juice.

2 tablespoons vodka

600 ml (1 pint) chilled apple juice

2 tablespoons finely chopped mint,
plus 4–6 small sprigs

1 Stir the vodka into the chilled apple juice. Pour into an ice-cream machine and freeze, following the maker's instructions, adding the chopped mint halfway through the freezing process.

2 Alternatively, pour the liquid into metal ice-cube trays (without the dividers), cover with foil and freeze for 45 minutes. Remove the sorbet and tip into a food processor or large bowl. Process briefly or beat with a wire whisk, then return to the container and continue freezing. Repeat the processing or whisking twice more, at 45-minute intervals, adding the mint during the last beating.

3 This is best eaten within the next 2 hours. Serve in small glasses and lay a tiny sprig of mint on each one.

Serves 4 to 6

apple jellies
with mint and almond sauce

As with the Apple Sorbet (see page 215), the quality of this simple dish depends totally on the excellence of the apple juice. On no account use those made with concentrates; buy the best pure apple juice.

1 Heat 125 ml (4 fl oz) of the apple juice in a small pan and dissolve the gelatine in it; do not let it boil. Remove from the heat once the gelatine has been added, and set aside until it has melted. Then mix with the rest of the apple juice and run through a strainer to catch any lumps. Pour into small tin moulds to set. (I use oval *oeuf en gelée* moulds holding 125 ml/4 fl oz each.) Chill in the refrigerator for 2–3 hours or overnight to set. To serve, turn out on to small flat plates and pour a little mint and almond sauce around each jelly.

Serves 4 to 6, depending on the size of your moulds.

750 ml (1¼ pints) apple juice
1 tablespoon powdered gelatine
6 small mint leaves
Mint and Almond Sauce (see page 175)

a tansy pudding

Tansy was very popular in the sixteenth, seventeenth and eighteenth centuries, although today it seems so bitter as to be almost unpalatable. This pudding was traditionally eaten at Easter. A more enjoyable version can be made by substituting 8 tablespoons chopped sorrel for the tansy, and omitting the sugar. The spinach juice is best made in a vegetable juice extractor; failing that, cook some spinach in a little water and use that.

1 Put the breadcrumbs in a bowl. Bring the cream, or milk and cream, to a boil, then pour over the breadcrumbs and leave, covered, for 15 minutes. Stir in the beaten eggs, the spinach juice, tansy, sugar and nutmeg. Turn the mixture into a buttered dish and bake in a pre-heated oven, 160°C (325°F), Gas Mark 3, for 45–50 minutes or until the pudding is firm.
Note: This pudding was sometimes baked under a joint of roast beef or lamb and served with it, almost like a Yorkshire pudding.

Serves 4

50 g (2 oz) soft white breadcrumbs
300 ml (½ pint) single cream, or milk and cream mixed
4 eggs, beaten
150 ml (¼ pint) spinach juice (allow about 375 g (12 oz) raw spinach)
2 tablespoons chopped tansy leaves
2 teaspoons sugar
½ teaspoon ground nutmeg

elderflower fritters

Elders are in flower in early summer. Only the young heads should be used or the dish will have a sickly flavour. Shake them after picking to get rid of any insects, but do not wash them unless you have to.

vegetable oil, for frying
about 20 elderflowers

Batter:

125 g (4 oz) plain flour
a pinch of salt
2 teaspoons caster sugar
2 tablespoons sunflower oil
150 ml (¼ pint) warm water
1 egg white, beaten

To decorate:

caster sugar
3 lemons, cut in quarters

1 To make the batter, sift the flour, salt and sugar into a food processor, switch on to blend, then add the oil through the lid gradually, continuing to beat. Then add the water slowly, still beating. Alternatively, sift the flour, salt and sugar into a large bowl, add the oil gradually, while beating with an electric beater or by hand. Continue to beat while you add the water. Leave for 1 hour, if possible, then process or beat again before using. Fold in the beaten egg white just before using.

2 Heat a deep pan three-quarters filled with oil until hot enough to brown a small cube of bread in 20 seconds (about 180°C, 350°F). Dip each flower head in the batter, scrape off the excess on the edge of the bowl, and drop into the hot oil. Cook a few at a time. Fry the flower heads for 2–3 minutes, turning once, then lift out and drain on kitchen paper while you fry the next batch. Sprinkle with caster sugar before serving, with lemon wedges.

Serves 6

rhubarb compote
with sweet cicely

4 tablespoons sugar
750 g (1½ lb) rhubarb, cut in 2.5 cm (1 inch) chunks
2 tablespoons chopped sweet cicely leaves

1 Put just enough water into a heavy saucepan to cover the base by 5 mm (¼ inch). Add the sugar and bring slowly to the boil and cook very gently until the sugar has melted. Add the rhubarb pieces and the chopped sweet cicely. Bring back to the boil, then stew very gently, half covered, until the rhubarb has just softened; remove from the heat before it starts to collapse. Turn into a serving bowl and leave to cool. Serve at room temperature or chilled, with cream, natural yogurt or vanilla ice cream.

Serves 4

chocolate cakes
with strawberries and mint

75 g (3 oz) butter, semi-melted,
plus a little for greasing
125 g (4 oz) plain dark chocolate,
such as Chocolat Menier,
broken in small bits
2 tablespoons plain flour, sifted
125 g (4 oz) caster sugar
3 eggs, separated

Filling:

200 g (7 oz) strawberries, chopped
1 heaped tablespoon chopped mint
250 ml (8 fl oz) double cream,
lightly whipped

1 Prepare 8 shallow round baking tins with flat bottoms, about 10 cm (4 inches) in diameter and 1.5 cm (¾ inch) deep. Rub them with butter, then line the bottoms with circles of buttered greaseproof paper. Heat the oven to 180°C (350°F), Gas Mark 4. Put the chocolate bits into a fairly large ovenproof bowl, and place in the oven until the chocolate has just melted, about 5–10 minutes. Remove from the oven (but keep the oven at the same temperature) and leave to cool for 5 minutes, then drop in the melted butter gradually, beating with a wooden spoon until amalgamated. Stir in the flour and sugar. Beat the egg yolks briefly and stir into the chocolate mixture, then beat the egg whites until stiff and fold into the mixture. Spoon into the tins to fill them by just over half. Bake for 15 minutes, then take out of the oven and leave to cool.

2 Later, when they have cooled, you will find the puffy crust that has formed on the top of the cakes has cracked and split. Lift off as much as you can, one cake at a time, and put 2 tablespoons of chopped strawberries in the centre of each cake. Sprinkle half a teaspoon chopped mint over each one, then spoon the lightly whipped cream over it. Replace most of the chocolate crust, and then chill in the refrigerator until you are ready to serve.

Note: The cakes may be made a day in advance, but the crust will be hard to lift off. It is better to remove it soon after baking, and reserve.

Serves 8

Right: Chocolate Cake with Strawberries and Mint, recipe above

elderflower tart

The blooms of borage or marigold may be substituted for the elderflowers in this summer dessert.

1 Make the pastry. Place the sifted flour in a bowl with the sugar, add the butter and rub in with your fingertips until the mixture resembles fine breadcrumbs. Add enough iced water to mix to a firm dough. Wrap in clingfilm and chill in the refrigerator for about 30 minutes. Turn the dough out on to a lightly floured surface and roll out and line a 20 cm (8 inch) flan tin. Prick all over with a fork, line with crumpled foil weighed down with beans and bake in a preheated oven, 190°C (375°F), Gas Mark 5, for 8 minutes. Remove the pastry case and reduce the oven heat to 180°C (350°F), Gas Mark 4.

2 To make the filling, heat the cream slowly with the elderflowers. When hot but not yet boiling, remove from the heat and stand, covered, for 10 minutes. Beat the egg yolks with the sugar, reheat the cream and pour through a strainer on to the eggs, beating well. Fold in the stiffly beaten egg white and then pour the mixture into the pastry case. Bake for 20 minutes, until puffy and golden brown. Serve the tart as soon as possible.

Note: If using marigolds instead of elderflowers, use the petals of 8 marigolds. A few petals may be reserved to scatter over the tart just before serving.

Serves 4

Pastry:

175 g (6 oz) plain flour, sifted
½ teaspoon caster sugar
75 g (3 oz) butter
2–3 tablespoons iced water

Filling:

300 ml (½ pint) single cream
3 elderflowers
3 egg yolks
50 g (2 oz) caster sugar
1 egg white, stiffly beaten

honey & ginger ice cream

This is made with a mixture of double cream and natural yogurt and is therefore less rich than a pure cream ice.

300 ml (½ pint) semi-skimmed milk

**I vanilla pod, halved and split in
4 pieces**

2 eggs

2 egg yolks

**I tablespoon vanilla sugar or
caster sugar**

**2 tablespoons clear aromatic honey
such as Greek or Mexican**

**2 tablespoons ginger syrup (from a
jar of preserved stem ginger)**

150 ml (¼ pint) mild natural yogurt

**150 ml (¼ pint) double cream
partly whipped**

**3 tablespoons chopped preserved
stem ginger**

1 Put the milk in a small pan with the vanilla pod, including the seeds. Bring slowly to the boil, remove from the heat and let stand, covered, for 20–30 minutes. When the time is nearly up, beat the eggs and egg yolks together, using an electric handbeater. Add the sugar gradually, continuing to beat. When the infusion time is up, reheat the milk, then remove the vanilla pod (rinse, dry and keep to flavour a jar of vanilla sugar).

2 Add the honey and ginger syrup to the milk as it is heating. When almost boiling, pour it on to the eggs and continue beating. Stand the bowl over a pan of simmering water and stir constantly until the mixture has slightly thickened. This may take 8–10 minutes. Remove from the heat and stand in a sink half full of cold water to cool. Stir now and then to prevent a skin forming.

3 When the mixture has cooled almost to room temperature, tip it into a liquidizer or food processor and blend with the yogurt and semi-whipped double cream. Then pour it into an ice-cream machine and freeze, following the maker's instructions, adding the chopped ginger halfway through the freezing time.

4 Alternatively, pour the mixture into metal ice-cube trays (without the dividers) or another metal container and place in the freezer or freezing compartment of the refrigerator. Freeze until lightly set all through: 2–3 hours, depending on the shape and thickness of the container and the power of the freezer. Add the chopped ginger after 1½ hours and stir with a metal spoon every hour or so. This method, although slow, produces a perfectly good ice cream, although the texture of the finished ice lacks the silky smooth quality of the machine-made product.

Serves 6

lavender ice cream

I prefer to make this with a simple honey, rather than the exotic scented varieties from Greece or Mexico.

1 Put the milk in a pan with the lavender. Bring it slowly to the boil, then cover the pan and remove from the heat. Leave for 20–30 minutes to infuse, then strain out the lavender and discard.

2 Put the egg yolks into a china bowl (preferably, not an ovenproof one) and beat them with an electric handbeater, adding the sugar gradually. Continue to beat for 2–3 minutes, then reheat the lavender-flavoured milk. At the same time choose a large pan in which the bowl can sit securely, and fill it one-third of the way with water, so that the bottom of the bowl does not touch the surface of the water. Remove the bowl and heat the water. When it is almost boiling, stand the china bowl in the pan. Adjust the heat so that the water barely simmers. Start to beat the egg yolks again and as the milk nears boiling point, pour it slowly on to the eggs, beating all the time. Using a wooden spoon now instead of an electric beater, stir constantly until the custard has thickened just enough to coat the back of the wooden spoon.

3 Lift the bowl out of the pan and stand it in a sink half full of cold water. Stir now and then as the custard cools to room temperature, to prevent a skin forming.

4 When the custard has cooled to room temperature, stir in the honey. Then fold in the lightly whipped cream and pour into an ice-cream machine and freeze, following the maker's instructions. Alternatively, pour the mixture into metal ice-cube trays (without the dividers) or another metal container and place in the freezer or freezing compartment of the refrigerator and freeze.

Serves 4 to 6

300 ml (½ pint) milk
2 sprigs lavender, plus flower heads
4 egg yolks
25 g (1 oz) caster sugar
4 tablespoons clear honey
300 ml (½ pint) double cream,
  lightly whipped

small iced cakes
with flowers

Crystallized flowers for the decoration must be prepared in advance. If making these seems too fiddly, freshly picked flowers or edible leaves, like nasturtiums, may be used instead. Failing flowers or edible leaves, small berries or currants may be used: red or white currants, blueberries and so on. Lemon juice may be substituted for the elderflower cordial.
To half-melt the butter you need to heat it gently, until it is quite softened but not melted.

2 eggs
approx. 150 g (5 oz) vanilla sugar or caster sugar
approx. 60 g (2½ oz) plain flour, sifted
approx. 60 g (2½ oz) ground almonds
approx. 150 g (5 oz) butter, half-melted

Elderflower Icing:

175 g (6 oz) icing sugar
approx. 3 tablespoons Elderflower Cordial (see page 226)
a few small Crystallized Flowers (see page 238), to decorate

1 To make the cakes, weigh the eggs in their shells and calculate the weight of the other ingredients accordingly: the sugar and the butter should each equal the combined weight of the eggs; which is the same as the combined weight of the flour and ground almonds.

2 Break the eggs into a large bowl and beat with a whisk. Add the sugar gradually, continuing to beat. Then fold in the flour and ground almonds, and stir in the semi-melted butter. Mix well, then spoon into well-buttered small round cake tins measuring roughly 6 cm (2½ inches) across and 2.5 cm (1 inch) deep. Bake them in a preheated oven, 180°C (350°F), Gas Mark 4, for 15–20 minutes until light golden brown with darker edges.

3 Take the tins out of the oven and leave to cool for 10–15 minutes, then lift out the little cakes and lay on a wire rack. When they have completely cooled, prepare them for icing. If they have risen into a dome shape, as sometimes happens, level them by cutting off the central tip. Then make the icing.

4 Sift the icing sugar into a bowl, warm the elderflower cordial and stir it into the sugar, beating hard until the mixture is absolutely smooth. Stop as soon as you have reached a spreading consistency. Spread the icing over the tops of the little cakes, using a palette knife dipped in warm water to smooth it out. Leave to cool and set before laying the crystallized flowers, or freshly picked flowers or leaves, on top.

Makes about 16.

drinks

elderflower cordial

This old-fashioned English cordial can be made only during two weeks in early summer when the elder is in flower. The elderflowers must be picked once they are fully open, for soon after that they start to develop an unpleasant, sickly scent. Elderflower cordial is now being made commercially, and there are several good brands on the market, but they lack the special charm of the one you have made yourself.

1 Put the water in a deep pan and bring to the boil. Add the sugar and the lemons and remove from the heat. Stir until the sugar has dissolved, then bring back to the boil. When it boils, add the elderflowers and the vinegar. Bring back to the boil once more, then immediately remove from the heat and leave to cool overnight.

2 Next day, strain the liquid into glass bottles – coloured glass is best, if you can get it – and keep in a cool larder or in the refrigerator. Kept in this way, it will last for 4–5 months; after that it starts to go fizzy. This delicious and refreshing drink can be mixed with vodka, gin or mineral water – either still or fizzy. Dilute to taste.

2.4 litres (4 pints) water
1.5 kg (3 lb) sugar
2 lemons, cut in pieces
20 large elderflowers
6 tablespoons white wine vinegar

Previous pages: clockwise from left, Yogurt Drink with Rose Petals, recipe page 229, Yogurt Drink with Mint, recipe page 228, Elderflower Cordial, recipe above, Moroccan Mint Tea, recipe right and Ginger and Lemon Drink, recipe page 229

Moroccan mint tea

This is a real mint tea, as made in North Africa, not just an infusion of mint, which is often called mint tea. If you cannot get Moroccan tea, which friends occasionally bring me, the best tea to use is probably one of the China teas, such as chunmee, gunpowder or Temple of Heaven, or an ordinary green tea. Be sure to use spearmint, the common or garden mint, and not one of the scented varieties. And do not be tempted to omit the sugar, or even cut it down much more than I have done already.

1 Warm a small teapot holding about 600 ml (1 pint), and put in the tea, sugar and mint leaves. Pour over enough boiling water to fill the pot, and stand for 5 minutes. Then pour from a height into 3–4 small glasses, and put a small sprig of mint in each one. Serve hot or warm. This is very refreshing on a hot afternoon, or drunk after a meal instead of black coffee. In this context, it also serves as a digestive.

Serves 3 to 4

I tablespoon Moroccan or green tea
3–4 tablespoons sugar
24 large spearmint leaves
3–4 small sprigs spearmint

yogurt drink with mint

Chilled yogurt drinks dominate the scene in Turkey, the Middle East and India during the hot weather. The most popular one, called ayran in Turkey and lassi in India, is made with yogurt thinned with iced water and garnished with chopped mint. It should really be made with a strong-flavoured yogurt like that found in Turkey but failing that, a sharp Greek yogurt is probably best.

1 Put the yogurt in a food processor or beat by hand, adding the iced water. Process or beat till blended, adding a little salt, then check the seasoning and the consistency. If too thick to drink easily out of a glass, add a little more water. Pour into tall glasses to serve, and sprinkle chopped mint on top of each glass.

Serves 2–3
Illustrated on pages 224-225

600 ml (1 pint) Greek yogurt
approx. 300 ml (½ pint) iced water
salt to taste
½ tablespoon finely chopped mint,
  to garnish

white wine cup

1 Make the sugar syrup by putting 75 g (3 oz) sugar in a small pan with 6 tablespoons water. Bring slowly to the boil, and then simmer gently, stirring, until the sugar has dissolved. Cool quickly, then pour into a glass jug and add the fruit juices, brandy and wine. Add the cucumber peel and chill in the refrigerator for 2–3 hours. Shortly before serving, add the mineral water, plenty of ice and the borage.

Serves 4 to 6

75 ml (3 fl oz) sugar syrup
  (see recipe)
75 ml (3 fl oz) lemon juice
250 ml (8 fl oz) orange juice
4 tablespoons brandy
I bottle semi-sweet, flowery white
  wine: Vouvray, Alsace, Riesling
  or Muscat
3 long strips cucumber peel
350 ml (12 fl oz) sparkling
  mineral water
3–4 stalks borage, with flowers

yogurt drink with rose petals

This is a sort of festive drink that might be served at a party in Turkey or in India. These sweet versions of the lightly salted, mint-flavoured yogurt drinks would normally be flavoured with rose water, but if you have already made some Rose Syrup (see page 239), this would be even better. When possible, use a few petals of a pink damask rose for a garnish.

1 Put the yogurt in a food processor or beat by hand until smooth and light. Add the rose syrup and iced water. (If using rose water, add the sugar and process or beat together, then taste for sweetness and check for consistency.) Add more rose syrup or rose water as required, and more iced water if the mixture is still too thick. Finally, pour into tall glasses and scatter a few rose petals over the top.

Serves 2 to 3
Illustrated on page 224

600 ml (1 pint) mild natural yogurt
3–4 tablespoons rose syrup or
  rose water
about 300 ml (½ pint) iced water
4 tablespoons caster sugar, if using
  rose water
8 rose petals, to garnish

ginger & lemon drink

This makes a good start to the day, especially after eating or drinking too much the previous night.

1 Put the sliced ginger and lemon in a mug, add the honey to taste, and fill up with almost boiling water. Stir well, and drink once it has cooled slightly.

Serves 1
Illustrated on page 225

2 slices unpeeled ginger, about
  2.5 mm (⅛ inch) thick
1 slice lemon, about 2.5 mm
  (⅛ inch) thick
½–1 teaspoon clear honey

preserves

dill pickles

These traditional accompaniments to salt beef and pastrami sandwiches are best made in midsummer, when gherkins are available and dill is plentiful. Homegrown dill is infinitely better than that sold in shops and supermarkets for this dish, which really needs thick stalks and flower heads as well as leaves.

1 Wash and dry a 1 kg (2 lb) glass preserving jar and place upside down on an oven rack. Turn the oven to 120°C (250°F), Gas Mark ½, and leave for 15 minutes. Then turn off the heat, leaving the jar in the oven. It should still be warm when you are filling it. Sterilize the lid by dipping in boiling water.

2 Pack the washed gherkins (or small cucumbers or wedges) into the sterilized preserving jar, with the garlic, dill and bay leaves scattered among them. Put all the ingredients for the pickle into a pan and boil for 3 minutes, then leave to cool before pouring over the gherkins.

3 Cool, then close the jar tightly. Keep for at least 2 weeks before eating. Once opened, the pickles should be kept in the refrigerator.

Makes 1 kg (2 lb)

1 kg (2 lb) gherkins or small
  cucumbers, or halved cucumbers
  cut in wedges
2 garlic cloves, thinly sliced
12 large sprigs dill, including flowers
  if possible
3 bay leaves

Pickle:

750 ml (1¼ pints) water
250 ml (8 fl oz) vinegar
25 g (1 oz) sea salt
12 black peppercorns
12 whole allspice berries

marinated goats' cheeses

These make a useful preserve to have on hand over a holiday. They also make a good present to take on a visit or for Christmas, especially when packed in a good-looking jar. Buy individual goats' cheeses, as slices from a log tend to disintegrate. And try to find young cheeses or the end result may be quite strong.

1 Pack the cheeses into a wide-mouthed glass jar, scattering the peppercorns and crumbled bay leaf among them. Slip the sprigs of rosemary and thyme down the sides of the jar, and add enough olive oil to cover the cheeses. Seal tightly, and label clearly with the date.

2 Allow 2 weeks before opening; the cheeses will keep for longer in a cool place but grow stronger the longer they are kept. Serve as a cheese, as part of a salad, or gently grilled and served on a bed of salad leaves.

6–8 small goats' cheeses,
  freshly made
12 black peppercorns
12 green peppercorns
1 bay leaf, crumbled
2 sprigs rosemary
2 sprigs thyme
approx. 450 ml (¾ pint) olive oil

Previous pages: from left, Dill Pickles, recipe above top,
Marinated Goats' Cheeses, recipe above

mint jelly

The leaves of sage, tarragon, thyme or lemon thyme may be substituted for mint. Use half as much sage as mint, but equal amounts of the others.

1 Wash and dry glass preserving jars and place them upside down on an oven rack. Turn the oven to 120°C (250°F), Gas Mark ½, and leave for 15 minutes. Then turn off the heat, leaving the jars in the oven. They should be warm when you fill them. Dip the lids in boiling water.
2 Put the apples into a deep pan with the mint. Add the water. Bring to the boil and simmer for about 30 minutes, until the apples are soft and pulpy. Scald a jelly bag by dipping it in boiling water, then pour in the apples and mint. Suspend the bag over a bowl to drain overnight.
3 Next day measure the juice and add 500 g (1 lb) preserving sugar for every 600 ml (1 pint) of liquid. Bring to the boil in a heavy pan and boil steadily until setting point is reached. To test for this, pour a tablespoon of the jelly into a saucer and chill quickly in the freezer or over ice. When it has cooled, push the surface of the jelly gently with a fingertip; if it wrinkles, setting point has been reached. This will probably take 20–30 minutes. Skim off the scum and remove the pan from the heat. Stir in the vinegar, lemon juice and chopped mint. Pour into sterilized jars and leave to cool completely, then close the jars tightly.

Makes enough to fill 3 x 250 g (8 oz) jars

mint sauce (a preserve)

125 g (4 oz) mint, leaves only
350 ml (12 fl oz) cider vinegar
125 g (4 oz) preserving or
  granulated sugar

1 Wash the mint leaves and pat them dry in a cloth. Chop them by hand, quite finely, then pack them into small jars. Boil the vinegar with the sugar until the sugar has melted, then pour it over the mint. Mix well and leave to cool, then screw down the lids and store in a cool, dark cupboard or in the refrigerator. To use, dilute with a mixture of lemon juice and water, to taste. Serve with roast lamb.

Makes 4 x 150 ml (¼ pint) jars

pickled ginger

Pickled ginger is the traditional Japanese garnish for eating with sushi. It is also delicious eaten with a variety of different foods, from boiled rice to sandwiches, and makes a splendid present. It is important to buy a supply of young, fresh and juicy ginger.

1 Prepare your preserving jars. Wash and dry glass preserving jars and place upside down on an oven rack. Turn the oven to 120°C (250°F), Gas Mark ½, and leave for 15 minutes. Then turn off the heat, leaving the jars in the oven until ready to use. They should still be hot or warm when you are filling them with the pickled ginger. Sterilize the lids by dipping them in boiling water.

2 Wipe the ginger with a damp cloth, then peel it and cut in the thinnest possible slices, cutting along the grain. Bring a pan of water to the boil, add the salt, then drop in the sliced ginger. When the water comes back to the boil, remove the pan from the heat and drain off the water. Cool the ginger quickly under cold running water, then drain again and tip into a bowl. Put the vinegar, sugar and water into a small pan and bring slowly to the boil. Simmer gently until the sugar has melted, then pour over the sliced ginger.

3 When the ginger and liquid have cooled, spoon them into warm, sterilized jars and leave to cool completely. Then close the jars tightly, wipe clean and label clearly. This simple preserve will keep for several months in the refrigerator.

Makes about 250 g (8 oz)

250 g (8 oz) fresh root ginger
1 tablespoon sea salt
250 ml (8 fl oz) rice wine vinegar
2 tablespoons soft brown sugar
6 tablespoons water

mint chutney

500 g (1 lb) cooking apples, peeled,
  cored and chopped

250 g (8 oz) onions, coarsely
  chopped

2 garlic cloves, finely chopped

1 yellow pepper, cored, deseeded
  and chopped

450 ml (¾ pint) white wine vinegar

25 g (1 oz) root ginger, bruised

250 g (8 oz) moist brown sugar

1 teaspoon whole coriander seeds

4 black peppercorns

4 whole allspice berries

½ tablespoon sea salt

4 tablespoons chopped mint

1 Prepare your preserving jars. Wash and dry glass preserving jars and place upside down on an oven rack. Turn the oven to 120°C (250°F), Gas Mark ½, and leave for 15 minutes. Then tûrn off the heat, leaving the jars in the oven until ready to use. They should still be hot or warm when you are filling them. Sterilize the lids by dipping in boiling water.

2 Put the apples, onions, garlic and yellow pepper into a heavy pan with the vinegar. Bring slowly to the boil and simmer until soft, about 30 minutes. Add the ginger, which you have tied in a piece of muslin, and the sugar, coriander seeds, peppercorns, allspice and salt. Heat the mixture gently until the sugar has melted, then simmer until thick; this may take as long as 1 hour.

3 When it is done, remove from the heat. Discard the the ginger and stir in the chopped mint. Spoon into warm sterilized jars and leave to cool. Then close the jars tightly, wipe them with a damp cloth and label them clearly.

4 To serve, spoon into a bowl and sprinkle some freshly chopped mint on top. It is excellent with rye bread and Cheddar cheese.

Note: To make coriander chutney, simply substitute chopped fresh coriander for chopped fresh mint.

Makes about 1 litre (1¾ pints)

grape jelly with lavender

The best grapes to use for this jelly are slightly unripe ones, both for their tart flavour and for their higher pectin content. Crab apples may be substituted for grapes, if more convenient.

1 Scald a jelly bag by dipping it in a pan of boiling water. Cut the grapes into small bunches – don't bother to pull them off their stems – and wash them well. Put them in a deep pan and add enough water to come level. Add the bunch of lavender and bring slowly to the boil. Boil steadily until the grapes are soft and pale in colour, then strain the contents of the pan slowly through a jelly bag suspended over a large bowl. (If you do not have a jelly bag, simply lay a square of double cheesecloth or closely woven muslin in a strainer.) Leave to drain for several hours or overnight. Do not attempt to hurry the process by pushing or squeezing, or the jelly will be cloudy.

2 Next day prepare your preserving jar. Wash and dry a 1 kg (2 lb) glass preserving jar and place upside down on an oven rack. Turn the oven to 120°C (250°F), Gas Mark ½, and leave for 15 minutes. Then turn off the heat, leaving the jar in the oven until ready to use. It should still be hot or warm when you are filling it. Sterilize the lid by dipping it in boiling water.

3 Measure the juice. For every 250 ml (8 fl oz) of juice, allow 250 g (8 oz) preserving sugar. Place together in a pan and heat, stirring constantly until the sugar has melted, then continue to boil steadily until setting point is reached. This will probably take 20–30 minutes, and can be ascertained by pouring a tablespoon of the hot jelly into a saucer and chilling quickly in the freezer or over ice. When it has cooled, try pushing the surface of the jelly gently with a fingertip. If it wrinkles, setting point has been reached.

4 Now skim off all the scum and pour the jelly into the hot, sterilized jar. When the jelly has cooled, cover it with a circle of greaseproof paper dipped in brandy, then screw down the lid. Wipe the jar clean and label clearly, then store in a cool, dry cupboard.

Makes about 1 kg (2 lb)

2 kg (4 lb) slightly unripe green grapes on their stems
10–12 heads lavender, tied together
approx. 500 g (1 lb) preserving sugar
1½ tablespoons brandy

garlic paste

This is a very useful standby to have in the refrigerator. It can be added to sauces for pasta or to vegetable soups, or spread on grilled bread, or used as a medicament for coughs and colds.

8 bulbs garlic (fresh, juicy ones are best)

2 small bay leaves, crumbled

3 sprigs thyme

6 black peppercorns

150 ml (¼ pint) olive oil

200 ml (7 fl oz) water

½ teaspoon sea salt

1 Break the bulbs into cloves; do not peel them. Lay them in a shallow baking dish and sprinkle them with the crumbled bay leaves, thyme and peppercorns. Pour the oil over them and add the water. Cover the dish with foil and bake in a preheated oven, 150°C (300°F), Gas Mark 2, for 1½ hours. When the time is up, pour off the liquid, discard the herbs, and push the garlic cloves through a medium food mill. Stir in the sea salt and pack into a screw-topped jar. The paste can be kept in the refrigerator for 6–8 weeks.

Makes about 300 ml (½ pint)

vanilla sugar

This is one of the most important staples to have in your larder, for commercial vanilla sugar is unsatisfactory and your own supply cannot be made overnight. It is also a useful way of storing used and unused vanilla pods. But make sure the pods are fresh when you buy them; they should be sticky inside and full of fragrance.

1 Start your supply with 1–2 kg (2–4 lb) caster sugar, 3–5 vanilla pods and a large glass jar. Pour the sugar into the jar, then slit a few of the pods lengthways with a small knife, and stick all the pods into the sugar so that they stand upright. Close the jar tightly and keep for 1–2 weeks before using.

2 As the sugar is used, replenish the jar with more caster sugar. And as you use vanilla pods in your cooking, rinse them, dry well by leaving on a sunny windowsill or near a radiator, then add them to the jar. After 2–3 years, empty the jar, throw away the vanilla pods and start again, using up the old stock of sugar before starting on the new.

crystallized flowers

These are not strictly speaking a preserve, since they can be kept for only 1–2 days. The most appropriate flowers to use are violets, small rose buds or petals, nasturtiums, sweet-scented geraniums, borage and bergamot. Young stems of angelica, sprays of red or white currants, and tender pea shoots can also be used.

1 Put the egg white on a plate, add a pinch of salt, and beat it lightly, using the blade of a knife. Stop before it gets frothy. Using a very fine paint brush, paint the flowers and shoots with the egg mixture, then dip them in the sugar, and shake off any excess. Lay them on a wire rack to dry overnight in a warm room. They can be used the same day to decorate an iced cake, ice cream or other dessert. Alternatively, they may be laid between layers of greaseproof paper and stored for 1–2 days in an airtight tin.

1 egg white
a pinch of salt
a selection of flowers, stems, shoots
25 g (1 oz) caster sugar

fig jam with lavender

I learnt to make this while staying on Gozo in early June, when there are purple figs in abundance.

1 Wash and dry a 1 kg (2 lb) glass preserving jar and place upside down on an oven rack. Turn the oven to 120°C (250°F), Gas Mark ½, and leave for 15 minutes. Turn off the heat, leaving the jar in the oven; it should still be warm when you fill it. Dip the lid in boiling water.
2 Peel half the figs, then chop them all roughly. Put them in a wide, heavy pan with the sugar, lemon rind and juice, ginger and lavender. Bring them slowly to the boil and then boil quite fast for 15–20 minutes, until the scum has vanished. (Don't bother testing for a firm set, as this jam sets remarkably quickly and has soon passed the point of no return.) Take off the heat, discard the lavender and stir in the pine nuts.
3 Spoon into a warm sterilized jar and leave to cool. Later, cover with a circle of greaseproof paper dipped in brandy, and close tightly.
Makes 1 kg (2 lb)

I kg (2 lb) ripe figs, purple for preference
I kg (2 lb) granulated sugar
finely chopped rind of ½ lemon
5 tablespoons lemon juice
I½ tablespoons finely chopped preserved stem ginger
10 heads lavender, tied in muslin
I heaped tablespoon pine nuts
I tablespoon brandy

rose syrup

Rose syrup may be used as a base for sorbets or ices, for sauces or drinks. This recipe is derived from recipes in cookery manuscripts from the fifteenth and sixteenth centuries. The rose used would probably have been either the damask rose (Rosa damascena) or the apothecary's rose (R. gallica officinalis). Still mineral water may be substituted for rain water.

1 Fill a large bowl three-quarters full with rain water. Then fill it to the brim by piling in freshly gathered rose petals. Stand the bowl over a broad pan of boiling water and continue to boil for 1 hour. Then lift out the rose petals with a slotted spoon, squeezing out the liquid, and put in a fresh lot. Repeat this process seven times, then measure the liquid that remains and add twice its volume of sugar. Boil gently until the sugar has melted, then strain through muslin, pour into bottles, and close tightly.

herb butters

These can be used as soon as they are made, and may also be frozen for future use.

parsley butter

250 g (8 oz) butter, at room temperature
2 garlic cloves, crushed
6 tablespoons chopped flat-leaf parsley
2 tablespoons lemon juice
sea salt and black pepper

Cream the butter in a food processor, adding the garlic, parsley, lemon juice, salt and pepper. Alternatively, pound the butter in a mortar, then add the other ingredients gradually, continuing to pound until all are amalgamated. Chill for 30 minutes to firm up. Form into a roll and cut in half. Roll each half in foil and freeze.
***Note:** This is sometimes called Maître d'Hôtel Butter. To serve with fish, replace the crushed garlic with ½ tablespoon finely chopped shallot.*

Serves 8

Above: Mint Butter, recipe right

coriander butter

Make as for Parsley Butter (see page 240), using coriander instead of parsley. Serve with grilled steaks or hamburgers, grilled tomatoes or mushrooms. To serve with grilled fish, omit the garlic.

dill butter

Make as for Parsley Butter (see page 240), using dill instead of parsley and omitting the garlic. Serve with poached trout, boiled asparagus, grilled tomatoes or new potatoes.

garlic butter

This is sometimes called snail butter or beurre d'escargot. Make as for Parsley Butter (see page 240), but omit the parsley and increase the garlic cloves to 8. Use on steamed shellfish, grilled sole, grilled mushrooms or tomatoes, boiled haricot beans or pasta.

horseradish butter

Make as for Parsley Butter (see page 240), using 125 g (4 oz) grated horseradish instead of the parsley and omitting the garlic, salt and pepper. Use on grilled steaks and with braised beef.

mint butter

Make as for Parsley Butter (see page 240), using 4 tablespoons chopped mint instead of the parsley, and 1 tablespoon finely chopped shallot instead of the garlic. Serve with grilled lamb chops or cutlets or grilled tomatoes.

mixed herb butter

Make as for Parsley Butter (see page 240), using 1 tablespoon each chervil, chives, dill, mint, tarragon and salad burnet instead of the parsley. Substitute 1 tablespoon finely chopped shallot for the garlic. Serve with grilled meat or fish or grilled vegetables.

mustard and dill butter

Make as for Dill Butter (see above), adding 1 tablespoon Dijon mustard, with or without seeds. Serve the butter with grilled steaks.

sage butter

Make as for Parsley Butter (see page 240), substituting 2 tablespoons chopped sage for the parsley, and 1 tablespoon finely chopped shallot for the garlic. Serve with grilled pork chops or whole baked onions.

herb oils

Although this is a practical way of preserving the flavour of a herb, I feel that with the high price of good olive oil, it is worth the cost in only a few instances. My two favourites are oils flavoured with basil and with garlic. The warm, fruity flavour of basil is so closely affiliated in our minds with olive oil that this seems an obvious choice. Garlic-flavoured oil, on the other hand, simply provides a speedy way of adding garlic to a dish when peeling and chopping 1–2 cloves seem too much of a hassle. For this reason I would choose a first-rate extra virgin olive oil from Italy, France, Greece or Spain for the basil oil, while a cheaper virgin oil would do very well for the garlic-flavoured one.

basil oil

4 tablespoons coarsely chopped basil
450 ml (¾ pint) extra virgin olive oil

Crush the basil by pounding briefly in a mortar. Add 2 tablespoons of the oil and pound again, then add the rest of the oil gradually. When well mixed, pour into a glass bottle – do not strain – and cork it tightly.

Keep for two weeks before using and shake the bottle every 2–3 days. Use to drizzle over pizza, tomato and mozzarella salad and pasta dishes just before serving. A little can be added to salad dressings, mixed with an unflavoured oil.

Makes 450 ml (¾ pint)

garlic oil

3–4 large cloves garlic, coarsely chopped
450 ml (¾ pint) virgin olive oil

Put the garlic in a mortar and pound briefly. Add 2 tablespoons of the oil and pound again. Add the rest of the oil gradually. Pour the oil into a glass bottle and cork it tightly.

Keep for 2 weeks before using, turning the bottle upside down once or twice every 2–3 days. Use to add to salad dressing, in pasta dishes, risottos and stir-frys.

Makes 450 ml (¾ pint)

Right: Basil Oil, recipe above

herb vinegars

This is one of the easiest and least expensive ways of preserving the flavour of certain herbs through the winter, especially useful if you make a lot of salads. And if you make your own vinegar, then it is an obvious choice. I find it best, however, to restrict myself to the few I really enjoy, as I resent my shelves getting cluttered with unused and unopened bottles.

I try to make just 2–3 each year: 2 savoury and 1 for sweet dishes. Instead of the classic tarragon vinegar, I make a variation that I call fines herbes vinegar, using equal parts of chervil, chives, parsley and tarragon. An old favourite, which I never see anywhere else, is salad burnet vinegar. This herb has a subtle flavour that goes well with a good white wine vinegar. For sweet dishes I make an elderflower vinegar.

fines herbes vinegar

20 g (¾ oz) chervil, chives, parsley and tarragon, leaves only, in roughly equal quantities
600 ml (1 pint) best quality French white wine vinegar

Chop the herbs roughly by hand, then put them in a mortar and pound until crushed. Heat one-quarter of the vinegar in a small saucepan. When it reaches boiling point, pour it over the herbs. Pound all together for a few moments, then leave to cool. Now mix it with the rest of the vinegar and pour, unstrained, into a wide-mouthed bottle or jar. Leave for 2 weeks, shaking every other day. Strain and rebottle.

Makes 600 ml (1 pint)

salad burnet vinegar

Make as Fines Herbes Vinegar (see above), using only 25 g (1 oz) salad burnet alone.

elderflower vinegar

freshly picked elderflowers, just at their prime
white wine vinegar

The proportions for this vinegar are not vital; they will depend on the size of the elderflowers and the jars. Wash the flowers if dusty and shake dry. Otherwise just pack them loosely into a wide-mouthed jar. Fill the jar with a good white wine vinegar; do not stint on quality. Seal tightly and stand in a cool, dark place for 2 weeks, then strain into a clean bottle. Use to add a subtle sweet-sour flavour to savoury or sweet dishes or salads.

Right: Classic Tarragon Vingegar

herbal teas

With the exception of Moroccan Mint Tea (see page 227), which may mean a real tea made with tea leaves and flavoured with mint, most herb teas are really infusions, made by pouring almost boiling water over a handful of fresh herbs or 2 teaspoons of dried herbs. Some of the most popular infusions are camomile, mint, lemon verbena and peppermint. Other good unusual herb teas are hibiscus, often combined with rose hip to make a beautiful dark red drink, and elderflower. All the above are produced commercially and can be bought in good grocers and health food shops. If using loose dried herbs rather than teabags, a useful gadget is a small round ball made of steel mesh, which holds the loose herb and facilitates its removal.

An alternative is to make herb teas with fresh herbs, gathered to order in your own garden. Sage makes a surprisingly delicious drink, as does fennel. Simply pick a small handful of leaves, put them in a small teapot or mug and pour almost boiling water over them. Leave them to infuse for 4–5 minutes, as you would for commercially prepared herb teas.

Some people adore herb teas, others loathe them. Yet they are a habit that should be encouraged, especially after dinner, in lieu of drinking coffee. Depending on the choice of herb, the tea may act as a digestive and/or a soporific, as opposed to black coffee, which can only be a stimulant. The most appropriate herbs to use in the evening, in that they act as sedatives, are Camomile (see page 247), fennel, lemon balm, lemon verbena and linden flowers (from the lime tree). This last is a bit insipid for my taste unless combined with mint (see page 247), as is done in France, where it is called tilleul-menthe. Good as digestives are camomile, mint and sage, but sage is also a stimulant, so should not be taken late at night unless you need to stay awake.

camomile tea

In former times camomile was made into an infusion and used as a final rinse when washing the hair, to keep fair hair light in colour. Nowadays it is used mainly in the form of camomile tea, also an infusion, to be drunk after dinner instead of black coffee, as a light sedative

If using commercially produced camomile teabags, simply put 1 in a cup or mug and fill up with almost boiling water. Stand for 5 minutes, then remove the bag. If using the loose dried herb, place it in a ball or other wire mesh container. Failing that, the tea is best made in a small teapot, allowing 2 teaspoonfuls of dried camomile to 175 ml (6 fl oz) of nearly boiling water, then strained into a cup. Fresh camomile may also be used in the same way.

Serves 1

linden-mint tea

This is a delicious combination of dried herbs, very popular in France where it is called tilleul-menthe. *It is one of the best infusions for serving after dinner, as the linden flowers are a sedative, while the dried mint acts as a digestive. But be careful to use ordinary mint, not peppermint, which would not mix well with the linden.*

1 teaspoon dried linden flowers (or ½ teabag)
1 teaspoon dried mint (or ½ teabag)

If using loose herbs, put them in a ball or other wire mesh container, and place in a fairly large cup or small mug. Fill up with almost boiling water, then let stand for 5 minutes before removing the herb.

Serves 1

drying herbs

Few herbs dry well and, unless you grow your own, there is little point in embarking on this somewhat time-consuming exercise. It is only worth drying herbs that have been grown in soil. I have tried using herbs bought in the supermarket (which are usually grown hydroponically— that is, in water), just for interest, and it is simply not worthwhile. Better by far to buy good dried herbs. However, if you have a herb garden, then you will wish to preserve at least a few herbs before they are past their best. Once the herbs have flowered, their leaves have lost most of their flavour, and new leaf growth will be greatly reduced. Even if you pick off the flowers as they form, and by doing this you lose much of the pleasure of growing herbs, there will be a marked loss of flavour.

I suggest you single out the few that retain their flavour and that you find useful in the kitchen, and harvest each one just before the flowers open. Choose from bay, marjoram, mint, oregano, rosemary, sage, savory and thyme. (The others may be preserved by other means, such as freezing; see page 250.)

Choose a dry day and pick the herbs soon after the dew has evaporated and before the sun has reached its peak. Use secateurs to clip the herbs neatly, choosing the tender young shoots and bearing the finished shape of the bush in mind. (This applies only to perennials; with annuals, and most biennials, you may pick as much as you can use.) When picking any of the labiates – this includes all the herbs mentioned above as eminently suitable for drying, except bay – do not cut the shoots right up to the old wood: leave one whorl of new leaves uncut.

Lay the herbs on a rack or large sheets of newspaper, keeping each variety separate. Cover with muslin to keep off the dust, and place in a warm, shady place. Shade is essential; avoid the sun at all costs. In the past people used to tie herbs in little bunches and hang them from the kitchen ceiling, often over the stove. This looked charming but was not very effective, as the air could not penetrate freely, and a smoky kitchen is hardly an ideal place. In hot climates, like the Mediterranean, a cool, airy shed is ideal, but in a damp climate some extra warmth is needed. Some people go so far as to use an airing cupboard or plate-warming compartment, but I find a warm room works reasonably well. Herb-grower Frances Smith has a fancy for drying bay leaves flat, like those sold in shops. To achieve this, she dries the leaves between pages of a telephone directory kept in an airing cupboard.

It is best to dry herbs separately and to mix them, if you must, as you use them. The exception is the classic mixture Herbes de Provence. This is usually made with equal parts of rosemary and thyme, and lesser parts of basil, marjoram, savory and/or tarragon. In a damp climate I am dubious about including basil or tarragon, which do not dry well under these conditions. In the dry heat of places like Provence, they have a more robust flavour.

Most herbs take about 1 week to dry, but this depends on the type of herb – thick stalks take longer than thin ones – and the weather, as herbs dry more quickly on warm, dry days than on cool, damp or humid ones.

Once dried, the herbs should be stored immediately. The twiggy ones with small leaves, like thyme and marjoram, may be left on the stalk and stored upright in glass jars. With the larger-leafed plants, like sage and mint, it is better to strip the leaves off the stalks and pack them into small containers. Coloured glass jars are best, as direct sunlight destroys the chlorophyll, causing the structure of the herb to collapse. Clear glass jars are satisfactory so long as they are stored in a cool, dark cupboard. The refrigerator is best, if you can spare the space.

freezing herbs

There are two basic methods of preserving herbs for use through the winter: drying (see page 249) and freezing. Drying is unsuitable for all the delicate soft-leafed summer herbs, such as chervil and dill, basil and tarragon, parsley and chives, which lose all vestige of their flavour and become as dry as dust. Luckily, they respond well to freezing, and this must be done at home since frozen herbs can only rarely be found in the shops.

There is no point in freezing herbs bought in the supermarket, for they just do not have enough flavour. Use only fresh herbs properly grown in soil. If you are freezing your own herbs, it is important to harvest them at the optimum moment. This varies slightly with each variety, the aim being to catch them when their flavour is at its fullest, just after the flower buds open and before they are fully in bloom. Cut the herbs in the morning after the dew has evaporated. Annuals and biennials may be picked wholesale, possibly leaving a few plants to self-seed; you can dig up and throw out the rest. Perennials should be treated with care: do not cut more than two-thirds of the leaves or the plant will die, and pay attention to keeping the plant in a good shape.

Have a good selection of plastic bags , foil and small sticky labels to hand. With large-leafed herbs like basil, simply pick the leaves off the stalks and make little piles of 12 at a time. Tuck these into small bags, tie up the bags, flattening them to force out as much air as possible, label and place in the freezer. Small-leafed herbs like chervil are best frozen in sprigs, with the leaves still on the stems.

I think it is better not to chop the herbs before freezing. Each time a herb is cut, a cell is broken open, allowing air in, which will oxidize. This process is repeated when leaves are frozen, as the cells expand and break open, and flavour is lost each time. It seems more sensible to freeze the leaves whole, then chop them immediately on taking them out of the freezer. Frances Smith gave me a useful tip, which works only with curly parsley. Pick the curly leaves off the stems and pack them in plastic bags, then freeze, leaving some air in the bag. When ready to use, remove the bag from the freezer and crush it with a rolling pin, which immediately breaks up the parsley into tiny particles and obviates the necessity of chopping.

If you still want to freeze your herbs already chopped, you may like to try the ice-cube tray method. Chop your herbs and half fill each compartment with them. Fill the tray with still mineral water. (Each ice cube holds about 1 tablespoon chopped herb and 1 tablespoon water.) To use, simply melt the ice and pat dry the chopped herb if, like me, you dislike the idea of using soggy herbs.

With the aid of modern technology, we are able to preserve our herbs quite efficiently by a number of different methods, each chosen carefully to suit the herb. A few will be dried, more frozen, others made into herb butters or pestos. Yet none will ever quite replace the delight of the fresh leaves of green herbs picked in early summer and stuck in a jam jar on the kitchen table.

Right: Frozen herbs using ice-cube tray method, see above

index

Author Acknowledgement
My sincere thanks to Frances Smith of Appledore Salads, who was kind enough to take me on a 'tunnel safari', and to share with me some of her comprehensive knowledge of herbs.

Publisher Acknowledgements
Our thanks to Rosemary Titterington of Iden Croft Herbs for allowing us to use her herb garden for photography and for her enthusiasm and help and to Pim Gleadle for supplying herbs to us at short notice.

Photographic Acknowledgements
Eric Crichton page 62; John Fielding page 25;
The Harry Smith Collection pages 66 and 68.

Notes

Both metric and imperial measurements have been given in all recipes. Use one set of measurements only and not a mixture of both.

Standard level spoon measurements are used in all recipes.
1 tablespoon = one 15 ml spoon
1 teaspoon = one 5 ml spoon

Eggs should be medium (size 3) unless otherwise stated.

Milk should be full fat unless otherwise stated.

Pepper should be freshly ground black pepper unless otherwise stated.

Fresh herbs should be used unless otherwise stated.

Ovens should be preheated to the specified temperature – if using a fan-assisted oven, follow the manufacturer's instructions for adjusting the time and the temperature.

POWERSHOP 5

new retail design

frame publishers
amsterdam

contents

ACCES
S

grey canopy

Where	Singapore, Singapore
Opening	May 2013
Client	LBL Investment Holdings
Designer	Grey Canopy (p.411)
Floor space	127 m²
Shop constructor	Falkon Interior
Photos	Andrew Phua

araldi 1930

It looks like a black and white photograph but the shapes are futuristic: this men's accessories boutique is finished in shades of super-glossy and matte grey, from gunmetal to gull and charcoal. Grey Canopy, tapped to create this grey space, with an interior that 'displays the display' to let the product sell itself. 'Manly and modern', the store's liquid-looking interior features boldface and geometric shapes. Araldi, 'the king of belts' asked the designers to showcase as many leather belts as possible, a brief the designers took to heart, constructing three belt towers of display that can showcase 380 belts and 180 buckles – for a total of 4000 product permutations. To avoid deforming the leathers, which is easy to do, the fit-out was designed to ensure that none of the products are pressed or bent. Each belt strip hangs 1100 mm with a curve of 70 mm diameter at the top where the tip of the leather clips into the tower while the other end is battened down with a butterfly pin. The belt display, which actually obscures a structural column that was an eyesore but could not be removed, form the central visual experience of the shop and, in fact, become not just a fashion accessory and product but an 'accessory' or ornament to the interior also.

Three belt display towers hold up to 4000 combinations of belts and buckles.

The client wanted as many belts displayed as possible, which the designers accomodated with large display towers.

The belt towers were inspired by a coiled belt.

it looks like a black and white photograph but the shapes are futuristic

A wall display for shoes and bags, and doors to storage areas are adorned, floor-to-ceiling, with a 'wall covering' of hollow wide tubes.

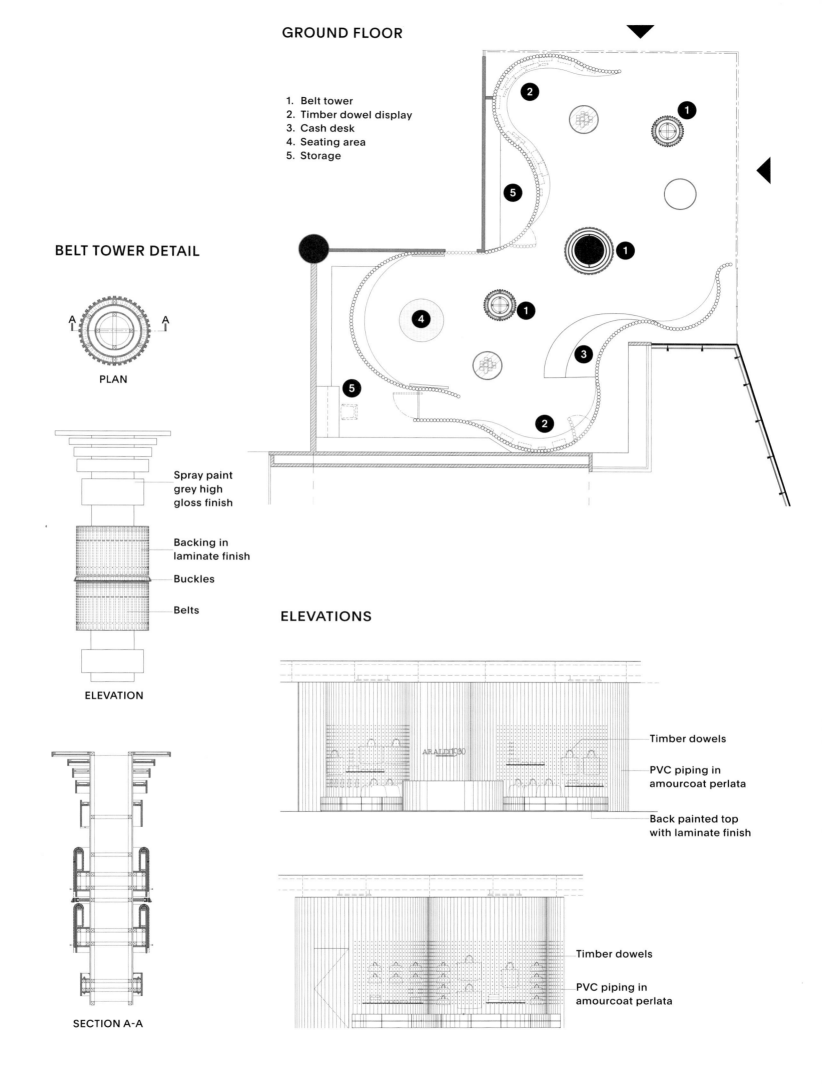

GROUND FLOOR

1. Belt tower
2. Timber dowel display
3. Cash desk
4. Seating area
5. Storage

BELT TOWER DETAIL

PLAN

Spray paint grey high gloss finish

Backing in laminate finish

Buckles

Belts

ELEVATION

SECTION A-A

ELEVATIONS

Timber dowels

PVC piping in amourcoat perlata

Back painted top with laminate finish

Timber dowels

PVC piping in amourcoat perlata

sid lee architecture

Where	Quebec, Canada
Opening	August 2013
Client	Birks
Designer	Sid Lee Architecture (p.415)
Floor space	158 m²
Shop constructor	SAJO
Photos	Stéphane Brügger

birks

Finishes like hickory wood, MDF, Corian and walnut are used in the design.

In 1879, Henry Birks opened his St. James Street shop. Five generations later, the family is still sourcing Canadian diamonds, creating nature-inspired jewellery and offering both luxury and accessibility, a 'warm prestige'. To imbue the architecture with the brand character, Sid Lee Architecture derived a fractal pattern from the volumetric shape of its famous blue Birks box, turning this pattern into a flexible grid system. This pattern was applied from facade to interior in a kaleidoscopic play on scale in which the proportions of the blue box are always recognisable. The facade, made of warm-white perforated metal panels, filters daylight through the 'concentration and dilution' of the pattern. Inside, the materials palette remains simple: hickory floors and stairs, walnut panelling and MDF in the Birks pattern on walls and white Corian and Starfire mirror for the furniture. A 46 × 46 cm grid formed from the box pattern determined the dimension of displays whilst a series of podiums at a different scale determined the shop's circulation. A lenticular film depicting a piece of jewellery sheaths the rear wall, but the centre of the store is anchored by a chandelier that is a jewel, in itself. Made from magnifying glass it provides an unusual source of gem-like light dispersion. Birks describes it as 'an icon in the form of an experience, rather than imagery.'

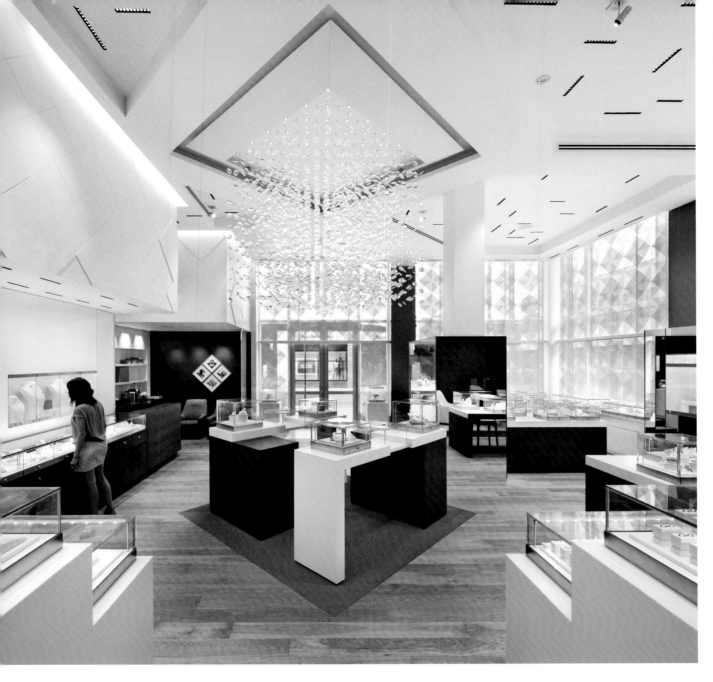

A chandelier made from magnifying glass makes a jewel of a centrepiece.

for five generations, the family has been sourcing canadian diamonds

A kaleidoscopic translation of the iconic Birks jewellery box is the basis for the sheer, light-filtering facade.

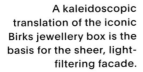

Sid Lee Architecture

Birks

The box pattern determines the grid that set the dimensions of the displays and organisation of the shop.

AXONOMETRIC DRAWING

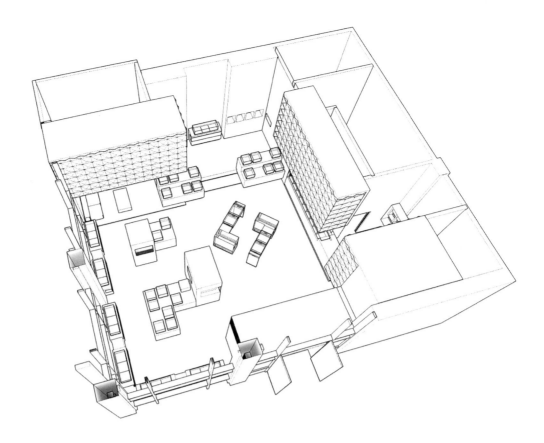

FLOOR PLAN

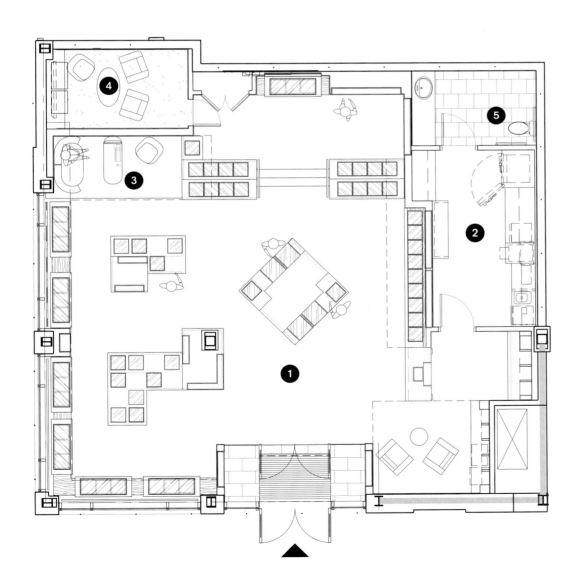

1. Main floor
2. Storage
3. Sitting area
4. VIP office
5. Restroom

ippolito fleitz group

Where	Shanghai, China
Opening	May 2015
Client	Xiamen Artgri Optical
Designer	Ippolito Fleitz Group (p.412)
Floor space	94 m²
Shop constructor	Fushida Company
Photos	Shuhe Architectual Photography

bolon eyewear

The cash desk is one of few deviations from the black, white and gold palette.

The longing for a bright, sunny day inspired the design of this eyewear shop where the products are presented like stars of the stage – in the limelight. This retail concept, which can be scaled from flagship to boutique, elevates the clarity, functionality and precision of display. Through the floor-to-ceiling glass storefront, most of the space is visible from the outside. The designers set small square white shelves at right angles to each other on the walls to establish a three-dimensional grid, each shelf showcasing a pair of glasses in its own miniature stage, with the lighting around each deftly drawn: each product sits before an illuminated background, so that the true colour of the lenses is easy to see while a tightly focused LED spot falls on each from a vertical panel hanging above, creating a soft aura around each item. The team selected high-quality materials to match the Chinese brand's emphasis on French refinement and fashionability: white marble floors are paired with black marble tabletop jewel box displays and service desk. Behind the consultation table, a leather-clad wall becomes a warmer focal point of the interior, along with the polished golden ceiling, which makes the entire shop luminous, recalling a day spent, not so long ago, playing in the waves.

High gloss is high elegance in this eyewear shop where pentagonal black marble displays are reflected in a golden ceiling.

the concept elevates the clarity, functionality and precision of display

The precisely lit display presents each pair of eyeglasses like an actor on a small stage.

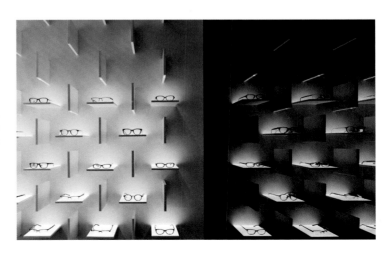

line-inc.

Where Tokyo, Japan
Opening April 2015
Client Weave Toshi
Designer Line-Inc. (p.412)
Floor space 116 m²
Shop constructor D. Brain
Photos Kozo Takayama

CA4LA

The interiors of the Shibuya shop for Japanese hat brand CA4LA has been renovated with special attention to current Tokyo trends in order to celebrate the tenth anniversary of this location. The existing space previously had dark flooring, a burgundy carpet, blackened steel and sheer black drapery, a classical look that was true to the brand. Line-Inc. decided, however, to make the new interior brighter and more contemporary. The challenge lay in altering the store while maintaining the general layout of furniture and preserving historical architectural elements. Line-Inc. assigned the ground and first floors – between which men's and women's products are divided – different fixtures and material palettes. The men's ground floor blends the new and old: the floor and walls have been replaced with black and white hexagonal tiling, but the pressed tin ceiling and brick wall were preserved and painted white. The first floor shop, dedicated to women, is softened and warmed with white and brown wall tiles, blonde oak floors, walls and ceilings, and bespoke brass pendant lights. The team also freed up the wall flanking the staircase in order to turn it into a millinery gallery, and applied white wall tiles and sconces in the storefront to establish the modern look immediately, as customers enter. Instead of the black curtains of the past, the windows now showcase ever-changing line-ups of headgear.

The ground floor is dedicated to different types of hats for men.

Part of modernising consisted of using new materials: on the ground floor, black and white hexagonal tiles mix with natural wood tables.

the renovation celebrates the tenth anniversary of this location

The team turned the wall along the oak staircase into a hat gallery.

Blonde wood dominates but softens the women's first floor surfaces.

rafael de cárdenas/
architecture at large

Where   London, United Kingdom
Opening   March 2015
Client   Delfina Delettrez
Designer   Rafael de Cárdenas/
           Architecture at Large (p.414)
Floor space 140 m²
Shop constructor Reflex Interiors Construction
Photos   Mark Cocksedge

delfina delettrez

New York-based Rafael de Cárdenas sought to turn Delfina Delettrez's jewellery designs into a darkly seductive walk-through experience. In this jewel box of a shop in London's Mount Street, de Cárdenas has applied the exuberance of his signature contemporary and multi-hued confections to a more classical, sedate and lushly crepuscular space. To achieve this, he turned to contrasting materials, ranging from satin finish brass, velvet and polished wood to stainless steel, a wallcovering in a jewel green malachite pattern that matches the stones in the jeweller's work and shearling lined display cases. Delettrez's dark storefront is set into a light stone facade and the shop draws visitors in with its sumptuous emerald walls. Meanwhile infinity mirrors behind the display counters multiply the surreal qualities of both the store and the jewellery it contains in bespoke vitrines made of glass and brass. The designer installed pinpoint lighting fixtures to illuminate the vitrines and amplify the lustre and sparkle of the pieces. The malachite wallcovering, at enormous scale, makes visitors feel as if they have walked into a precious mineral cavern. Encrusting the flanking and rear wall of the shop, it draws visitors down to the lounge-like basement where the jewellery is 'magnified, multiplied, reflected' to increase the sensation of being inside a jewel, and still mining for more gems.

The malachite patterned walls draw visitors down into a subterranean lounge where they may further mine for precious stones.

The black metal storefront is set into the old stone building facade like a gem.

visitors are drawn in by the sumptuous emerald walls

stefano tordiglione design

Where	Hong Kong, China
Opening	November 2013
Client	Dinh Van
Designer	Stefano Tordiglione Design (p.415)
Floor space	15 m²
Shop constructor	Permastellisa
Photos	Courtesy of Dinh Van Paris

dinh van

The compact shop is faced with graphical
Parisian landmarks, recalling the jeweller's romantic roots.

When French jeweller and Cartier apprentice Jean Dinh Van launched his eponymous atelier in Paris in 1965, his work was an intimate expression that felt both lifelike and modern. Stefano Tordiglione Design's creative team designed a graphical Hong Kong shop for Dinh Van that is as compact and elegant like a artisanal showcase. The designers mined Dinh Van's romantic Parisian roots to depict the city's iconic architectural landmarks across the surfaces of the store. These sketch-like illustrations unfurl over a feature wall in the form of a charcoal grey and white silhouette of the Eiffel Tower, along with reproductions of black and white prints of the Pantheon and the Place de la Concorde that were used in a long-ago Dinh Van advertising campaign. The jewellery display cabinets also celebrate all things Parisian through their resemblance to the fretted iron tower, itself, with industrial-looking bases that are supported by thin tapering metal rods, recalling small-scale cross-sections of its architecture. To accommodate the boutique's pocket-size location, the designers tucked an indented sales area into the wall and gracefully downsized the cash desk. Against the metallic surface of the facade, which is also wrapped by the ribbon of hand-sketched illustrations, the silhouette scales up into a cross-hatch pattern of architectural struts.

The sales area is softened with all the edges and corners in order to make economical use of the compact space.

the graphical shop is compact and elegant

Stefano Tordiglione Design   Dinh Van

ippolito fleitz group

Where	Titisee-Neustadt, Germany
Opening	July 2015
Client	Drubba
Designer	Ippolito Fleitz Group (p.412)
Floor space	430 m²
Shop constructor	Ganter Interior
Photos	Zooey Braun

drubba moments

In a little town at the edge of a lake in the Black Forest lies another, smaller, forest. This forest resides in a family-run luxury watch boutique called Drubba and offers a momentary rural respite for citified Asian tourists. Drubba started as a kiosk in the 1950s where visitors could rent boats by the hour and, later, buy traditional cuckoo clocks and high-end wristwatches that could tell them the hour. The interior 'concentrates' the shopping experience for tourists on a tight itinerary whilst unifying diverse brands in one coherent display. Ippolito Fleitz Group ranged branded areas around a central zone overhung with square spruce rods that descend from and ripple over the ceiling, an abstraction of the forest outside that forms the emotional heart of the shop. Here, a cafe, a watchmaker's atelier, and a showcase of high-quality timepieces focus on craft more than logos. In the same way that the shop sits amidst the forest, this centre is encircled by the discrete brand zones, all of which share certain features: wall niches provide texture and rhythm whilst the subtle complexion of large-format hexagonal floor tiles let the perimeter of the space recede, offer a neutral backdrop for display and reinforce the interior's polygonal plan. This unbranded space becomes a handsome centrepiece, but without overshadowing the branded areas around it.

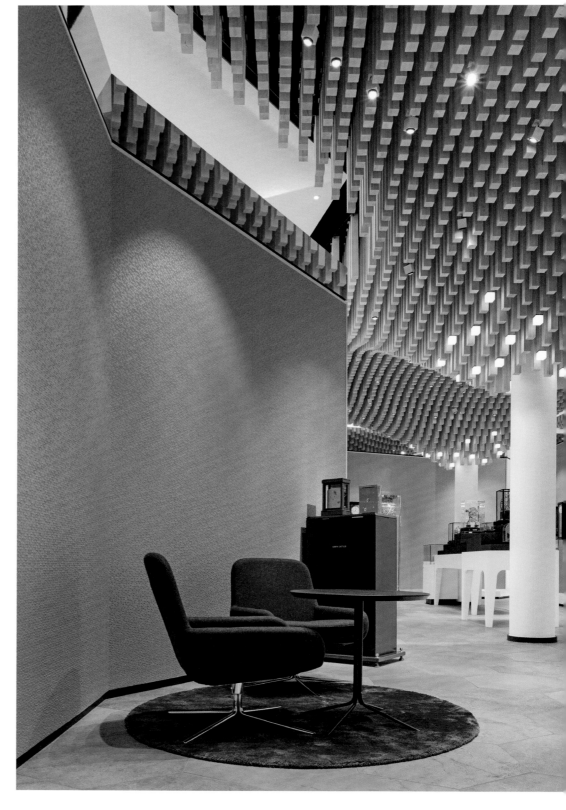

The tips of some of the spruce rods are fitted with static light sources.

Spruce rods wave over the ceiling like upside-down saplings, a sculptural interpretation of the nearby forest.

square spruce rods descend from and ripple over the ceiling

studio david thulstrup

Where	Munich, Germany
Opening	May 2015
Client	Georg Jensen
Designer	Studio David Thulstrup (p.415)
Floor space	250 m²
Shop constructor	MJ2
Photos	Hampus Berndtson

georg jensen

Founded in Denmark in 1904, legendary silversmith Georg Jensen's history provides fertile ground for inspiration. Studio David Thulstrup was asked to create a new template retail interior concept to showcase Jensen's hollowware, jewellery and watches. The design took its cues from the Art Deco geometry so richly portrayed in the brand's early designs. This suggested the design of black Deco-derived arches, which return the bright white, gallery-like interiors to a more intimate visual scale and help punctuate the transition and circulation between spaces. Looking to Scandinavia, floor-to-ceiling vertical timber slats were designed for the private sales and men's areas, where semi-transparency indicates a relaxed Nordic sensibility. They also relied on other warmer natural materials, such as stone and wood paneling, to contrast with the sharp black steel framing geometry on the walls. Elsewhere rough hammered terrazzo gives a quiet nod to the art and techniques particular to silversmithing. Zoned spaces broadcast the spirit of each product type, while these individualised spaces are nonetheless subsumed by the Jensen-defined spirit of the shop, as a whole. The bespoke furnishings include a finely crafted wood and silver table by Laura Bergsøe and wall-integrated jewellery display boxes, which establish a minimalist, geometric frame to underscore the nuanced details of each piece.

Grainy wood panels and vertical screens dramatically frame the much smaller scale product windows in the private sales area.

In the men's area, pale asymmetrical wall displays are offset with warmer, darker materials like walnut.

A detail from one of the bespoke wood and silver tables crafted by Laura Bergsøe.

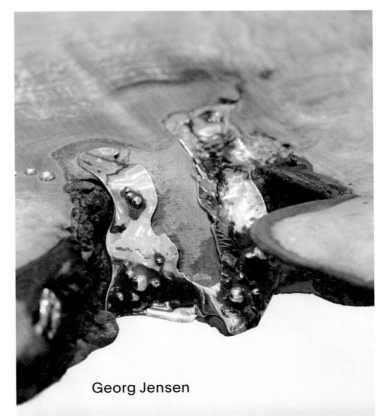

027   Studio David Thulstrup

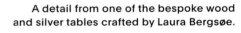

Georg Jensen

Accessories

individualised spaces are subsumed by the jensen-defined spirit

Softly textured white walls contain integrated jewellery display boxes trimmed in black.

The shop design is inspired and characterised by geometry, Art Deco and Scandinavian references.

　　　Studio David Thulstrup　　　　　　　Georg Jensen

AXONOMETRIC DRAWING

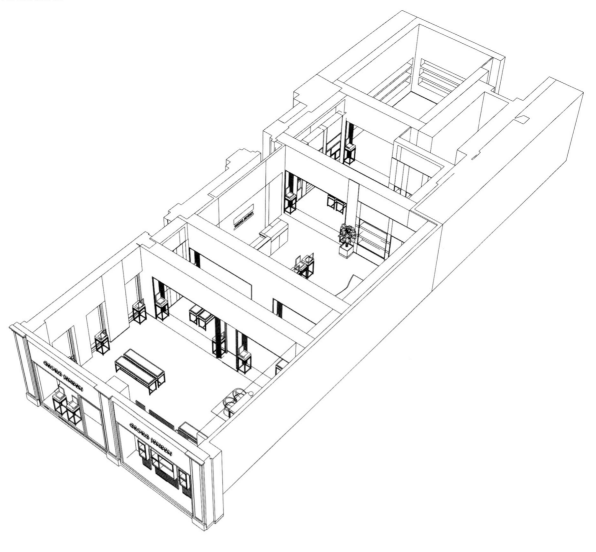

SECTION A-A

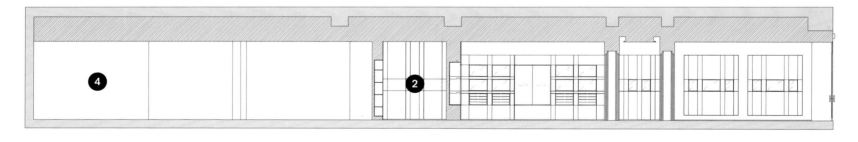

SECTION B-B

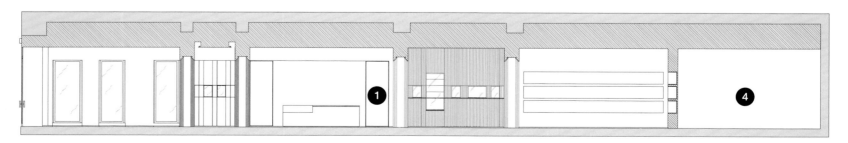

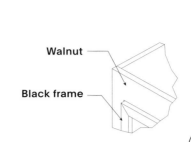

The custom made displays are minimalistic and focus on highlighting the jewellery.

Walnut

Black frame

FLOOR PLAN

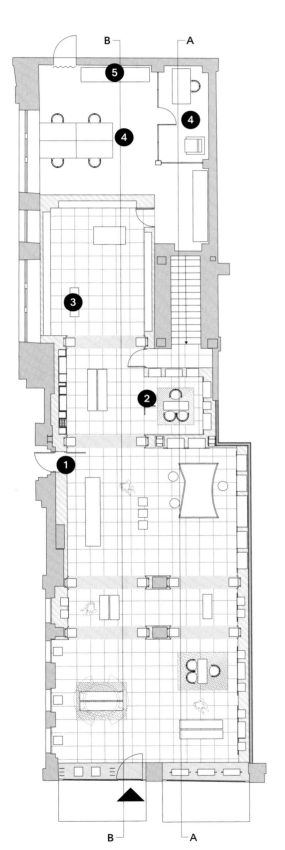

1. Fire escape
2. VIP area
3. Cash desk
4. Office
5. Storage

Semi-transparent timber slats indicate a relaxed Nordic sensibility.

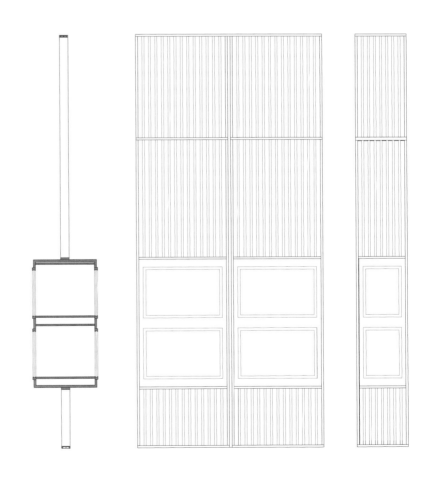

studio arthur casas

Where	New York, United States
Opening	June 2015
Client	H. Stern
Designer	Studio Arthur Casas (p.415)
Floor space	215 m²
Shop constructor	Michilli
Photos	Ricardo Labougle

h. stern

This fresh series of concept stores for the international jeweller evokes the cosmopolitan Brazilian identity that characterises the brand. Studio Arthur Casas designed an architectural jewellery box that complements the finely crafted product while containing it. An interior assembled from a profusion of details, the shop has an unexpected homogeneity that draws all those details together with elegant consistency and clarity. The range of blonde, beige and honey tones, as well as a mix of wooden panels, natural materials, and the curvaceous organic forms of cantilevering displays and counters, and luxuriously upholstery are reminiscent of mid-century Brazilian Modernism. (The Milo Baughman chairs, however, pay homage to mid-century American Modernism, Arthur Casas says.) The designers created the gridded, diagonal facade pattern from the client's logotype 'S' in polished metal panels that resemble scales and, like those of a fish, change as ambient light changes. Inside, the lighting was designed by l'Observatoire International to emphasise the beauty of the jewels both while on display and while clients try them on. Overhead the ceiling is gently domed, which makes the interior feel lofty, bright and open. Its smoothness lends uniformity above eye-level to an otherwise subtly chiaroscuro interior that uses spotlights artfully to create a hierarchy throughout the space.

The use of organic materials and forms with friendly textures – wood, fabric, leather, and metal – mark the design as Brazilian.

this architectural jewellery box complements the finely crafted product

A subtly domed white ceiling gives the space an airy brightness.

christophe carpente CAPS architecture interior design

Where	Shanghai, China
Opening	December 2014
Client	Hearts On Fire
Designer	Christophe Carpente CAPS Architecture Interior Design (p.409)
Floor space	85 m²
Shop constructor	Rich Honour International Design
Photos	Courtesy of Hearts On Fire

hearts on fire shanghai

Patterns from the brand's famous diamond cutting are incorporated into graphics, packaging and mirrored shop walls.

This Boston-based jeweller entered the Chinese market in 2014 with a shop in Shanghai. Christophe Carpente CAPS Architecture Interior Design created a new Hearts On Fire identity and then applied it to retail space, furniture, visual merchandising, lighting and graphic design. Instead of conforming to the first shop's concept which represented the store as a jewellery box, this interior more broadly represents a world of diamonds, which starts in the earth where diamonds are hidden for millennia, continues in the hands of artisans who smooth, cut and polish raw diamonds and ends with the people who give and wear them as symbols of human relationships. The brand's unique method for cutting diamonds leaves them expertly proportioned, forming a perfect pattern of eight hearts when viewed from below and a series of eight arrows when viewed from above. These perfect heart and arrow patterns in 20 variations became the brand's new graphic, interpreted for packaging and as an interior finish above the jewellery counters. Christophe Carpente etched the patterns into two layers of reinforced glass backed with a mirror, giving them depth, dynamism and sparkle.In window displays and above the store's oval counters and customer seating areas, jewellery-like chandelier fixtures symbolise the starry, moonlit sky. In contrast with this, the floors are cut from pilarguri, an irregular Norwegian stone that polishes to a rough sheen, and are offset with plush rounded wool carpets.

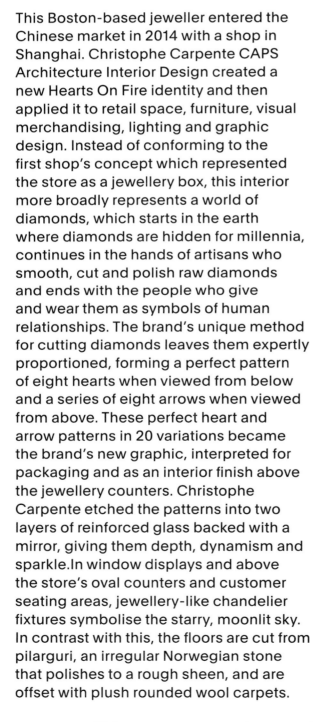

this interior represents a world of diamonds

Christophe Gernigon
Architecture Interior

Shanghai

christophe carpente CAPS architecture interior design

Where	Taipei, Taiwan
Opening	August 2015
Client	Hearts On Fire
Designer	Christophe Carpente CAPS Architecture Interior Design (p.409)
Floor space	31 m²
Shop constructor	Rich Honour International Design
Photos	Courtesy of Hearts On Fire

hearts on fire taipei

Christophe Carpente CAPS Architecture Interior Design has designed nine Hearts On Fire jewellery stores. This boutique is a shop-in-shop in the chic, 24-hour, concept bookstore Eslite in the Xinyi district, which is a distillation of the larger format concept in a limited space. In contrast to the Shanghai shop, which feels more flashily luxurious, this location is devoted to bridal jewellery for young, educated and discerning customers who come to the larger bookstore to find items unrelated to jewellery. This shop's glamour is more nuanced and refined. The perfect heart and arrow patterns are derived from the unique look and light dispersal produced by the Hearts On Fire diamond cutting technique and are reproduced as glass partitions, but with greater subtlety. In the Eslite store, the shape of narrow maple wood vertical panels, or fins, echoes the arrow patterns. In Taipei, because the fins hide side lights, the effect is less dazzling and more organic. Christophe Carpente also rendered a 3D diamond motif in a bronze lacquer wall finish, a colour scheme also used in the furnishings. At the heart of the room, a communal table promotes a more intimate conversational ambience than typical jewellery counters and lets clients share their opinions with each other.

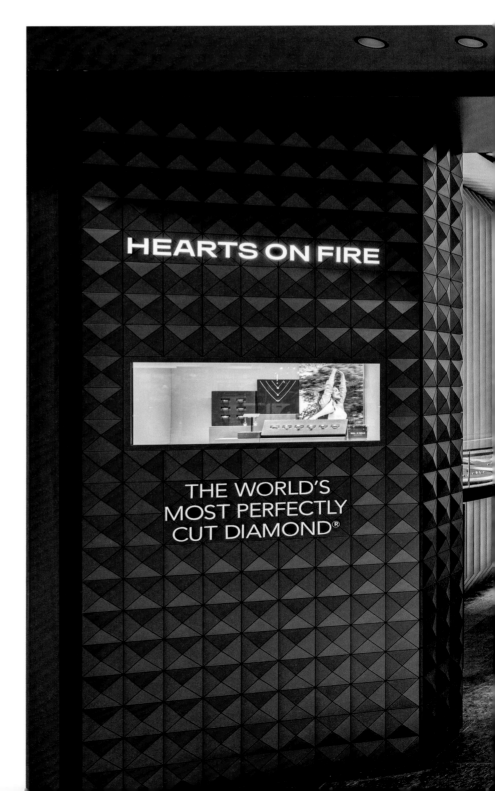

the glamour is more nuanced and refined

Every surface is highly textured and shaped like the oval counters and globular lights.

Christophe Carpente designed this jewellery brand as a space-limited, boutique within a bookstore.

Christophe Carpente CAPS
Interior Design

burdifilek

Where	Toronto, Canada
Opening	February 2014
Client	Mark Lash
Designer	Burdifilek (p.408)
Floor space	157 m²
Shop constructor	Lash Design Build
Photos	Ben Rahn

mark lash flagship

A sumptuous materials palette combines with modern forms and a simplified layout to give this jewellery boutique a 'quiet confidence'.

Burdifilek calibrated the eponymous flagship of a Canadian fine jeweller to the material and creative beauty, and the timelessness, of Mark Lash's work. The team partitioned the shop into three zones to make the clientele feel most lavishly served. Immediately on entry, glossy smooth-lined vitrines line the showroom, luring the visitor's gaze backwards, over the product, past a cantilevering fixture that stands in the middle of the floor. The cash desk and ear piercing area are separated from the retail floor in order to maintain a sense of undiluted sophistication, while the engagement room, which does double-duty as a personal consultation area, becomes the jewel in the crown of the flagship. The designers layered this space with dichroic glass and bronzed mirror, giving it a gentle iridescence 'to heighten the sensory connection to a magical ethereality.' Alone or in concert, each element mimics the luxurious, subtle nature of the jewellery. Choreographed to frame the small but precious products, 'Moments of pause' is an exploration facilitated by floor-to-ceiling mirrors which slide down the length of a room. Fine jewellery continues to maintain its strong connection to the highest levels of craftsmanship and luxury, which is echoed in the opulent finishes, but here it is also pointedly paired with contemporary forms and function.

each element mimics the luxurious, subtle nature of the jewellery

The engagement room is finished with a subtly iridescent layering of dichroic glass and bronzed mirror.

The interior is scaled and detailed to frame the, high-value product, even graphical marble walls pop petite jewellery displays onto the eye.

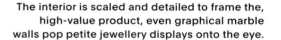

pinkeye

Where	Beerse, Belgium
Opening	December 2014
Clients	Kristel van Gorp and Karel Vandeputte
Designer	Pinkeye (p.414)
Floor space	300 m²
Shop constructor	Gielissen
Photos	Frederik Vercruysse

optiek van gorp

Pinkeye's interior for this purveyor of eyewear puts the glasses front and centre in its latest boutique, framing them with rich materials, subdued colour and soft pattern. A lens motif and allusions to the sense of sight are used in various ways throughout, in bespoke light fixtures, tables, displays and accessories. Even the brand's logo, which decorates the rear of the store with its blurred text, 'pays homage to the eye'. The shop's grey colour scheme is richly accompanied with American walnut veneer and a titanium bronze pigment used to paint six large screens visible from the entrance. Behind the consulting tables, perforations bored into this series of Trespa panels depict celebrities, wearing glasses, who became famous for making eyeglasses cool: Buddy Holly, James Dean, Woody Allen, Marilyn Monroe, John Lennon and Audrey Hepburn. The same moiré pattern that the designers used for the logo, the facade, and to stipple the faces of low cabinets was used to 'draw' these portraits, a use of pattern that establishes a coherent look and feel throughout the boutique. The glasses, themselves, appear to levitate in their amorphous illuminated niches, another bespoke solution: Pinkeye hung each pair from a bar kitted out with small clips that support the glasses. They're almost impossible to see.

A detail from one of the Trespa panel portraits. Similar ombre perforations were used on cabinets and the facade.

Perforations strategically punched into Trespa screens resolve themselves into six portraits of famous eyeglass wearers.

Annick Van Gorp

glasses appear to levitate in their illuminated niches

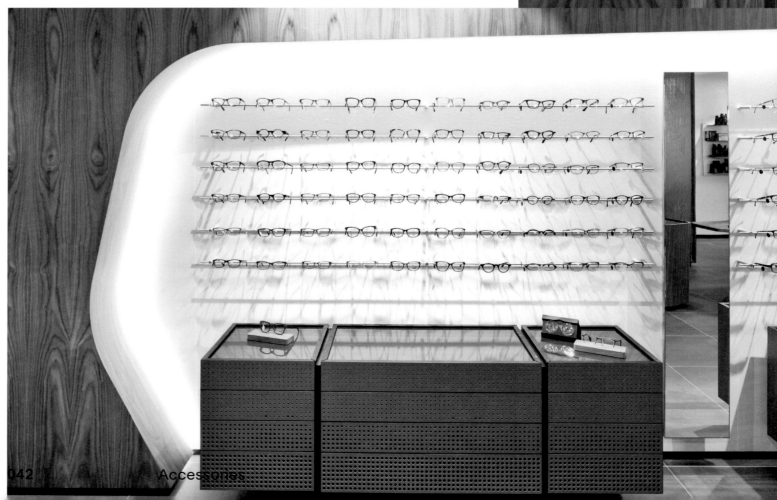

Contour-lit recesses in the walnut veneer wall
panelling make the product the focal point of the space.

Throughout the shop, numerous references to the sense of sight flesh out the design concept.

ippolito fleitz group

Where	Moscow, Russia
Opening	November 2013
Client	N.N.
Designer	Ippolito Fleitz Group (p.412)
Floo space	10 m²
Shop constructor	AO Engeocom
Photos	Zooey Braun

the tailor shop

The gem-shaped cabinets boast opening mechanisms as sophisticated – and invisible – as those in the brand's jewellery.

This materially rich jewellery boutique is, indeed, suggestive of a little gem in a big Russian shopping centre. Essentially a walk-in jewellery box, the Tailor Shop has been tucked cleverly into a converted ventilation shaft in Moscow's Atrium Mall that measures a mere 10 m². Because the shopping centre was completely leased, the owners were forced to come up with a creative way to 'find' additional retail space within the strictures of the existing, overbooked floor plan. When Ippolito Fleitz Group understood the compact size of the site, however, they decided to make a virtue of this lack of space. To do this, the designers built a shallow storefront in which customers can feel as if they are browsing not just through, but inside of, a (very large person's) jewellery box. The creative team laid down a classical wooden parquet floor and then adorned the walls with hexagonal panels cushioned in plush purple velvet. These textile 'tiles' alternate along the walls with embedded mirrors and display cabinets of the same shape that have complex, but invisible opening mechanisms. In one corner, the diminutive cash desk – itself about as big as a display podium – recalls the mineral form of a growing crystal.

this is essentially a walk-in jewellery box

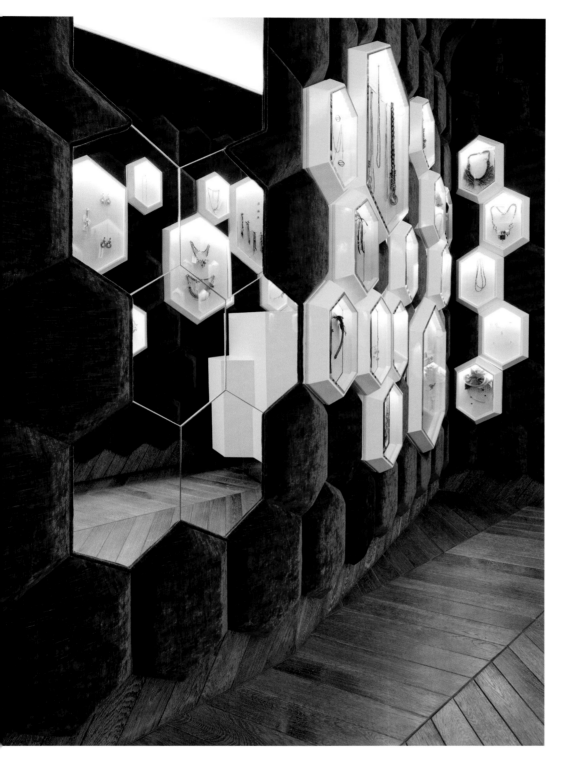

The walls are covered in hexagonal panels of fuschia velvet interspersed with mirrors and displays.

This jewellery shop was squeezed into 10m², making its size its key feature.

pinkeye

Where	Leuven, Belgium
Opening	June 2015
Client	Nathalie Bladt
Designer	Pinkeye (p.414)
Floor space	75 m²
Shop constructor	BM Projects
Photos	Kathleen Claes

toop

The billowing yellow ceiling hints at the presence of big Mama Toop, who is said to live on the building's first floor.

For children's optician Nathalie Bladt, Pinkeye designed a fantasy world in which tubby character toys the colour of sunshine play the role of exuberant designer eyewear displays. The shop's name Toop refers to the mole, a creature renowned for its poor eyesight, and for which its characters and display stands are named. Working with BM Projects, part of the studio's brief was to design a mascot for their client, translate it into character toys with a backstory and turn all of it into a retail environment. The result is that, inside, the designers hint that a family of these larger-than-life characters resides upstairs where the weight of the hefty Mamma Toop makes the ceiling bulge downward into the street-level shop. Wearing many shades of yellow, the Toop kids love to help kiddie customers choose their new eyeglasses and even help by trying them on first. The characters, who populate much of the interior in 2D or three, dominate visuals down to the shop's packaging, and are even available for purchase (so that, at home, they can serve as a toy or 'a nightstand guardian' for the kids and their extra eyes). The interior, which features a mural narrating the Toop story further, is expressive but not frivolous, sweet, but not saccharine.

pinkeye designed
a fantasy world

Toop designer toys positioned around
the store are used as eyeglass displays.

The interior tells the story of a family of chubby
moles with poor eyesight called the Toops.

The toys can be bought to bring home as the guardians of kids' new glasses.

A large mirror reflects and divides the room without making the space feel cramped.

VIU

Where	Berlin, Germany
Opening	July 2015
Client	VIU Ventures
Designer	VIU (p.416)
Floor space	65 m²
Shop constructor	VIU Ventures
Photos	Sandra Kennel

VIU flagship

Industrial but not muscle-bound, the furniture was made by a local studio called Atelier Haussman.

'Framing Characters.' That's the tagline of Swiss eyewear label VIU, which by now frames the eyes of characters all over the globe. Because the design of each VIU boutique rests on a foundation of clarity, simplicity and especially context when designing the VIU flagship in Berlin, creative director Fabrice Aeberhard started with the local people, culture and architecture. He wanted the interior retail environment to mirror the existing architectural facade. In the 65 m² shop, the ground floor facade is a gridded white stone wall. To mirror it indoors, Aeberhard installed a storefront glazed from floor to ceiling, through which the gaze is drawn inward past a minimal, subdued canvas of bright-white walls and ceiling to the 'eyewear wall', which was cut from four tonnes of Cipollino Greco green marble. This crisp application of natural materials mixed with bareness and clean lines is well-suited to the brand's 'modern classic' aesthetic. The interior, with its tonal whites and beton cire floor, is also furnished in a spartan way that leaves the shop feeling emphatically airy and expansive. The table and stools used for customer consultation were designed and made by local studio Atelier Haussman. Their industrial-looking frames provide a gentle contrast to the warmly naked space, however, the table top – crafted from green Greek marble – is a perfect match to the adjacent marble display wall.

The gridded white stone facade finds its echo in a white and marble interior.

051   VIU   VIU Flagship

natural materials are mixed with bareness and clean lines

The display wall was cut from 4 tonnes of stacked green Cippolino Greco marble.

BODY
HEALT

einszu33

Where	Munich, Germany
Opening	October 2015
Client	Aesop Germany
Designer	einszu33 (p.410)
Floor space	110 m²
Shop constructor	Ganter Interior
Photos	Bodo Mertoglu

aesop munich

In this skincare shop, austerity and forthrightness of display become elegant; contrasts, a virtue; and empty space, intimate. Soberly mixed materials and untamed textures generate a feeling of balance and tension simultaneously: a rough concrete ceiling and screed floor find their counterpoint in polished, pale surfaces, brass floor inlays and fixtures, upholstered wooden cabinets and a textile wall in a blushing hue. Anchoring the 110 m² shop, a massive 7 m concrete point-of-service island topped with Italian Pergamena marble and a recessed concrete washbasin becomes the heart of the store. Around this symbol of the timeless call to ablutions, clerk and client consult. Behind it, signature amber apothecary bottles line the marble slabs of barely-there metal shelving that rises on thin legs from floor-to-ceiling. The design has its origins in a quotation from German composer Gustav Mahler: *Tradition ist die Bewahrung des Feuers und nicht die Anbetung der Asche.* ('Tradition is not to worship the ashes, but to pass on the flame.') In the historically fraught centre of Munich, between places of present indulgence and the overwhelming guilt from past periods, the challenge was to build a space of profound well-being. The solution: a synthesis of contrasts that radiates calm.

This skin care boutique plays with balance and tension using disparities in material and texture.

A sleek marble counter contradicts and complements the oversized concrete island.

untamed textures generate a feeling of balance and tension simultaneously

Upholstered cabinets and brass details oppose coarser elements in cast concrete.

Fine bronze details frame the washbasin.

Body and Healthcare

The interior layers hard and soft, heavy and light, coarse and clean, create a sense of calm through contrast.

A super-slender matte
powder-coated metal shelf
offers another sleek element
to contrast with weightier,
rougher furnishings nearby.

Body and Healthcare

FLOOR PLAN

1. Sales area
2. Point-of-service
3. Testers
4. Storage
5. Office
6. Kitchen
7. Restroom

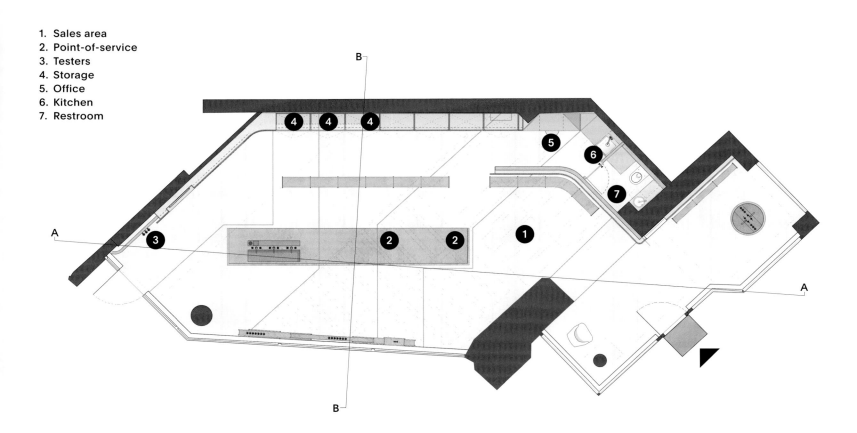

SECTION A-A

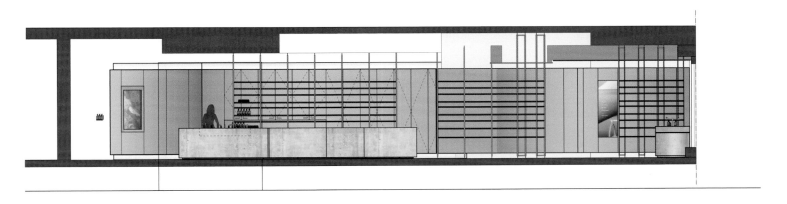

SECTION B-B

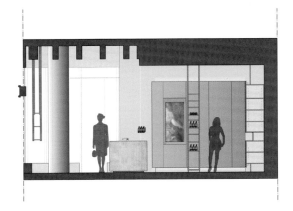

genesin studio

Where	Adelaide, Australia
Opening	July 2014
Client	Aesop Australia
Designer	Genesin Studio (p.411)
Floor space	100 m²
Shop constructor	Aesop Australia
Photos	Jonathan VDK

aesop rundle street

This shop interior for an outpost of the design-savvy Australian skincare and cosmetics brand was fit 'casually' into its heritage context in order to enable customers to understand the product in its native setting. Echoing the quality of natural light in luminous Adelaide, the Genesin Studio team kept the interiors fresh and light. From the existing high Victorian ceiling, they suspended bespoke long-drop blackened steel pendant lights of the studio's own design, along with drop, or trapeze, shelving, knitting the high and low of the lofty space together visually. The designers considered how to put the building's historical materials to contemporary use, eliciting nostalgia while updating the space. Circulation flows around three tablet-shaped islands and a central hand-wash basin lined with green stone. The tablet form, used later by Vincent van Duysen in the Hamburg store, tidily synthesises lines and curves. Durable and native to Australia, Tasmanian oak was used in the plank flooring, timber sales area wall and veneered counters. The blonde warmth of the wood complements the space's honey tones, while contrasting softly with the signature amber apothecary bottles. Genesin Studio, who calls scent design 'the next level of the retail experience', added an aromatic component to the Aesop interior template by concealing 10 oil-burning scent diffusers under the floor grates, branding the shop through fragrance.

This bright, modern skincare shop celebrates and updates the heritage building in which it is located.

Hard-wearing Tasmanian oak is used to plank the floors and to clad the marble-topped islands.

A hand wash basin is inset with green marble and fitted with custom brass faucets.

A frill-free apothecary-like display of Aesop's amber bottles contrasts with the other blonde, warm colours in the space.

Body and Healthcare

genesin studio kept the interiors fresh and light

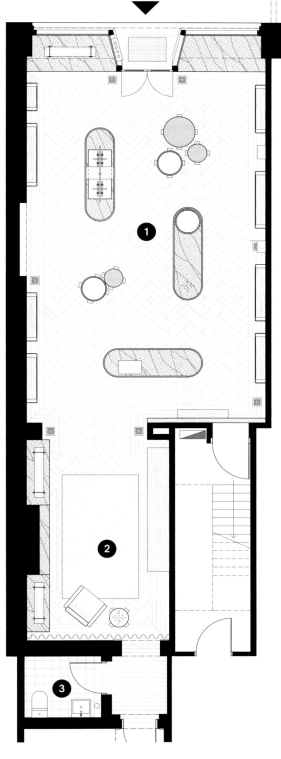

FLOOR PLAN

1. Retail area
2. Lounge
3. Restroom

inblum architects

Where	Tallinn, Estonia
Opening	August 2014
Client	Crème de la Crème haute parfumerie
Designer	Inblum Architects (p.411)
Floor space	61 m²
Shop constructors	Spectum pro and Solid supply
Photos	Darius Petrulaitis

crème de la crème perfume lab

Inblum Architects designed this fragrance, cosmetic and skincare shop to appear simultaneously 'cold as ice, but radiant and vibrant with life.' The greatest challenge the architects faced lay in having to display hundreds of diverse perfume brands together in a single diminutive space without creating any visual 'noise'. The client asked that the interior feel relevant enough to engage Northern Europeans, while preserving the familiarity of recognisable brands. The resulting interior combines a coldness that derives from its styling as a sterile laboratory environment with a perception that it is, nonetheless, rather lavish. It constantly conveys two distinct emotions and moods. Most immediately, this effect has its origins in the combined use of brushed aluminium and marble ornamented with the vivacious colours of the perfume packaging, which is warmer and more variegated. The wooden detailing of the occasional oak shelving and drawers is also warm, but uniform, and intended to appeal to a northern sensibility. The elongated, frame-like displays, which stand as robust and slender as dominoes, create a sense of powerful precision and, at the same time, delicacy. The architects' solution emphasises sustainability, aesthetics that allude to history and distinct cultural backgrounds, along with quality, keen detailing and a fresh approach to the shopping experience.

The interior contrasts a lab-like bareness with luxury, colour and wood with brushed aluminium and marble.

The bold but slender shelving units lend a sense of order to the proliferation of packaging.

a sterile laboratory
environment
that is lavish

Inblum Architects   Crème de la Crème Perfume Lab

creneau international

Where	Genk, Belgium
Opening	October 2014
Client	Enzo Riggio
Designer	Creneau International (p.409)
Floor space	140 m²
Shop constructor	Creneau International
Photos	Arne Jennard

r hair salon

Guests waiting on an overstuffed leather sofa in front of the dozen cutting stations enjoy the building's generous – six-metre – ceiling height.

Creneau International's designers considered Enzo Riggio – the Italian-born owner of this hair salon and a teacher at hair shows, schools and salons – as 'the headmaster of hairdressing'. When Riggio found space to expand his salon, they decided to create an environment that was part luxury salon and part academy, using classroom-like details and furnishings. Dressed in black and white zigzag graphics and modernist typography, the scheme capitalises on the hyper graphic quality of old school barbershop stripes by using them in bold repetition. The space was divided into an island of twelve central cutting stations, six washing stations, a waiting area, a product bar, a prep area and a discrete office volume. The 6 m ceiling height makes the interior airy and light but also offers a challenge in a type of space where clients expect to enjoy privacy while letting their hair down. The space is divided into multiple areas defined by different floor finishes and floor levels to resolve this: in front of the cutting stations – ornamented with library catalogue drawers and vast mirrors hung from oversize leather straps – a waiting room furnished with an overstuffed sofa feels exposed and light-washed. But above a tall island containing the service stations, the ceiling has been, effectively, lowered by a large, low-hanging mirror mobile.

the enviroment is part luxury salon and part academy

At the freestanding cutting stations, the airiness of the waiting room closes down into a more human-scale environment because a large mirrored mobile hangs very low from the ceiling.

There is a bright, voluminous waiting area where guests can order something cleansing at the salon's intimate black marble 'bar'.

dfrost

Where	Berlin, Germany
Opening	September 2015
Client	Oliveda
Designer	dfrost (p.410)
Floor space	24 m²
Shop constructor	Josef Bott
Photos	Ulrich Schaarschmidt

the olive-tree pharmacy flagship

The bare simplicity of the interior reflects brand values and facilitates the brand experience.

'Natural, minimalist architecture meets thousands of years of knowledge,' sums up the interior for this pharmacy, which makes cosmeceuticals focused on 'olive-tree therapy'. Using high-quality all-natural materials like their client, the designers gave the 24 m² space an unfussy, modern, Mediterranean character that is also bright, unisex and welcoming. The product mantra is essentially 'less is more' if applied expertly. For the interior: dfrost preserved existing historical elements and architectural details, restoring the brick walls and old wall panelling and then whitewashing them. The focus of the shop is a floor-to-ceiling apothecary cabinet in black-painted wood. On its shelves and drawers, they ranged the brand's eminently simple brown glass flacons and jars labelled in simple black and white, recalling historical tinctures and elixirs instead of cutting-edge cosmetics. Clerks use a brass ladder that slides on a rail to reach products, but first customers try the products at a counter trimmed with olive wood. An illustration by Italian artist Michele Tranquillini is illuminated from the rear on one wall of the shop, facing a product shelf dedicated to the brand's most popular cosmeceuticals, the green of its olive-shaped glass unit matched with the colour of the pharmacy's 'cell elixir'.

the design preserves existing historical elements and architectural details

A glass display shelf – in a green that matches one of the elixirs – allows visitors to focus on best-selling products.

The products are displayed in simple brown glass flacons and jars that recall historical tinctures.

open air studio

Where	Bangkok, Thailand
Opening	March 2015
Client	Unilever
Designer	Open Air Studio (p.414)
Floor space	500 m²
Shop constructor	Creful
Photos	Wison Tungthunya

unilever network

Unilever Network is responsible for the multinational brand's premium beauty and wellness product ranges. This multi-brand concept store features its cosmetic brand, Aviance, its vitamin label Beyonde, Unilever Home, its cleaning detergent and a toothpaste line called I-fresh. Situated at the company's Bangkok headquarters, the shop's display needed to showcase an image of the brand associated with 'timeless elegance'. To cultivate this ambience, Open Air Studio started with oval forms, with which the team created sequences of product displays bounded by curtain-like floor-to-ceiling black fins. They also built a more intimate stand-alone display volume shaped like a house and placed Beyonde products on shallow shelves set into the flanks of rectangular columns lit from within. The designer chose to keep the palette spare, crisp and clear, using matte white surfaces on walls and ceiling, a glossy white floor, the black fins and a grainy wood to line the interior of the 'house'. To express the brand identity, they also used accents of a bright-deep blue, the same as the Aviance packaging, for the line's wall logo which, against the white background stands out like a jewel. A second brand colour is a pale blue that is used in doses throughout the space on some backlit walls and globe chandeliers that were custom-made to echo the form of the Unilever Network logo.

Each product area takes a different form: Beyonde products are displayed in columns, iFresh takes the form of a house.

The bespoke chandeliers glow in one of the brand colours and is shaped to echo Unilever's logo.

The deep bright blue of the Aviance product range and packaging is used to highlight and decorate its display area.

the designer chose to keep the palette spare, crisp and clear

The design keeps sightlines across the large retail floor plan.

Oval shapes and glossy black fins supporting shelves serve to define various product areas.

BOOKS

square one

Where	Bucharest, Romania
Opening	February 2015
Client	Carturesti bookstore
Designer	Square One (p.415)
Floor space	1000 m²
Shop constructors	M.C.R Invest and Square One
Photos	Cosmin Dragomir

carturesti carusel

Wandering ultramodern railings at mid-level billow outward in irregular curves, underscoring the sinusoidal shape of the floor.

This concept bookstore is a confection that seems to have been made from solid oak, white paint, and vanilla buttercream frosting. The designers grafted liquid-looking contemporary elements and added functionality onto the already robust beauty of an historical building. Inspired by the painting *Golconda* by Renee Magritte, the architects synthesised elements of Steampunk and the Surrealism of the films *Brazil* and *The City of Lost Children* with 1930s, and bits of 1970s, Bucharest. A long central atrium leads from the entrance echoed by an extensive skylight far overhead. Book and product storage fully exploit the 5-m-high walls, wrapping the whole perimeter. Consonant with the brand, Square One used a broadly open plan and sculptural shapes without obstructing the existing architecture. But to make the most of limited space for product display and circulation on the middle floors, a sinusoidal floor and railing was added to generate more space between the pillars for stationary and other displays. The monolithically monochromatic treatment of almost the entire building interior reinforces the lighting scheme, a significant part of the plan. Warm-spectrum fixtures punctuate the ceilings, composed seemingly at random, but in a composition that was calculated precisely to accommodate the projected level of intensity demanded by each different display. This installation of the fixtures also mimics the starry sky viewed through the central skylight.

Historical and new architectural details are rendered in white to highlight the calculated lighting.

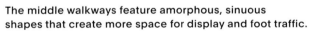

The middle walkways feature amorphous, sinuous shapes that create more space for display and foot traffic.

Carturesti Carusel

Above-ground, light fixtures mimic the night sky seen through the roof skylight but were actually arranged to provide specific levels of light in each area.

In the basement, large cabochon-like lights are set into a delicate structure that artfully cages the ceiling.

the architects were inspired by the painting golconda by renee magritte

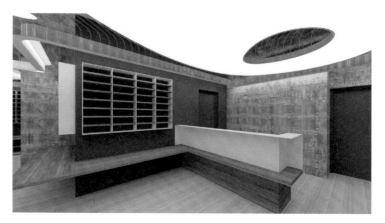

SECOND FLOOR

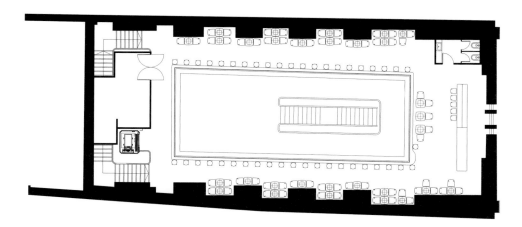

FIRST FLOOR

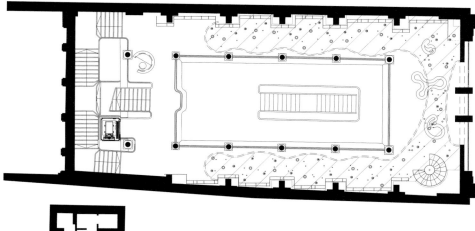

GROUND FLOOR

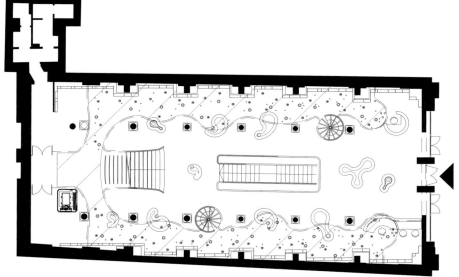

BASEMENT

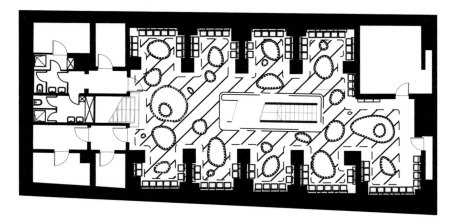

Organic flowing railings line the ground floor and first floor mezzanines. The bookstore is designed to accommodate a variety of activities for visitors: a multimedia centre in the basement, an art gallery on the first floor mezzanine and a bistro on the upper-most floor.

savvy studio

Where	Mexico City, Mexico
Opening	November 2013
Client	Casa Bosques
Designer	Savvy Studio (p.414)
Floor space	56 m²
Shop constructor	Savvy Studio
Photos	Alejandro Cartagena

casa bosques

Preserved in all its architectural house-ness, this bookshop looks and feels more like someone's home. Savvy Studio relied on the beautiful bones and flourishes of the original architectural shell, keeping its relaxed domesticity. The cosy atmosphere is lined with mismatched rugs and coffee tables, sofas and potted plants, reading lamps, cacti and window panes that are decoratively leaded, but not coloured. The addition of warmly stained wood is the only reminder that this is a shop because it is the primary material used to build bookshelves and magazine racks, and so quietly highlights them. The project is the result of a collaboration between Rafael Prieto, director of Casa Bosques and Savvy Studio and Jorge de la Garza, a multidisciplinary artist, who saw a hole in the cultural fabric of Mexico City. The domesticity suits their business' educational, simple, friendly, community-building and straightforward ethos: more than a book merchant, the space may be the city's first library dedicated to a curated but inclusive selection of independent publishers in Mexico. It boasts a catalogue ranging over a spectrum of creative fields, from art and design to photography, film, music, criticism and theory and promotes exchanges amongst local and international editors, artists, designers and academics, in the form of book readings, lectures and workshops.

This bookshop has
a welcoming
feeling of a home.

The house feel and its warmth
suit the business' accessible,
community-building character.

it looks and feels more like someone's home

The book and magazine displays are made from natural grainy wood.

Blocks of wood are stacked end-wise unevenly into the wall, forming a mosaic of sorts in addition to a magazine display.

Savvy Studio   Casa Bosques

anagrama

Where	Monterrey, Mexico
Opening	November 2015
Client	Conarte
Designer	Anagrama (p.408)
Floor space	90 m²
Shop constructor	Artliplano
Photos	Estudio Tampiquito

libreria conarte

This bookstore for the city's Council for Culture and Art is imagined as a nook where visitors can lose themselves in a book. The client, Conarte, supports, stimulates and preserves the arts. This particular space was designed to promote the experience of reading, with an emphasis on 'experience'. Located in a renovated hacienda, the design preserves existing stone walls, wooden ceiling beams and old window frames. The architects poured the floors and stairs in concrete and crafted the new furniture and bleachers from pine plywood. The concept of the interior focuses on manufacturing an environment capable of wrapping the reader up comfortably, activating the imagination and welcoming them to spend more time there, not just to make a purchase, but to enjoy the act of reading. Aside from holding books, in a nimble act of trompe l'oeil, the shelves knit together and bend fluidly to form a dome under the ceiling that recedes into the remote distance of the not-so-far-away rear wall, playing with visual perspective. Two additional elements help to reinforce the forced perspective: tiers of stair-like bleachers painted with a colourful ombre finish also create a perception of depth and, at the very back, a simple, illuminated half-circle on the wall serves as the vanishing point of the composition.

The bookshelves rise from the floor and torque slightly holding the books at unusual angles.

Two arcing shelves create a forced perspective along with bleachers painted in a gradient and a neon light that serves as a vanishing point.

The bookstore – in a former hacienda – preserves old elements while adding modern patterns that lend emotion to the otherwise serene space.

INITIAL SKETCHES

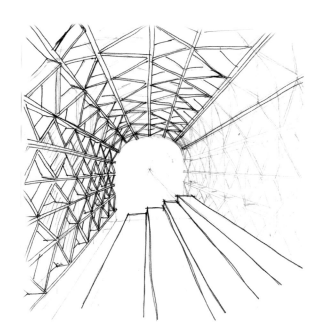

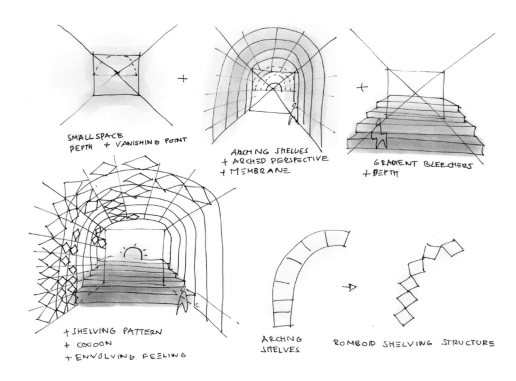

SMALL SPACE
DEPTH + VANISHING POINT

ARCHING SHELVES
+ ARCHED PERSPECTIVE
+ MEMBRANE

GRADIENT BLEECHERS
+ DEPTH

+ SHELVING PATTERN
+ COCOON
+ ENVOLVING FEELING

ARCHING
SHELVES

ROMBOID SHELVING STRUCTURE

this environment is capable of wrapping the reader up comfortably

FLOOR PLAN

1. Cash desk
2. Book shop
3. Reading area

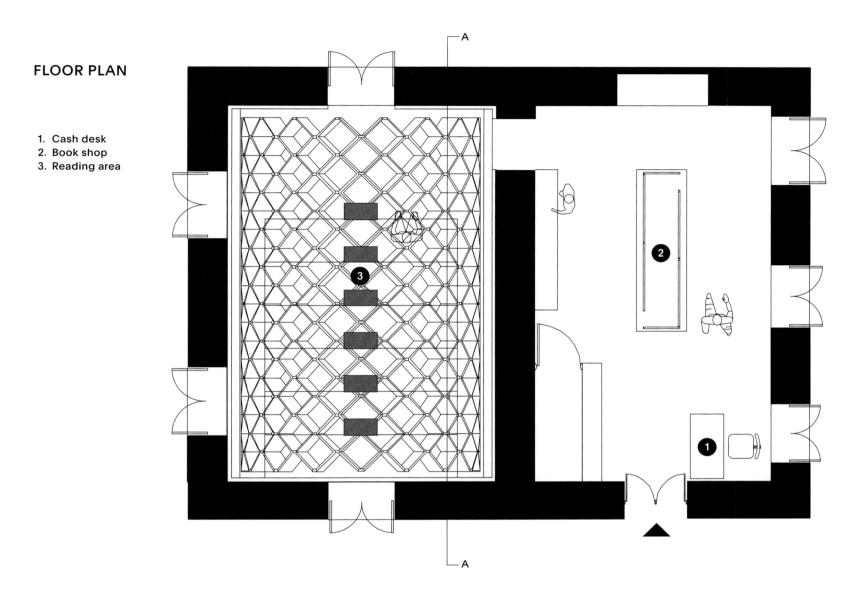

SECTION A-A

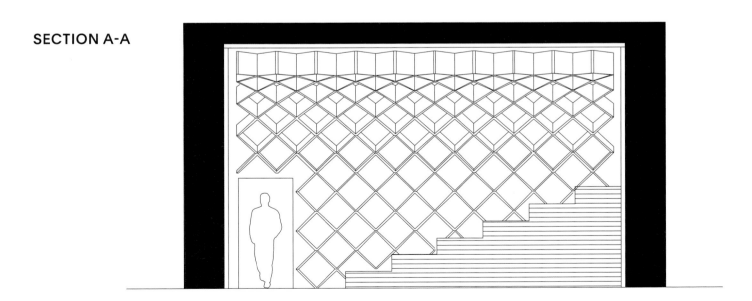

studio arthur casas

Where	Rio de Janeiro, Brazil
Opening	December 2012
Client	Saraiva Bookstore
Designer	Studio Arthur Casas (p.415)
Floor space	2000 m²
Shop constructor	LAR Construtora
Photos	Fernando Guerra

saraiva bookstore

Part public plaza, part library, part restful space, this four-floor bookshop has a simple, cosy, versatile architecture. The plan organises a great deal of information, letting books and new media co-habit the shelves without dominating them or becoming monotonous. The displays in this '21st century space' were designed to ensure that no single book will eclipse the others, encouraging visitors to browse. Some shelves are suspended by rails and can be easily rearranged, while various platforms have different heights, tables are organised by themes that range books together with whimsical objects, and the shelves closer to the floor are inclined so their titles can be read by anyone standing above them. Historical Brazilian furnishings – the Paulistano Chair by Paulo Mendes da Rocha, the Beg Armchair by Sergio Rodrigues and C26. C210 armchairs and ottomans by Carbono Design – create a space that is elegantly comfortable, inviting visitors to settle in for an extended read. Brazilian walnut warm surfaces remain a neutral canvas over which the myriad colours and textures of the books glow. Multimedia spaces, a cafe and an auditorium are on the basement floors with the kids' area, where a multi-coloured ramp interrupts the grey neutrality of the rest of the store in a space scaled down to child-size. For smaller readers, trapezoidal niches also translate the more grown-up architectural language used elsewhere.

Brazilian walnut and neutral grey provides a backdrop for shelves crowded with diverse colourful books.

The bespoke ceramic floor reflects
lighting under the millwork,
brightening the space in a subtle way.

Studio Arthur Casas   Saraiva Bookstore

Iconic Brazilian furniture – both chic and laid-back – invites shoppers to stay awhile to read that first chapter or two.

shelves are suspended by rails and can be easily rearranged

The bookstore has a simple, cosy and versatile architecture.

First floor

Ground floor

Basement 1

Basement 2

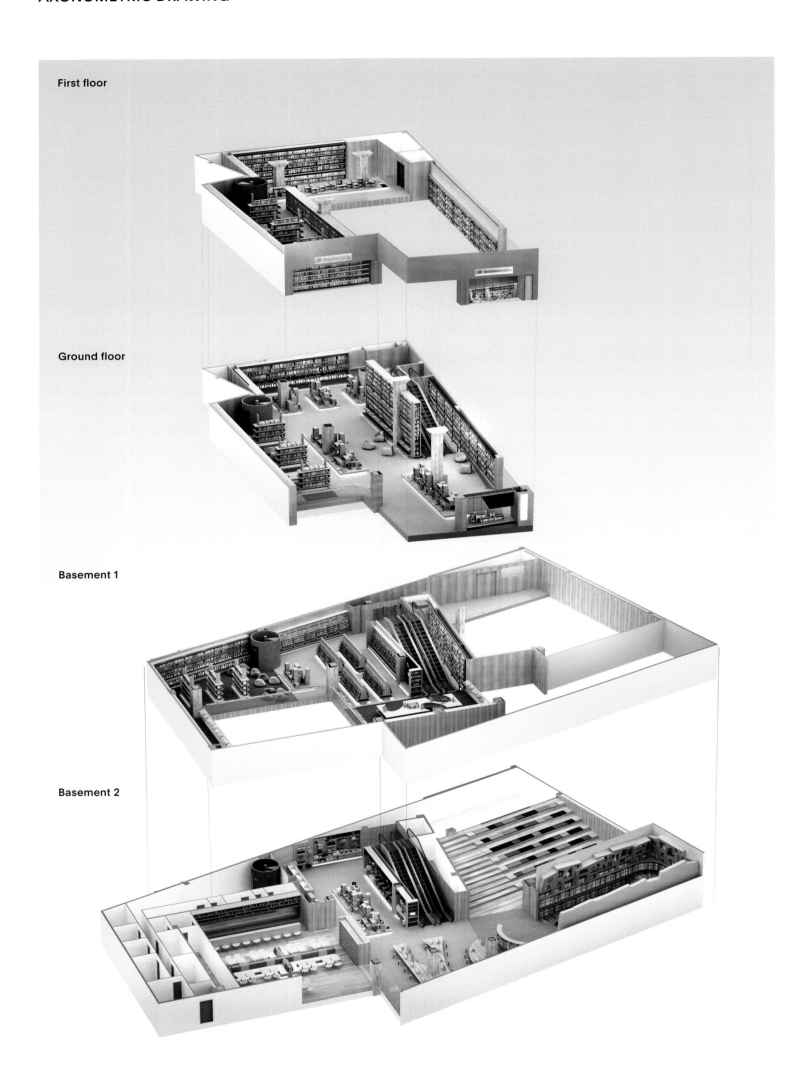

BASEMENT 1

1. Storage
2. Kitchen
3. Bar
4. Restaurant
5. Stationary shop
6. Kids area
7. Auditorium
8. Cash desk
9. Games
10. Accessories
11. Cameras and video
12. Books and reading

FIRST FLOOR

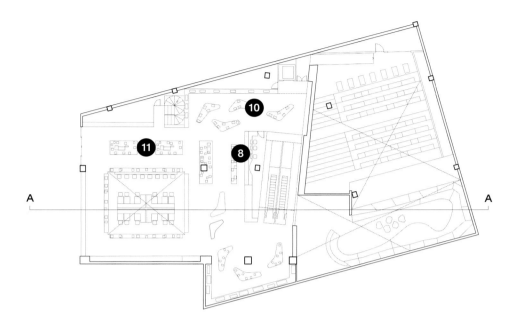

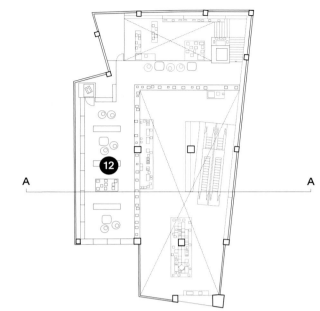

BASEMENT 2

GROUND FLOOR

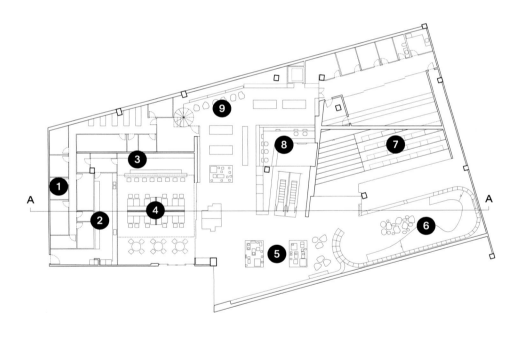

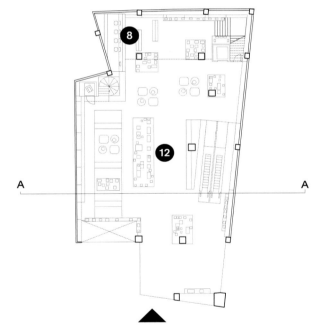

SECTION A-A

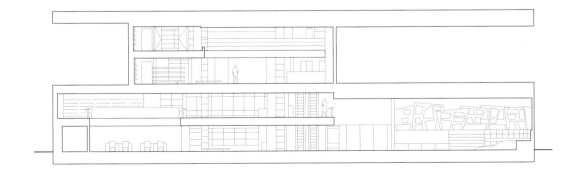

CORE

STORE

schmidhuber

Where	Berlin, Germany
Opening	February 2015
Client	Audi
Designer	Schmidhuber (p.414)
Floor space	25 m²
Shop constructor	Raumtechnik Messebau & Event Services
Photos	Marcus Zumbansen

audi ultrastore

The Audi Ultrastore is intended to serve several purposes: it is a brand immersion, a pop-up shop – Audi's first – contained in a box, and an illustration of how the automobile manufacturer innovates to unite lightweight construction processes with efficiency and design. The minimal interior of the space, designed by the Munich-based Schmidhuber architecture office, includes a seemingly featherweight sculpture reminiscent of a vastly scaled-up mesh. Located in the 'concept mall,' Bikini Berlin, where the emphasis is on renewing and reinventing the contemporary shopping experience, the scalable Ultrastore box was built to turn a 2D message about Audi's synthesis of technological performance with 'invisible' efficiency into a walkable 3D space. Inside a cargo container-size wooden frame, the boxes sculptural 'mesh' forms a super-porous membrane of branching aluminium pieces around heavier, opaque white displays containing the Audi Sport product range, which are made from powder-coated sheet aluminum. These units – ribbon-like and rhomboidal with large window-like apertures – allow the products to be viewed from both inside (clearly) and out (just enough to draw passers-by inside). The Schmidhuber design team also mounted a screen to the wooden ceiling beams to show films about the brand and to showcase accessories, including backpacks and duffle bags, sunglasses and wallets, and even model cars.

a pop-up shop contained in a box

The brand experience is articulated in a three-layer box: a wooden exoskeleton lined with a large sculptural 'mesh'.

Exposed timber beams strike a contrast amongst the aluminium membrane, tastefully combining a medley of materials.

hidden fortress

Where	Berlin, Germany
Opening	October 2014
Client	Catherine Pfisterer
Designer	Hidden Fortress (p.411)
Floor space	85 m²
Shop constructor	Majo Ertel
Photos	Courtesy of Hidden Fortress

bazar noir

The design is a flexible, open space, whilst keeping its existing loft-like character.

This 'concept store for hard-to-get goods' is a versatile space with a strong, dualistic character. In Bazar Noir, cherry-picked objects and interior accessories from around the world are showcased in a 'black-and-light' two-floor environment whose jet colour takes its cues from the name of the shop (making the design team work hard to maintain a consistent black tone over a variety of surfaces, materials and production methods). Meanwhile, through the contrasting black and blonde surfaces, they established two flip-side retail faces. Hidden Fortress used maritime pine – in its original barely finished blonde – to create this emphasis, sewing together two retail spaces that recall a single lined garment. The designers also made the space easily reconfigurable via a flexible shop system that lets store managers make constant tweaks to a constantly changing constellation of products. To complement the cost-efficient pine wood, which clothes most of the space, they trimmed it lightly with more noble materials like copper, Corian and glass, which help to warm the store's minimalism. They did this in the staff kitchen, for example, which, to make the most of every metre, also serves as a showcase of kitchen products. A cantilevering staircase becomes the focal point of the store, however, linking the stair with the upstairs mezzanine whilst distinguishing both from the monolithically black surfaces of the ground floor.

The monolithic use of blonde pine continues from the staircase into the room to contrast the black colour in the first floor, giving the dark even more impression.

The colour black unifies the almost windowless shop.

Concept Stores

accessories are showcased in a 'black-and-light' environment

The functioning kitchen serves two purposes: as a staff kitchen and a living showcase of kitchen products.

In the kitchen, the cost-effective black surfaces are accented with higher brow materials like copper.

FIRST FLOOR

1. Sales area
2. Restroom
3. Kitchen
4. Light shaft
5. Storage

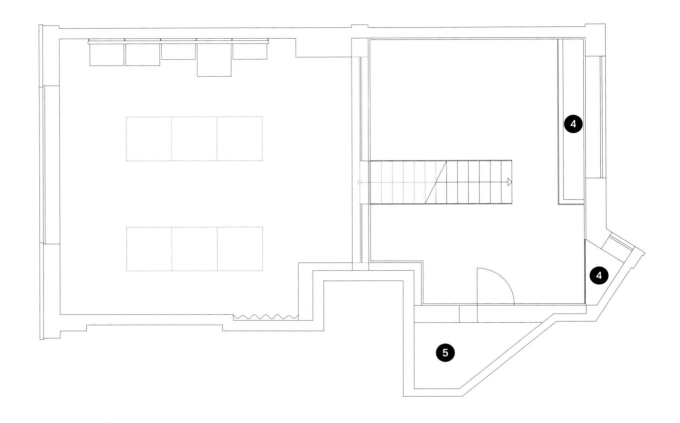

GROUND FLOOR

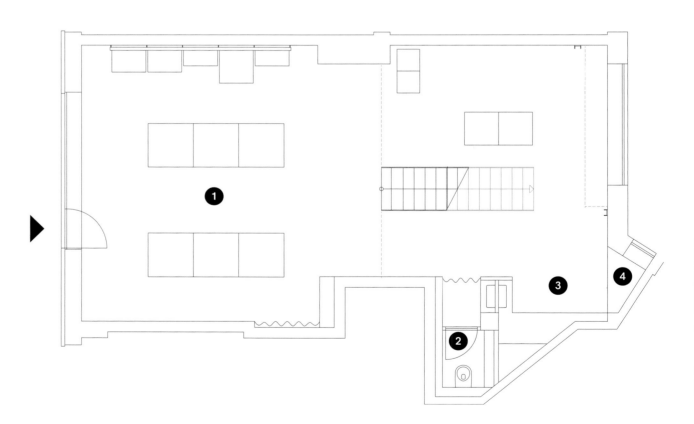

SHELVING SYSTEM

DISPLAYS

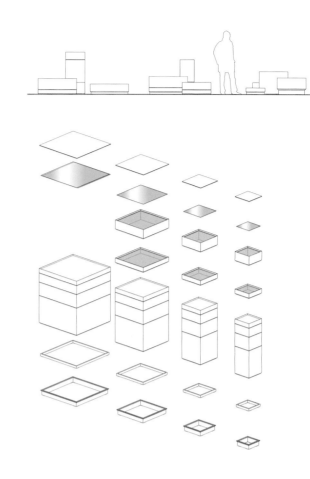

EXPLODED AXONOMETRIC

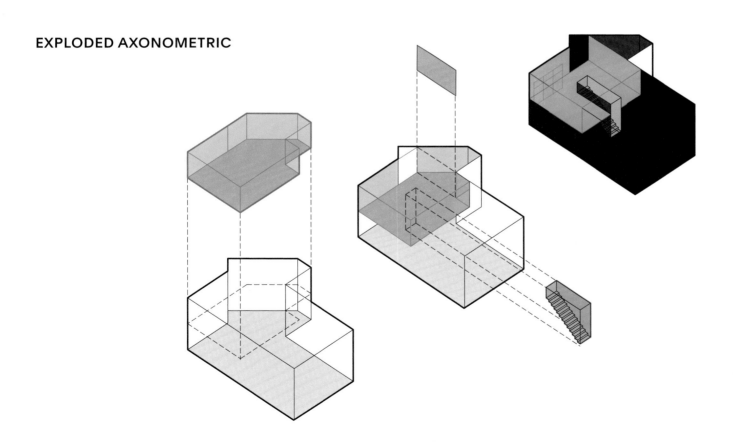

dalziel & pow

Where	London, United Kingdom
Opening	April 2014
Client	Jigsaw
Designer	Dalziel & Pow (p.409)
Floor space	511 m²
Shop constructor	Garenne Shopfitting
Photos	Courtesy of Dalziel & Pow

duke street emporium

Inside a Queen Anne-style, Grade II listed building, Dalziel & Pow delivered a flagship statement in 511 m². Between Oxford Street and the prestigious boutiques of Mayfair, the client, Jigsaw, wanted to mesh the progressive creativity of East London with the West End. The resulting concept clothing store for the innovation-championing brand is essentially a lifestyle destination, not just for fashion but also the work of emerging British artists. Duke Street Emporium is a place 'to linger and socialise'. The bold, eclectic interior unites a coffee shop by Fernandez & Wells, a browsable book nook, and a shop-in-shop called The Shop at Bluebird. Dalziel & Pow designed the brand identity and in-store communications, using handwritten price labels with stamped and blind-embossed branding to match the tailoring and craft of the clothing. The designers sourced 33 pieces of found furniture, a signature interior element familiar from the client's previous stores, however for Duke Street, Italian 1950's designs were chosen to complement the space. Art, however, becomes the fulcrum of the concept: installations and artwork populate the two-floor store, curated to complement the brand, as well as the heritage building. Instead of creating a gallery-like white box, the team preserved the original layout, with its niches, nooks and brick-lined construction, and then used a light monochrome colour scheme as a background to the art and graphics.

The designers kept the original brickwork and domestic, warren-of-rooms layout.

the store is essentially a lifestyle destination

While making reference to its location and history, the store also uses progressive design pieces and art to keep it contemporary.

In a listed building, Dalziel & Pow combined clothes, a coffee shop, books and art.

i29 interior architects

Where	Amsterdam, the Netherlands
Opening	April 2014
Client	Frame Publishers
Designer	i29 Interior Architects (p.411)
Floor space	180 m²
Shop constructor	Set Company
Photos	Ewout Huibers

frame store

Unusual views through the shop include stairs that go nowhere and mannequins that survey it all.

More than a shop, the Frame Store is a creative platform meant to offer a three-dimensional experience of its namesake Dutch interiors magazine over two retail floors and a gallery. Frame Publishers teamed up with Foam Photography Museum to open the canal-side creative centre in the historic Felix Meritis building. The publisher-turned-retailer needed to showcase not just new products but emerging talent and innovative brands, mixing up fashion, art and design with media, beauty and food. Inside, the original rafters, beams and floor planks, showcase the old school grandeur of the space. i29 Interior Architects added plinths, mirrored panels and two reflective fitting rooms, a small art gallery and stairs leading to a landing that surveys the space (whilst generating a surreal image for shoppers below who see only the torsos of those at the top of the stairs). The mirrors absorb the new volumes into the existing space where they become another of the stories written into its architecture. With glimpses of the ultramodern products on display, old and new are enriched by the contrast. The use of many mirrors also represents the Frame magazine's role in broadcasting images of important design to the world. Just so, old architecture and new products are broadcast throughout the monumental, space.

The historic building features the original rafters, beams and floor planks.

Mirrored stand-alone panels reflect the excavated heritage building as much as the products, fusing them together.

mirrors absorb the new volumes into the existing space

Products are displayed elevated above ground level.

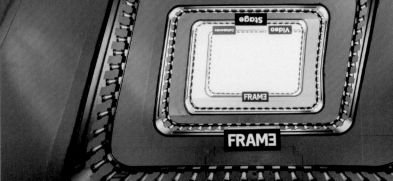

Logos and signage hover in the void
formed by the spiralling grand staircase.

i29 interior architects

Where   Amsterdam, the Netherlands
Opening   October 2014
Client   Frame Publishers
Designer   i29 Interior Architects (p.411)
Floor space   90 m²
Shop constructor   Brandwacht en Meier
Photos   Ewout Huibers

frame store

Artist Niek Pulles' graphical work explores
multidimensionality on the square white panels of the exhibition space.

A second retail space for Frame Publishers also broadcasts creativity, innovation and discovery whilst remaining highly versatile. Located on a canal at the publisher's original location, this interior has flip sides the way a coin does: contrast is conveyed succinctly in a black and white space that represents the self-conscious juxtaposition of culture and commerce, art and design. In a single space, the architects meshed two opposite shops into each other, transposing a blank-paper white and rectangular space over another that is black as ink and diagonal. The white space recalls the emptiness and fierce neutrality of a museum or gallery whilst the black side offers a product-fuelled shopping experience. From the entrance, hovering in the whiteness, white panels and black frames are suspended from or mounted to the walls, floors and ceiling. These serve as a white canvas onto which creative content can be exposed or easily changed out by invited artists and designers who simply replace the front panels with their own bespoke work. On the other hand, viewed from the rear, the shop assumes a radically different aspect: black wooden triangular boards display the store's products behind the white panels. Everywhere contradiction is expressed through interior elements: black vs. white, square vs. triangular, empty vs. full, 2D vs. 3D.

this interior has flip sides the way a coin does

Displays – white from the front, black behind – are mounted to the floor or wall or suspended from the ceiling.

FUTURE TRIBES
NIEK PULLES

STUTTERHEIM
MUUTO
THE WHITE BRIEFS
FIRST OF AUGUST
MONTALE
USLU AIRLINES
É T U D E S
TOILETPAPER
HOUSE OF DAGMAR
AVELON
SMEDLEY

maurice mentjens

Where	Eindhoven, the Netherlands
Opening	September 2015
Client	House of Smart
Designer	Maurice Mentjens (p.413)
Floor space	84 m²
Shop constructor	Timmerfabriek Hees
Photos	Arjen Schmitz

house of smart

The 'grey matter'-themed colour palette makes large display counters less conspicuous.

The Intelligent Community Forum (ICF) once dubbed Eindhoven the 'world's smartest region'. Partly to reflect its location at the technological heart of Holland, Maurice Mentjens designed this stimulants shop as an abstraction of the brain. Its monolithic but irregular latticing of walls and ceiling suggests neural pathways. Even the colour scheme refers to the cerebral cortex, or 'grey matter'. Mentjens' previous smart shop interiors were modelled on an alchemy lab and spiritual space; at Eindhoven, the shop theme is richly and energetically layered: inside, old brick walls were left exposed, linking the new design to a larger history of time and place. The generously sized storefront windows are not just about a view to sales, but about transparency, literal and metaphorical. The myriad cross-hatched wooden beams, which create a deep texture, refers not just to streams of thought, but to labyrinths, holography and the local lighting industry, computer chips and motherboards; they even function as narrow shelving, presenting product samples. LED 'beams' that match the dimensions of the wooden beams suggest the firing of synapses but also, of course, enlightenment, pure and simple. 'The realm of creativity is chaos,' says Mentjens. 'An open mind is of vital importance for true renewal.'

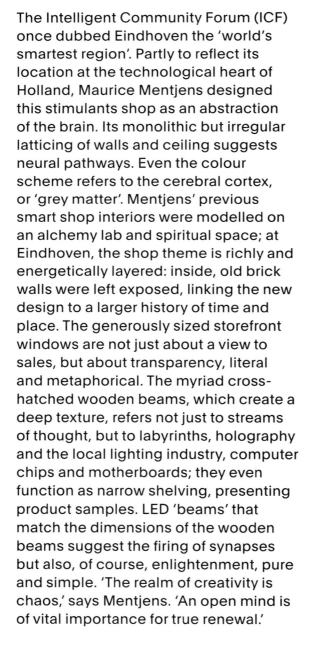

Minimal LED light strips blend into the wooden beams and allude, in part, to the firing of synapses.

All walls and the ceiling have been panelled with a
network of 65 mm wooden beams that also serves as display surface.

this shop is an abstraction of the brain

The interior recalls the structure of the brain reflecting its location in the technological centre of the Netherlands.

Concept Stores

studio sklim

Where	Singapore, Singapore
Opening	January 2015
Client	Emporium of the Modern Man
Designer	Studio Sklim (p.415)
Floor space	68 m²
Shop constructors	Idealhomes and Mint Garden
Photos	Khoo Guo Jie

rattan clouds

Clouds hanging from the ceiling on brass pulleys can be cranked up and down.

The interior of this contemporary lifestyle goods retailer can be changed up constantly to accommodate its changing merchandise. Designed by Singaporean design firm Studio Sklim, Rattan Clouds is a versatile solution that makes the shop not just reconfigurable but 'multiconfigurable'. The Rattan capsules are bent into spheres by traditional artisans and finished in a variety of stains that can be used whole or split into hemispheres for seating, storage, display and lighting. Passers-by can view the entire shop through the floor-to-ceiling glass facade before entering the white space dressed with a matte-finish polyurethane concrete screed floor and a concrete floating cash desk. Brass fixtures – fittings, garment racks along with hinges and chains on the capsules – complement the concrete and Rattan. As luminaires the Clouds house halo like bulbs and cast 'shadow textures' against other surfaces. Those suspended from the 4.7 m ceiling can be raised and lowered by a mechanical crank to make space for exhibitions, installations and gatherings. The repetition of the form over diverse applications and the emphasis on the Rattan spheres, creates an art installation as visual merchandising and a space that is not only commercial but cultured. The arranging and rearranging of the space makes the store feel as ephemeral as a cloudy sky.

rattan capsules are used for seating, storage, display and lighting

From the street, the shop looks more like a gallery with an uninterrupted, full-height glass storefront.

The shop interior consists of a single well-crafted form repeated artfully across all furniture types.

d'art design gruppe

Where	Bielefeld, Germany
Opening	October 2015
Client	Schüco International
Designer	D'art Design Gruppe (p.410)
Floor space	750 m²
Shop constructor	kohlhaas messebau
Photos	Lukas Palik

schüco showroom

Schüco claims to turn 'houses into homes' with its energy-saving system solutions for building envelopes: windows, doors, facades, security, automation and so forth. The design of this showroom at the company's headquarters, which is visited primarily by brand partners and specialised members of the trade, took its cues from the architectural concept of the brand's recent trade fair booth. That booth, described as a work of 'mediatecture' by D'art Design Gruppe, who designed it, became a microcosm of the showroom's intuitive user experience. Laid out in three complementary areas over a white epoxy resin floor, three zones – Studios, Brandwalk and Product Labs – highlight products and expertise accompanied by interactive media stations. These areas, for example, demonstrate the facade elements of the company's 'Parametric System' and showcase new approaches to construction. Dart's team works collaboratively across disciplines to create a holistic brand experience that better addresses today's 'complex, multisensorial' world. In this case, its media designers created an 'expert table' featuring software applications controlled by interaction with objects on the table, which serves as an archive of the brand's collective knowledge. This becomes a useful tool for the sales staff along with Schüco's Augmented Reality applications in a space under the rubric of 'Housing'. Combining the spatial scheme, applications that support the staff, and interactive displays, the showroom is designed to unite both experience and interaction.

Clean lines, a limited palette and generous use of blank space enhances the customer experience.

Three product zones present the brand's sustainable architectural solutions.

System solutions are directly incorporated in the design of the rooms to showcase company products.

the showroom is designed to unite both experience and interaction

The showroom's design is dotted with interactive media stations to explain the products.

D'art Design Gruppe Schüco Showroom

coordination asia

Where	Shenzhen, China
Opening	October 2015
Client	TCL Telecommunication Equipment
Designer	Coordination Asia (p.409)
Floor space	263 m²
Shop constructor	Ming Gao Decoration
Photos	Courtesy of Coordination Asia

TCL electronics

For all the brands abandoning physical retail for digital, there are also 2D brands turning to 3D. TCL an electronics company, once exclusively e-commerce, asked Coordination Asia to create an 'offline retail haven' for tech geeks and electronics fans. The result is a tech-savvy concept store that lets visitors feel as if they are stepping into a video game instead of just playing one. Part gaming terrain, part laid-back domestic environment, the design allows shoppers to buy online and off, linking the two business platforms and saving time. The concept can be adapted to any future retail space via a multifunctional and modular floor, wall and ceiling system, the dimensions of which may be sized up or down to accommodate varying sites. Wall-mounted display cabinets hung at various heights make it easier for customers to compare products while background walls painted in a monochrome push products into the foreground. Modernity and innovation are expressed in slices of vivid colour that contrast with predominantly dark surfaces. Both the brand's visual identity and the interior, feature dynamic diagonal stripes and interior modules that can be configured to cross the room in different directions. This (ever-convertible) juxtaposition of contrasting materials disrupts any perception of linearity that could become boring, which ensures that the shop looks clean and simple, but never inhibiting or inflexible.

Diagonals, black and white stripes and colourful anodised aluminium frames suggest a digital landscape.

an 'offline retail haven' for tech geeks and electronics fans was created

Hyper graphical surfaces obscure the shape of the room slightly so that all the lines inside, do not have a sense of dull linearity.

Between digital flatland and cool 3D clubhouse, this windowless shop provides a window into the world of electronics.

Oversize graphics adorn the
floor-to-ceiling shoe displays.

coordination asia

Where	Beijing, China
Opening	August 2015
Client	Nike Sports
Designer	Coordination Asia (p.409)
Floor space	1200 m²
Shop constructor	Genera-tions Production
Photos	Courtesy of Coordination Asia

the nike studio

Men's sportswear is showcased in gallery-like half-rooms.

Part exercise in branding, retail and exhibition design and part plain old exercise, the Nike Studio is a high-impact fitness centre and athletic-wear showcase that brings together a series of workout studios with experiential product displays. In a spartanly furnished 1200 m² gallery, Nike showed off its autumn/winter 2015 collection called *Holiday 15* while making allusions to infinity, speed and empowerment. Guests were encouraged to 'find their fast' in a minimalist but high-impact series of spaces. To draw visitors through an exhibition-like product gallery and to create a sense of energy and motion, the designers darkened workout areas and struck a contrast with stand-alone product installations and screens in dramatic forms. Coordination Asia embodied speed and infinity in reflective display cases and booths, LED grids and hyper linear frames and display structures installed in repetitive or mirror-image rows. The design team showed Nike uniforms in four mirrored containers and installed *Zoom* apparel behind rows of semi-transparent screens. Rectilinear lights arch over the locker room while treadmills are 'contained' in an LED light 'box', creating a human scale space within the larger room, suggesting freedom and shelter at the same time. Elsewhere an athletic sensibility prevails with benches and footwear bars, as well as pep-talk imperatives in muscular graphics.

A large LED wireframe girds the ceiling and walls of the otherwise dark studio with light.

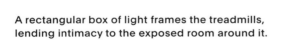

A rectangular box of light frames the treadmills, lending intimacy to the exposed room around it.

a contrast is struck with stand-alone product installations and screens in dramatic forms

In the locker room, strong graphics make bold statements and LED lights arch overhead like an arcade.

creneau international

Where	Antwerp, Belgium
Opening	September 2015
Client	ID&T
Designer	Creneau International (p.409)
Floor space	220 m²
Shop constructor	Creneau International
Photos	Arne Jennard

tomorrowland boutique

One installation consists of clusters of real books hung open on the black wall.

'Dream-like' describes this dark but cheerful pop-up shop, which is designed to complement a local dance festival known for its otherworldly atmosphere and fantastical scenography. Walking inside, over the black dance floor at the entrance, visitors are greeted by enlarged letters taken from literature that feel as if they are embarking on 'a journey full of things to discover' in a double-height space that nonetheless feels cosy: products, objects, music, art, flying printed matter, interactive mirrors and other novel and unexpected elements ornament each room. Conceived around the Tomorrowland Festival's mythology regarding a 'book of wisdom', the space is filled with books, books and more books in various forms and installations: at the top of a staircase with a classical lathe-turned balustrade, a large wall-mounted library wraps the upper mezzanine from floor-to-ceiling. There, actual books can be found mid-flight along with crowded-bookshelf patterned wallpaper. Most furnishings are black and the walls and stairs painted black. The walls are hung with illustrated pages or venerable old volumes cracked open and artfully composed. Creneau International designed all the furniture and, because the Tomorrowland identity is based in music, dance and entertainment, the designers also included a bar and a DJ booth at the rear so that the shop can be transformed into an events space, as well.

Creneau preserved the existing staircase leading up to a real library and printed words on the black dance floor at the entrance.

novel and unexpected elements ornament each room

In the storefront, Tomorrowland is represented by a fairy-tale forest in silhouette.

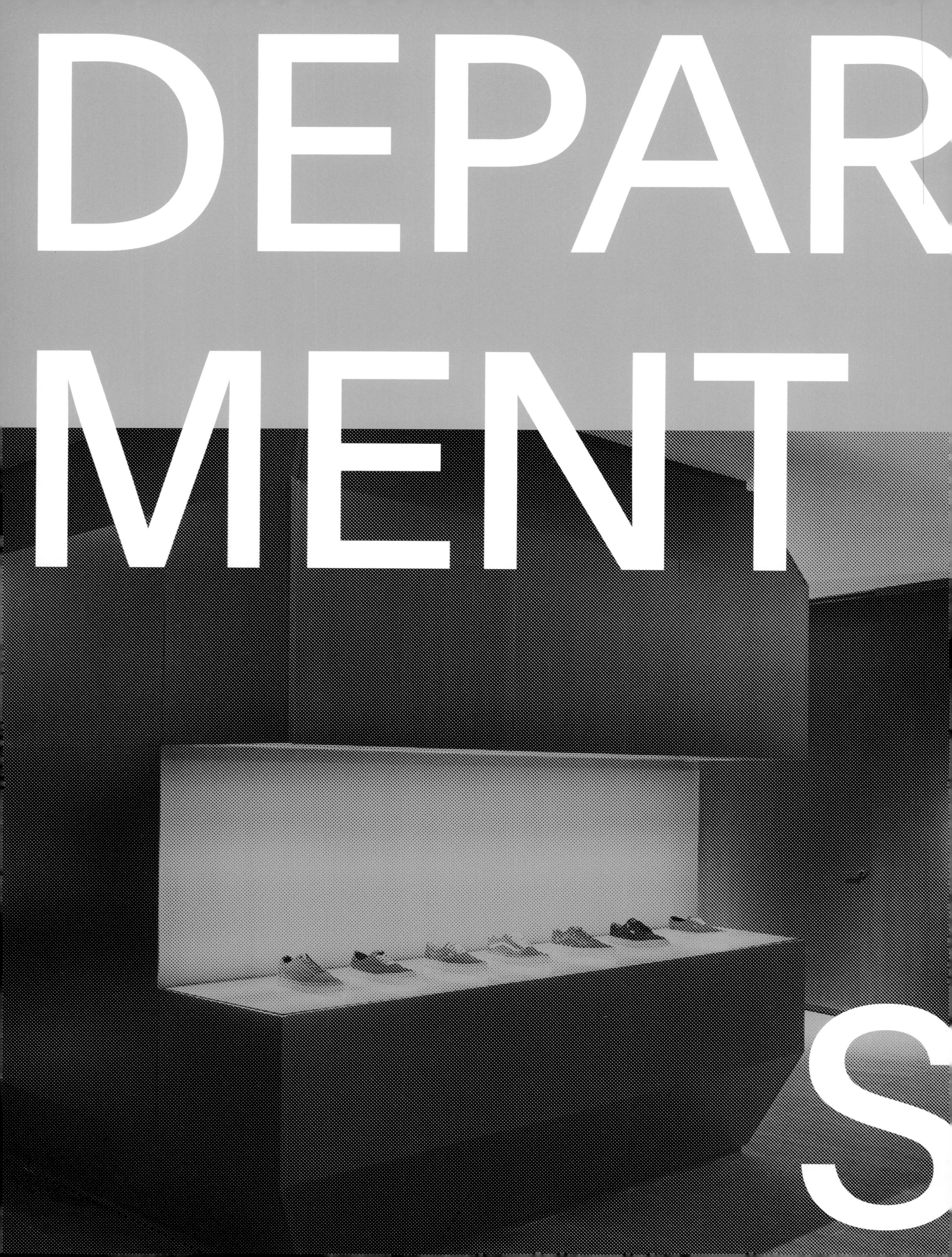
DEPAR
MENT
S

T

TORES

campaign design

Where	Eindhoven, the Netherlands
Opening	June 2015
Client	De Bijenkorf
Designer	Campaign Design (p.409)
Floor space	3238 m²
Shop constructor	Vizona
Photos	Roman Thomas

de bijenkorf

De Bijenkorf is one of the largest shopping emporiums in the Netherlands, each of whose stores is designed by a different architect. Mid-century icon Gio Ponti designed the Eindhoven building, located in an historic industrial area, featuring a 3 dimension cladded exterior made of green glazed tiles. The proportion, scale and forms of the facade, along with the rough luxe graphical work of furniture designer Piet Hein Eek, inspired Campaign Design's redesign of the second floor. Here the kids, bed and bath, kitchen and home accessories department communicates a tranquil layer of modern luxury marked by clean shapes and colours. To link the interior and its industrial roots, Campaign exposed the ceiling and columns and provided a powder coated lighting channel in a geometric pattern that underscores the space's volume and structure. They applied resilient geometric patterns to the Art Deco-inspired escalator and the porcelain tile floors (radiating sunburst stripes, bold chevron parquet) and borrowed the colour of Ponti's bespoke tiles. To distinguish departments, the designers chose representative structures – like the outline of a gabled house called the 'Plywood Playhouse' in the children's clothing area – to define each while serving as a display element. This also allows many seasonally changing products to be showcased while keeping sightlines uncluttered.

Raw unfinished concrete columns blend into the sleek and modern interior.

The kitchen department is in between a 3D cubic structure and a chevron patterened floor.

The external facade inspired the screen that decorates the escalators.

modern luxury is marked by clean shapes and colours

Kids' clothes hang from trestle-like racks inside the Plywood Playhouse.

blocher blocher partners

Where	Mannheim, Germany
Opening	November 2015
Client	Engelhorn
Designer	Blocher Blocher Partners (p.408)
Floor space	15,000 m²
Shop constructor	Blocher Blocher Partners
Photos	Courtesy of Blocher Blocher Partners and Engelhorn

engelhorn

For this multi-brand Mannheim fashion house, Stuttgart-based Blocher Blocher Partners redesigned and expanded its flagship by 3000 m². The 'less is more'-driven makeover divided menswear and women's into two retail levels that mix a cocktail of social, commercial and culinary pleasures: the clothing floors are complemented with a gold-flecked champagne bar called Moments, a Michelin-starred restaurant, Opus V, and a lounge called Dachgarten, all of which privilege experience of the space and brand, while expressing Engelhorn's revitalised mantra: 'be different, be incomparable.' The building's extensively sky lit roof makes the hospitality and shopping areas airy and saturates them with natural light. The men's section is dominated by masculine materials and colours while women find bright welcoming hues and nudes strategically highlighted with gold and dark chrome. The distinctive concept that organises the space is the transposition of the components of the brand's virtual shop into a physical space. The curated concept areas at the centre of the retail floors are designed, like an e-commerce site, to be easily modified to introduce fresh themes and aesthetic ranges. It is bespoke mechanisms that achieve this, most importantly a versatile ceiling made from a gridded system of aluminium profiles to which a variety of display modules, shelving and components carrying lighting or room-partitioning textile panels, may be affixed.

Each area in the store has a unique atmosphere. Brand shops have been avoided largely.

A golden champagne bar and two restaurants – one Michelin-starred – mix shopping with socialising, and commerce with culture.

a sky lit roof makes the hospitality and shopping areas airy and saturates them with natural light

Bright colours mark the womens design department on the fourth floor.

Department Stores

The ceiling grid allows lighting, displays and room-dividing elements to be easily changeable.

All presentation modules are highly flexible.

HMKM

Where	Beijing, China
Opening	October 2013
Client	Galeries Lafayette
Designer	HMKM (p.411)
Floor space	47,000 m²
Shop Constructors	China Construction First Building Group and Beijing Yuan Architectural Decoration Design
Photos	Jonathan Leijonhufvud

galeries lafayette

A digital version of the original store's grand dome crowns the amorphous void of the atrium on a large LED screen.

The Beijing outpost of this historic high-end department store is a dynamic blend of the original Parisian flagship's glamour with high-technology and a modern Chinese take on luxury that addresses the high-powered local market. The 47,000 m², six-floor building – each floor distinguished by a different colour, material and theme – comes with its own auspicious history as the former Bank of China headquarters. HMKM stacked two vitrines atop each other on the ground and first floors and wrapped the double-height entrance with larger-than-life LED screens. Dramatic lighting and audio visuals by London-based PJC helps to draw visitors through the store and showcase products sumptuously. A second screen suspended over the atrium parallel to the floor depicts the Beaux Arts steel-and-glass coupole that has become a symbol of the original Boulevard Haussman emporium. Beneath the digital dome, the coupole is repeated in various forms throughout the building at client touch-points and on in-store displays. All of the programmable LED panels remain exposed and shift frequently to engender a dynamic sense of movement and change. In addition to the high-tech visuals, the designers also translated the shop into a vastly elegant, Parisian apartment, incorporating modern, fresh details that update leitmotifs borrowed from the Haussman shop's grand Art Nouveau spirit.

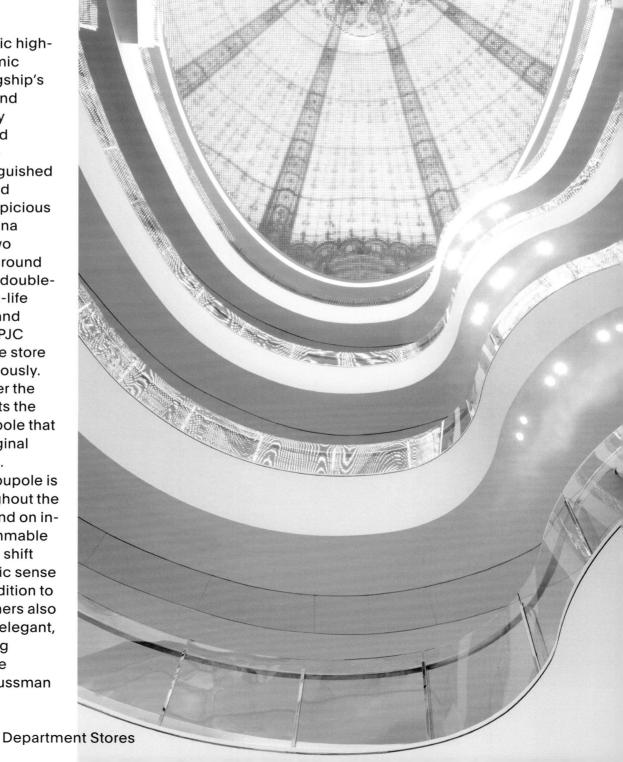

The retail areas modernise decorative motifs that once embellished the original Art Nouveau department store.

a dynamic blend of the original parisian glamour with a modern chinese take on luxury

The design synthesises the glamour of the historic emporium with technology and a specifically Chinese version of luxury.

HMKM

Where	Bangkok, Thailand
Opening	June 2014
Client	The Mall Group
Designer	HMKM (p.411)
Floor space	5000 m²
Shop constructor	–
Photos	Courtesy of Paragon PR team

paragon beauty hall

Divided into abstracted petal panels, the drop ceiling contains unobtrusive spotlights.

HMKM effected the graceful renewal of a 5000 m² space dedicated to beauty. The interior features a refined international look that shimmers like the subtlest eyeshadow in champagne and golden hues. These warm colours, with materials like etched glass and mirror, lend an aura of glamour to the experience. Visitors meander freely through what might have been an overwhelming clutter of premium and mid-market make-up and skincare counters, as well as a new fragrance destination. To establish order in a large-scale space showcasing a profusion of brands, the designers shrank each brand's canopy to clear sightlines, making browsing easy and avoiding the feeling of being cramped or mind-boggled with options. Visual merchandising zones and an artful repeating ceiling ornament draw customers across the floor. The bespoke drop ceiling consists of discrete panels in an eight-petal floral pattern. The petals hold spotlights in some areas whilst, in others, the flowers turn into chandeliers adorned with clusters of long illuminated acrylic rods. In the fragrance department, HMKM designers took cues from faceted perfume flasks to create display furnishings, trimming the space with champagne-colour metalwork and designing a floor gondola that gives the space a unique character. By backlighting the shelves, they also ensured that the scents remain at the centre of the senses.

this look shimmers like eyeshadow in champagne and golden hues

The faceted display shelves and furnishings were inspired by perfume bottles.

The colour scheme and finishes makes the space feel elegant and glamorous.

In lieu of dictating traffic patterns through the shop, distinctive sculptural forms are one of the wayfinding tools.

burdifilek

Where	Seoul, Korea
Opening	March 2014
Client	Hanwa Galleria
Designer	Burdifilek (p.408)
Floor space	9920 m²
Shop constructors	Hanmi Interior, Gawon, Daewon, Samwon and Shinhan ID
Photos	Ben Rahn

the galleria luxury hall west

Third-party shop-in-shops were eroding this department store's identity and with it, an emphasis on good value and convenience that identity had signalled to customers. Burdifilek managed to create a coherent single-brand design featuring flexible curated pockets of display which embolden shoppers to explore unfamiliar brands 'without prejudice', an unusual strategy on the Korean market. Displays with a unified look on the perimeter and in the middle of the retail floor are constructed to be highly adaptable to different product placement, shops, sensibilities and seasonal shifts without diminishing or diluting the store's overall presence. The designers also removed the traditional department store 'hard boundaries' that typically rely on well-defined aisles to dictate circulation and thereby promote shallow grazing, so to speak, instead of allowing customers to choose their own shopping adventure. The resulting interiors – over four floors – add both volume and depth to the browsing experience while bringing a large retail space down to a more human scale. This approach may prove especially valuable to the Korean market because the country is a portal through which new brands reach Asian consumers. Instead of losing partnerships with international brands by strengthening its own identity, this interior design actually facilitates the introduction of new third-party brands and encourages their discovery by meandering shoppers.

Although the department store is spread across four large floors, the new interiors bring the shopping experience to a more intimate scale.

volume and depth enhance the browsing experience

Coherent single-brand areas can be created in reconfigurable pockets of curated product that encourage wandering and discovery.

Versatile displays make it easy for the store to change things up according to season, look or label.

Accessory displays are graphical and bold to express the client's identity while forming a blank canvas for shop-in-shop products.

FASHIO

d'art design gruppe

Where   Mainhausen, Germany
Opening   January 2014
Client   adidas Group
Designer   D'art Design Gruppe (p.410)
Floor space   1000 m²
Shop constructor   Projektpilot
Photos   Lukas Palik

adidas and reebok showroom

Neuss-based D'art Design Gruppe designed two adjacent brand zones for athletic footwear and apparel brands adidas and Reebok in a single space in a Mainhausen wholesale order centre. The larger adidas area is rendered in black and white, emphasising a purity of form, colour and material. Facing the entrance, a curving LED wall is intended to 'emotionalise' the entrance and draw visitors in. This is the source of most of the adidas area's graphical treatments and digital media content. Dart organised the space using biomorphic wall modules to define product range displays. These clean-lined modules, complete with highlight platforms that can be neatly terraced, recuse themselves, allowing the garments and footwear to dominate the store's visual landscape, as well as being neutral enough to accommodate the seasonal change of products and trends. Both spaces share a smooth light flooring made from concrete and exposed ceilings where building equipment is visible. Reebok's section of the showroom has a look that is less finished and pared-down but it still has a clarity of forms and composition. The display system consists of black steel shelving and plywood boxes, as well as bold wall graphics that organise and identify various product areas. Because easy re-configurability is crucial to the buying process, Dart also developed mobile stations that can be installed as needed.

Aside from a colourful wall logo, the adidas areas are primarily black and white.

A LED wall greets visitors to the adidas side of the showroom.

D'art Design Gruppe adidas and Reebok Showroom

Plywood and black steel displays are backed by large bold graphics.

biomorphic wall modules define the product range displays

The Reebok area of the two-brand showroom features a rougher finish than adidas.

D'art Design Gruppe   adidas and Reebok Showroom

denis košutić

Where	Vienna, Austria
Opening	July 2014
Client	Vipro
Designer	Denis Košutić (p.410)
Floor space	600 m²
Shop constructor	Vipro
Photos	Lea Titz

amicis women

High-gloss marble floor and mirror polished stainless
steel display tables glitter against the occasional matte surface.

Denis Košutić, who believes that 'nostalgia and fantasy are the future', is exploring what he calls a 'new classicism' in the design of this luxury women's boutique. The core of this aesthetic, he explains, is 'understatement, not overstatement' and indeed, the shop is lushly naked. A two-level, mostly two-colour space was stripped down to its fundamental structure. One level consists of a long railroad room, narrowing and sharpening the focus of visitors. On the other level, the designer established a precisely planned series of more intimate rooms. Then Košutić brought vintage furniture and product highlight areas featuring bright yellow upholstery to create soft, warm focal points in the black and white space. Befitting such a narrow linear space, the line became the most important element in his toolkit. Used alone or in aggregate, the geometry of the line informs both functional and ornamental aspects of the project. The designer also relied on materials and surfaces to generate severe contrasts: for example, beyond the black and white palette, a mix of high-gloss with the unpolished and the muted, Baccarat wall lights and Nero Marquina marble alongside custom stucco elements, flat-black bar-shaped pendant lights and matte-lacquered MDF wall display boxes. In places, minimal presentation tables and vitrines are fashioned in glass and mirror-polished stainless steel to shine and glint against matte backgrounds.

The design incorporates functional and decorative elements in a highly geometric fashion.

the core of this aesthetic is 'understatement, not overstatement'

Yellow upholstered armchairs, stools and wooden tables
inject the black and white space with a gentle shot of colour.

claudio pironi & partners

Where   Baku, Azerbaijan
Opening   February 2014
Client   Avenue
Designer   Claudio Pironi & Partners (p.409)
Floor space 1343 m²
Shop constructors MonkeyDu and
                   Pasha Construction
Photos   Gianluca Dorio

avenue coliseum

Luxury and welcome co-exist in this 1343 m², two-floor, multi-brand fashion and accessories store which locates itself 'on the new luxury frontier'. As usual with a multi-brand merchant, the challenge lay in balancing opposites: the need to define and broadcast the brand as a dynamic, homogenous and omnipresent unit versus the necessary profusion of diverse labels and logos. As a solution, Claudio Pironi & Partners, in collaboration with architect Gianluca Dorio and Stefano Severi with Quadrastudio, created a boutique feel in a massive space, conceiving the store as a jewellery box that offers a tactile, multisensory, eclectic, emotional experience of shopping. The architects used a limited but bright palette of colour and materials – Carrara Gioia matte finish marble floor, walls in white wood Boiserie, white marble and punched metal in tons of white – and differentiated zones through the use of various finishes that range from synthetic to natural and smooth to rough. At the entrance, the luminous, transparent acrylic outline of a hemispherical cupola becomes 'an almost absent volume' that is nonetheless present enough to serve as both the structure of and storage for a luxury accessories station. Roses ornament the walls of the bridal boutique along with fabrics, marble and steel, while the men's lounge has been rendered in wood and situated on the ground floor next to fragrances.

Variety is expressed through finishes.
A lace-textured cylindrical partition is
echoed by a sleek marble cash desk.

A wireframe-like 'cupola' of transparent acrylic at the entrance contains a shoe and accessories display.

a tactile, multisensory, eclectic and emotional experience

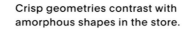

A copper accessories display with intricate detailing, showcases shoes and small purses.

To create a clear, consistent expression of the larger brand despite a profusion of small labels, limited colour and materials palettes are used.

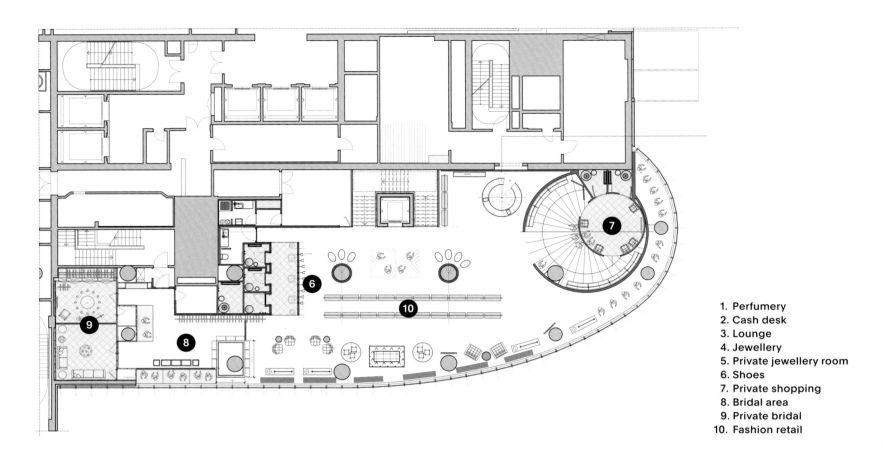

1. Perfumery
2. Cash desk
3. Lounge
4. Jewellery
5. Private jewellery room
6. Shoes
7. Private shopping
8. Bridal area
9. Private bridal
10. Fashion retail

GROUND FLOOR

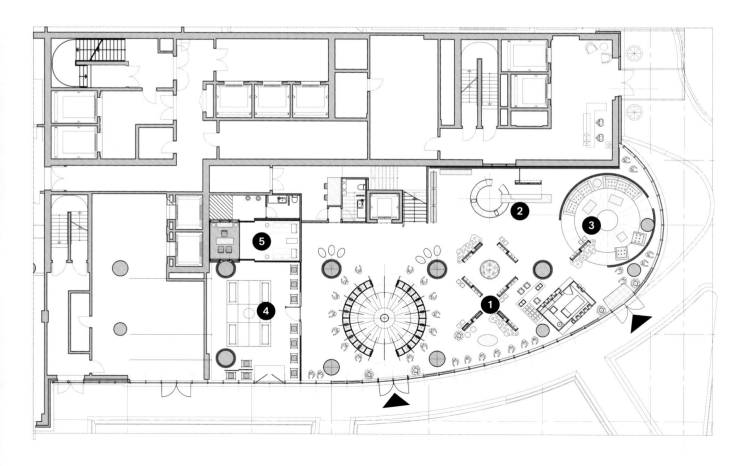

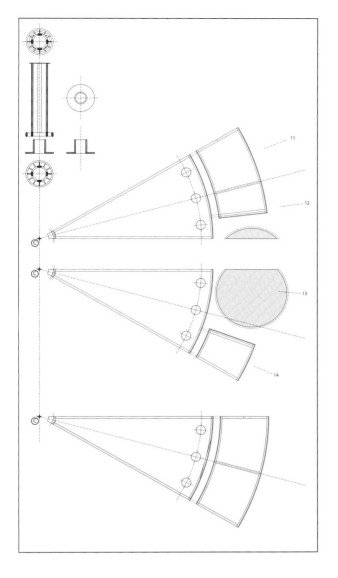

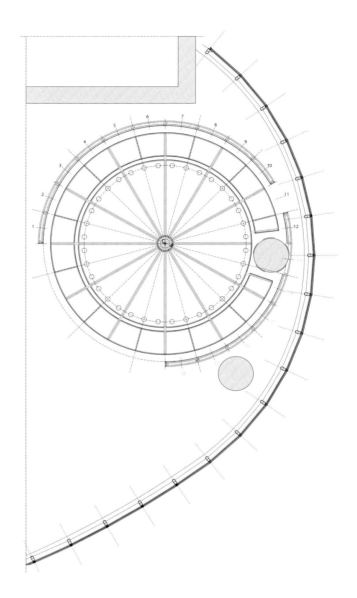

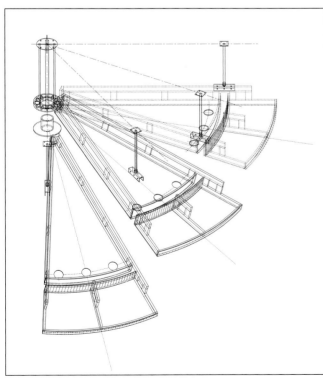

snarkitecture

Where	Los Angeles, United States
Opening	November 2015
Client	COS
Designer	Snarkitecture (p.415)
Floor space	465 m²
Shop constructor	1100 Loft
Photos	Noah Kalina

COS

The cut-outs of the garments in the steel displays underscore the architectural character of the clothes' construction.

Snarkitecture's second commission from minimalist ready-to-wear fashion label COS was a temporary retail space that showcased its A/W 2015 collection in a downtown Los Angeles design gallery. Inside, the designers played with reflections and monochromaticity. Guests enter an all-white room arrayed with an offset grid of bespoke displays made from bent powder-coated steel and concrete. Silhouettes of some of the collection's garments have been cut out of each sheet of metal, emphasising the robust, architectural forms of COS designs. At the centre of the room, a single display rack exhibits an additional selection of pieces in shades of white and grey. The interior is anchored around a 6 m tall wall, panelled with mirrors on both sides, bisecting the double-height space. The mirrored wall serves as a 'threshold' between the first all-white room and the second room, whose composition precisely mirrors that of the white room but is painted monolithically pale pink. The colour references the warm copper and rose tones of the current collection and, on this side of the mirror, the additional garments shown are hung in gradations of pink. The goal, the designers explained, was to create an unexpected world for visitors to experience, themselves, and then share with others.

This temporary COS shop showcased the A/W 2015 collection and featured silhouettes of some of the new pieces cut out of standing steel sheets.

Beyond a 6 m high wall sandwiched between mirrors, a second room painted entirely pink is a mirror reflection of the first.

an unexpected world was created for visitors to experience and to share with others

corneille uedingslohmann architekten

Where	Stuttgart, Germany
Opening	September 2014
Client	Sevens Görgens
Designer	Corneille Uedingslohmann Architekten (p.409)
Floor space	1332 m²
Shop constructor	Formlos Designstudio
Photos	Michael Neuhaus

elb

This multi-label fashion 'showroom' in the city's Gerber shopping centre mixes raw modern elements with vintage to create an airy, bright and laid-back environment. The interiors, which contain apparel that is a combination of premium fashion and contemporary design, are marked by natural materials and details. The designers were asked to create an open and warm environment and achieved this by bringing in light colours and materials like recycled wood, along with concrete blocks and raw black steel that generate a clean and 'progressive' vintage aesthetic. Long plinths of concrete block or salvaged wood stack up to form the cash till or to display garments while defining different zones. The Cologne-based design team decided to preserve the existing screed floor, but sanded and sealed it, enshrining the existing colour differences and visible cracks and thereby lending a sense of authenticity to the space. The generous retail floor is laid out in zones that are each bounded by a carpet and kitted out with pendant lamps and a highlight podium showcasing a single mannequin. Unique hand-picked objects also help to brighten and lighten the space, including white vintage bicycles, an oversized plastic cactus, carpets and printed cushions, vases and lamps.

Concrete blocks stack up to form a cash counter with crispness that balances out the relaxed warmth of the wooden walls and floors.

Woven wicker lamps hang over raised wooden platforms that display folded garments.

raw modern elements are mixed with vintage

The ceiling's glowing glass discs guide visitors through the multi-level shop.

studio david thulstrup

Where	Hangzhou, China
Opening	January 2012
Client	Elegant Prosper
Designer	Studio David Thulstrup (p.415)
Floor space	581 m²
Shop constructor	Shanghai Nanhai Construction
Photos	Peter Krasilnikoff

elegant prosper

Bespoke furnishings and mirror polished steel display
boxes glow beneath a ceiling illuminated through glass discs.

The interiors of the Elegant Prosper flagship in Hangzhou appear as if they have been fashioned from slices of puffy white clouds, giving visitors the sensation of being brightly enveloped in a space of air and light. The high-end Asian womenswear brand asked Danish architect David Thulstrup to imbue more than 500 of its retail spaces on the Chinese mainland with a more cosmopolitan and international character along with warm simplicity of Scandinavia. Elegant Prosper announces itself to the street with a radiant, classically adapted facade with large LED wall panels at the entrance. The store was given a completely new multi-floor plan and intelligent circulation, accompanied by bespoke furnishings and display fixtures, and a sumptuous material palette. This palette embraces bright materials for an elegant but contemporary finish: Italian white marble stucco, natural blonde wood with flooring and stairs crafted from raw concrete. Thulstrup's team tucked indirect lighting and recessed spotlights into ceiling pockets and grooves, but the most intriguing and significant light source takes on a diffused form, across the ceiling with suspended fields of luminous glass discs. Arranged on a tight grid, the overhead trail created by these glass discs help to guide shoppers deeper into the store and up onto the floors above.

Elegant Prosper

bespoke furnishings and display fixtures

The interiors surround shoppers with space, air and light.

Layout of the materials used to create a light and airy space.

Garment niches are alternated in some areas with textured white wall panels.

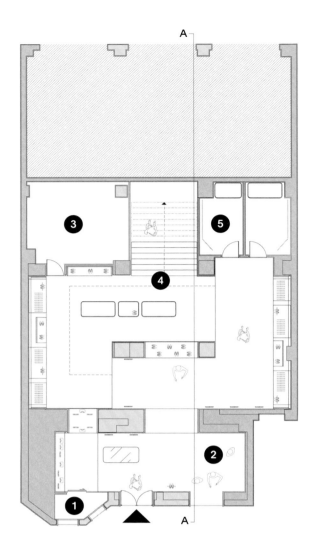

The building's arched Italianate facade
is a synthesis of the classical and the modern.

Rendered illustration to show the blend
of natural light wood and Italian white
marble complementing one another.

GROUND FLOOR

FIRST FLOOR

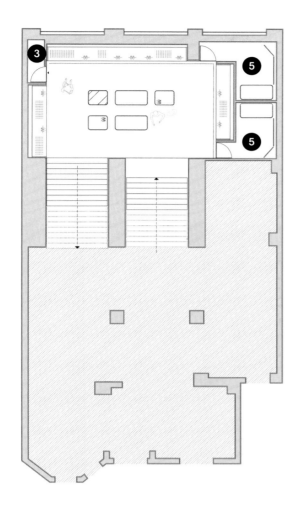

SECOND FLOOR

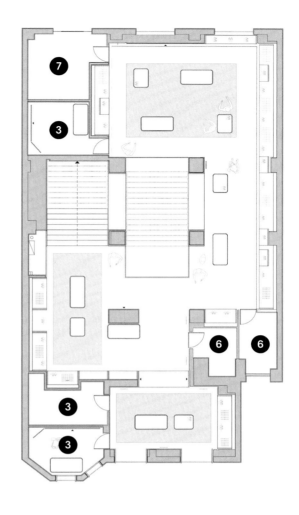

SECTION A-A

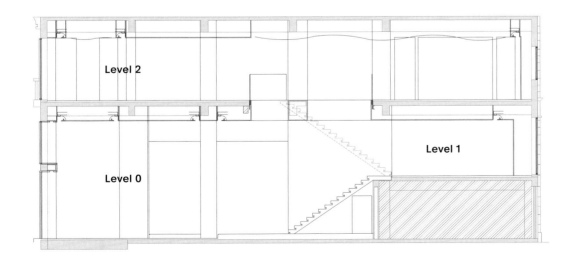

Level 2

Level 1

Level 0

1. Cash desk
2. Window display
3. Storage
4. Stairs
5. Fitting rooms
6. Restroom
7. Staff room

studiojosvandijk

Where	Amsterdam, the Netherlands
Opening	August 2015
Client	ETQ Amsterdam
Designer	studiojosvandijk (p.415)
Floor space	300 m²
Shop constructor	studiojosvandijk Construction Management
Photos	Katrien Franken

etq store

The lighting system is a network of fixtures designed to be controlled one-by-one.

Spartan, industrial, geometric, solid versus see-through, heavy versus light: as Jos van Dijk began to design this retail space for a mono-brand online shoe shop, his work helped them to expand into a high-end multi-brand retailer. In the former Roxy discotheque on the Singel Canal, Jos van Dijk relied on minimalism of, and truth to, both detail and material to create a synthesis between the building, the brand, the product and his design philosophy. In part, his challenge was to 'add by deleting', to get rid of all unnecessary details – not a single screw is to be seen in the entire store – and to develop a strong streamlined architectural identity for ETQ. Jos Van Dijk designed the lighting fixtures to be programmed and controlled individually to create precise lighting scenarios. The space features monumental volumes cast from concrete, including floor, stairs and walls, as well as massive white concrete furniture, some pieces of which weigh up to 2000 kg. The 30 cm thick anthracite concrete walls and ceilings had to be raised and the concrete stairway had to be moulded twice to achieve the optimal colour and texture. In fact, it required an emphatic reinforcement of the building's structure to prevent the ground floor from collapsing under either the concrete or cranes.

The design of this footwear shop is based on minimalism and attention to detail.

Minimalism is paired with heroic volumes of cast concrete – the stairs had to be moulded twice – craned into the building, which was reinforced for that purpose.

Beside the lightweight displays, some of the solid white concrete furnishings weigh up to 2000 kg.

Fashion

monumental volumes are cast from concrete

A grid of wall display components are visible almost only because they cast shadows across the wall.

The minimalistic materials and details complement each other in the design of the store.

GROUND FLOOR

1. Cash desk
2. Cage display
3. Seating and display
4. Fitting room
5. Wall sneaker grid
6. Storage
7. Office
8. Kitchen
9. Wall displays
10. Wall racks
11. Concrete display

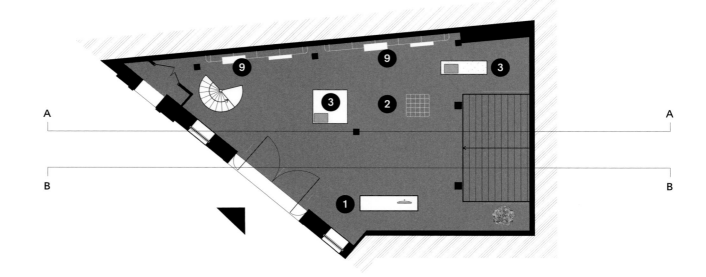

BASEMENT

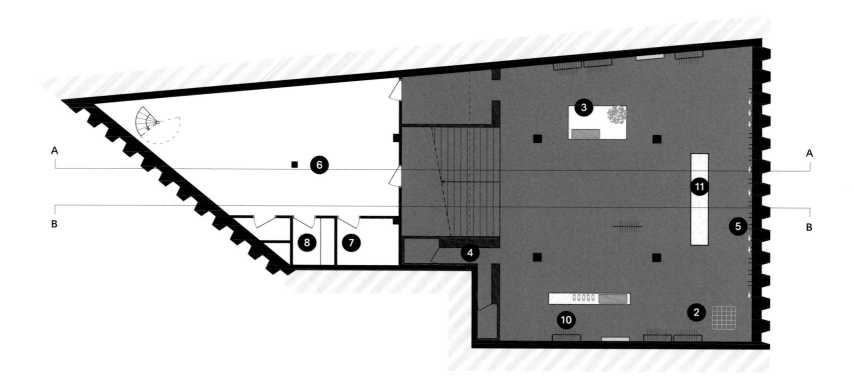

SECTION A-A

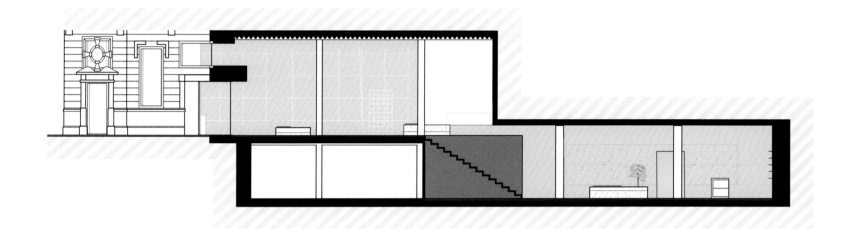

SECTION B-B

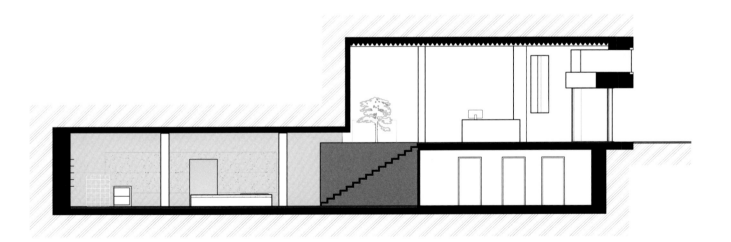

anagrama

Where   San Pedro Garza García, Mexico
Opening   May 2015
Client   Kindo
Designer   Anagrama (p.408)
Floor space   128 m²
Shop constructor   Artliplano
Photos   Estudio Tampiquito

kindo

The goal of the design was to make what might have been a dull shopping experience feel like play-time for children and their parents.

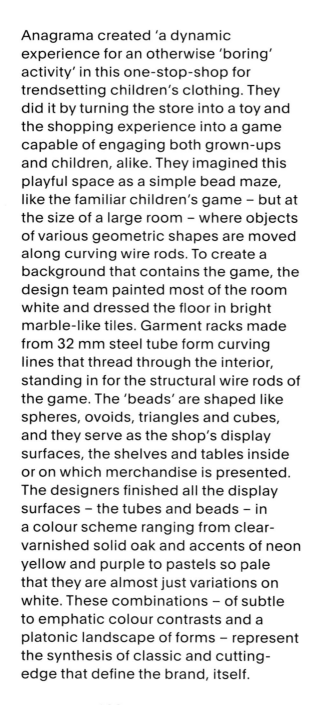

Anagrama created 'a dynamic experience for an otherwise 'boring' activity' in this one-stop-shop for trendsetting children's clothing. They did it by turning the store into a toy and the shopping experience into a game capable of engaging both grown-ups and children, alike. They imagined this playful space as a simple bead maze, like the familiar children's game – but at the size of a large room – where objects of various geometric shapes are moved along curving wire rods. To create a background that contains the game, the design team painted most of the room white and dressed the floor in bright marble-like tiles. Garment racks made from 32 mm steel tube form curving lines that thread through the interior, standing in for the structural wire rods of the game. The 'beads' are shaped like spheres, ovoids, triangles and cubes, and they serve as the shop's display surfaces, the shelves and tables inside or on which merchandise is presented. The designers finished all the display surfaces – the tubes and beads – in a colour scheme ranging from clear-varnished solid oak and accents of neon yellow and purple to pastels so pale that they are almost just variations on white. These combinations – of subtle to emphatic colour contrasts and a platonic landscape of forms – represent the synthesis of classic and cutting-edge that define the brand, itself.

The retro childrens game replica is a combination of wood pieces with painted pastel beads and neon tubes.

This kids' clothing shop is a scaled-up version of the iconic children's bead maze toy.

this playful space is a simple bead maze

Throughout this human scale bead maze, clothes and accessories are displayed on racks, shelves and tables in geometric forms.

FLOOR PLAN

1. Shoes
2. Accessories
3. Cash desk
4. Toy display
5. Fitting room
6. Restroom
7. Storage

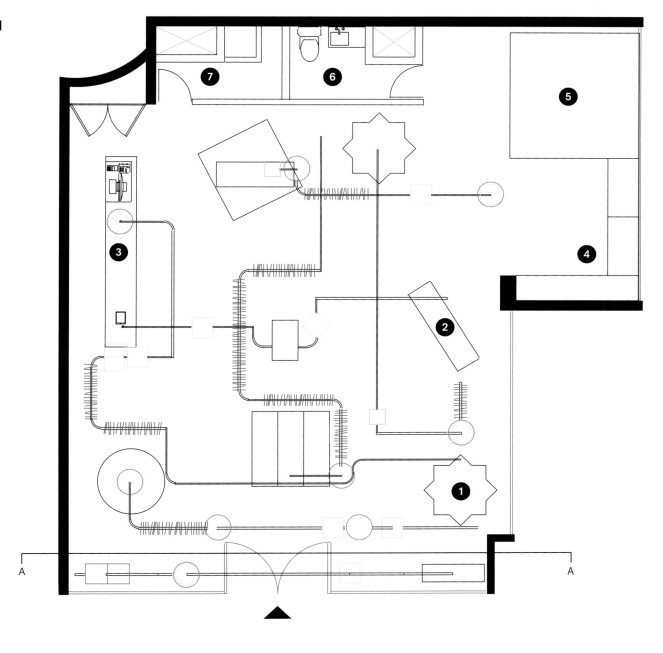

SECTION A-A

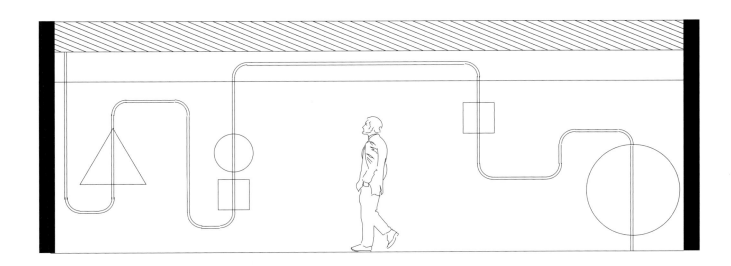

corneille uedingslohmann architekten

Where — Hagen, Germany
Opening — October 2014
Client — J.P. Görgens
Designer — Corneille Uedingslohmann Architekten (p.409)
Floor space — 1092 m²
Shop constructor — K. Storck
Photos — Michael Neuhaus

kult

For this multi-label clothing store at a shopping mall in land-locked Hagen, the designers looked to the beach to create a modern environment that is light and colourful. They embellished the interiors with maritime elements, including woven basket pendant lights, shutters, worn ladders and rope and, on entering, shoppers make their way past palm trees, blue skies and a vividly coloured two-story glass-brick wall. On the first floor, a large retail area is bisected by a wood-plank boardwalk into adjoining men's and women's areas and lined with fitting rooms that resemble a cheerful series of beach cabanas with varnished pastel doors. Mannequins and marquee products are showcased atop wooden highlight boxes while, overhead, the team exposed the concrete ceiling and services for a loftier look that is both organic and industrial. Against a background of grey sanded and sealed screed flooring and the exposed concrete ceilings, small product areas are buoyed up by various textures and materials, including varnished recycled wood boards, metro tiles and shipping crates that were used to create stand-alone furniture and display platforms. Along the walls, the designers installed white powder-coated steel, wooden boxes and ornamental cinder blocks. Even the cash desk – clad in sea-blue tiles and unfinished wood – emphasises the breezy contentedness of this fictional world.

A wooden boardwalk divides the large sales floor into men's and women's sections with cabana-like fitting rooms that broadcast a beachcomber spirit.

this light and colourful environment was inspired by the beach

A large floor-to-ceiling colourful glass brick wall welcomes shoppers into the store.

genesin studio

Where	Adelaide, Australia
Opening	January 2013
Client	Lax Fashion
Designer	Genesin Studio (p.411)
Floor space	200 m²
Shop constructor	Sean Clarke
Photos	Jonathan VDK

lax

A faceted wooden denim display showcases the label's most popular product.

Genesin Studio describe this fashion retail environment aptly, as a 'ply-on-ply saturated space that folds and twists around the ever-changing fashion world'. Because the label's focus is street clothing and lifestyle accessories, the designers were asked to avoid making the shop appear expensive or pretentious. The resulting space, 'saturated with a single material', is both understated and bold: its monolithic use of high-grade plywood humble and unconventional – a striking gesture – while also providing a simultaneously neutral, and uniform, canvas for the constantly rotating roster of garments. The creased geometric formation of the walls and ceiling was conceived as 'growing, collapsing, folding and twisting' from the storefront around a honed concrete floor, to the rear, where it morphs into a fitting room and denim display. Even the bespoke displays are made from plywood and fitted with casters to make them mobile and to make the visual merchandising highly adaptable. The services and other equipment like air, speakers and lighting are hidden inside the joinery but also articulated in the tectonic structure of the ceiling. Even the fitting rooms feature invisible tapered door pulls. As much as the team's drawing capabilities, Genesin Studio's creative use of 3D surfaces stretched the skills of the tradesmen who built the shop and who began by string-lining the ceiling and then building the walls up to meet it.

The irregular plywood box of the shop becomes a focal point for mall shoppers.

the space folds and twists around the ever-changing fashion world

The custom shelving and table displays are set on wheels for versatility of merchandising.

burdifilek

Where	Quebec, Canada
Opening	October 2015
Client	Mackage
Designer	Burdifilek (p.408)
Floor space	185 m²
Shop constructor	Axxys Construction Group
Photos	Ben Rahn

mackage flagship

The simplified layout is anchored with strong visuals and warm sheltering materials and colours to define a distinct zone for each collection.

Mackage's original success with outwear was the product of life in chillier climates, and it has been parlayed into a lifestyle label that is refined, sexy and modern. For the flagship interiors, Burdifilek was inspired by the urban sensibility of the modern ski chalet. To translate this scheme into the space, materials such as Oak are used in bare but warm surfaces to express a cosy, textural and comforting tone. The design emphasises on shelter while embracing a simplified layout that feels airy and free, bringing the skied aplhine landscape indoors. To echo the label's creative process and detailing, every object in the store is bespoke. Some furnishings make reference to snow, ice and wintry nature: some in abstractions, including an irregularly faceted white marble cash desk that resembles an iceberg and others in more literal ways, like a wall-size backlit photograph capturing a view over the top of the Rocky Mountains, glowing behind a row of garment racks. The affect is one of purity, comfort, quality craftsmanship and made-to-measure detailing. In refining the image of the chalet, the design team has also provided a sanctuary, if not from the elements, at least from the typical visually cluttered shopping experiences around it.

The flagship makes references to the celebration of colder climates like this backlit wall mural overlooking the Rocky Mountains.

highly textural materials and comforting tones emphasise the feeling of shelter

Subtle references to cold climates are also abstracted in furnishings like the cash desk, which looks like ice.

Where	London, United Kingdom
Opening	April 2015
Client	Max Mara Fashion Group
Designer	Duccio Grassi Architects (p.410)
Floor space	900 m²
Shop constructor	Fiera Contract
Photos	Jamie McGregor Smith

max mara

This luxury boutique – which expands the brand's flagship London store – 'looks like a real place to live, not a built scenography,' says the Milan-based architect who designed it. On the outside, Duccio Grassi's team redesigned the facade, adding the first floor while, inside, they took advantage of a gently ascending staircase that spirals sculpturally between floors (the proper term is 'helicoidal'), visually linking various levels and rooms. The staircase – elegantly sober, modern but expressive – is 'the explanation of the journey inside the shop' and of the brand persona, Grassi explains. The three-floor shop has been rendered in grey honed stone and acid-etched iron, Paulownia wood and smoked oak, black marble and concrete, light linen in subdued hues and brass, which brightly frames garment racks but, around the fitting rooms, has been finished with a 'stone effect'. These make the space one of high contrast and allows each floor to assume its own character: the feel is intimate, wide windows pour light over the street level oak flooring in Hungarian herringbone and Castelnovo patterns, while the floor above it wraps around a flat roof garden, bringing light and views of vivaciously green plantings. Dotted throughout with intimate and variegated vignettes of furniture, the shop offers living room-like respite for weary shoppers.

Floor-to-ceiling polished brass display elements frame garments sculpturally and contrast with highly textural stone walls, floor and columns.

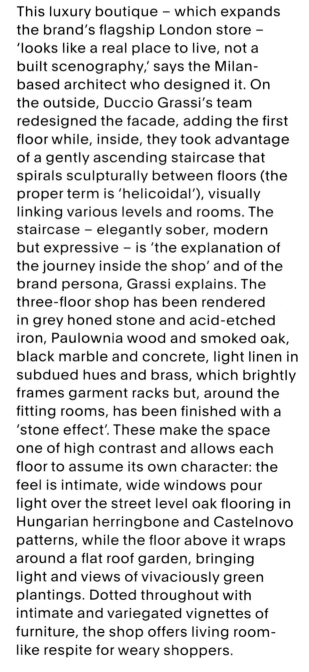

Smoked oak is laid out in a Hungarian herringbone pattern.

Opposites frame each other: clear acrylic handbag shelves are framed by polished brass atop a wooden credenza.

a seamless ambience merges the inside and outside in an elegant ensemble

Many seating areas with various furnishings add to the high-contrast space.

The fitting rooms are faced with stone-finished brass walls and fronted with a sofa and tables in a salon-like setting.

Furry carpet defines another living room-like area, looking onto floor-to-ceiling windows and a roof garden that filters light into the first floor along with greenery.

Duccio Grassi Architects

mark't

Where	Amsterdam, the Netherlands
Opening	June 2014
Client	Men at Work
Designer	Mark't (p.413)
Floor space	450 m²
Shop constructors	Brandwacht & Meijer and Store3D
Photos	Ewout Huibers

men at work

The cash desk is playful and fun.

Fun is the word for this playful basement boutique. Against a bright white background, contrasts, custom furnishings, bold graphics and typography and doses of primary colours dominate along with neon signs that recall the 1980s and allude to the city's famous Red Light District. A neon sign above the denim department, for instance, reads: Blue Light District, while another over the men's shirt racks reads 'Girls Girls Girls'. A high podium that brings mannequins' heads to just below the ceiling, is actually an old illuminated cinema marquee on which messages can be easily changed. Mark Theeuwes co-opted the basement's industrial features, including a structural ceiling and columns, and installed garment racks made of pipe and heavy construction lighting overhead to match. The men's area is distinguished by distressed green surfaces and steel while women have a vividly coloured fitting room lounge and soft surfaces – emerald sofa and drapes, lemon yellow chairs, red polka dots, a Berber boucherouite rug. The omnipresent white surfaces underneath it all, which feel loft-like, help to set off the designer's measured use of colour, making the furnishings – custom-made by Brandwacht & Meijer (with choice vintage props and other pieces) – stand out like works of Pop Art. The white fuses all the elements together, making it, as Theeuwes has exuberantly said, 'a white fresh crispy fun big boutique.'

The white-surfaced boutique features neon signs like that over the denim area.

Neon vintage pieces are complemented by architectural features like box green construction lights.

The gorilla is a vintage prop while the garment racks were made with pipes to suit the basement's original industrial character.

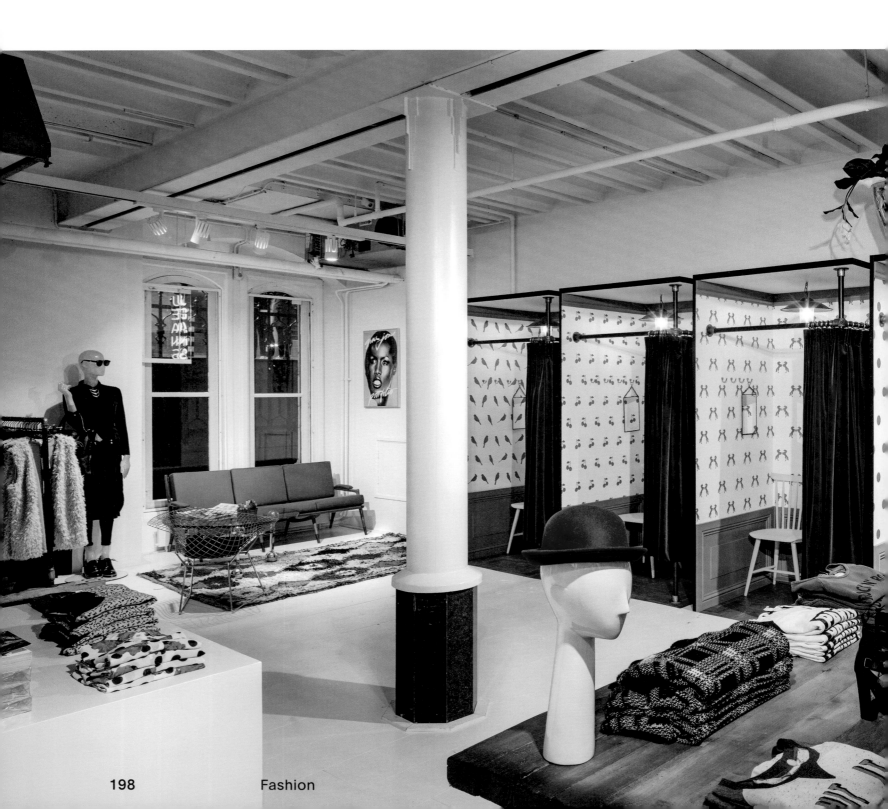

Theeuwes made a display podium from an old cinema marquee, another of the carefully vetted vintage props.

CONGRATS ON YOUR FACE

I WANT TO HAVE TEXT WITH YOU

fun is the word for this playful basement boutique

The women's fitting rooms and lounge are defined by colour and soft materials.

A forest stands over the accessories and under a light fixture made of gold party tinsel.

monki store concept

Where	Stockholm, Sweden
Opening	November 2015
Client	Monki
Designer	Monki Store Concept (p.413)
Floor space	560 m²
Shop constructor	H&M Construction
Photos	Fredrik Sweger

monki

Vertical slices of mirror panel the wall beside the candy-coloured Rainbow Staircase.

The founders of this exuberantly eclectic clothing label describe it as 'a storytelling brand'. Indeed, Monki stores are stories: they knit together imagination and mystery, 'spatial confusion' and the surreal to offer whimsical experiences to its young 'snap-happy' female customers. The Kungsgatan store contains as many fictional Monki World destinations as possible, each represented in the ten storefront vitrines: a field of turning Turbine Flowers, a Rainbow Staircase above which jellyfish float and a 'disco-sparkly' Crystal Cave with a golden floor located in the Ruby Mountains under a ceiling dressed in bubbles that confound the room's dimensions with an infinity of reflections. The Onion City in the Clouds is a shoe destination where footwear hovers atop spaceships instead of shelves whilst accessories shelter in a forest of gnarled trees beneath a chandelier made of gold party tinsel. Fitting rooms stand amidst the Forgotten Forest where shoppers can view clothes from all angles and lose themselves in more reflected reflections. There is a wide diversity of imaginary places, materials and finishes within the space. Details and furnishings – ranging from Tom Dixon mirror ball pendants and the Form Us With Love Ogle lamp to walls, stairs and furniture designed by the Monki team – make it a shop where customers discover more than just new fashions.

footwear hovers atop spaceships instead of shelves

Shirts are displayed on a miniature carousel in Monki's Stockholm store.

Fashion

The eclecticism of materials, finishes and furnishings makes it a shop that can be explored over many visits.

The Crystal Cave features a mirrored bubble-clad ceiling with reflections that make the space feel simultaneously expansive and intimate.

Monki

claudio pironi & partners

Where	Dalian, China
Opening	February 2015
Client	Linxiang Group
Designer	Claudio Pironi & Partners (p.409)
Floor space	220 m²
Shop constructor	Winner Group
Photos	Alen Dong

philipp plein dalian

The grandest grandeur: behind a strikingly illuminated retail facade clad with black glass hexagons that looms 21 m above ground, Philipp Plein Dalian shop appears almost diaphanous. Claudio Pironi & Partners, with the participation of architect Gianluca Dorio, created a space where soft translucence meets hard transparency and obsidian blackness throughout. Even the signature Philipp Plein Swarovski crystal skull is rendered in black, encased in a large extra-clear hexagonal glass case in the form of a column and placed to divide the ground floor retail into symmetrical halves. To enter the shop from the adjacent mall, shoppers pass through a black marble 'portal' garnished with lateral light-boxes. The shop floors and walls are clad in black and white marble and the so-called precious furniture and display shelving, which are made in glass, polished stainless steel, waxed iron and Carrara Gioia white marble with a matte finish. The two-floor, 220 m² store is accessorised with these signature details, along with geometric displays and hexagonal folding tables, while a grandiloquent staircase is set in smoked mirror. Pinpoint spots in the ceiling are composed into a constellation of stars. On the first floor, the space is dressed in white arabesque marble, polished stainless steel and mirrored displays. This floor features a lounge furnished with hexagonal chairs upholstered in black crocodile leather beneath the signature handcrafted Murano clear-crystal chandelier.

The huge Swarovski crystal skull watching over every Philipp Plein shop is rendered in a sultry black in the Dalian shop and divides the street-level floor in two.

The signature handmade Murano crystal chandelier conforms to the brand's template for its international retail interior design.

a space where soft translucence meets hard transparency

This boutique sits behind a monumental 21-m-facade made of black glass hex tiles and an illuminated logo.

Claudio Pironi & Partners   Philipp Plein Dalian

claudio pironi & partners

Where	Dubai, United Arab Emirates
Opening	September 2015
Client	Bugatti Group
Designer	Claudio Pironi & Partners (p.409)
Floor space	180 m²
Shop constructor	MonkeyDu
Photos	Loe Russel

philipp plein dubai

'Glittering in the Mall of the Emirates,' this Philipp Plein shop is an embellishment on the Plein retail template, a concept that finds itself at home in Dubai. Claudio Pironi & Partners describes fashion houses as 'temples of the new order' and the interior design as scenography. For this shop Claudio Pironi, with the participation of Stefano Severi with Quadrastudio, broadcasted the brand's characteristic flash by using sharp, hard glittering surfaces and frames, recalling diamonds and their settings: the boutique boasts Philipp Plein's signature oversize Swarovski crystal skull, a handcrafted Murano crystal chandelier, black and white marble floors and walls and furniture in polished stainless steel, waxed iron and glass, Arabescato white marble and leather. The shop is a glossy theatre of display furnishings in the form of framed boxes repeated over and over again, a design by Claudio Pironi called the 'Box in the Box' that has a cross-frame structure developed with the technology department of MonkeyDu. The women's section wears white marble, stainless steel and clear mirror. The men's has been tailored in black marble, burnished iron and smoked mirror, but greeting children in front of the Kids' section is a kid-size faceted golden teddy bear. To show off accessories, Claudio Pironi sought 'a perfect material and formal symmetry' where silver metals are replaced with the gold of brass detailing.

A huge Swarovski crystal skull and hand blown Murano chandelier anchor the interior template for Philipp Plein shops around the world.

fashion houses are 'temples of the new order'

Colours, materials and hexagons are repeated with great
consistency throughout from floor tiles to partitions and boxy
display shelves.

Claudio Pironi & Partners

Philipp Plein Dubai

dittel architekten (DIA)

Where	Stuttgart, Germany
Opening	September 2015
Client	Das Gerber
Designer	Dittel Architekten (DIA) (p.410)
Floor space	9 m²
Shop constructor	Heikaus Interior
Photos	Martin Baitinger

pop up box

An integrated lifting system lets the owner move three of the four modules anywhere desired.

It's been a while since we've heard 'form follows function', but this is a fair description of the clever system behind this expandable fashion boutique. The first Pop up Box popped up as a convertible mobile retail space that offers retailers and exhibitors a customisable, self-contained presentation area. The cube reanimates empty areas of the shopping centre without interrupting its look and feel, accommodates a wide array of display needs, and conforms to any brand identity through a changeable material palette. To enable the Box to pop up, the architects used an integrated lifting system that allows retailers to open, move and arrange three of the four modules anywhere they like. This creates a wheelchair-accessible retail floor of about 20 to 30 m² out of a box that compacts down to only 9 m² when closed. The modules into which the cube breaks offer a flexible shop-fitting system inside, enabling display fixtures to be attached where and when needed to create shelves, drawers, hangers and tabletop surfaces. After business hours, the branded perforated metal panels in the walls allow glimpses inside and exterior monitors continue to broadcast brand content. The shop is powered through floor boxes and relies on integrated batteries that are charged overnight, creating enough energy to power the ceiling spotlights and product illumination throughout the day.

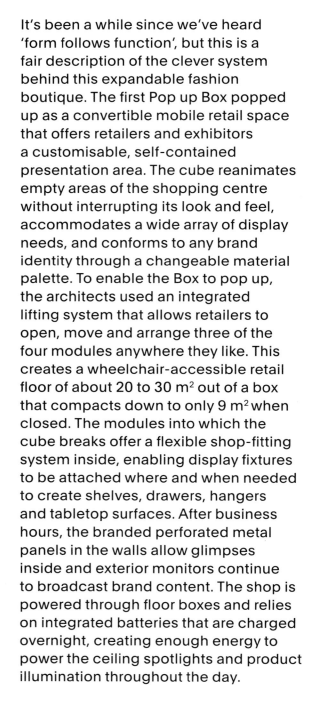

there's a clever system behind this

This little boutique has no door; after hours, the modules of the boutique box close together like puzzle pieces.

Versatile modules can be reconfigured into shelving, tabletops, hanging display or drawers.

Perforated metal panels offer glimpses inside and exterior monitors offer insight into the brand while the shop is shuttered.

When open, the 9 m² box becomes a wheelchair accessible 30 m² retail floor.

SECTION

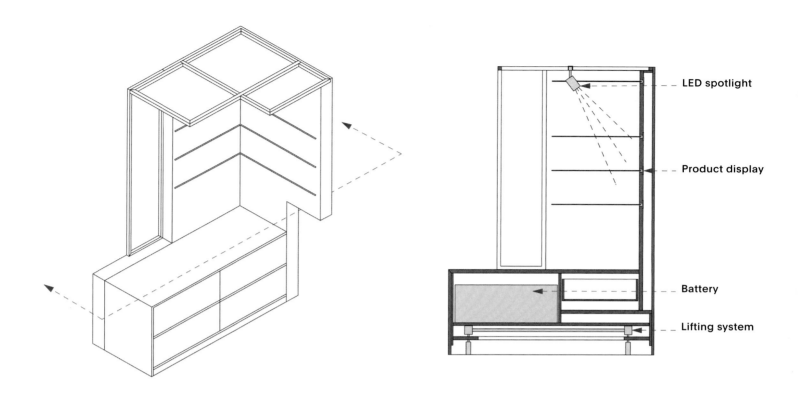

LED spotlight

Product display

Battery

Lifting system

EXPLODED AXONOMETRIC

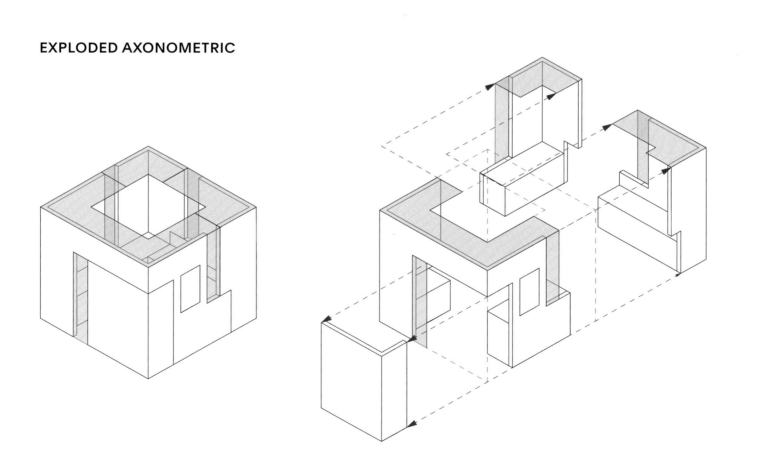

dalziel & pow

Where	Madrid, Spain
Opening	October 2015
Client	Primark
Designer	Dalziel & Pow (p.409)
Floor space	12,300 m²
Shop constructor	ICA
Photos	Dalziel & Pow

primark

The octagonal atrium features a 360-degree 'cinema experience' with eleven transparent LED screens through which product and architecture are still visible.

Credits for this clothing retail project include lists of artists as much as architects. Design consultancy Dalziel & Pow preserved a Grade II listed Madrid building, reconnecting rooms that had been divided and cut off from each other, and restoring it via traditional methods and materials – horsehair plaster and allusions to Moorish patterns and tiling. Meanwhile, they united digital design with bespoke art commissions to construct a wholly contemporary 'urban sanctuary' where visitors can find inspiration and shop the latest trends. Enlisting the help of O'Shea & Moro, Dalziel & Pow employed some of the city's talented artists to make the store eclectic, expressive and local. The voluminous, light-saturated, four-floor, octagonal atrium features a glass roof, original ironwork and mouldings. Here, a 360-degree cinematic experience flows across eleven massive, transparent LED screens programmed with bespoke audio and visuals – from fantasy forest to catwalk scenes. By embedding the content strategically within the architecture, the digital content appears to be happening live in store – for example kids peeking around the columns and fashion models walking around the floors. The technology is engaging, unexpected and truly appropriate. This is retail theatre at its best.

digital design and bespoke commissions are combined

The beautiful, storied structure houses five floors of fashion and features 131 cash desks, 15 escalators, 91 fitting rooms and 300 mannequins.

From street art to an installation of coloured paper origami, Dalziel & Pow brought elements of surprise throughout the store, inspired by the breadth and creativity of Madrid.

pablo rodriguez

Where	Berlin, Germany
Opening	November 2015
Client	Puma
Designer	Pablo Rodriguez (p.414)
Floor space	420 m²
Shop constructors	Demolhuber, G4 Architects, F&S, Teamwork and Studio 38
Photos	Adriano A. Biondo

puma flagship

The *Forever Faster* graphics mix illustration, inspirational texts and celebrity imagery.

This flagship design for footwear and athletic apparel giant Puma, narrates stories using Puma products instead of props and encourages the customer's strong engagement and interaction with products on show. The retail space contains a great deal of Puma collections, but is an expression of energetic simplicity: in 420 m², Pablo Rodriguez brought two retail lines together. They kept the concepts, directions and identities of *Forever Faster* and Select (Puma's collaborations with outside designers) distinct, identifying the former through its black stained pine plywood surfaces and the latter through its white oriented strand board. Materials, forms and colours had to fit the brand closely, but the lighting design and technology became crucial to cultivating the right mood. To introduce the *Suede Sole* shoe pattern the designer used laser cut steel plates in this pattern on the staircase and a wall unit system. He relied on merchandising set-ups on the stair landing and a Flip Dot sign to increase foot traffic between the ground and first floors. The interior concept demonstrates to the customer that Puma is a serious sports brand with a storied past that can be recounted by some of the fastest products and athletes in the world. This history is celebrated in a 'DNA Wall' that depicts athletes who have collaborated with Puma in the past and present. Puma Global Retail Environment team, Ermanno Modonessi, Oudry Aldana and Yannick Torfs, worked together in the Berlin concept execution with Pablo Rodriguez.

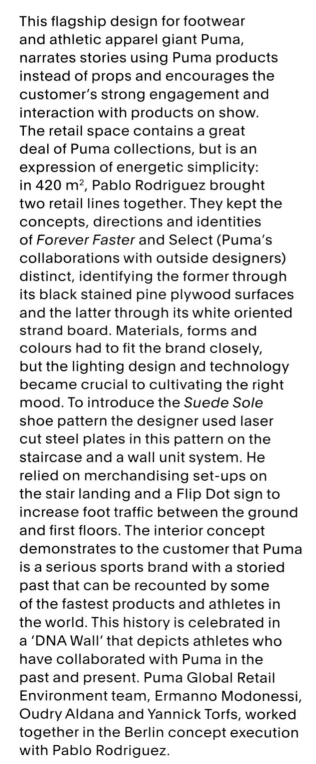

A separate area showcases the Puma Select envionment within the *Forever Faster* concept.

The retail space features products from Puma's collaborations with unique assorted design houses and street fashion designers.

Carefully considered LED lighting creates the right ambience throughout the store.

the retail space is an expression of energetic simplicity

FIRST FLOOR

1. Cash desk
2. Storage
3. Fitting room
4. Window wall unit
5. Emergency exit
6. Running area
7. Women's restroom
8. Male restroom

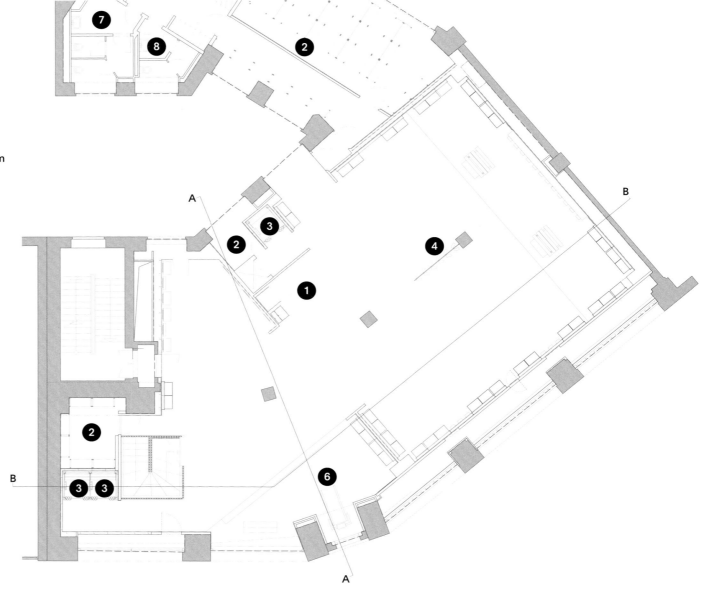

GROUND FLOOR

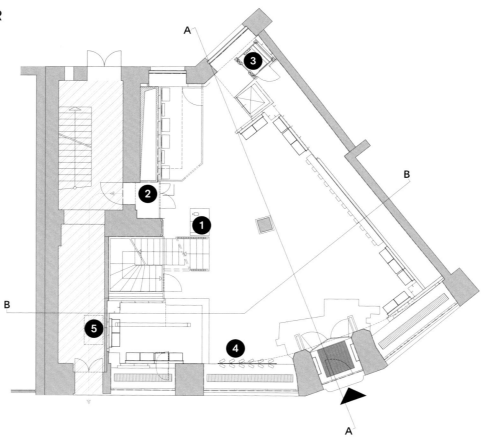

SECTION A-A

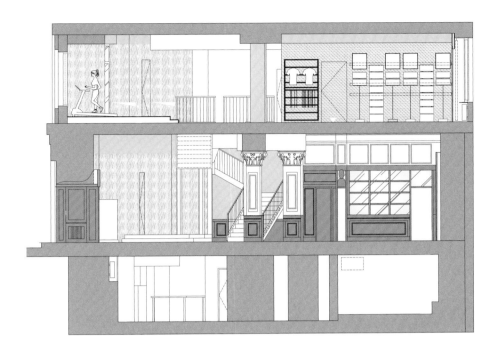

SECTION B-B

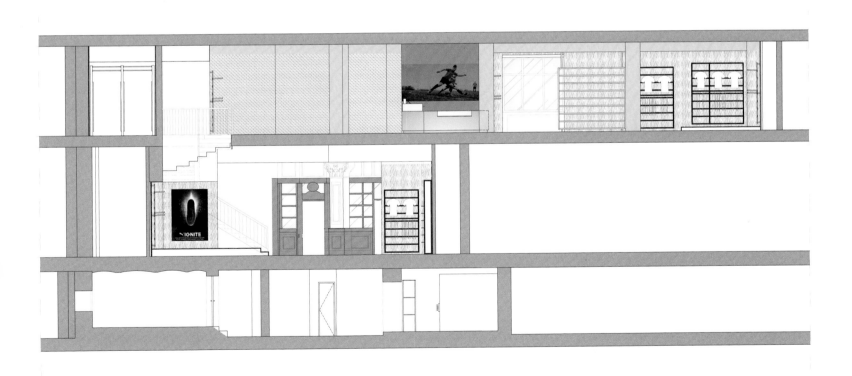

Pablo Rodriguez   Puma Flagship

brinkworth and wilson brothers

Where	Johannesburg, South Africa
Opening	August 2014
Client	Puma South Africa
Designers	Brinkworth (p.408) and Wilson Brothers (p.416)
Floor space	195 m²
Shop constructor	Designamite
Photos	David Ross

puma select

To showcase athletic apparel brand Puma's luxury product range, Brinkworth and the Wilson Brothers eschewed the use of luxe materials in order to focus on 'honest' materials that would put the product in the foreground. The designers, who believe that todays' retail space must be flexible, created a modular concept that is versatile, scalable, precise and pared-down, while using its construction as an ornamental pattern. It's smooth but explicitly structural and carpentry look also gives a nod to Britain's craft traditions. The designers elevated that familiar and modest material, pegboard, by digitally engineering it in spruce plywood to create a 'tool kit' of modular elements. This Puma pegboard features square perforations set wide apart and rendered in a two-tone chevron pattern. These panels serve as perimeter walls, interior walls cum partitions and as louver displays – in the 'Sneaker Peek' section – that can fold down perpendicular to the wall to form a small shoe shelf or fold up flush with the rest of the panel to rejoin the pegboard system. The rest of the display surfaces repeat this material palette and structural detail over and over again – even fitting room curtains are printed with the same pattern of two-tone chevrons and dark squares. Powder-coated inspection lamps (typical on construction sites) slot into the pegboard to reinforce the shop's workshop spirit and to provide colour.

Panels inspired by pegboard are used as merchandising walls and interior partitions with fold-down sections that double as footwear displays.

The pegboard pattern is repeated everywhere from the walls to the pattern on fitting room curtains.

To show off a luxury product range, the designers decided not to use luxury materials.

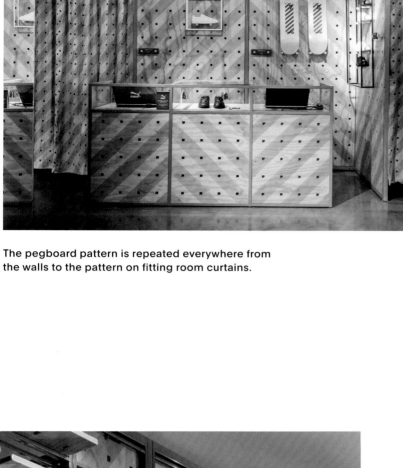

the smooth but explicitly structural look gives a nod to britain's craft traditions

UXUS

Where	Doha, Qatar
Opening	February 2013
Client	Qatar Luxury Group
Designer	UXUS (p.416)
Floor space	785 m²
Shop constructor	Lead Construction
Photos	Adrian Haddad

qela

UXUS enmeshed this plush emporium in fine art, design and handcraft, interleaving the characteristics of a world-class art gallery with a couture salon 'to redefine luxury as a cultural experience'. The creative team at UXUS borrowed the undulating forms and fluid curves of Qatar's 'calm, pure' arid landscapes and rendered them in a colour scheme dominated by desert tones and luxe materials – bronze, solid walnut, travertine and nero d'avola stone slabs, bespoke hand-knotted silk rugs and satin and linen drapery. The designers also blended traditional hand-carving with state-of-the-art manufacturing techniques to create elaborate detailing and, with a bow to the brand's Arabic roots, generated a *moucharabieh* pattern assembled from parts of the Qela logo. The facade of the store is made from this pattern, as well as stand-alone bronze screens, which mark curated product areas throughout the store and take their form from an abstraction of *dhow* sails. Overhead, a 'celestial vault' or wooden cupola has also been elaborately hand-carved with the *moucharabieh* pattern and eight-pointed stars. Precision-engineered freestanding cylindrical vitrines give a theatrically staged 360-degree view of collections upstairs. By displaying products on solid wood and stone plinths the designers put nothing but air between consumer and product, making the shopping experience feel more intimate.

The luxury space synthesises art gallery and couture salon.

Arabian allusions like the carved cupola caps the atrium with spotlights resembling stars around it.

The couture jewellery can be viewed in 180 degrees through cylindrical vitrines.

Under a tinted globe chandelier, a living room-like setting allows shoppers to rest both feet and eyes.

Upstairs, layers of drapery, classically polished stone floors and columns of glass create a materially sumptuous environment.

there is nothing but air between the consumer and product

Hardwood plinths are used
to display products.

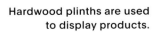

Abstract imagery to glossy surfaces and curiosity-inducing jewel box wall displays describe luxury.

GROUND FLOOR

1. Gallery
2. Office
3. Storage
4. Plant room
5. Control room
6. Fire place
7. Seating area
8. Restroom
9. Fitting room
10. Private salon
11. Atelier
12. Kitchen
13. Janitor room
14. Vestibule

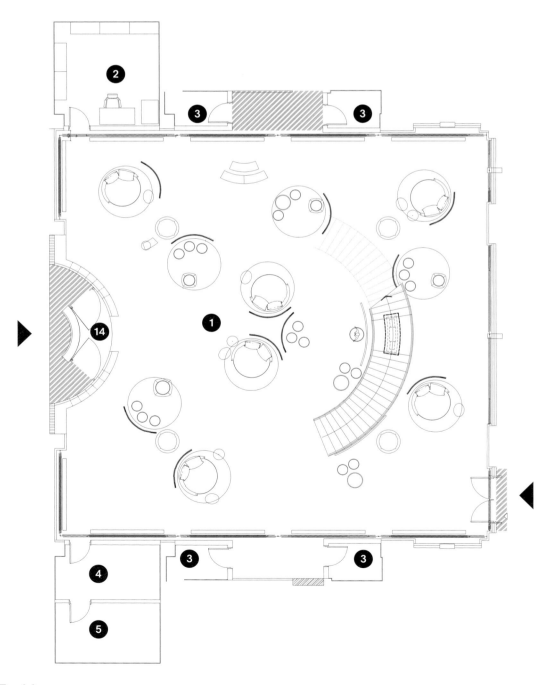

ELEVATION

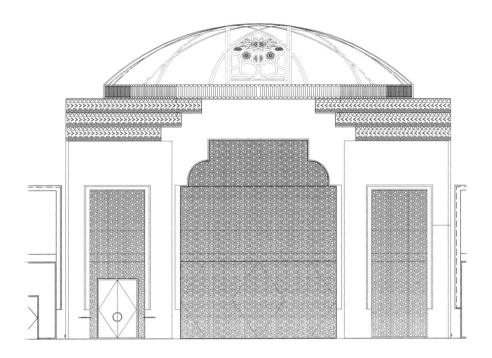

FIRST FLOOR

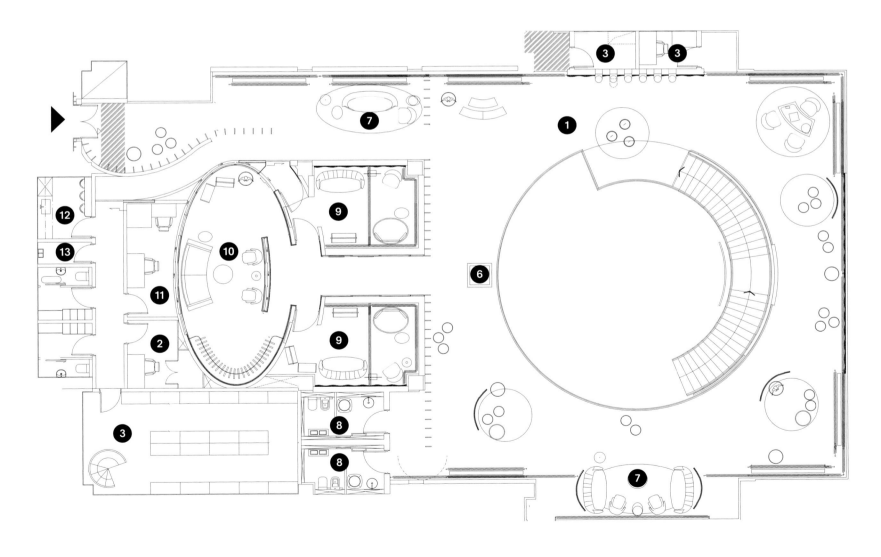

clemens bachmann architekten

Where	Munich, Germany
Opening	January 2014
Client	Kauai Textilvertriebs
Designer	Clemens Bachmann Architekten (p.409)
Floor space	1300 m²
Shop constructor	R+Z Schreiner Meister
Photos	Bernd Ducke

quiksilver, roxy and dc shoes

Clemens Bachmann Architekten took inspiration from the industrial heritage of the building it's in to create this footwear showroom for three brands. They stripped down two of the four walls so that the scale, the light from the north-facing roof, the trussed ceiling structure and the industrial character were well and truly revealed. Then they complemented these with maritime pine floors and walls that will be burnished, appropriately enough, by foot traffic. To suit the identities of the brands and the vintage spirit of their existing stores, the designers added only simple, subtle materials like pine, which becomes a natural canvas for the colourful clothes and shoes on show. In order to accommodate special events like fashion shows or skating days, the only interior volume that was installed permanently is the office area, which surveys the showroom floor and is partitioned into rooms by freestanding, ceiling-high, black MDF walls that will accommodate new hires and staff changes, as needed. One meeting 'box' for staff meetings or customer presentations was installed, house-like, perched on stilts. The kitchen at the centre of the room can either be closed by tracked curtains made from truck tarpaulins (with a transparent strip sewn in at eye-level so that customers are never neglected) or kept open and used as a secondary meeting space.

The vintage industrial feeling of the existing interior was augmented with fresh maritime pine on the walls, stairs and floors.

Products are displayed on stand-alone tables, shelves and racks in the middle of the warehouse-like space.

Two steps up from the showroom floor, the offices' windows maintain a connection between staff and customers at all times.

Most structures inside are not permanent, which maintains the versatility of the space.

subtle materials like pine, becomes a natural canvas for the colourful clothes and shoes

A central kitchen can be closed off by truck tarpaulin curtains or left open to serve as another meeting area.

Clemens Bachmann Architekten   Quiksilver, Roxy and DC Shoes

FLOOR PLAN

1. Offices
2. Restroom
3. Meeting room
4. Showroom
5. Kitchen
6. Storage

SECTION A-A

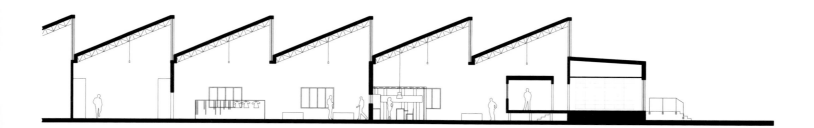

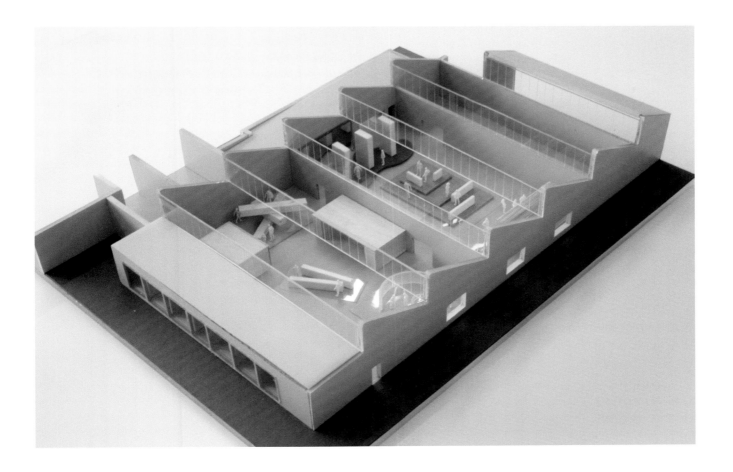

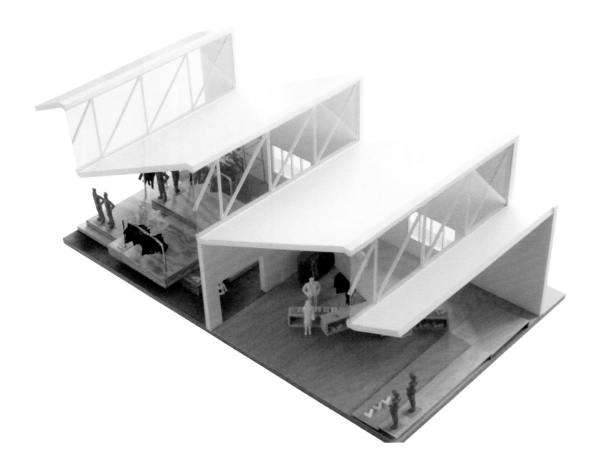

Clemens Bachmann Architekten   Quiksilver, Roxy and DC Shoes

qwstion studio

Where   Zurich, Switzerland
Opening   June 2015
Client   Qwstion contemporary backpacks
Designer   Qwstion Studio (p.414)
Floor space   320 m²
Shop constructors   Qwstion Design Team and Daniel Gafner
Photos   Nico Schärer

qwstion invites

Qwstion Invites, co-founded by creative director Christian Paul Kaegi, is a flagship store for a Swiss backpacks and bags brand that sells furniture, fashion and eyewear by like-minded designers. In an increasingly virtual world, Kaegi wanted the space to serve as an analogue celebration of simplicity in design. The interior is influenced by minimalist American artist Donald Judd, who approaches every object as a functional sculpture. Kaegi respected empty space, preserved the generous windows and original aluminium frames and used a limited but diverse range of basic industrial materials including wood, gypsum panels and aluminium tubes combined with mirrors and glass. He poured a concrete floor and painted the concrete ceiling white, designed large, bespoke light fixtures and constructed modular walls made from perforated and expanded sheet steel. These sheer walls double task as display surfaces and porous partitions between the retail floor and development department and archives, which are also tucked into the shop's 320 m² and remain visible to shoppers browsing the retail floor. Kaegi fashioned display surfaces from construction wood, anodised aluminium, mirrors, Autopole extendable columns and cage fixtures by Italian manufacturer ALU. The designer slathered one wall floor-to-ceiling with a black and white photographic mural of a tiled wall, creating a minimalist but highly textured trompe l'oeil.

The shop represents the brand values of questioning convention and melding functionality gracefully with form.

A chunky wood block floor serves as the storefront display while perforated expanded sheet metal and custom hooks provide bag display.

The bags are sold alongside work by other labels to let shoppers experience contemporary design over a range of goods.

Fashion

the space serves as an analogue celebration of simplicity

A mirrored credenza, metal mesh and crisply orthogonal tables front a trompe l'oeil photo mural, confusing the perspective.

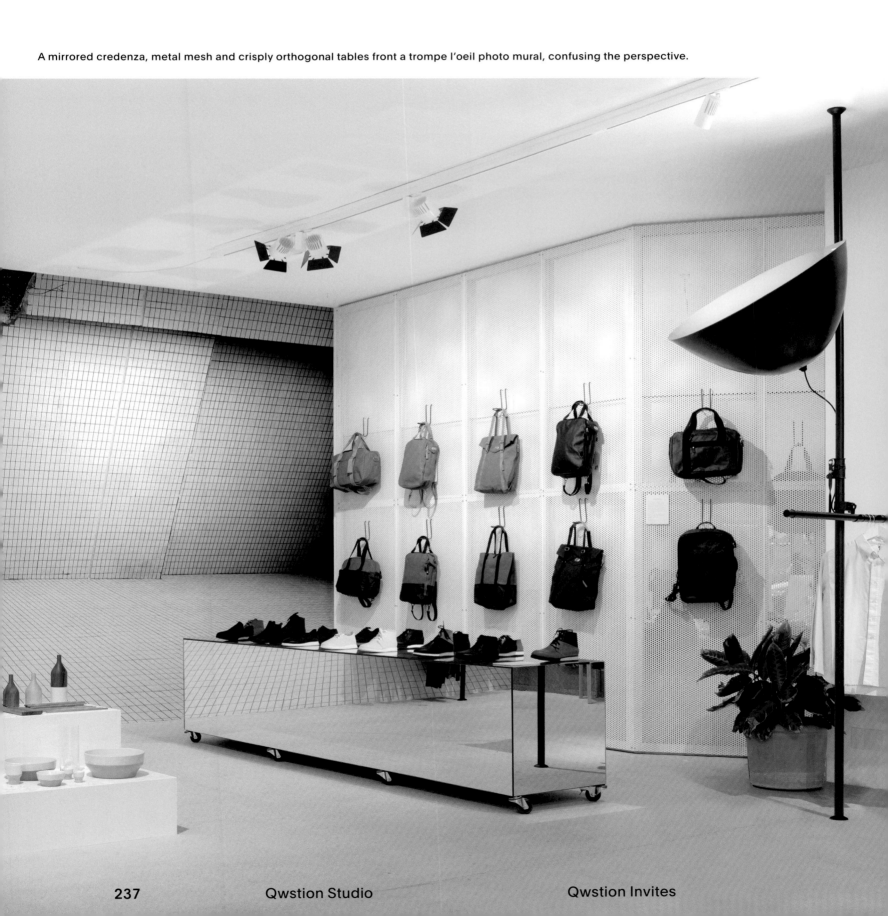

d-raw

Where	Toronto, Canada
Opening	June 2015
Client	Reiss
Designer	d-raw (p.410)
Floor space	223 m²
Shop constructor	CIS
Photos	Richard Leeney

reiss

The rippling ceiling, rendered in a bespoke stretch fabric, softens the space from above.

The interiors of this materially robust, yet almost austere, retail environment for fashion label Reiss alternate between light and weighty, translucent and hard. This places the emphasis on form, colour and finish while shaping the contours and character of the space in a manner calibrated to match the client's re-invented identity. The shop's sculptural look contrasts cool and dark with lofty and sheer in a space modelled on a showroom or gallery. D-raw created a marble portal at the entrance featuring large shards of angular, asymmetrical glass panels that float behind the floor-to-ceiling glazing of the storefront. Inside the designers deliberately exposed concrete columns which serve as boldface graphical gestures that allude to the clothing's origins in design-driven tailoring. A shallow ripple of origami-like waves soften the ceiling above a series of pivoting screens that partition the 223 m² store into more intimate, enclosed spaces. This intimacy is amplified into a feeling of privacy in the fitting rooms where the ceilings have been lowered, generating spaces more human in their scale. Here, in lieu of the terrazzo and marble elsewhere, the floors are softened with rugs. Measured doses of lush materials, including a blue agate cash desk and white Corian furniture, as well as surfaces in sycamore, smoked glass, bronze-trimmed mirror and mirror-polished concrete, echo Reiss' investment in the beauty of restraint.

a shallow ripple of origami-like waves soften the ceiling

A detached vitrine with large, irregular, laminated glass panes hover over mannequins in the storefront.

brinkworth

Where	Rotterdam, the Netherlands
Opening	August 2015
Client	Run2Day
Designer	Brinkworth (p.408)
Floor space	158 m²
Shop constructor	Shell Works
Photos	Louise Melchior

run2day

The variety of materials and textures also serves to define product zones and provide a familiar background for display.

This particularly site-specific shop – a running apparel retailer – merges materials and history that make up the fabric of the city outside with the materials that fill its interiors. Brinkworth incorporated objects and materials – street finishes and sports flooring added at the bases of rails, plinths and cash desk – that recall an entire history of running in the city. Marketing company Maradona created a History Wall that is diplayed on the tiled wall of the running strip that hems behind a mesh screen on one side of the store. For this small track, the designers used white tiles, lighting details and architectural forms that recall the local Maastunel, which is a point along many running routes through the city. The passion of local runners for experiencing their city on foot and in motion is celebrated by walls, floors and even furnishings rendered in concrete, herringbone grey cobblestone, worn red brick and brick pavers, hot-rolled steel mesh display screens and oak slats. The materials also define zones, vary the floor texture and background particular ranges of product. 'We looked at the streetscape that the people of Rotterdam experience on their runs and applied these qualities within the store,' says Brinkworth director Sonny Cant, 'reflecting their city back at them in a different context.'

This highly site-specific store that brings gritty outdoor urban materials – brick, cobble, concrete – into its interior, reflecting the local urban running experience.

the passion of local runners for experiencing their city is celebrated

Timber slats provide display space for garments while screening the History Wall and gait analysis track.

HMKM

Where	London, United Kingdom
Opening	June 2013
Client	Selfridges
Designer	HMKM (p.411)
Floor space	2416 m²
Shop Constructors	Duala International, Vizona Shopfitters and Beck Interiors
Photos	Marcus Peel

selfridges denim studio

By mining early architectural details like ceiling coffers and original windows, the team mixed modern with the store's iconic 107-year history.

In Selfridges, HMKM turned the third-floor children's department into the British emporium's dedicated denim destination. Showcasing 11,000 models by 60 brands proved to be both a virtue and challenge: the team tapped technology to elevate service, making the experience accessible and memorable while avoiding a warehouse-like display of products. They opened and brightened the floor by excavating the original coffered ceiling and windows, exposing the rich history of the iconic 1909 West End building through its early architectural details. Multiplicity reigns in this democracy of denim, where a luxurious marble and leather concession contrast along with its express self-checkout till. Angled lines and planes, folds and gradient tones give the displays a sense of energy, exemplified by a long tube of indigo light that threads its way from the entrance of the Denim Studio through the Fit Studio and a traditional atelier where tailors personalise jeans for customers in real time. With London designers, Kin, the Studio created an interactive 'Jeanius Bar' table in the fitting area where visitors may dive digitally into the vast inventory to search for products and view them on an integral elevated display or to compile a wish list of favorites to email to themselves.

multiplicity reigns in this democracy of denim

A tubular blue light leads through the Denim Studio into the Fit Studio and tailor's atelier.

prospace asia

Where	Xiamen, China
Opening	October 2015
Client	Septwolves Menswear
Designer	Prospace Asia (p.414)
Floor space	1330 m²
Shop constructor	Septwolves Construction Team
Photos	Max

septwolves flagship

One of China's most popular premium menswear labels, Septwolves boasts 3000 locations throughout China and a reputation for pioneering the first mix of Chinese fashion culture with an international design sensibility. This flagship store integrates five sub-brands into a coherent shopping environment that includes a tailor's zone, cafe, fashion lounge, gallery, 'chill-out zone' and designer boutique. The layout is designed to avoid the 'one lap and exit' dilemma common to many men's retail stores. The products and displays have been presented in fresh, friendly, eye-catching ways that highlight fabric, construction and design. Prospace Asia created themed displays that draw from various developments in the arts and fashion in order to create 'multi-sensory experiences' in the store. A central circular 'stage area' links the two floors where it can easily be reconfigured for temporary fashion events. Another link between floors is a wall of greenery that rises alongside the wide main staircase. The designers have created a space that is simultaneously contemporary, sophisticated, masculine, active and worldly, where men can feel at home – or as if they're in a gentleman's club where a bespoke zone featuring luxe leather furnishings recalls the real thing. RFID technology is integrated into the physical store, uniting the online and offline retail platforms, enlarging the shopping experience and making the store 'multi-experiential'

The shopfront is striking but also transparent enough to show off the strong interior architectural elements to passers-by.

At the entrance to the store, a window display fronts the broad, forest-like staircase lined with oak timber plinths and a large plant wall.

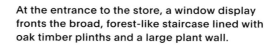

The wolf icon is representative of the brands identity and is used on products and displays.

men feel as if they are in a gentlemen's club

The shelving units around the central stage have the graphic beauty of simplified Chinese characters.

Glass, mirrors and light create a 'transitional' space when customers cross the first floor stage area.

It was important to create a number of 'non-retail' spaces in the store in order to present different spatial experiences.

doepel strijkers

Where	Antwerp, Belgium
Opening	September 2015
Client	Stills
Designer	DoepelStrijkers (p.410)
Floor space	95 m²
Shop constructor	MAAQ
Photos	Teo Krijgman and Kaj Van Geel

stills

A view through the two-level glazed storefront reveals the single continuous design element – an unbroken square tube – that rises past the slab of the mezzanine.

A continuous 'ribbon' of square steel tube threads over the two floors of this clothing boutique, organising circulation and providing both hanging display racks and sculpture, while using a minimum of material. The ribbon is visible from the street through double-height glazing which looks into the store as if it were a cut-away revealing the floor slab of the mezzanine. Presentation platforms sometimes elevate that continuous straight line off the floor but in other places it extends onto the upper level without any support, tracing parts of a 3D grid. This means that shoppers are able to experience the fashion and accessories on different levels and from distinctly framed and various points of view. For a brand that honours unusual combinations and subtle contrast in its own designs, DoepelStrijkers emphasised the transformation of the space and the coexistence of both the original space and the new interior concept. They did this by juxtaposing preserved remnants of the old space with the new design scheme: grey paint covers the walls from the floor to half a metre from the ceiling, leaving a ragged edge so as to emphasise the existing wooden surfaces.

The single display element as it threads its way from the street level floor upward to a double-height ceiling.

remnants of the old space are preserved with the new design

The line displays hanging garments, suggests a route through the shop and is, simply, sculptural.

rosie lee

stride

Where	Moscow, Russia
Opening	May 2015
Client	A3 Retail Group
Designer	Rosie Lee (p.414)
Floor space	188 m²
Shop constructor	–
Photos	Katie Khromova and Rosie Lee

A visually energised space is created, using concrete, plastic-coated timber, steel and plywood.

This shop for Stride, a new premium running brand, was designed to convey speed, strength and motion in every detail. The scheme integrates digital technology and modular design to cultivate a socially welcoming space for runners of all abilities. The designers used the negative space of a running gait to create the Stride logo and this same dynamism flows visually through the retail space. At the entrance visitors find a wooden Motion Wave ceiling installation drawing them into the store. Inside, the concrete, steel and plywood interior includes a faceted concrete 'community wall' in front of which guests can photograph themselves and friends in selfies to share on social media. A treadmill for in-store gait analysis is embedded flush in the floor and accompanied by a post-mounted iPad for recording the runner. Garment displays are minimal but just as visually dynamic as the logo: they include clothing rails continuing in irregular lines that could represent a series of short steep climbs or EKG heart rate readouts, and an easily reconfigurable slot system used to hold garments in place. Modular footwear boxes hang at the same angle as the logo's runner and slot into a wall of pegboards, which can also be used to post information, like running routes, using wooden pegs and cord.

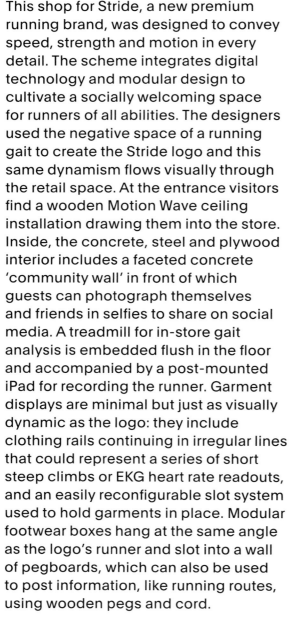

An undulating wooden ceiling installation establishes a sense of speed and motion at the entrance to the store.

garment displays are minimal but just as visually dynamic as the logo

Pegboard walls use wooden pegs and cord to serve as modular shelving or a bulletin board.

The faceted concrete Stride logo wall at the entrance is a backdrop against which customers take photos to share on social media.

Merchandise is displayed on clothing rails that continue in irregular lines.

The units are designed to deliver an adaptable and readily reconfigurable retail space.

Rosie Lee   Stride

montalba architects

Where	Los Angeles, Unites States
Opening	May 2014
Client	The Row
Designer	Montalba Architects (p.413)
Floor space	409 m²
Shop constructor	Shawmut Design and Construction
Photos	Dominique Vorillon

the row

The architects and designers created bespoke fixtures and vitrines and paired natural materials, textures and tones with concrete and metal.

The founding flagship of fashion label The Row bathes in the sundown glow of California Modernism. The architectural team of Montalba Architects worked with owners Ashley Olsen and Mary-Kate Olsen to dovetail indoor and outdoor spaces. The shop is part gallery and part residence with a foyer, courtyards, floor-to-ceiling structural glass doors, native plantings and living room-like sitting areas, one complete with a fireplace. Visitors enter through a double-height courtyard and an oversize glass door with a bespoke bronze knob. Here the foyer looks onto a poolside parlour where natural light saturates the surrounding galleries via sliding or pivoting glass doors and a 7 m long skylight. Montalba Architects and The Row created bespoke fixtures and vitrines and hemmed the perimeter of the space with brushed stainless-steel garment rails and steel-blade accessories shelves. Beyond these custom fixtures, the mid-century furnishings that raise the residential quotient throughout the space, were found by the clients, who also chose vintage light fixtures that complement the recessed lighting. The team's choice of richly austere materials – organic textures like Tung oil-rubbed walnut display podiums and antiqued limestone paired with matte white concrete, fields of barely framed glass and brushed metal – aligns with The Row's 'polished minimalism' and refinement of details, a warm and textural but pared-down sensibility and its nuanced tonal palettes.

Most of the mid-century and vintage furniture was found by the fashion designers, themselves.

the team worked with owners ashley olsen and mary-kate olsen to dovetail indoor and outdoor spaces

Salon-like sitting areas, fireplaces, a skylight, courtyards and glass doors make the boutique feel distinctly residential.

Wooden podiums that display accessories, echo the richly minimal quality of the clothes.

SECTION A-A

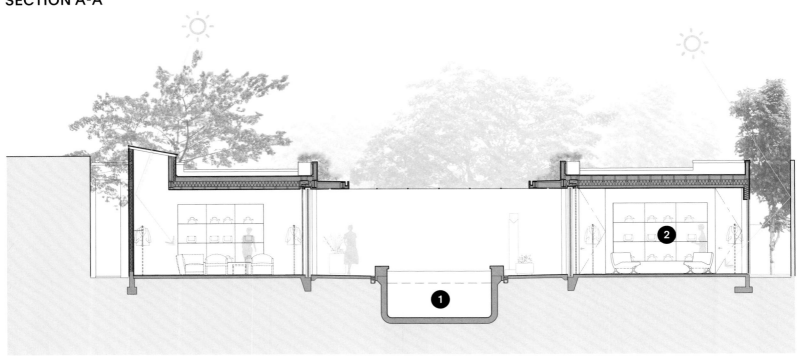

FLOOR PLAN

1. Pool
2. Sitting area
3. Fitting room
4. Courtyard

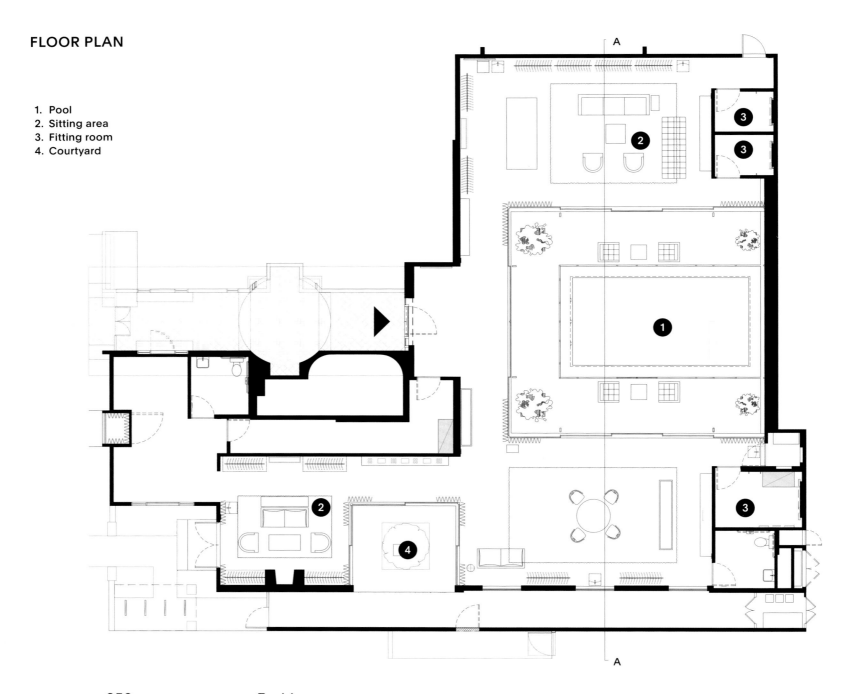

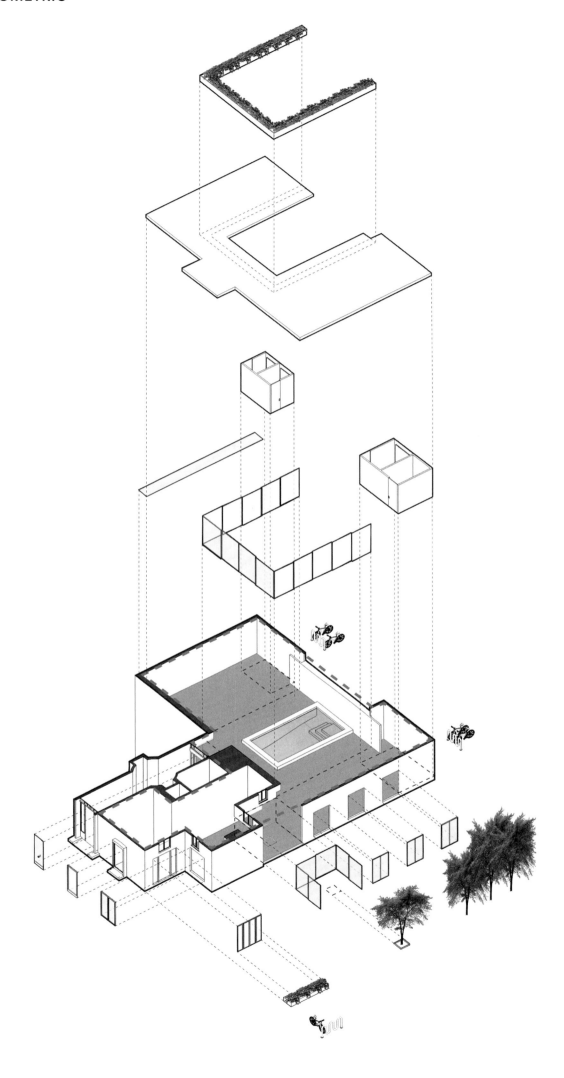

line-inc.

Where	Tokyo, Japan
Opening	November 2014
Client	Your Sanctuary
Designer	Line-Inc. (p.412)
Floor space	65 m²
Shop constructor	Sogo Design
Photos	Kozo Takayama

the secretcloset

The boutique emphasises blank spaces in order to showcase the garments and accessories.

This clothing boutique was Line-Inc.'s fourth retail interior for the brand, based on a template concept to which they were asked by the client to add something fresh. At only 65 m², it was a smaller space, but it boasts lofty 4-metre ceilings, so the designers used both qualities to their advantage. Line-Inc. created a welcoming living room scenario – complete with a cushy sofa, soft rug and oak furniture – basing it on the boutique owner's London flat, and to pique the curiosity of passers-by's, designed the storefront so that the contents of the shop are not entirely visible from the street. To do this, bespoke display cases are placed on either side of the entry which, along with 3.5 m tall displays for mannequins and floor-to-ceiling shelving at the centre of the room, give the interior a low-key symmetry. As the most recent shop, it features materials that diverge from the earlier boutiques, making it look and feel more modern: its sleek surfaces consist largely of glass, blackened steel and mirror finish steel. Marble is used for furnishings like the cash desk and table tops and, instead of timber flooring, Line-Inc. installed mortar-grey tiles. The designers also focused on composing moments of emptiness in the knowledge that empty space can prove the simplest way to highlight products filling the rest of the space.

empty space
can prove
the simplest
way to highlight
products

ito masaru design project/SEI

Where	Tokyo, Japan
Opening	September 2015
Client	Ueno-Shokai
Designer	Ito Masaru Design Project/SEI (p.412)
Floor space	260 m²
Shop constructor	CPO
Photos	Kozo Takayama

ware-mo-kou

There is a mix of traditional materials like gourds, as lamps, with new industrial materials like wooden shipping pallets, used for display.

'Subtly Japanese' is an apt description for this shop tucked into an alley near Shibuya's main boulevard. In an area that is quintessentially Tokyo, in that it is as Japanese as it is cosmopolitan, the store was designed as a space in which indigenous culture – fashion, art, music, books and food – can be presented, based on seasonal themes, alongside that imported from around the world. Ito Masaru used traditional and ancient materials – plaster-covered walls, gourds turned into pendant lamps, washi paper, stone and tatami – together with modern materials and details whilst preserving the minimalism of the whole. Set into a softly tiled facade, the entryway and storefront display run diagonally to the street (just as shipping palette displays inside are placed diagonally to the walls), subtly distinguishing it from its neighbours. To enter, visitors pass through a tunnel that serves as a palate cleanser between the outside city and the whole world contained inside. A gallery in the rear of the ground floor contains themed exhibitions over a mortar floor so thickly coated with resin that it might be mistaken for water, which the designer says 'lends a nothingness to the spirits of those who step on it,' amplifying the mental immersion of the visitor. Downstairs, in the basement, through a mash-up of fashion, art and cherry-picked international books, the shop is designed for meandering.

The designer describes the shop as 'subtly Japanese.'

The shop is minimal, as it combines new and old, and Japanese with international cultures.

indigenous culture can be presented, based on seasonal themes

In the gallery, exhibitions are mounted on shelving balanced with weights over a resin-coated floor that resembles water.

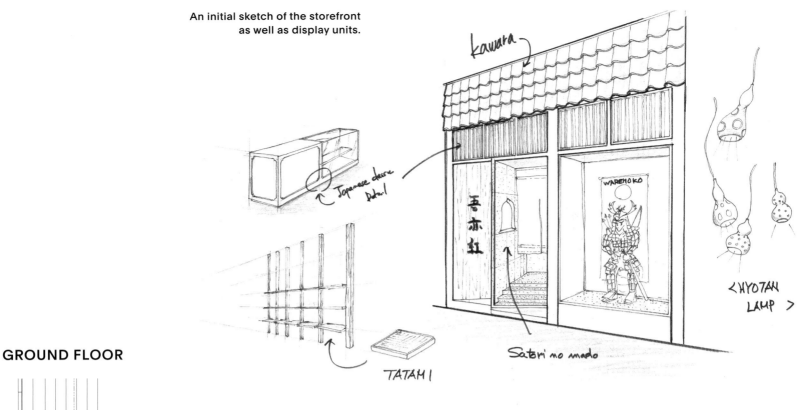

An initial sketch of the storefront as well as display units.

kawara

Japanese door Detail

吾赤虹

WAREMOKO

Satori no mado

TATAMI

〈 HYOTAN LAMP 〉

GROUND FLOOR

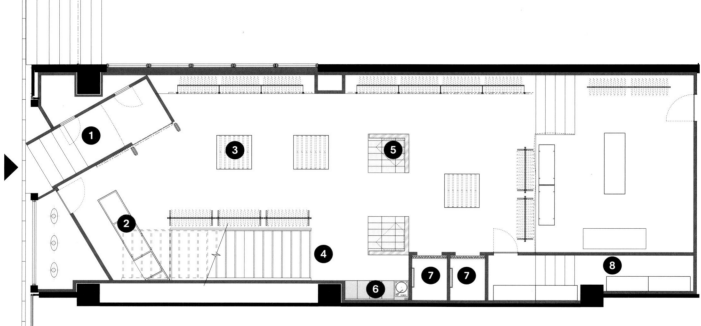

BASEMENT

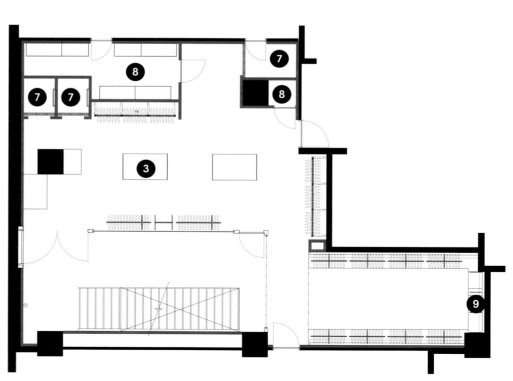

1. Entrance tunnel
2. Cash desk
3. Shelf displays
4. Stairs
5. Speakers
6. Gramophone record display
7. Fitting rooms
8. Storage
9. Mural shelf

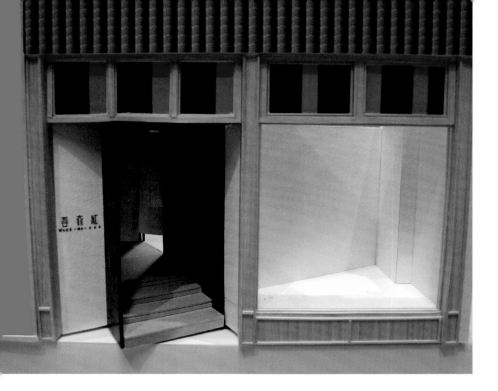

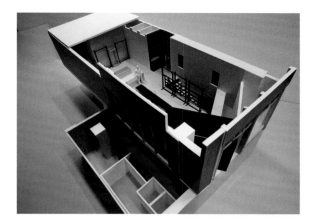

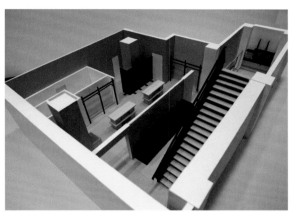

Since the initial model of the design, the entry and storefront display run diagonally to the street.

Renderings illustrate the medley of traditional and modern material used to create a minimalistic space.

A model of the store showcases the spatial and vertical layout.

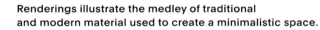

The use of tatami pays tribute to traditional Japanese material.

267   Ito Masaru Design Project/SEI   Ware-mo-kou

FOOD

BEV

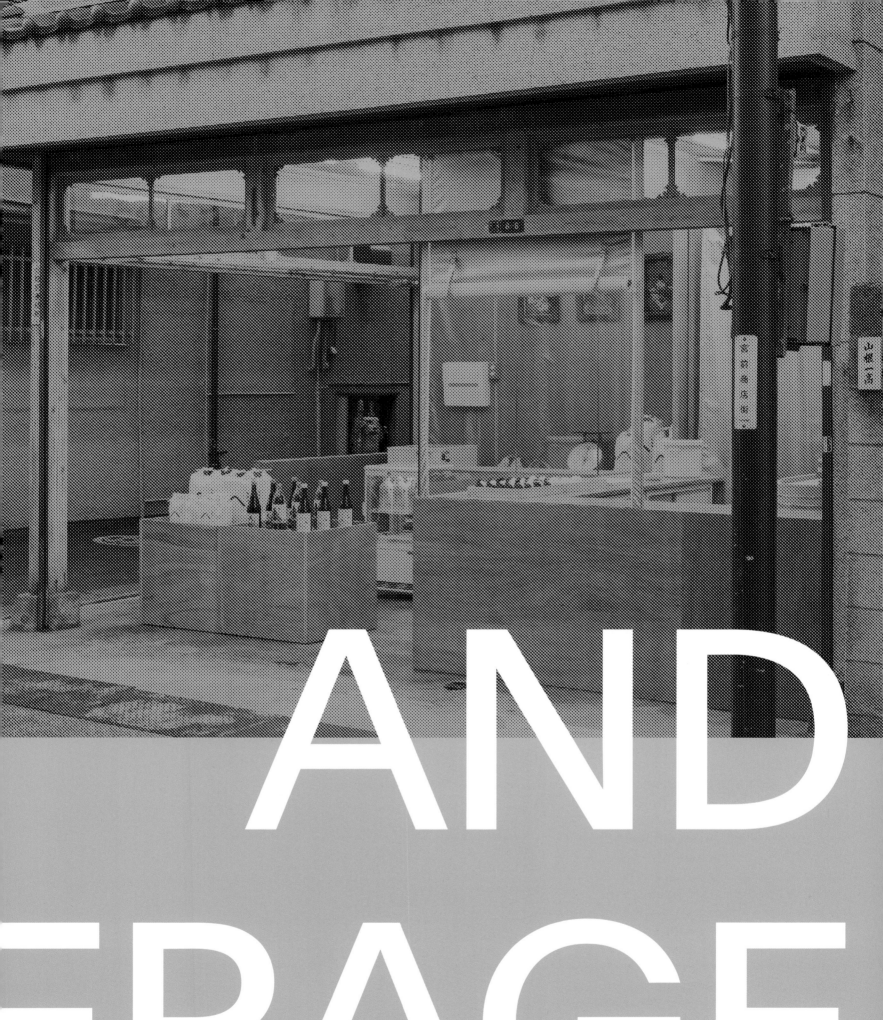

AND
ERAGE

kplus konzept

Where	Hagen, Germany
Opening	October 2014
Client	Bears & Friends
Designer	kplus konzept (p.412)
Floor space	40 m²
Shop constructor	Schleifenbaum Design & Project
Photos	Kratz Photographie

bears & friends

The teddy bear-shaped tasting shelf behind the cash desk is flanked by a custom-printed polka dot wallpaper in candied hues.

In this sweets shop, kplus konzept cultivates the perception – in the fresh juiciness of colour and voluptuousness of form – that shoppers are 'entering a bag of jelly bears'. Bavarian confectioner Bears & Friends sells more than 100 flavours of fruit gums, but it faces serious competition. To distinguish the brand from its rivals, kplus konzept was asked to transform it into a human scale, walk-through experience that would feel 'dense and intense' in just 40 m². The interior sums up the diversity of Bears & Friends offerings tidily through a profusion of candy colours custom-printed on the wallcovering and floor along with highlight bears in the walls and large cut-foil bears on the storefront. On the rear wall behind the cash counter, the designers mounted a tasting shelf that is also shaped like a bear. Although this sweetly expressive theme suggests a birthday party, because the exuberant visuals are ranged over a structural grid, the interior feels balanced and homogeneous and the eye is not lost in pattern. The layout of the shop, with entrances on two sides, also concentrates the customer's focus. Throughout, a circular pastille shape is repeated in the oversize plate-shaped Delta pendant lighting fixtures and offset or 'fanned' display trays. These trays, set in the centre of the room, anchor the whole composition brightly.

A circular pastille shape is repeated throughout many aspects of the sweets shop.

shoppers are 'entering a bag of jelly bears'

triad china

Where	Harbin, China
Opening	September 2014
Client	Yuanda Holdings
Designer	Triad China (p.416)
Floor space	2700 m²
Shop constructor	Meitu Building Decoration Engineering
Photos	Tim Franco

home park

Triad's design of this upmarket supermarket chain, where gourmet ingredients, imports and local delicacies are all to be had in one place, features a 'room-to-room' concept. The hypermarket has a 'market hall' format and formal dining hall. The designers first considered the perspective of where a gourmet chef would buy groceries and brought their answers together – a farmer's market, fishmonger, butcher, artisanal deli, patisserie – under one roof. Each room is distinct in fit-out, furniture and graphic implementation and has a name that suggests a narrative and a community of food crafters: customers enter through The Barn, where fruits and vegetables can be found. The Butcher sells meat and The Fish Market, seafood. La Cave is the wine section whilst The Warehouse, with the industrial look that its name suggests, is where drinks, snacks and imported and specialty goods are located. The homely dining area consists of a modern teahouse and other eateries offering international cuisines. In each room, environmental graphics reinforce that room's spatial narrative and make each feel welcoming. 'Vast attention' was given to the visual communications in order to educate customers about their options, ranging from unfamiliar Western products to the beloved local ones. The infographics – about different cuts of meat, nutritional benefits, recipes and food preparation tips – embroider the interiors and enlighten shoppers in a playful manner.

The design highlights Triad's multidisciplinary interior design and visual communications skills.

The market includes a variety of food options that are complemented by material and lighting features.

environmental graphics reinforce each room's spatial narrative

The beauty and health products area has a sleek and unified look.

Traditional wall panelling, warm whites and a wooden parquet floor draw shoppers into the old-school Let's Bake bakery.

Overhead lighting is fixed into barrel drums over the shopping aisles.

Infographics elucidate anything from cuts of meat to nutritional information and recipe ideas.

SKETCH OF
'THE BARN'

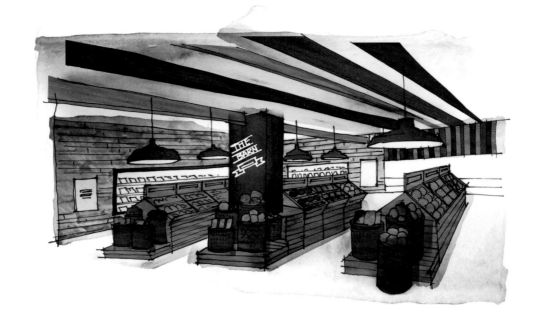

SKETCH OF
'THE BUTCHER'

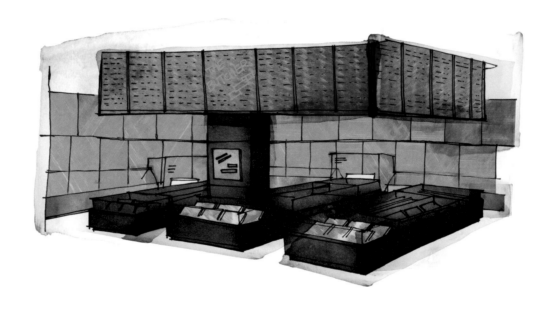

SKETCH OF
'THE CORNERSHOP'

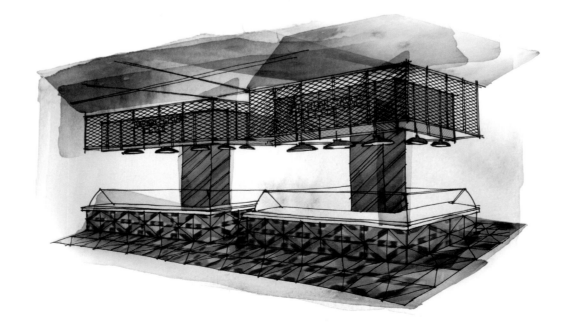

FLOOR PLAN

1. Cash desks
2. Restaurant
3. Bakery
4. Open kitchen
5. Retail area

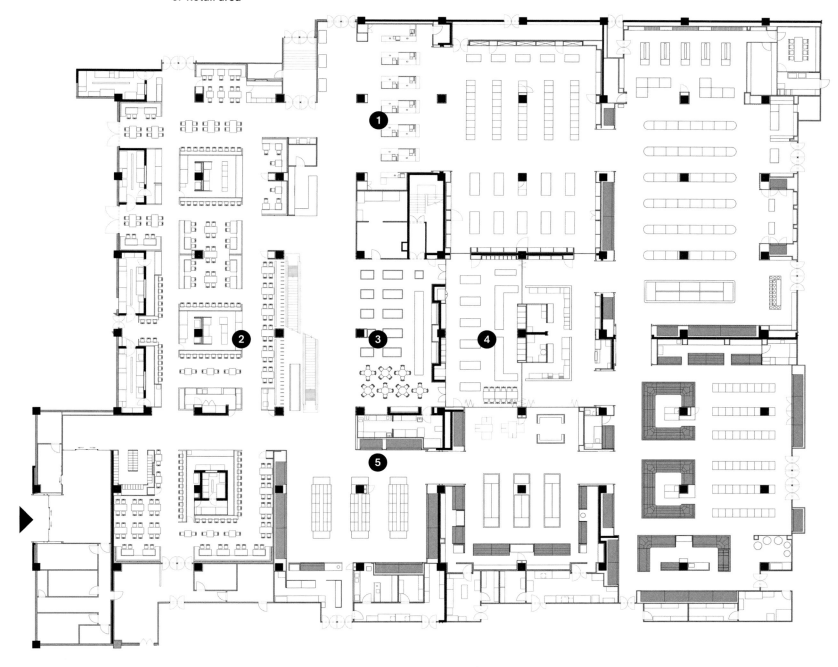

SKETCH OF 'THE FISH MARKET'

triad china

Where	Shanghai, China
Opening	December 2015
Client	Hunter Gatherer
Designer	Triad China (p.416)
Floor space	580 m²
Shop constructor	Modernspace
Photos	Tim Franco

hunter gatherer

The Hunter Gatherer marketplace and restaurant is a proponent of the 'safe food' movement in China. The idea is to provide chemical-free foods controlled from 'seed to table', something Hunter Gatherer is calling 'real food'. Much of the market's produce comes from the company's own farms in Chongming and Yantai, China and often arrives covered in the soil it was grown in. Triad China realised that shoppers didn't understand the science, labour and care going into real food production so their solution was to focus the design on explanations about food sources, the science of farming and the Hunter Gatherer mission. Entering the 580 m² market through a series of full-height barn doors, visitors arrive at a bright open restaurant space where guests eat together at communal tables under the beams of a sprawling barn roof and pendant lighting in a scene akin to a harvest festival. Flanking the entrance, farm window frames fitted with LED screens play live-stream video of work going on at the Hunter Gatherer farm in Yantai, Shandong. Like the restaurant's menu, Triad chose its materials – like natural saw-cut lava basalt stone walls – for their natural textures and flavours and created a white background that foregrounds both food and products.

The barn-based visuals at the entrance represent central elements of the seed-to-table concept.

A barn roof rises over the restaurant and its communal tables, creating a rustic community vibe.

The cold-press juicer is showcased in a glass room with text and visual information.

natural textures create a foreground for both food and products

The wine selection is displayed in timber shelving with signage that educates the consumer about the product.

Visual communication is a prominent part of the whole design.

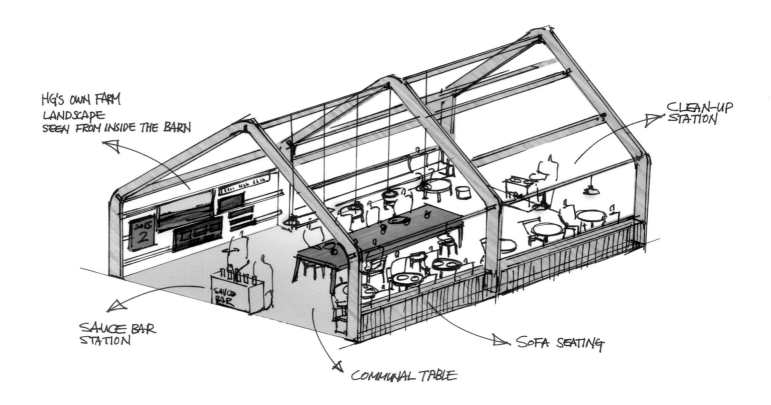

HG'S OWN FARM
LANDSCAPE
SEEN FROM INSIDE THE BARN

CLEAN-UP
STATION

SAUCE BAR
STATION

SOFA SEATING

COMMUNAL TABLE

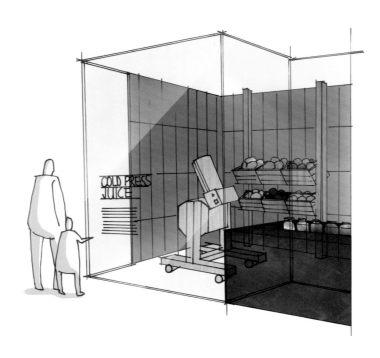

FLOOR PLAN

1. Cash desk
2. Cafe
3. Retail area
4. Open kitchen
5. Juice room
6. Produce area
7. Storage
8. Office
9. Back kitchen
10. Seating area

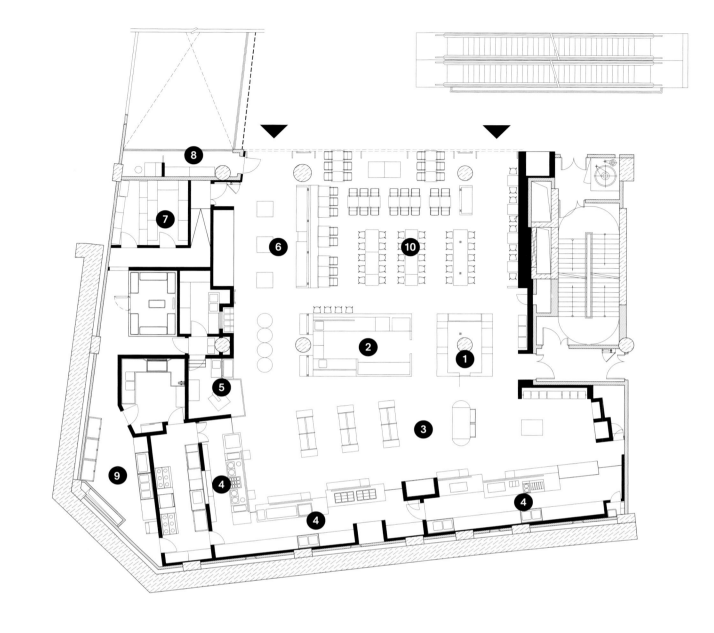

BIRDS-EYE VIEW RENDERING

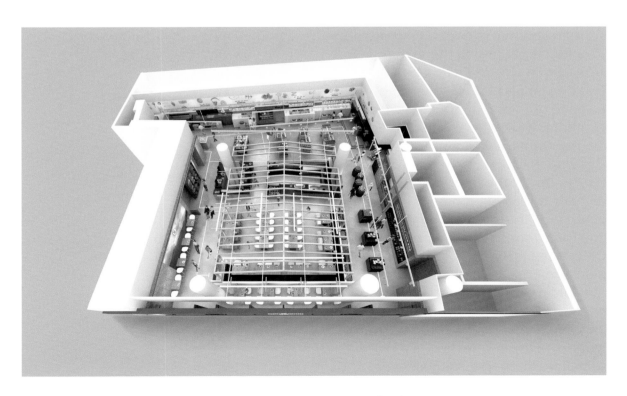

moriyuki ochiai architects

Where	Tokyo, Japan
Opening	June 2015
Client	Dream Dairy Farm
Designer	Moriyuki Ochiai Architects (p.413)
Floor space	98 m²
Shop constructor	Aslego
Photos	Atsushi Ishida

momom store

This highly textural – even tactile – interior translates the vital force of nature wed to the man – and handmade into a dairy shop and eatery. The space visualises the freshness of the milk that comes from dairy cows on the nearby farm and the magical animus of trees in the surrounding forest. Moriyuki Ochiai considered the care with which each dairy product is crafted, as well as the beauty of the natural world to create an expressive space. He applied cedar wood tiles to the floor and ceiling, and brushed on wall paint that 'blends earthen and milky tones' in a gradation of colour highlighting the texture of the wood while evoking a ripple of milk. Two egg-shaped tables have a green to white gradient, another reference to nature, while three tree-shaped fixtures form towers of green and white shelving. Rising vertically as if forming the canopy of the tree, white splashes of 'milk' brim over, fountain-like, into overhangs that conceal lighting and into the surfaces of adjacent shelving. On the ceiling, Ochiai painted timber planks in dark and light greens and overlaid them with short slats of unpainted wood to form a canopy of 'branches' that provides the warmth of wood and the suggestion of a rhythm, as of light filtering through leaves.

This dairy shop pays poetic homage to the handcrafted and to the vitality of nature by evoking fresh milk and the trees of the forest nearby.

Tree-shaped towers with crowns shaped like milky splashes serve as both shelving and light fixtures.

beauty of the natural world is embraced to create an expressive space

Over cedar wood surfaces, gradations of a special white paint that emphasises wood texture recalls the rippling of milk.

Moriyuki Ochiai Architects   Momom Store

luchetti krelle

Where   Sydney, Australia
Opening   October 2014
Client   Nutorious
Designer   Luchetti Krelle (p.413)
Floor space   25 m²
Shop constructor   Promena
Photos   Michael Wee

nutorious

This nut boutique is designed to recall a humble market stall, which sets it miles apart from the sleek fashion boutiques surrounding it. In fact, the designers' creative concept came from this relatively posh context. They recalled inspiration from old shops, where the front counter once multitasked as a viewing window. This draws customers through the shallow storefront to where freshly roasted nuts are on show, making the compact space as economical as it is small and entirely avoiding the look of a mall kiosk. Instead it has assumed the face of a high street shop. The brief also included the creation of a calm, ordered and streamlined environment, whilst retaining the welcoming warmth of the original store. Chocolates, which the brand had never sold before, are now placed in the curve of the counter. Overall, the designers restricted the colour scheme to creamy shades reminiscent of Kraft paper or nut butter. They used timber dowel in the joinery and then cast the countertop from concrete. The rest of the shop is primarily steelwork and glazing. These materials, along with the colour palette and modern equipment visible inside, suggest an old-time industrial space where things that 'just aren't made like that anymore', are, indeed, made just like that.

'things just aren't made like that anymore'

The restrained materials palette creates a neutral appearance while standing out from its neighbours.

A small but efficient display of what's currently on offer flanks the left side of the door.

jo nagasaka/
schemata architects

Where	Tokyo, Japan
Opening	December 2014
Client	Owan Inc.
Designer	Jo Nagasaka/ Schemata Architects (p.412)
Floor space	16.5 m²
Shop constructor	Todo
Photos	Kenta Hasegawa

okomeya

There are rare moments in design when pragmatism and simplicity become, without exaggeration, a fine art. This tiny rice shop is located on a shopping street in Togoshi Koen that has been in decline, turning into a 'shutter street', on the verge of extinction. As part of an ongoing effort to reanimate the local commercial ecology, Jo Nagasaka rehabilitated a narrow wooden building that was once a vegetable shop with the grocer's home in the back. In the area, small business owners support each other in various small ways that are big community builders, which became the focus of the architect's creative process. At just under 17 m², the shop has the virtue of being operable by a single person as a simple, low-cost affair. The building itself was old, so Jo Nagasaka did a thorough refurbishment, sanding existing wooden surfaces and structural elements like the columns until they matched the tone of the Lauan plywood from which he built the store's furniture. Today, in the revitalised space, the street and store become one, and the old and new seem indistinguishable. The shop seems to recuse itself from notice, but, to anyone paying attention, the extraordinary level of craftsmanship and humble beauty of the design and construction imputes a similar authenticity and superior quality to the business and the product, as well.

Jo Nagasaka preserved and sanded the old wooden surfaces and columns to match new furnishings made in Lauan plywood.

This humble corner rice shop is part of a community-wide effort to revitalise a declining shopping street.

the street and the store become one

The 16.5 m² shop is so small, it can be run by a single person, keeping costs down.

The street and shop floor overlap, which reflects the character of the streets' mutually supportive business community.

Jo Nagasaka/Schemata Architects   Okomeya

lautrefabrique architects

Where — Jeddah, Saudi Arabia
Opening — November 2015
Client — Patchi Saudi Allied
Designer — Lautrefabrique Architects (p.412)
Floor space — 110 m²
Shop constructor — Dal Al Arabia
Photos — Luc Boegly

patchi

Confections are displayed like jewels in a jewellery box.

This Lebanese chocolate shop and 'concept boutique' has siblings in 35 countries. Within its 110 m², in the region's first open-air mall, Lautrefabrique Architects re-sculpted the brand's image of 'extreme elegance', blending a dollop of warmth with sensuality and a bit of the baroque. Fashioned to look like a black marble jewellery box and decorated with copper letters, asymmetrical windows and lights that recall traditional lanterns, the facade mixes strong visuals with precious materials. On the threshold, a full-height copper screen wraps visitors, its pattern fashioned from the Patchi logo. A long linear glass 'jewellery' counter shows off confections that are reflected in a mirror-polish copper ceiling panel. Overhead, mapped directly above the glass counter, matte black Tom Dixon pendant lights lined with radiant hammered copper, give the space another warming glow. Around a broad, black, lacquered reception desk and an ebony wall, Patchi's recognisable anise and black packaging fills shelves with candy colours while multi-hued sweets glow from illuminated niches limned in black. The space feels sumptuous and yet orderly, mouth-watering but disciplined, because the architects based its proportions on Nature's Golden Ratio. Elitis wallcoverings and a Toulemonde Bochart carpet that dresses the beige floor give the chocolate-free surfaces texture while furniture by Danish label Hay injects the space with almost edible colour.

The pattern of the copper screen abstracts the shop's monogram, knitting it into an ornament at the threshold.

The black marble facade announces the opulent quality of the product inside.

the furniture injects the space with almost edible colour

STOREFRONT ELEVATION

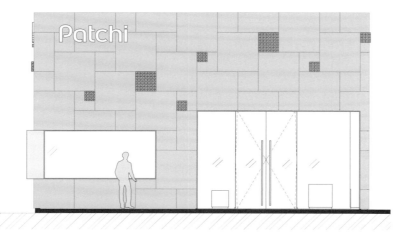

Lightboxes on the facade are modern updates of the traditional moucharabieh latticework common to the region.

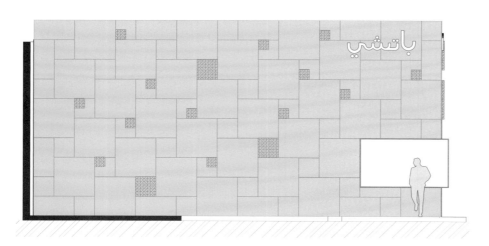

FLOOR PLAN

1. Chocolate counter
2. Cash desk
3. Wrapping room and storage

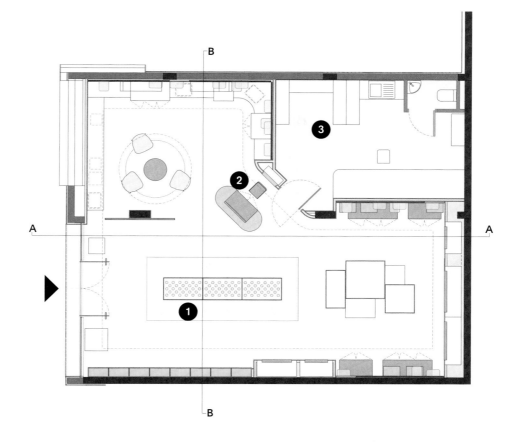

SECTION A-A

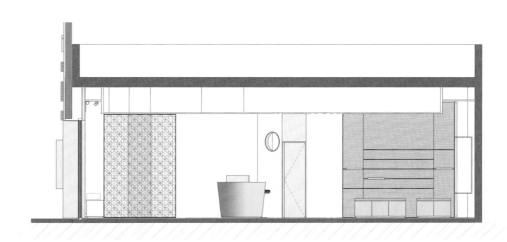

SECTION B-B

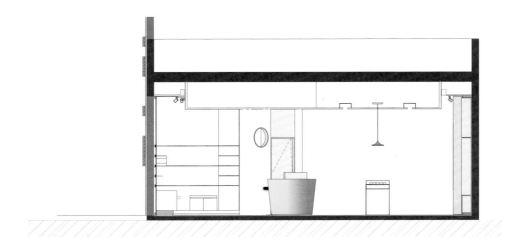

3deluxe

Where	Frankfurt, Germany
Opening	February 2014
Client	perfect day
Designer	3deluxe (p.408)
Floor space	165 m²
Shop constructor	Graf Müller
Photos	Sascha Jahnke

perfect day

It is old news that living sustainably and living aesthetically need never be mutually exclusive, but this flagship in an international airport terminal for a socially conscious coffee store makes the point once again. As a social entrepreneur, perfect day looks out not just for the planet, but for people too by supporting bio-organic cultivation, forging lasting relationships with local producers and raising the awareness of coffeehouse patrons. 3deluxe looked to these mindful, world-bettering values to design the space, combining organic forms, contrasting hues and tough high-quality materials – solid walnut wood and white stone composite – with atmospheric lighting programs that shift depending on time of day, creating a light-filled biomorphic interior. The voluptuous contours of the bespoke furnishings – the service counter and lilac banquettes – form a smooth ribbon that begins in the sales and service areas at the front and curls into the rear lounge with its view onto the tarmac. Matching these curvaceous lines, amorphous shapes are applied to cut-out wall shelves, free-form waterjet-cut floor tiles and a drop ceiling fitted flush with surface-mounted suspended down lighting. Photographic adhesives depict flora found in the coffee cultivating region of mountainous southern India where perfect day sources its beans. The colour palette also borrows from the rainforest's lush natural hues: the white coffee flower, the ripe purple bean and the emerald canopy.

A natural colour scheme is incorporated into the design of the shop.

The furnishings and drop ceiling curve organically into intimate pockets of seating in an otherwise exposed space.

organic forms are combined with contrasting hues and high-quality materials

Wall illustrations and nature photography as well as lilac banquettes warm the tarmac-side lounge.

triad china

Where	Shanghai, China
Opening	August 2015
Client	Stonefresh Holdings
Designer	Triad China (p.416)
Floor space	140 m²
Shop constructor	Modernspace
Photos	Tim Franco

stone fresh

Bespoke picnic stools and tables give an air of rusticity and fresh-air outdoors.

In spite of its small size and mall-bound location, this cheerful frozen yogurt, juices and energy snacks shop for the American healthy lifestyle brand takes the form of a metaphorical getaway. Triad China incorporated a vivid colour scheme and hypergraphic origami shapes that are rendered in contrasting shades of green and purple: grass green, grape, the lilac of evening falling into an enchanted forest, refreshing hues (and the brand's own purple) that should make passers-by hungry. The floor's earth-tone hexagonal tiles map a path of escape into a fairytale mountainside, or a sunny hand-crafted world (think: kids' paste pots and safety scissors). The anchor of the space is a camping trailer full of yogurt toppings, surrounded by wooden picnic furniture, pine cone pendant lamps and rope-swing-seats whilst the yogurt self-serve wall jags with the outline of a mountain ridge and snowflakes. All of this abstract imagery runs through the shop's packaging, prints, app, social media and web presence, too. Warm lighting makes for a warm welcome that never becomes overripe. Each of the fixtures stores equipment and enables store employees to easily run and maintain the shop. The modular format also enables its roll-out on varying square footage sites and the accommodation of increasing numbers and types of product.

Colour and graphical shapes come together in a cheerful terrain to create this healthy lifestyle snack shop.

The entire shop is a metaphorical holiday.

hyper graphical origami shapes are rendered in contrasting shades

HERE'S HOW TO CLIMB THE
YOGURT MOUNTAIN
优格山登山指南

GRAB A CUP
自取杯一枚
PICK FLAVORS
口味任意选
ADD TOPPINGS
顶料随心添
WEIGH IT
最后齐称重
ENJOY IT!
尽享新滋味

Embellishing the picnic theme are
two seats in the form of rope swings.

Triad China   Stone Fresh

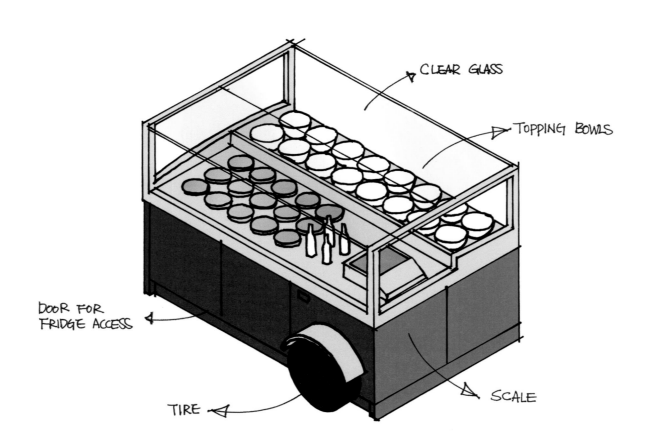

FLOOR PLAN

1. Cash Desk
2. Frozen yogurt
3. Seating area
4. Back kitchen

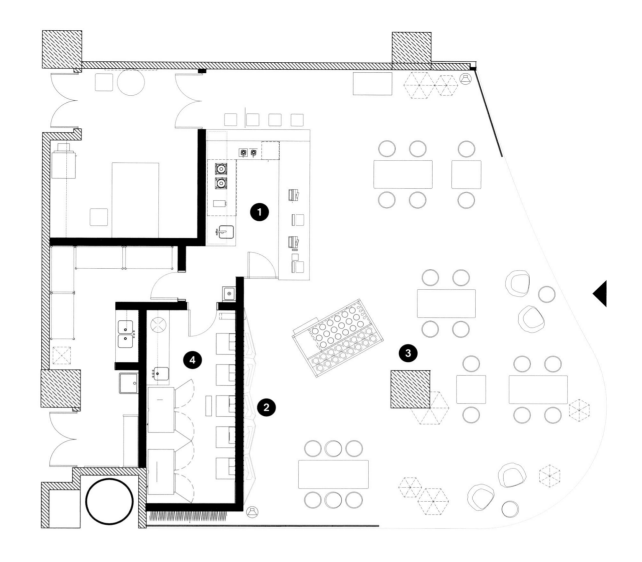

BIRD'S-EYE VIEW RENDERING

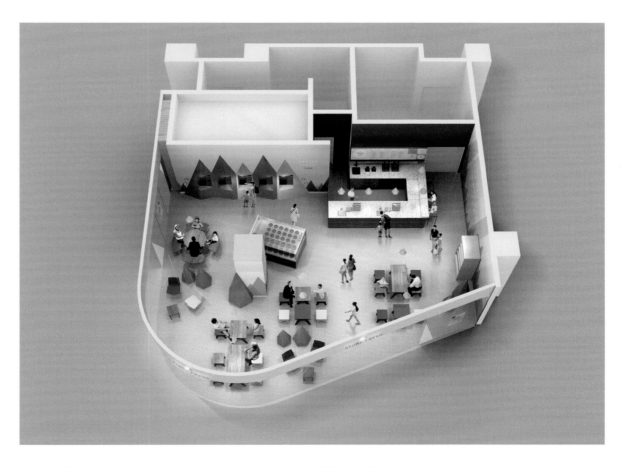

landini associates

Where	London, United Kingdom
Opening	April 2014
Client	T2
Designer	Landini Associates (p.412)
Floor space	95 m²
Shop constructor	AWESO
Photos	Andrew Meredith

T2

Landini Associates designed this tea salon as 'an antidote' to the sleekness of traditional British teahouses and in homage to the ancient art of tea making and drinking, but the first international outpost for the Australian brand is meant to educate its patrons and roll back the mysteries, if not the magic, of the ancient beverage: it boasts a tea library of 250 varietals, tasting stations and aroma tables, where visitors taste, touch and smell various ingredients, and a brew bar with brew master, who demonstrates brewing methods. Transparent display counters consist of layers of interwoven welded steel, so that the mechanism of the drawers is revealed from pulls to brass pipes, fittings and sinks. T2's signature orange packaging is framed by an industrial colour scheme that includes the blackened, oxidised steel and copper mesh of the library (a metal interior that reaches onto Redchurch Street and wraps the storefront). Because the ceiling height was relatively low, the designers relied on floor-to-ceiling shelving, or libraries, along with mirrored ceiling panels to make the shop feel larger. The building the shop is in was cobbled together over centuries and had an intimidating 'labyrinth of columns', but these too were put to efficient use in the plan, directing instead of hindering circulation.

mirrored ceiling panels make the shop feel larger

The tea library has more than 250 blends of tea ranged in bright boxes that pop out of dark industrial surfaces.

FURNIT
AND
FUPRROI

open air studio

Where	Bangkok, Thailand
Opening	September 2015
Client	Air&Craft
Designer	Open Air Studio (p.414)
Floor space	60 m²
Shop constructor	Chang Da
Photos	Varavudh Lattanand

air&craft

Air&Craft is a poetically named, tightly curated lifestyle shop and cafe in Bangkok that showcases furniture, lighting and accessories that embrace the values of wood and metal craftsmanship from various regions, with an emphasis on the best of local makers and designers. Each selection and display emphasise not just the product, but the production process behind each object, any heirloom techniques used in its fabrication and the qualities that make the piece unique. Bangkok-based Open Air Studio was tasked with articulating these values in a showroom, which they converted from the disused garage in which it is now located. Open Air transformed it into a shop and eatery with a simplified material palette that makes the small retail floor easy for the eyes to parse. Open Air's approach to the project focused on the structural and material integrity of the environment by, for example, exposing the existing concrete slab ceiling and using wooden beams to conceal all of the electrical conduits and ductwork. The creative team also installed a handsome red wood parquet floor, mounted metal shelves directly into the concrete and used removable oak planks to give the displays – and the walls – their warmth and tactility.

Converted from an abandoned auto repair garage, the interior focuses on structure and materiality.

the design embraces the values of wood and metal craftsmanship

The showroom relies on a pared-down palette of materials, emphasising its relationship to wood and metal crafts.

studio mokum

Where	Amsterdam, the Netherlands
Opening	April 2015
Clients	Friederike Joppen and Thijs Box
Designer	Studio Mokum (p.415)
Floor space	70 m²
Shop constructor	Heeremans Bouw
Photos	Jolanda Kruse

de balkonie

Two alcoves in the flanking walls contain balcony decor vignettes on pallet podiums.

Ever heard of a balcony furnishings and decoration store? The Dutch hadn't either. Usually balconies are neglected, taken up with cumbersome bits of storage and smokers banished to the outdoors. Enter Studio Mokum, which designed this 'stylish casual green store', along with its identity and graphic design, which were based on the pen illustrations of Peter-Paul Rauwerda, a friend of the owners. As its name would suggest, the shop sells contemporary plants, furniture and accessories suited to the diminutive sizes and restricted conditions of most city balconies. To design retail space around this, Studio Mokum set up balcony vignettes in the store's alcoves and filled the space to brimming with potted plants to create the organic character of a nursery instead of just a design boutique. Matching the emerald complexion of the space, they restored the existing sand-colour terrazzo floor, painted the walls a soft gull-wing grey, rescued shipping pallets for use as display podiums and installed patina copper green vintage shelves to hold accessories. They also curated a furniture collection that synthesises vintage and contemporary design objects. At the centre, a large table carves out ground for an informal meeting area (which, however, is usually appropriated by the neighbour's cat). The shop's great virtue is that one wants to linger there, making it a paradigm of its products' application.

rescued shipping pallets are used as display podiums

This shop is devoted to the urban balcony, a part of the home that is often little more than a ledge and sorely underappreciated.

d'art design gruppe

Where	Dusseldorf, Germany
Opening	March 2015
Client	Henkel
Designer	D'art Design Gruppe (p.410)
Floor space	700 m²
Shop constructor	D'art Design Gruppe
Photos	diephotodesigner.de

henkel global experience center

The space is embedded with interactive technology without feeling overwhelming.

Clean, fresh, modern and natural are good words to describe the look and feel of this global experience center of the laundry and home care business unit at Henkel. Its designers suggest that the bright blank-paper-white space 'throws a daring glance into the future'. The purpose is to offer a comprehensive overview on Henkel's expertise in the laundry and home care category that draws on all senses, offering a clear look at everything from product innovation, digitisation and sustainability to category management. D'art Design Gruppe's goal with this spacious interior – which includes a green wall and interior columns that resemble trees blowing in a breeze – was to create a space with a strong sensorial experience choreographed through architecture, scenography and visual language. Technologies and interactive moments – including multimedia and touchscreen stations, opportunities for visitors to make and test their own products, a 270 degree cinema, and even eye-tracking glasses – are embedded transparently into the interiors, perceptible and easily used without overwhelming visitors. Light canals outline many architectural elements using LEDs programmable via iPad so that various lighting scenarios can be selected during presentations.

the bright white space 'throws a daring glance into the future'

A living green wall is the background to images of nature as well as interior columns shaped like trees.

The space informs about consumer behaviour and how this knowledge is incorporated into formula developments.

nomura/ryutaro matsuura

Where	Osaka, Japan
Opening	November 2013
Client	Koizumi Lighting Technology
Designer	Nomura/Ryutaro Matsuura (p.413)
Floor space	1279 m²
Shop constructor	Nomura
Photos	Nacasa & Partners

klos

After filtering natural light by using various media,
Ryutaro Matsuura showcases coexistence with the artificial light.

Most lighting showrooms banish natural light in order to showcase the artificial. Instead, however, Nomura re-examines our experience of light by saturating this LED lighting store with sunlight filtered through various media. Luminous, pale and poetic, defined not by walls but by frames, shadow and sheer bespoke fabric panels hung between ceiling and floor, the space is effortlessly layered and forms small mist-like rooms around the fixtures. Nomura took advantage of existing windows on all sides to bring ample natural light deep into the space to 'co-exist' with artificial light. As one delves deeper into the room, however, the sunlight becomes weaker and the synthetic light, stronger. Because the fabric panels progressively diminish the amount of sunlight penetrating the back of the space, each space between panels assumes a different 'quality of brightness'. Designer Ryutaro Matsuura used the fabric layers to give 'form to the light, allowing the light to be touched by the hand'. The bespoke textiles contain patterns – squares of various sizes in a thinner, more translucent, weave – that suggest windows, adding texture to the space. The square niches can actually be moved depending on where it's needed. Matsuura also made it possible for sales people to modify media content by putting all information into digital form, accessible on unobtrusive projectors, tablets and touchscreens.

the space is effortlessly layered

Instead of walls, translucent bespoke floor-to-ceiling fabric are used to give 'form' to light.

Nomura/Ryutaro Matsuura   Klos

The movable fabric panels let visitors reconsider the beauty of sunlight while contemplating the potential of LED light.

As daylight diminishes deeper into the store, the LED light has an increasingly strong presence.

Narrow hallways are created in-between the lightly hung fabric panels.

Furniture and Home Products

FLOOR PLAN

1. Entrance hall
2. Video area
3. Reception room
4. Light and furniture display
5. Meeting rooms
6. Office

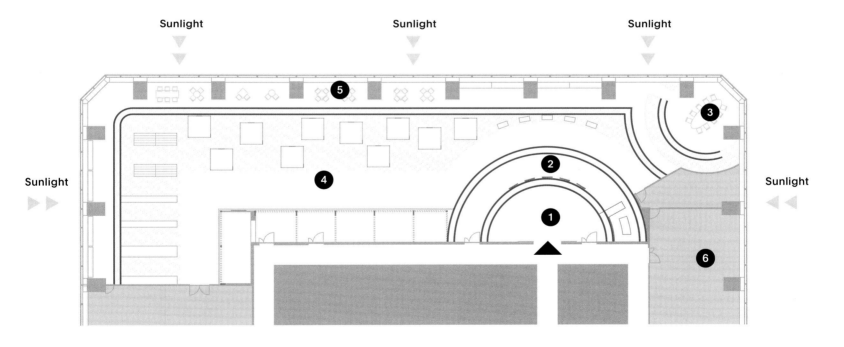

Sunlight

Sunlight

Sunlight

Sunlight

Sunlight

SECTION

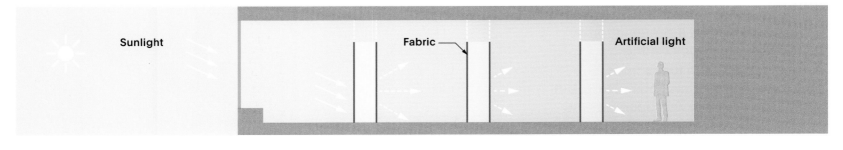

Sunlight

Fabric

Artificial light

Nomura/Ryutaro Matsuura   Klos

BEHF corporate architects

Where   Vienna, Austria
Opening   June 2014
Clients   KAPO and Neue Wiener Werkstätte
Designer   BEHF Corporate Architects (p.408)
Floor space 500 m²
Shop constructor Neue Wiener Werkstätte
Photos   Paul Ott and Rupert Steiner

neue wiener werkstätte

This furniture flagship for a brand inspired by the iconic Wiener Werkstätte is situated on the historic Vienna Ring Road, its interiors synthesising the contemporary and the historic. A ceiling-height wall, painted monolithically yellow and glowing through the store, defines the space, making a building-within-a-building the first focus. Just as the brand's products do, the wall abstracts and integrates both traditional and contemporary design elements, whilst symbolising the primacy of its long embrace of craftsmanship. The wall partitions the retail floor into interior and exterior halves, private and public living space, styled into hotel suites and bedrooms on one side and kitchens and living rooms on the other. The value of craftsmanship is represented by the seamless transitions that occur as the wall zig-zags through the room, shifting a section of facade complete with fenestration into a piece of specialist built-in furniture or a kitchen. At the same time that these spaces morph from public into private, they also transition from brand-new into old school. Away from the wall, the rest of the showroom recalls industrial joinery facilities with epoxy coated floors and an expanded metal grid ceiling. The design scheme establishes a simultaneously sophisticated and welcoming atmosphere through furnishings, composition, materials and lighting, but exploring the yellow wall becomes the biggest attraction of the space.

The flagship's storefront is set into an historical facade.

The yellow wall morphs into kitchen countertops and cabinetry.

Inside, a wall resembling a building-in-a-building has a library section featuring yellow floor-to-ceiling shelving.

spaces morph from public into private

The kitchen counter leads to a vertical green wall.

The living room section of the wall is detailed with old-fashioned wall mouldings that frame modern furniture.

FLOOR PLAN

1. Lounge
2. Bedroom display
3. Kitchen display
4. Meeting room

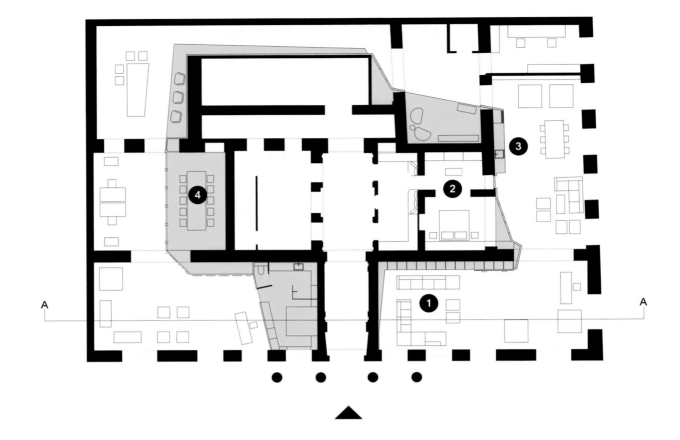

SECTION A-A

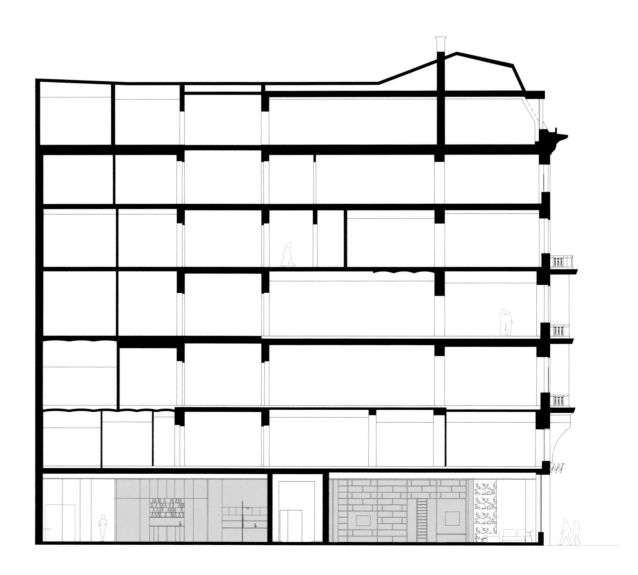

VISUAL CONCEPT

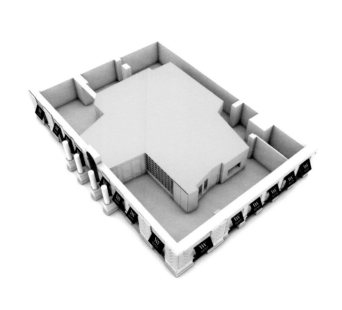

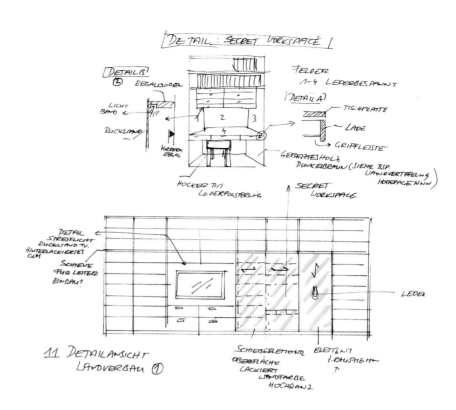

FRONT FACADE

creneau international

Where	Genk, Belgium
Opening	May 2015
Client	Sleep Design
Designer	Creneau International (p.409)
Floor space	200 m²
Shop constructor	Creneau International
Photos	Arno Roncada

sleep design

While lounging on test mattresses, visitors find that the black ceiling glows with a Milky Way of stars.

In front of this custom bed and mattress showroom, drivers pull into a parking spot whose parallel painted lines have been turned into the outlines of a bed equipped with a pillow and downturned duvet. Creneau International's design team wanted to associate the interior design with 'the main event in any bedroom: dosing off into dreamland.' In lieu of the white, open-plan stores with not a modicum of privacy where one must usually try beds, this shop is dark, cool and quiet. This may be because the designers took some cues from Belgian Surrealist painter René Magritte and used 'nightscape' colours – black, midnight and middle-of-the-night blues. The team dreamed up armchairs made from quilted mattress textiles, dotted the shop with small blue sheep and mounted a series of wall niches that explain the raw materials that go into a mattress. A galaxy of stars is created that glows out of the black ceiling above a surreal 12 m-long test-bed, as well as sleep and dream quotations to be read while reclining. (Another 12 m mattress in the long storefront window resembles a crawling caterpillar.) The test beds are tucked into an area screened by floor-to-ceiling panels made of sheer fabric printed with a subtle ombre of those puffy clouds often found in the happiest of dreams.

A little blue model sheep stands in front of the material wall where raw mattress materials are displayed in midnight blue niches.

Sheer floor-to-ceiling panels printed with clouds screen the test beds.

it's dark, cool and quiet.

A surreal 12 m-long mattress arches across the dark storefront behind a parking spot whose embellishment has turned it into the outline of a bed.

OBILITY

office AT

Where   Nakonpatom, Thailand
Opening   March 2015
Client   Nakornchaisri Honda Automobile
Designer   Office AT (p.413)
Floor space   10,000 m²
Shop constructor   Energy Construction
Photos   W Workspace

honda showroom

Visible from the road was the main aspect of the project brief. This auto showroom, however, goes energetically above and beyond the call of duty. Its futuristic form wasn't created to merely boggle the mind of the contractor building it. The Honda showroom's location on a busy thoroughfare was not to be wasted: Office AT designers imagined a fluidly jagged form – vector-like – on its own shallowly terraced plaza. The 10,000 m² site is divided into two main structures that include a showroom, sales office, reception area and, at the rear, a car maintenance garage, and enough floor space to park 100 vehicles. The long narrow main showroom, including the primary car display and sales floor, lies folded alongside the road for easier viewing. These areas have also been divided into two parts, bisected by a large, planted courtyard that captures sunlight to increase the site's energy efficiency. This disjuncture also generates a more compelling visual approach to the dealership for customers and an elevated room that becomes an illuminated car display during the night. This is connected to the ground floor which serves as the main showroom by a ramp. Behind this lot is the second building where car repair and maintenance is done and where cars not on display can be parked.

The design has enough floor space to park 100 vehicles.

The owner wanted this Honda showroom to be visible from the adjacent main road.

a planted courtyard captures sunlight to increase the site's energy efficiency

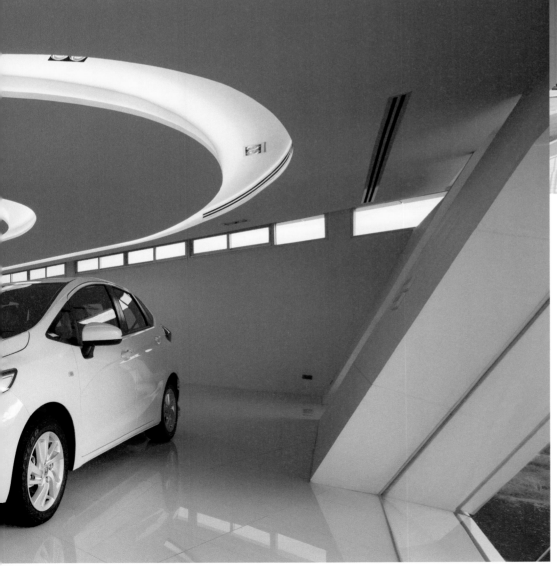

A courtyard draws in light to increase the dealership's energy efficiency.

The building includes a sales office and a lounge-like reception area.

EXPLODED AXONOMETRIC

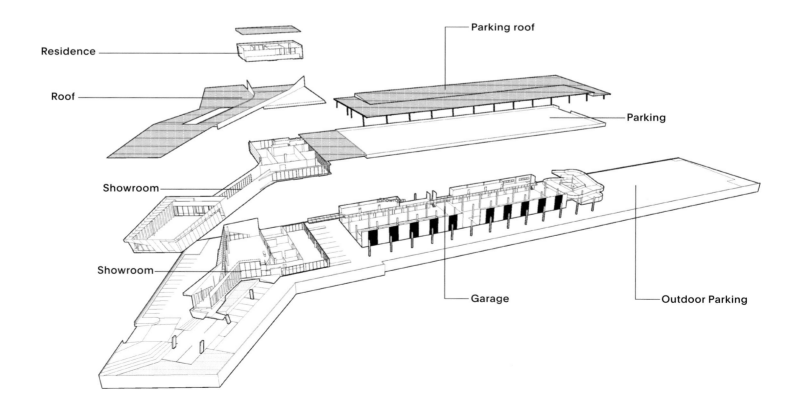

Residence

Roof

Showroom

Showroom

Parking roof

Parking

Garage

Outdoor Parking

SECOND FLOOR

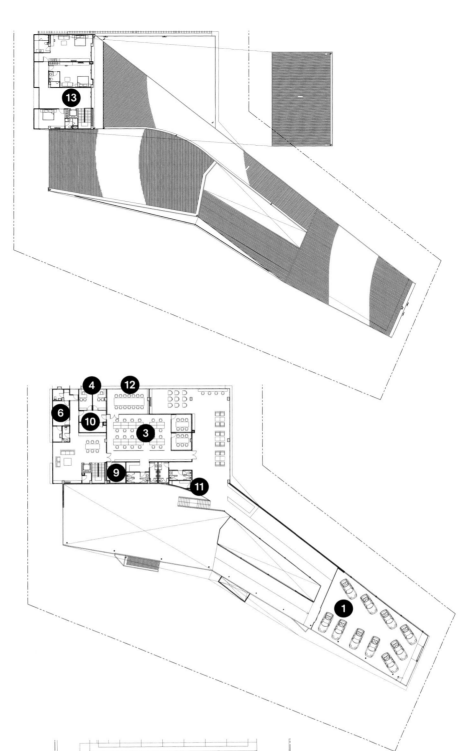

FIRST FLOOR

GROUND FLOOR

1. Showroom
2. Lobby
3. Office
4. Private office
5. Seating room
6. Restroom
7. Server room
8. Parking
9. Storage
10. Control room
11. Pantry
12. Meeting room
13. Residence

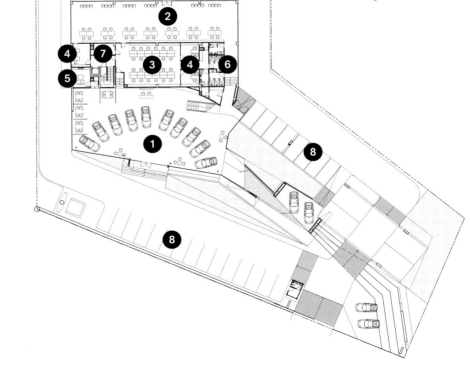

KMS blackspace

Where	Frankfurt, Germany
Opening	September 2015
Client	Audi
Designer	KMS Blackspace (p.412)
Floor space	1714 m²
Shop constructor	KMS Blackspace
Photos	Stefan Bösl

matrix pop-up store & club

For the introduction of Audi's A4 car, KMS Blackspace turned a trade fair booth into a sleekly sci-fi pop-up shop and functioning nightclub. Eschewing typical auto show conventions and turning its back on the fairgrounds, Audi set up shop in the city centre where a stand-alone showroom could be made accessible to both industry insiders and the public. Partnering with local businesses and using virtual reality tools, they kept the Matrix (space) open around the clock, making it convertible from a daytime retail hub to a nightclub open to all. In some areas, a fibreboard and laminate floor feature milled white stripes, in others carpets accompany unfinished concrete. The space features a large bar lit with LEDs, lifts sheathed in mirror foil, windows coated with one-way mirror film and a Chesterfield sofa, pallet pieces and furniture by Vitra and Walter Knoll. Donning VR glasses, visitors find themselves in a digital Matrix while standing in the real one. In this real-virtual space, the A4 materialised, a four cylinder engine built itself, LED headlights extruded into the space, and observers enter a virtual cockpit before being dropped off inside the analogue Matrix. This double reality, which could be experienced 24/7, linked the pop-up's day and night aspects while confusing virtual and actual space.

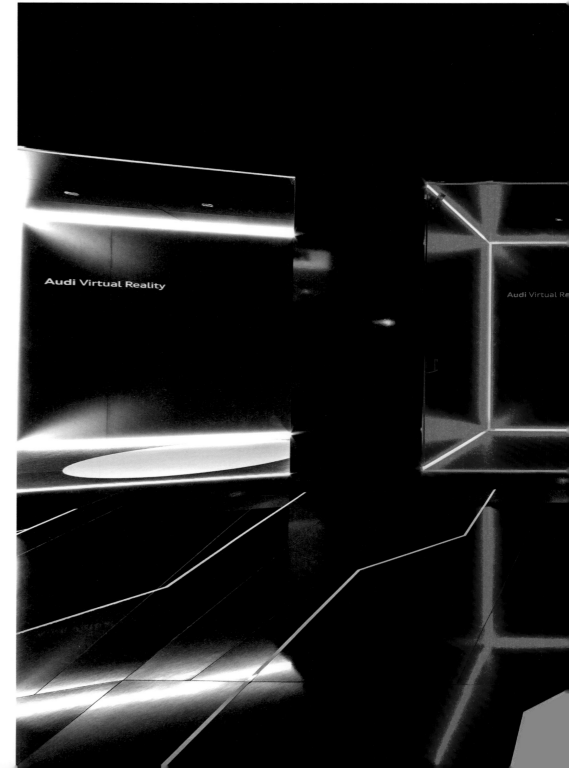

The dramatically lit club entrance is analogue, but looks almost digital.

Audi Virtual Reality glasses and niches link the real interiors to virtually real interiors.

eschewing typical auto show conventions into a sleeky sci-fi pop-up shop

The futuristic showroom, showcases laminate floors with milled white stripes, which add to its sleek sci-fi look.

In some areas, instead of laminate floors, the concrete floor is unfinished and furnished like a lounge.

suppose design office

Where	Tokyo, Japan
Opening	December 2014
Client	Kanto Mazda
Designer	Suppose Design Office (p.416)
Floor space	1517 m²
Shop constructor	Fujita Corporation
Photos	Toshiyuki Yano

mazda showroom

Interspersed throughout the sales floor are cafe tables and auto displays, pleasantly merging its functions.

Sometimes in design, constraints turn out to be virtues. Even though they were working with an irregularly shaped site along an arterial road, with strict height restrictions, Suppose Design Office turned this Honda showroom in Meguro Himonya for the Japanese auto giant into a space of comfort, convenience and novelty. They created an environment capable of engaging people who are deeply interested in cars as well as those who may not have a particular interest, but may still have a need. The result integrates an automobile showcase with cosy cafe and living room-like areas. Passers-by, who get a view inside because the site has a long boundary line abutting the road, may look in and wonder if it is a cafe or a showroom. This complementary contrast is also paralleled in the materials used, which synthesise sharpness and soft organicism through the use of timber with stone and black glass. Even the 'hard' glass of the facade has a soft curve in it where the building bends obtusely in the rear. The designers also made the garage attached to the showroom brighter and more expansive than the typical garage, which was possible partly due to that initially daunting footprint of the site, which when put to use didn't seem so 'irregular' anymore; instead it turned out to be just what they needed.

This auto showroom has a distinctly domestic feeling to it.

In areas around the car display, there are spaces that look like living rooms or lounges.

341   Suppose Design Office   Mazda Showroom

The irregular property lines, which had seemed problematic at first, became a design strength.

Contrast is expressed by a soft bend in the 'sharp' glass of the facade.

they created an environment capable of engaging people

The attached garage is bigger and brighter, with more exposure, than is typical.

GROUND FLOOR

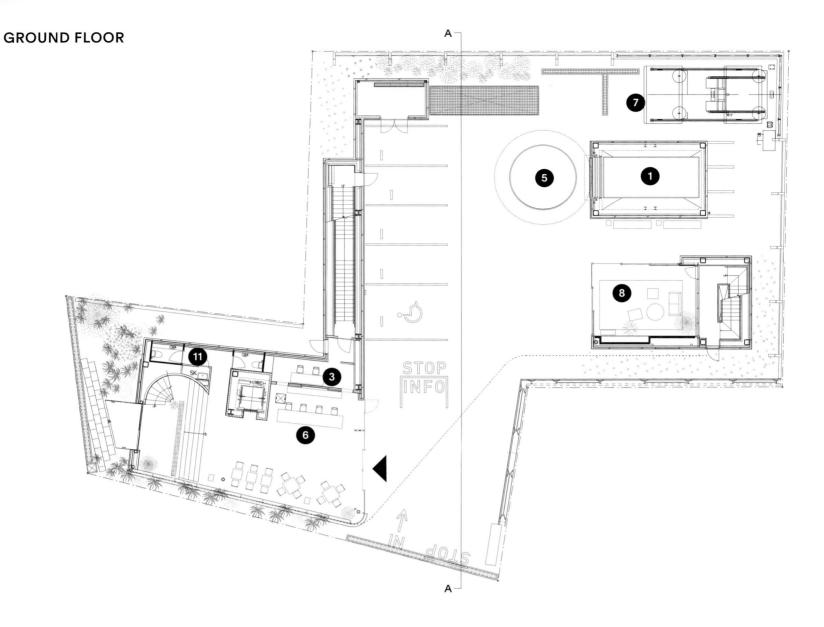

BASEMENT

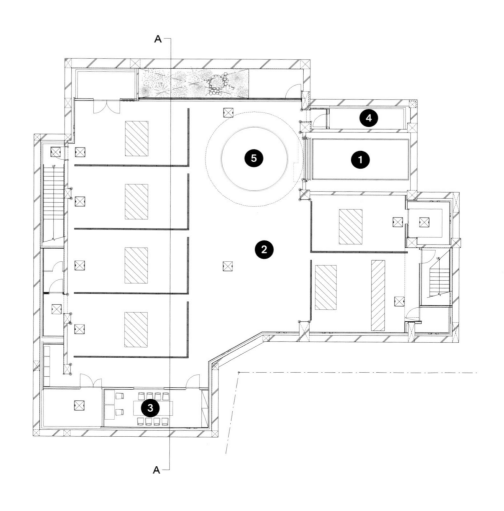

1. Car elevator
2. Auto service station
3. Office
4. Machine room
5. Turn table
6. Reception
7. Car wash
8. Brand garage
9. Kitchen
10. Cafe
11. Restroom

FIRST FLOOR

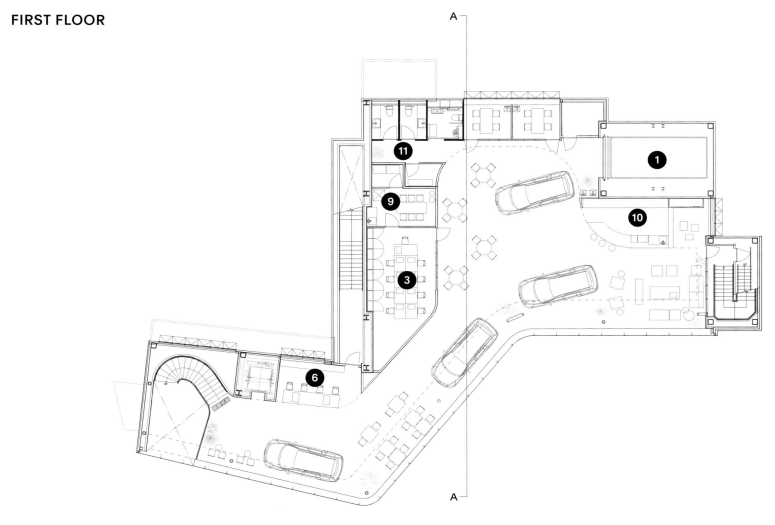

SECTION A-A

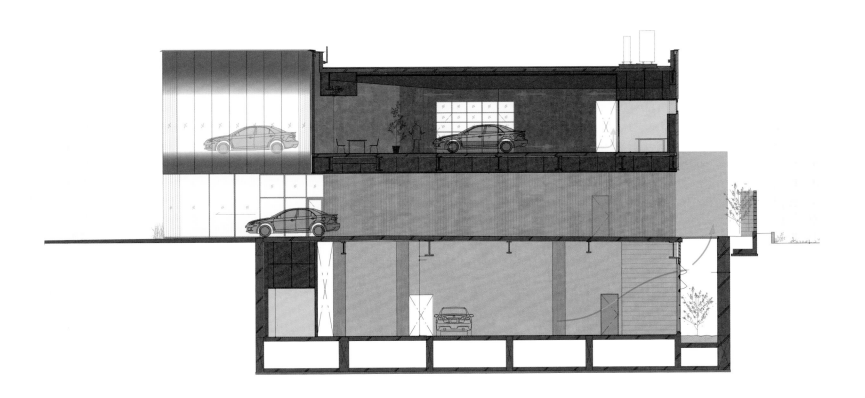

kauffmann theilig & partner and atelier markgraph

Where	Hamburg, Germany
Opening	May 2014
Client	Daimler
Designers	Kauffmann Theilig & Partner (p.412) and Atelier Markgraph (p.408)
Floor space	350 m²
Shop constructor	Ganter Interior
Photos	Daimler

mercedes me store

For the legendary car manufacturer, the design team engineered a first-class retail template to be launched worldwide in high-traffic urban areas. These modular and versatile multipurpose stores designed by Kauffmann Theilig & Partner (architecture) and Atelier Markgraph (communication and media), each combine vehicle presentations with restaurant facilities, events, information and personal dialogue as well as a media show and interactive exhibits. In combination with a web platform, the shops serve to inspire visitors with 'tailored individual offers', whether they are Mercedes-Benz owners or not. The Hamburg Mercedes me Store – so-called because it was designed to put the customer at the centre of its world – was the harbinger of the series. At the core of the scheme are two spatial concepts: the 'envelope' and the 'sheath'. The 'envelope' refers to the neutral shell of the store, consisting of floors, walls and ceilings constructed from high-grade unfinished concrete. In contrast with these surfaces, the 'sheath' is made from roughly hewn oak and serves as an adaptable modular interior of mixed-use areas kitted out with custom furnishings. The store area is sectioned into three spaces: a generous public restaurant where cars are presented and lifestyle events, from gastronomical presentations and fashion defiles to lectures and concerts, are hosted; a more intimate half public consultation and shop zone; and a discreetly private consulting room.

The car display is integrated into the public exhibition and event area.

The restaurant and shop are built to communicate with visitors whether they own a Mercedes – or any car at all.

Kauffmann Theilig &
Partner and Atelier Markgraph

Mercedes me Store

The city store features a modular interior that accommodates catering, consultation, showroom and sales.

A bistro extends the city store to the pedestrian zone and completes the public event and exhibition area.

the shop serves to inspire with 'tailored individual offers'

FLOOR PLAN

1. Exhibition and event area
2. Bistro
3. Shop
4. Lounge
5. Consultation

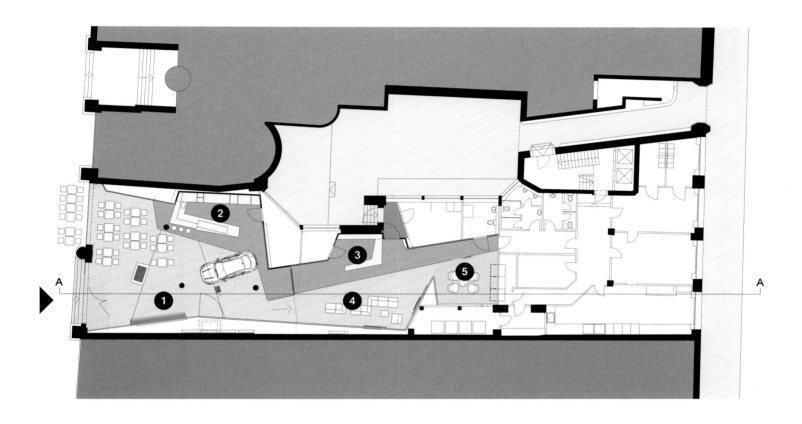

SECTION A-A

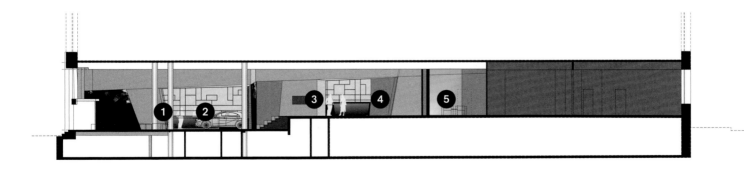

Kauffmann Theilig &
Partner and Atelier Markgraph

Mercedes me Store

SHOES

marco costanzi architects

Where	Rome, Italy
Opening	November 2015
Client	Calzaturificio Casadei Spa
Designer	Marco Costanzi Architects (p.413)
Floor space	90 m²
Shop constructors	C.M.I. and AFA Arredamenti
Photos	Andrea Martiradonna

casadei flagship

Marco Costanzi imagined the Casadei flagship as a velvet lounge encompassed by marble, brass, silver, root wood and light. He looked to the character of the brand and synthesised its qualities: sensuality, luxury, quality, innovation, geometry and creativity, stressing the luxury and sensuality with the use of blonde and root-wood milled panels to dress the walls, and creating a lush jewel box. By using alternating fields of brass and silver or using the two together, he lightened and brightened the space, conveying a sense of grandeur and providing precious frames for the displays. Given a long narrow space, the architect paid close attention to geometry: diagonal lines form a pattern that crosses the ceilings and floors while black channels are carved into the white ceiling to carry spotlights. The flooring too is a composition of lines: marble strips lined with brass plate. Costanzi framed mirrored walls in brass, which also serves to frame shoes that appear to float atop a wall of transparent shelves. Reflected in the mirror, a series of illuminated displays with brass and silver profiles showcase the collections along with shallow platforms in Fior di Pesco marble along the floor. Running down the spine of the shop, upholstered day beds and armchairs in petroleum and dove grey velvets allow visitors to try shoes in rich comfort.

Offset trays of brass-enriched root wood
and marble serve as displays.

Even the palatially scaled front door has a subtle (and literal) twist to its design.

Daybeds upholstered in petroleum and dove grey velvets provide individual areas for trying shoes.

the space conveys a sense of grandeur

Rich materials in nuanced patterns – cut into geometric shapes – make this shoe shop feel luxurious and intriguing.

household

Where	Santa Monica, United States
Opening	April 2015
Client	Christian Louboutin
Designer	Household (p.411)
Floor space	86 m²
Shop constructor	Hurst Siebert
Photos	Mark Humphrey

christian louboutin

This high-end women's footwear label – whose every shop interior varies – is situated in an outdoor mall, but needed to fit into the larger neighbourhood's rustic canyon architecture and feel native to its wealthy, and often celebrity, Brentwood clientele. The character of this clientele means that the merchandise is less trend-driven than other Louboutin locations and focuses primarily on casual-chic apparel and beachwear. The shop's two storeys flank a double-height atrium, with a VIP lounge upstairs, and a lush red statement carpet, the same scarlet shade as Louboutin's iconic soles, which is the only constant in the brand's otherwise diverse retail spaces; everything else differs: Household created a 'casual-chic' environment where glamour is nothing more and nothing less than it needs to be and added a maritime motif appropriate to the coastal location. The sea is evoked in details like mother-of-pearl wallpaper, nautical rope and displays that resemble ships' masts made from reclaimed timber. These 'masts' hold whitewashed displays and have a porosity that allows customers to catch a glimpse of what's beyond, inviting further exploration. The plinths, along with salvaged furniture reupholstered in blue velvet, underscore the casual atmosphere while the natural wooden elements communicate quality and authenticity. Authentic is right: One of the sofas belongs to Louboutin, himself.

The design utilises natural wooden elements to communicate quality and authenticity.

Mast-like displays, a hull-like cash desk, mother-of-pearl wallcoverings and rope suit the shop's Oceanside location.

MATERIAL PALETTE

The VIP lounge upstairs has a lush red statement carpet.

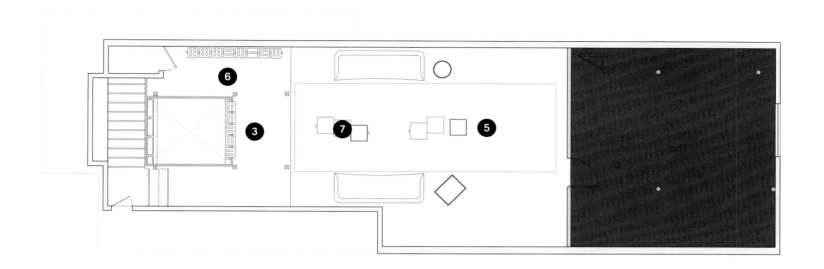

GROUND FLOOR

1. Mall entrance
2. Cash desk
3. Womenswear
4. Street entrance
5. VIP lounge
6. Menswear
7. Beauty products

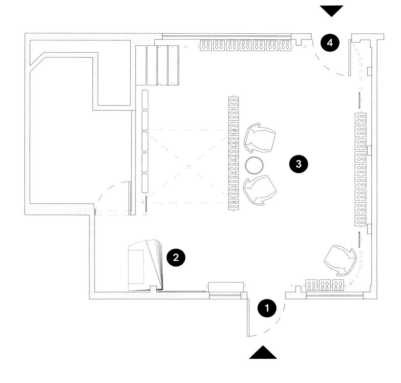

one of the sofas belongs to louboutin, himself

BIRD'S-EYE VIEW SKETCH

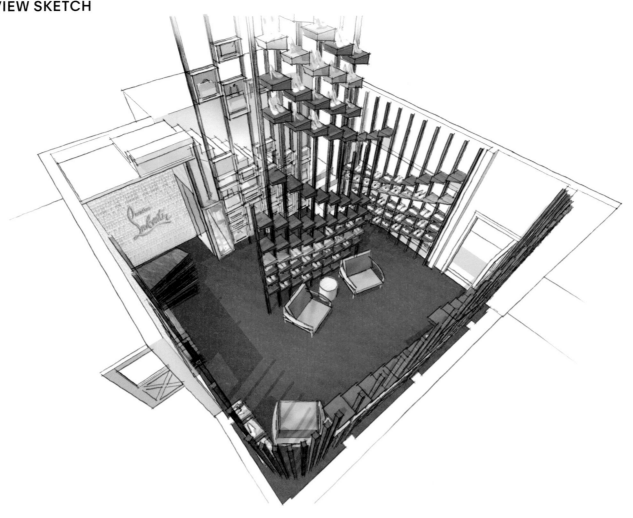

DIGITAL SKETCH OF DISPLAYS

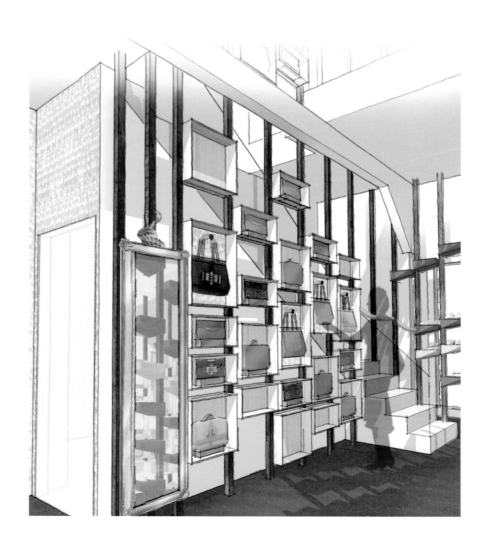

VIP LOUNGE

campaign design

Where	London, United Kingdom
Opening	July 2015
Client	Kurt Geiger
Designer	Campaign Design (p.409)
Floor space	330 m²
Shop constructor	Clements
Photos	Nick Hufton

kurt geiger harrods

Cylindrical platforms serve as tree trunk-like displays.

In a booming retail space, footwear brand Kurt Geiger briefed Campaign Design to create a bold and memorable shop-within-shop concept that would be tucked into Harrods department store. The resulting solution serves as play space and a realm of the imagination for the 'mini-adult' – both kids and parents – within the very grown-up Harrods environment. Campaign's creative team envisioned it as a 'luxurious and magical space' inspired by the Japanese animation *My Neighbor Totoro* about two girls who embark on a series of adventures with woodland spirits. This abstracted world is complete with a forest of enchanted trees, a furry woodland seating area, a forest canopy consisting of folded polished aluminium tiles and a digital storytelling and entertainment zone. The austere visual language manages to balance refinement with a perception of lavish whimsy that is articulated in the tropes of this fantastical forest. Beneath the abstract white trees, which grow toward the ceiling to support a 'canopy' of creased chrome 'leaves', kids can climb on a series of plush seats dressed in green mink to play on iPads while their parents browse. Like a glade in a forest clearing, the configuration of trees wraps a central teal lounge. The material chosen support this luxe but minimal aesthetic with a marble cash counter, mirrored columns, terrazzo floors, cowhide and faux fur.

The kids' designer shoes are displayed under an abstract forest of folded metal 'leaves'.

Green Mink conkers are the focal point within the enchanted forest.

a realm of imagination for the 'mini-adult'

abraham chan

Where	Hong Kong, China
Opening	October 2014
Client	Pedder Group
Designer	Abraham Chan (p.408)
Floor space	126 m²
Shop constructor	Ardes Design Associates
Photos	James Fung

on pedder men

To emphasise the curatorial quality of the broad array of products on display, Abraham Chan camouflaged the first menswear flagship for Pedder as a collector's apartment. The shop features a swank 'living room' furnished with a highbrow collection of international furnishings by big-name designers that reflects the international character of the brand, including pieces by Polish-Brazilian architect Jorge Zalsupin, French designer Christophe Delcourt, Austrian Marco Dessi and German Sebastian Herkner. This tony domestic setting encourages visitors to stay longer and explore. The 'living room' hosts the main footwear collection beside the fireplace, along with small accessories showcased in displays set into limestone walls and wooden portals that contain secret display niches. From the parlour, these two large 'portals' open into a narrow gallery. Display podiums highlight the latest products as well as a wall of sunglasses. Informal and friendly material and colour palettes contrast with megabrand retail spaces nearby: white painted walls, a pale ash wood floor and large wooden passageways. Hand-crafted details also add to the human scale and warmth of the store. In fact, the traditional mannequins were tattooed by local artists, a form of artwork that matches a rotating collection of work by emerging international artists, including local favourite, Michael Lau.

The design of the shop resembles a living room.

The colour palette and materials were chosen to feel friendlier than the more intimidating starchy shops nearby.

hand-crafted details add to the human scale and warmth

Handcrafted details like real tattoo art on mannequins introduce art alongside works by emerging artists.

abraham chan

Where	Singapore, Singapore
Opening	October 2015
Client	Pedder Group
Designer	Abraham Chan (p.408)
Floor space	1860 m²
Shop constructor	Pushing Tin
Photos	Allen Tan

pedder on scotts

Pergola-like structure makes the lighting scheme more versatile.

In the city's wildly popular Orchard Road shopping district, Abraham Chan, Ply Union and the in-house Pedder design team sought to evoke the feeling of spending a pleasant day in a modern, but rather quirky, gallery. The creative teams parcelled this Pedder store into zones, each with a distinct look and feel, but all linked both visually and spatially around an atrium. This establishes a circular path that distinguishes itself from the rather dull sequential arrangement of the conventional department store. The zoning feels orderly but, within that tidy structure, visitors feel free to wander and browse without becoming overwhelmed. This design solution allowed the teams to define stylistically unique areas – think hypergraphic blue rooms with striped walls, woven pendant lamps and a turquoise wood-grain carpet, a room arranged around an Airstream trailer and old wood furnishings turned into unconventional display tables – that highlight the qualities shared by the diverse brands 'curated' together in each retail area. In the meantime, there are also particular design gestures – softly relief patterned walls, wood surfaces or muted colours – that provide a more neutral backdrop against which products pop. In the end, each zone is styled radically differently, almost as if each were a different – and very expressive – store, and yet the spirit of each seems of a kind.

An Airstream trailer is used for display and movable track lighting for precision illumination.

Abraham Chan

Pedder on Scotts

each zone is styled radically differently

A showcase of pyramidal glass-topped chest of drawers, a hanging bike and a wooden wall cut in faceted relief.

In this exuberantly blue room, curated brands and products are displayed.

Pivoting glass doors, slathered with graphical, handwritten messages, open both into the shop and into the mall.

abraham chan

Where	Hong Kong, China
Opening	January 2015
Client	Pedder Group
Designer	Abraham Chan (p.408)
Floor space	77 m²
Shop constructor	Ardes Design Associates
Photos	James Fung

pedder red flagship

Each room is bright, pale and smooth with accents of colour in the form of the showroom rug and a window display.

Abraham Chan describes this shoe and accessories flagship as 'a small shop designed to act like a big one'. At only 77 m² with a ceiling height of 2.3 m, this heavily trafficked store in the Harbour City Shopping Centre highlights the sales desk, keeps shoppers moving fluidly through its two entrances and showcases a large, changing inventory that they made easily restockable. The design team divided the space into three rooms, including a long rectangular gallery that is the primary retail floor, the narrow walls of which give it the illusion of height; a smaller anteroom where purchases are made; and a super-compact stock room in the rear. The room divisions establish a hierarchy of spaces that encourage browsing. The display and sales rooms are distinguished subtly by their complementary but distinct finishes: the display room is lined with grey oak, bespoke wooden shelving, a natural oak floor and a custom cut-pile wool area rug in jewel tones that injects colour into the space. The point of sales area is a bright white space with a monolithic white marble counter that, through the windows, also serves as what the designers think of as a 'beacon' for the flagship.

Chan's team partitioned this little, low-ceilinged shop into three rooms to show a high volume of merchandise.

hierarchy of spaces encourage browsing

The design combines a variety of distinct finishes that complement each other.

Abraham Chan

Pedder Red Flagship

TELEC
AND
SER

fabrice ausset
interior design

Where	Nanterre, France
Opening	May 2015
Client	BNP Paribas Cardif
Designer	Fabrice Ausset Interior Design (p.410)
Floor space	200 m²
Shop constructor	Candelas
Photos	Eric Legrand

cardif lab

Large screens are embedded in the walls of each room.

'200 m² to be connected to the world' is how Fabrice Ausset describes this showroom of technological innovations and a future work space that is mobile, connected and immediately adaptable. The space shows off the high-tech by using very low-tech material: Ausset composed the walls of the lab from cardboard and Corian. It is precisely the perceived contradiction between the organic and the technological, respectively that he co-opts to create an environment geared towards comfort and discovery simultaneously. From the entrance, Ausset dovetails technology and architecture 'to disrupt the concept of space': an individual visitor accesses the lab through an 'airlock' that is lined with mirrors set into a chevron pattern. In the bright white room beyond, large screens are tiled into the walls, on which the visitor may watch an interactive animation. The space is simple, strongly material, modular and accessible. It consists of subtle colours, textures and lighting intended to pleasantly pique the curiosity and promote the process of discovery. Natural materials and the honeycomb of the cardboard range through beige to brown tones while the tan and green carpet suggests both the mineral and the world of plants. Colours – green signage, yellow and orange – and bright lights dot the white lacquered wood or Corian to create a playful effect.

Visitors enter the lab through an 'air lock', passing a phalanx of mirrors.

Fabrice Ausset Interior Design   Cardif Lab

The lab blends technology, natural materials and colours to express the environmental and sustainable concerns of the client.

the space shows off the high-tech by using very low-tech materials

A contrast of high-tech backlit Corian with the warmer, more organic look of the honeycomb texture of cardboard are showcased.

io studio

Where — Prague, Czech Republic
Opening — December 2014
Client — ČSOB Bank
Designer — IO Studio (p.411)
Floor space — 240 m²
Shop constructor — DCH-Sincolor
Photos — Jonáš Mlejnek

era bank

Without severing sightlines or space, the columns seem to shelter both meeting and lounge spaces.

With Era Bank, IO Studio refreshed the typically wearying banking experience. In spite of the advanced technologies tucked into it, the space has great clarity while looking analogue and welcoming. Instead of practically bullet-proof teller counters that seem to anticipate a run on the bank, there are slim workstations. Instead of plastics and vinyls, natural materials – wooden timbers, woven flooring – and organic forms prevail. This is a bank that bespeaks shelter, security and optimism: breaking up the interior without cutting spaces off from each other or overly interrupting sightlines. Together with the design team, founder Luka Krizek relied on biomorphic softly linear shapes and stripy sculptural details made from oak timber slats over walls and columns that recall the image of a breeze running through robust but supple trees. Circulation is created and navigation guided intuitively via a lamellar wooden wall that partitions the bank into five specialised areas like small glades opening up in a forest. The mapping of the furniture within the individual areas means that a banker is always nearby, but without impinging on each client's sense of privacy. IO Studio used TON and Vitra furniture but also installed the wooden ARBO light designed by the studio for Halla and created bespoke furniture solitaires in a bright white Corian, that give the space bright lightness.

The space is both private and accessible.

io studio refreshed the typical weary banking experience

Close-up detail of the Corian furniture.

The glass face of the store makes much of it visible from the outside.

doepel strijkers

Where	Haarlem, the Netherlands
Opening	May 2015
Client	KPN Retail
Designer	DoepelStrijkers (p.410)
Floor space	90 m²
Shop constructor	Bpr retail
Photos	Teo Krijgsman

KPN

The shop is framed by LED and interactive smart walls, which connect the virtual brand space that is online to the physical shops.

DoepelStrijkers believe that printed fly posters, paper-borne graphics and information and quaint items such as price tags have become obsolete in commercial ventures today. The designers were asked to move the telecommunications brand KPN's stores away from being 'product-oriented shops with intangible services' toward being environments focused precisely on both experiences and services. A clever interior solution encompasses a template that can be rolled out to all the brand's stores. It consists of a versatile structure made up of minimalist modular elements, the units of which serve as seating, work surfaces and display for products or information. The designers describe the scheme as being 'future-proof', by which they mean that the scheme allows for extremely easy scalability and adaptations even those that cannot yet be anticipated but which may become necessary later. Another important aspect of the concept was for the designers to link the company's virtual telecommunications shop, which customers are accustomed to using extensively online, to the physical one by turning entire walls of the store into LED and interactive surfaces that operate using infrared and Kinect technologies. These have the virtue of being programmable on-site or remotely and are capable of reacting to the movements of the shoppers.

the scheme allows for easy scalability and adaptations

Between the colourful smart walls of the shop, modular white units form a single surface that serves as seating, display or screen to countertop.

concept i

Where	Bangkok, Thailand
Opening	May 2015
Client	Bank of Ayudhya
Designer	Concept i (p.409)
Floor space	230 m²
Shop constructor	Pharapatch Construction
Photos	Owen Raggett

krungsri bank

This 70-year-old Thai bank got not just a new name and new customer-technology interfaces, but a new face too, one that appears contemporary while still conveying its venerable age. Concept i defined three 'sensual zones': at the bank entrance, the first is a dark area highlighting interactive screens intended to 'inspire customers to stop, think and try something new.' The second zone is where the tellers are located and where clients wait to be served in a lounge-like space of cushy benches and chairs embraced with a curtain, so to speak, of brass rods. The third is a wayfinding zone that aids navigation with clear signage. The designers chose materials that update the bank in order to draw in a younger customer: dark 'Colour Core' glass panels were matched to the existing brand colour, a maroon grey, dark-stained engineered oak clads the floor and ceiling highlights while the remaining walls were sheathed in 3 m film to match the establishment's 'graphic pathway'. Concept i custom designed all the furniture in light grey upholstery with yellow highlights to match the brand identity. The crowning element is a large, colour-toned black-and-white photograph of the renowned Ayudhya temples by an accomplished local photographer Marc Schultz. Of course, the photographer gilded its temple stupors by hand – they too echo the brand palette.

the design provides a new contemporary banking experience

This area is an 'exploration' zone, where clients have access to tellers who can explain services and products.

A wall-size mural of famous Thai temples hand-gilded by the local photographer in the brand's primary colour.

The lounge seating is decked out in the brand's colours and screened by a curved 'wall' of brass rods.

The foyer provides a dimmed environment that emphasises interactive screens.

andrea lupacchini architetto

Where	Rome, Italy
Opening	October 2013
Client	Promesse Viaggi
Designer	Andrea Lupacchini Architetto (p.408)
Floor space	400 m²
Shop constructor	S.D.B 2000 Construzioni
Photos	Francesco Galli

promesse viaggi

'The conquest of the customer must be complete and must involve all the senses,' says Andrea Lupacchini who designed this travel agency, which he also describes as a concept store for travel. The building is a formally exuberant collage of deconstructed geometric shapes and robust material contrasts in neutral tones, what the architect calls a 'kaleidoscopic container, ever-changing and flexible.' This expressive construction is more than good advertising: it lets visitors imagine the journey, not just through geography but through the emotions, as well. He grafted a patchwork of parallelepipeds made of micro-perforated sheet metal onto the concrete building to serve as screens that carry imagery. The facade can be radically altered by its RGB lighting according to colour, image and which sections of the building are lit. Inside, a hidden air conditioning unit wafts pleasant scents into the office, drawing on the senses right away. Surfaces are finished with either white gelcoat or black resin, sometimes matte, sometimes glossy. The ceiling of one floor is crowned with a starry sky of pinpoint lights and the workstations are not just desks but plastic forms cut out of the ceiling above them and pulled downward, drawing light down with them. It is the third floor roof garden that provides illumination for the skylit lower floors and where events are hosted day and night.

Pixel-like windows also recall portholes on the facade of this building for a travel agency.

The formal eccentricities and material contrasts complement one another.

Andrea Lupacchini Architetto   Promesse Viaggi

The design is expressive and formal with a variety of deconstructed volumes and contrasting materials.

the kaleidoscopic container is ever-changing

One part of the ceiling features a starry sky of pinpoint LED light spots.

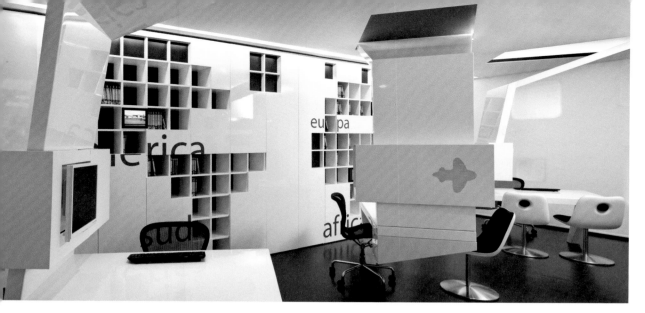

Geometric shapes and sleek finishes creates a modern space.

GROUND FLOOR

1. Catalogue exhibition
2. Travel agent
3. Office
4. Restroom
5. Small pond
6. Garden
7. Apartment space
8. Skylight
9. Conference space
10. Seating area
11. Control room
12. Kitchen

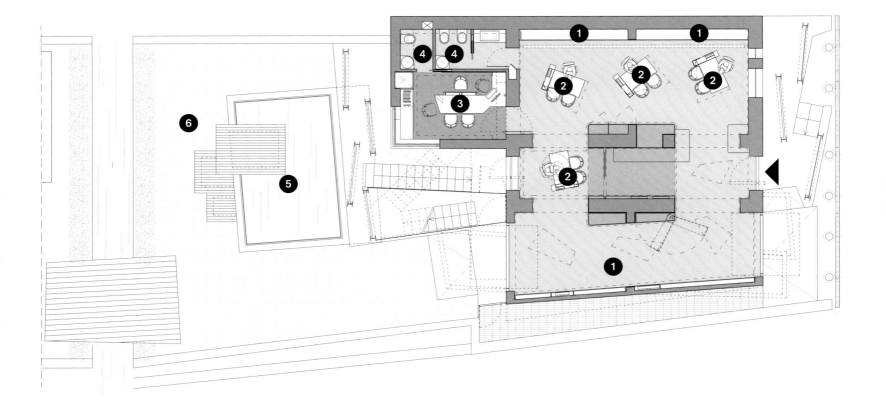

The organic white panels are arranged to hold advertising, promotion and communication on a large scale.

A glossy sculptural red staircase accesses each floor from the rear of the building.

SECOND FLOOR

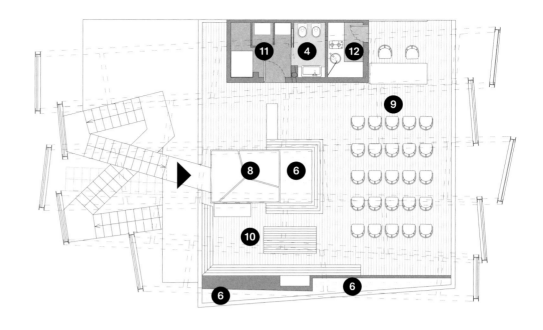

FIRST FLOOR

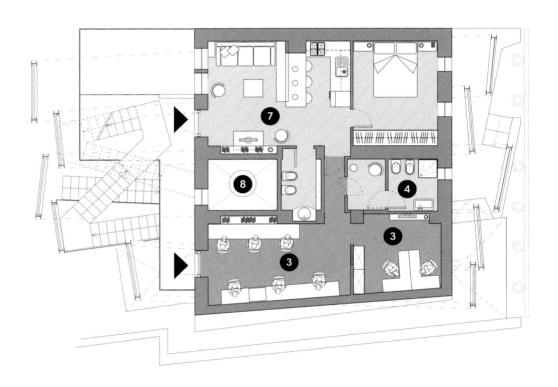

DISPLAY CASE VISUAL

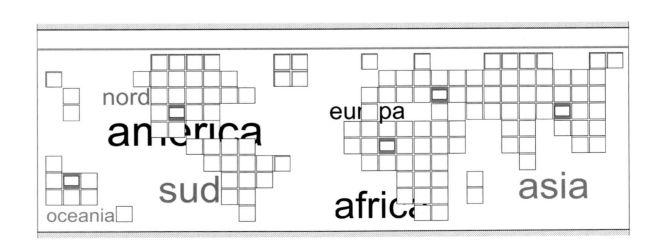

Bolts of blue streak across the backdrop
of white-stained wooden surfaces.

haf studio

Where	Reykjavik, Iceland
Opening	January 2015
Client	Síminn
Designer	Haf Studio (p.411)
Floor space	150 m²
Shop constructor	JP Innrettingar
Photos	Gunnar Sverrisson

síminn

The bespoke display units are mobile to allow for day-to-day requirements or to open up the space for events.

Haf Studio has designed a flagship store for the Icelandic telecom brand Síminn, creating a unique customer experience in a contemporary interior. The goal was to present the latest tech gadgets in a space that has a warm, homely feel. Incorporating the client's identity in an engaging way was another high priority, which is where the beguiling shade of blue comes in that ties a thread throughout the whole retail scenography. This is teamed with white-stained ash and pine surfaces that give the space a particularly Nordic feel. An additional material palette of concrete and felt, is completed with all-Scandinavian furnishings, from the light fittings and furniture to the design details. 'What is interesting about this project is that we worked from the aspect of experience design, in particular focusing on every little detail to make the customer experience unique, with consideration given to the interaction with sales representatives,' comments the design team. Cue the bespoke, and a little bit quirky, display units that are flexible in form and function. The mobility in the base units offers staff the option to move them around ensuring the workstation layouts adapt to the requirements on any particular day. This answers the design brief accurately, which called for the store to be interchangeable and capable of being adaptable to various events, from conferences and presentations to musical performances.

A warm, inviting space has been created for users to try out the latest tech gadgets or engage with the interactive light wall.

the designers worked from the aspect of experience design

The flagship store for telecom brand Síminn is decked-out with Nordic design details.

pinkeye

Where	Ghent, Belgium
Opening	January 2015
Client	Telenet
Designer	Pinkeye (p.414)
Floor space	125 m²
Shop constructor	Beerens Winkelbouw
Photos	Verne

telenet

For Belgium's star telecommunications operator, Pinkeye created a flagship that bespeaks 'seamless connectivity'. The interior presents a friendly, family-oriented, fun-loving client who offers experiences instead of opaque technology; a provider of human connectivity, entertainment and empowerment instead of just a 'provider'. Pinkeye designed 'from outside to inside', building two yellow-framed 'portals' into the shop and creating an unconventional high street storefront to engage people from the outside. Inside, the aim was to allow visitors to explore instead of just waiting and queuing and to apply technology in an understated manner, scaling it to suit customers instead of overwhelming them. In lieu of entrenching store clerks behind counters and desks, the designers established 'informal but informational' loci throughout the shop where consultations and conversations take place in a more collegial fashion. The resulting space has clarity, lightness, warmth and, yes, connectivity: in part this is discernible in the intuitive circulation and an unusual wayfinding tool: clusters of pendant light fixtures run across the ceiling, dropping down at points of interest to customers. Turning to accessible materials like ceramic and wood, vintage furnishings dressed in American walnut and a full-colour print wallcovering, the team cut down on marketing messages and logos and let the brand express itself through a human interface instead of a hard sell.

Flos lights guide visitors through, hanging lower at strategic sales or info points.

A house-shaped element shelters the tellers' desks providing intimacy in a relatively open space.

Telecom and Services

Customer and clerks can meet at small tables, informally and collaboratively.

a flagship that bespeaks 'seamless connectivity'

The design presents a source of entertainment, empowerment and connection amongst people.

KMS blackspace

Where	Cologne, Germany
Opening	July 2013
Client	Vodafone Deutschland
Designer	KMS Blackspace (p.412)
Floor space	200 m²
Shop constructor	KMS Blackspace
Photos	Jörg Hempel

vodafone flagship

Working closely with the national heritage office, KMS Blackspace needed to balance busy retail with a compelling brand experience in this telecommunications flagship in an historic building in Cologne's city centre. Largely by reducing the amount of branding over its surfaces, the mostly glass facade exposes and frames activities on both floors inside for passers-by on the pedestrian mall below: energetic product display in the Product 'theme world' on the ground floor and, upstairs, the Service theme world which hosts technical support, customer service and a cosy coffee shop. To allow the store to be easily reconfigured, the creative team created a modular furniture system along with lighting channels containing spots that can be managed by pre-programmed smart scene control. In identifying the primary points of interface between customer and brand and rethinking the visitor's journey through the building, a central brand wall with interactive media display was created to connect both floors. The brand wall influences the look and feel of the interiors whilst remaining flexible and welcoming interaction between customers and the client. This type of versatility – in scalable furnishings, brand space, media panels and communications elements – is key to the solution and allows for a high degree of adaptability, an adaptability that will be exploited as this template is re-created in subsequent shop interiors, trade show stands and industry events.

The ground floor is devoted to product information and display.

Modular furniture systems, specifically made for the store, allow for flexibilty within the space.

Technical support and customer service include a small coffee bar on the first floor.

A central red brand wall with interactive media display connects the two floors.

a glass facade exposes and frames activities

The transparent facade, largely free of signage, broadcasts activities on both floors to passers-by on the mall below.

FIRST FLOOR

1. Welcome desk
2. Consultation
3. Display wall
4. Cash desk
5. Coffee bar
6. Customer service desk

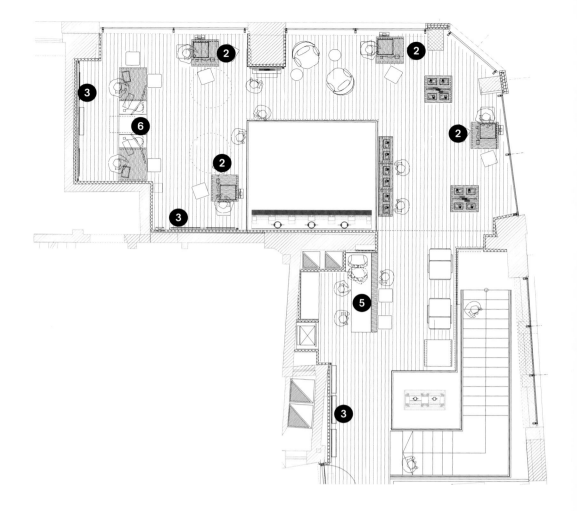

GROUND FLOOR

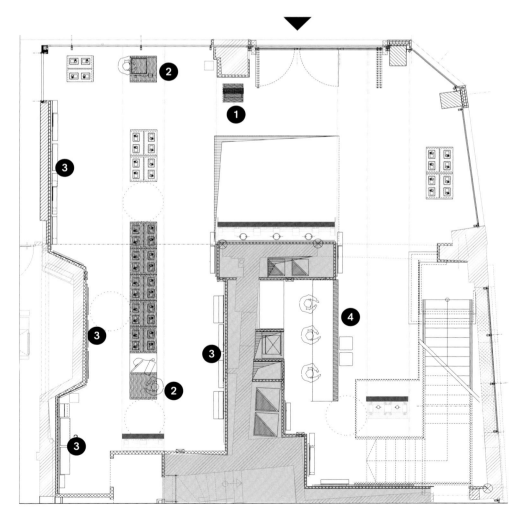

3deluxe
3deluxe.de

For more than two decades, Weisbaden-based 3deluxe has worked at the intersection of design, architecture, art and pop culture, in what the practice describes as 'transdisciplinary design'. The international office develops design concepts that cross creative boundaries and media with a bold formality and distinctive aesthetics. 3deluxe follow a creative philosophy that informs their multifaceted process and keep them attuned to social and cultural shifts that inspire and inform their work.

Abraham Chan
abraham-chan.com

From Toronto, Abraham Chan creates spaces to improve quality of life. The design office takes a human-centric approach to designing small to medium retail, residential and commercial spaces. Chan, himself, earned his architecture degree at the Rhode Island School of Design and, before launching his studio in 2014, managed projects at Yabu Pushelberg, ranging from the Louis Vuitton VIP Suites Hong Kong and the Waldorf Astoria Beijing to Miami condominiums and a Bangkok concept shop. / Photo by Maxime Bocken

Anagrama
anagrama.com

Based in Monterrey and Mexico City, since 2008, Anagrama has done high-impact branding, architecture and software development for an international clientele. The three founders, Sebastian Padilla, Mike Herrera, and Gustavo Muñoz started the studio in Muñoz's house; today, they direct a staff of more than 30 creatives and programmers along with new partners, Roberto Treviño and Danie Garza. Their approach focuses on solutions based on creative detail, the analysis of data and the integration of multidisciplinary teams.

Andrea Lupacchini Architetto
lupacchini.it

Roman architect Andrea Lupacchini graduated with honours in architecture from the University of Rome 'La Sapienza.' Since 1992, he has taught architecture, environmental design and classes about spatial design, food and well-being. He has also published books about food design, ergonomics and comfort and quality of life in the home. The studio's diverse commissions include commercial and residential architecture, domestic interiors, offices, restaurants, public spaces like parks, plazas and exhibitions.

Atelier Markgraph
markgraph.de

A leading agency for spatial communication, Atelier Markgraph combines interdisciplinary design and planning. Located in Frankfurt am Main the office creates tangible spatial experiences for clients that enables the user to experience companies, brands and themes in a three-dimensional context. With the use of leading technology, Atelier Markgraph incorporates disciplines such as the economy, culture and science to create spatial productions varying from exhibitions, media to corporate architecture. / Photo by Axel Jansen

BEHF Corporate Architects
behf.at

Armin Ebner, Susi Hasenauer and Stephan Ferenczy came together as BEHF Corporate Architects in 1995. Today, with 100 employees, they are commissioned to create both small and large-scale projects. For individuals up to multinational corporations like Deutsche Bank and Telekom Austria. The office works on retail and office space, shopping centres, listed building refurbishment, residences and hospitality calling on skills that range far beyond design into site supervision, tendering and procurement activities, lead consulting and project management. / Photo by Markus Kaiser

Blocher Blocher Partners
BlocherBlocher.com

Launched in 1989 by Dieter and Jutta Blocher, Blocher Blocher's practice makes an art of 'interlocking' their expertise in architecture and interior design, respectively. Based in Stuttgart, Mannheim and Ahmedabad, commissions range from commercial, residential and mixed-use projects, shopping malls, hospitality and retail design to their realisation. Daughter brands Blocher Blocher Shops and Blocher Blocher View extend the practice into branding, mono-brand and decor conception, corporate and graphic design, communications and visual merchandising.

Brinkworth
brinkworth.co.uk

Brinkworth is the eponymous design consultancy founded by Adam Brinkworth in London. Since 1990, the firm's international commissions have crisscrossed a range of creative disciplines, including architecture, interior, graphic and brand design and worked on production and market strategy. Brinkworth teams have worked with a wide variety of clients to imagine retail, branded environments, hospitality, office and residential space at every scale from unique spaces to global concepts. / Photo by Louise Melchior

Burdifilek
Burdifilek.com

Based in Toronto, Burdifilek is an interior design consultancy founded by creative director Diego Burdi and managing partner Paul Filek. Burdi and Filek have designed internationally, partnering with retail, real estate, and hospitality brands for more than two decades. Their approach folds together 'sophistication and creative intelligence', seeking inspiration in travel, art and artisanry. The resulting expressive interiors transcend trends and have the relevance to engage audiences from all over the world.

Campaign Design
campaigndesign.co.uk

'We believe in thinking differently.' Philip Handford founded London and Shanghai based Campaign Design in 2008. His 12-person team of retail savants is expert in fashioning handsome, intelligent, memorable retail spaces that broadcast the brand message for clients like Burberry and Virgin. The team's commissions run the gamut from product launches, pop-up shops and sumptuous flagships with global rollouts to creative direction, production and the hosting of narrative 'event experiences', emphasising the strategic, collaborative nature of creativity.

Christophe Carpente CAPS Architecture Interior Design
caps-architects.com

Christophe Carpente is a retail architect who, since 1997, has completed more than 500 high-end stores, involving international roll-outs of store templates, as well as graphic, furniture and lighting design for a stellar client list that includes international luxury brands De Beers, Cartier, Swarovski, Vertu, Hugo Boss and Christian Lacroix. The architect imagines compelling, expressive, deeply detailed retail environments that pinpoint and communicate the essence of each client's identity and commercial vision. / Photo by Arnaud Baumann

Claudio Pironi & Partners
studiopironi.com

'We Create Solid Dreams,' is the mantra of architect Claudio Pironi, who launched Forli-based Studio Pironi in 1997. In opening the office, Pironi sought to create 'synergies' between the fields of architecture and design. By 2005, he had established an eponymous firm offering services that integrate fashion, architecture and interior design in the realms of retail, luxury real estate and the hospitality industry. Today, the office consists of 32 architects, planners, interior and industrial designers. / Photo by Marco Onofri

Clemens Bachmann Architekten
cbarchitekten.com

Established by architect Clemens Bachmann in Munich in 2004, Clemens Bachmann Architekten is a multidisciplinary practice working internationally on architecture and design, both on residential projects and office space. Today Bachmann's creative team is made up of seven people, including both architects and interior designers. Some of the most recognisable CBA projects include the Restaurant Olympiasee in Olympic Park, Munich, the Business Club in the Allianz Arena and the Premium Lounge of FC Basel.

Concept i
concept-i-design.com

Executive director Geoff Morrison launched his studio Concept i in 1996 and has watched it grow into a multidisciplinary design practice with offices in Bangkok, Shanghai and Istanbul, areas of the world that have, themselves, been growing and changing fast. Concept i has been responsible for more than 1,000,000 m² of built projects that focus on high-visibility commercial, retail and leisure projects with a special emphasis on retail dining and entertainment space.

Coordination Asia
coordination.asia

Tilman Thürmer studied architecture at the Berlin University of Arts and, in 1994, began to design international museum and exhibition environments with an emphasis on transforming these institutions and archives into 'living communities'. Thürmer co-founded Coordination Berlin with architect Jochen Gringmuth and product designer Flip Sellin and then, in 2008, opened sister practice Coordination Asia in Shanghai. Today the 13-person team specialises in the creation of high impact museum, exhibition, retail and hospitality environments. / Photo by Coordination Asia

Corneille Uedingslohmann Architekten
cue-architekten.de

In 2002, Yves Corneille and Peter Uedingslohmann brought their names and talents together to form Corneille Uedingslohmann Architekten in Cologne, Germany. The two designers dedicated themselves and their office to exploring comprehensive architectural design, especially in the niche of retail interiors, using canny choices of material, texture and color to create small world's not just pretty shopping space. The studio has been working nationally and internationally ever since with an emphasis on cultivating long-term relationships with its clients.

Creneau International
creneau.com

Creneau International is a global agency that connects brands, spaces and consumers through design concepts. Established in 1989, the Hasselt-based office provides a full service, from concepts and consultancy to graphics, interiors, and F&B support for projects including hospitality, retail and branding. / Photo by Philippe van Gelooven

Dalziel & Pow
dalziel-pow.com

Working for the likes of Primark, Samsung, Next, John Lewis and O2 for 30 years, Dalziel & Pow creates engaging brands all around the world. The London agency's retail design experts excel at retail and experience strategy, brand definition, and interior, digital and graphic design. Creating innovative concepts, formats and environments, Dalziel & Pow defines brands and designs engaging experiences at the vanguard of a rapidly changing retail landscape.

D'art Design Gruppe
d-art-design.de

Because today's world is complex and saturates all of the senses, the D'art Design Gruppe is a spatial communications agency where design is developed through interdisciplinary collaboration. The Neuss, Germany-based office creates brand experience and 'adventure' spaces incorporating digital media – in fact, marrying various media channels – as well as modern graphics for clients such as adidas, Amtico, Bogner, Electrolux, Gabor, Grundig, Henkel, Lloyd, Panasonic, Philips, RWE, Schüco, Turck, Würth and Zaha Hadid. / Photo by D'art Design Gruppe

Denis Košutić
deniskosutic.com

Through the fantastical and minimalist lens of Vienna-based Denis Košutić, traditional notions are re-examined and renewed. He describes his work as 'prêt-à-porter-architecture', a translation of modern trends and fashion industry habits into spaces that treat everyday life with whimsy and inspiration. His work may begin with the strategic creation of a fresh – thoroughly modern – brand image and corporate identity and continue through the design of restaurants, nightclubs, shops, hotel apartments and modern furniture, as well as residential space. / Photo by Dobromir Zagorov

dfrost
dfrost.com

Founded in 2008 by Nadine Frommer and brothers, Christoph and Fabian Stelzer, dfrost creates brand spaces by translating identities into realms of experience. The retail identity agency is dedicated to designing the point of sale, the actual moment in space where the decision to purchase is made. Now 50 strong, dfrost's staff or 'brand companions' collaborate in interdisciplinary teams to design retail window display, visual merchandising, retail architecture, POS events, visual communication and comprehensive all-channel digital solutions. / Photo by Ramon Haindl

Dittel Architekten (DIA)
di-a.de

Founded in 2005 by Frank Dittel, Dittel Architekten (DIA) 'creates, defines and differentiates brands' in close consultation with its clients. Today, the office consists of 30 architects, interior and communication designers, who focus on the creation of 'an intriguing, characteristic and exclusive look' for each brand. From concept through construction and finish, Dittel's practice is interdisciplinary and takes on architecture, design and branding commissions in the areas of corporate, hospitality and retail space. / Photo by Dittel Arkitekten (DIA)

DoepelStrijkers
doepelstrijkers.com

Dutch design firm DoepelStrijkers is driven by a fascination for aesthetics with substance. They strive to generate works that create social, ecological and economic value. This duo create bold, monolithic commercial interiors that optimise user experience while capturing the essence of the brand identity. Their design solutions are not intuitively conceived, each project is the result of an extensive iterative design process. This scaleless, multidisciplinary approach often results in intriguing hybrid solutions. / Photo by Yvonne van Brandwijk

d-raw
d-raw.com

This architectural and interior design collective situated at the heart of London boasts a diverse client list and an equally great variety of bespoke design projects. Beyond their architectural skills, the d-raw team members, who reserve a special place in their hearts for less conventional commissions, are also experts in creative branding, retail design and renovation. The reach of their creativity and building capabilities is also extended by a satellite team of specialists dispersed across the globe.

Duccio Grassi Architects
ducciograssiarchitects.com

Based in Milan and Reggio Emilia, Duccio Grassi's architecture practice creates materially rich boutiques and showrooms for fashion clients like Max Mara and Zara. Commissions for the 20-person team run from the domestic to the commercial, from private villas to restaurants and jewellery shops. But they also move deftly between scales, building large shopping centres and offices, including Wafi City Mall in Dubai and Al Yasra headquarters in Kuwait, while also designing furniture for brands like Emmebi and Minotti Cucine. / Photo by Andrea Martiradonna

einszu33
www.einszu33.com

Einszu33 is a Munich-based firm for architecture and interior design, launched in 1999. Directed by Hendrik Müller and Georg Thiersch, a team of 18 works internationally on projects in the field of corporate architecture and brand communication, creating brand experience and temporary environments. The project portfolio includes showrooms, retail spaces, exhibition stands as well as work environments and hospitality concepts. Their clients are mostly premium brands in various industries like domestic appliances, automotive, cosmetics, fashion, food or hospitality. / Photo by Bodo Mertoglu

Fabrice Ausset Interior Design
fabriceausset.net

A sculptor, colourist and collector who deftly synthesises opposites, Fabrice Ausset studied the fine arts in Nîmes and architecture in Marseille. His early choice of projects – huts, sheds, textiles – privileged the obscure challenge over the obvious. In 1987, with partner Eric Bougaud, Ausset founded Zoevox Studio. Today the diverse team does interior design, furniture and digital environments, luxury apartments, scenography, hotels, concept shops, even the refurbishment of a castle. Ausset also created his own studio in 2015 which is a mix of art gallery, architecture and artist lab. / Photo by Philippe Garcia

Genesin Studio
genesin.com.au

In 2008, Ryan Genesin launched his eponymous studio to create practical, bespoke and meticulously detailed spaces. As the creative director, Genesin directs a burgeoning staff of five creatives who look to 'reinvent' themselves with every architecture and interior design project they do whether residential interiors, hospitality or retail. The progressive design team emphasises the importance of experimentation, of understanding artisanal processes and materials and of creating spaces and details capable of eliciting moods and nostalgia. / Photo by Jonathan VDK

Grey Canopy
greycanopy.com

Grey Canopy is a design studio founded in 2009 by two self-described 'true-blue Singaporeans', Sam Ang and Sal Chua, who say they 'live, breathe and play' design. The commissions closest to their hearts include boutique resorts, retail environments and commercial offices. Grey Canopy focuses on what they call 'prototypical designs' and client-specific creative strategies. Their approach can be summed up by the acronym ACE: aesthetically-driven, designed for the convenience of users, and as environmentally-friendly as possible.

Haf Studio
hafstudio.is

Haf Studio is a multidisciplinary design studio run by designers Karitas Sveinsdóttir and Hafsteinn Júlíusson. The company was founded in Milan, Italy in 2010 and is currently located downtown Reykjavik. All Haf Studio projects are based on creative and constructive teamwork that involves diverse professionals led by Hafsteinn and Karitas. / Photo by Baldur Kristjánsson

Hidden Fortress
hidden-fortress.com

Jan Maley, Björn Meier and Ingo ‚Kalle' Strobel launched Berlin's Hidden Fortress interior and experience design studio in 2013, catering to iconic names like adidas, Bugatti and Absolut Vodka. Their approach is sustainable, cued by context, well-crafted and comprehensive, from concept through production, whilst their process focuses on both the needs of the client and the client's client, the end-user. They describe their work 'as the attempt to verify and unify' all aspects of each complex assignment. / Photo by Sebastian Doerken

HMKM
hmkm.com

HMKM is a retail-focused design consultancy founded in 1990 and based in Soho, one of London's most fertile retail districts. The practice creates 'Total Retail' brand environments, as well as spatial experiences at all scales, and considers design to be a powerful business tool and sales locomotive. Because it operates under the aegis of the Interbrand Group, it can also provide localised services that are supported by a global network of 34 offices.

Household
household-design.com

Julie Oxberry, Sarah Page and Michelle Du-Prât came together as Household in 2004 and describe their office as a 'customer experience design agency' that enables client brands to dominate their retail niche: the Household creative team designs environments that are brand experiences, as well as doing communications, for a portfolio of clients, including Amazon, Dunhill, Harrods, Tesco, Unilever and Vodafone. Today Household's 32 designers work internationally from offices in London and Los Angeles.

i29 Interior Architects
i29.nl

Ouder Amstel-based i29 Interior Architects was founded in 2003 by Jaspar Jansen and Jeroen Dellensen, who create robustly experiential space without being bound to costly materials or opaque technologies. Their design is responsive to multiple needs simultaneously and tells a conceptual tale about their client, the space and the individuals who will inhabit that space. Known for making much of very little, the studio works on a variety of commissions that range from commercial, retail and hospitality space to exhibition design.

Inblum Architects
inblum.com

Inblum is an architecture and design practice based in Vilnius, Lithuania. Established in 2005, the studio is directed by architects Dmitrij Kudin and Laura Malcaitė, who work on both public and private projects. Their practice is devoted to the creation of original spaces capable of inspiring their inhabitants, and spaces that pay keen attention to the intimate relationship between an architectural object or architectural space and its user. Their environments are distinguished, in particular, by their emotional power. / Photo by Lina Albrikienė

IO Studio
iostudio.cz

IO Studio was established in 2007 in Prague as a design and architecture office under the aegis of founder Luka Krizek and, since 2011, Radek Blaha. In 2013, IO Studio moved house into the historic centre of Prague, connecting the practice directly to a showroom, where the studio's furniture and product design are exhibited and sold. The firm's commissions vary widely across a spectrum of residential projects to public contracts and work for multinational corporations.

Ippolito Fleitz Group
ifgroup.org

Multidisciplinary, international design studio Ippolito Fleitz Group is based in Stuttgart. This creative team of 50 designers works in ever-shifting project-based teams over a broad spectrum of design, ranging from strategy to architecture and landscape architecture, interiors, product and graphics. Their commissions are celebrated for their simultaneously warm and cool glamour, elegance of form and finish, artful colour schemes, the hypnotic repetition of form and a restrained, noble palette of materials like brass, marble and lush textiles.

Ito Masaru Design Project/SEI
itomasaru.com

Osaka-born Ito Masaru graduated from Tokyo Zokei University in 1987. After working in the Kawasaki Takao Office, Ito Masaru established his own studio, SEI (Sensitive Erotic Intelligent) Co. in 1991, eventually giving the studio his own name in 2005. Working both in Japan and internationally, he has become known as a maverick in the interior design industry and for creating unusual spaces through understated novelty instead of overdesign. / Photo by Miki Murata

Jo Nagasaka/Schemata Architects
schemata.jp/

Jo Nagasaka founded Schemata in 1998 on graduating from the Tokyo University of the Arts and then the collective creative office HAPPA nine years later. In Tokyo's Aoyama district, he takes on diverse projects ranging from furniture and interiors to architecture. Some of the studio's most recognisable work includes the Flat Table for the Sayama Flat (2008), the Aesop Aoyama shop (2011), the House in Okusawa (2009) and an exhibition stand for VITRA in Milan (2015). / Photo by Taro Hirano

KMS Blackspace
kms-blackspace.com

Munich-based KMS Blackspace reinvents brand interiors and designs unique brand experiences. KMS Blackspace creatives acquire a deep intimacy with the nature of brands and brand space, create inventive and engaging touch points and have what they call 'a sovereign control of all media'. The studio works on spatial communication, motion design and customer experience design commissions, doing tradeshows and events, shops and showrooms, corporate headquarters, exhibitions, museums and cross-over events for businesses of any size or industry.

kplus konzept
kplus-konzept.de

kplus konzept, in Düsseldorf, is well-versed in the creation of brand-distinguishing shop interiors, brand communications that touch all the senses, and compelling shopping experiences for malls, healthcare and hospitality projects. Interior designer Bettina Kratz founded kplus konzept in 2005 with communication designer and photographer Markus Kratz. Today, its 20 creatives range from interior, 3D, web and product designers to writers, photographers and communications experts. Their client list includes fashion label Esprit and Santander Bank. / Photo by Markus Kratz

Kauffmann Theilig & Partner
ktp-architekten.de

Kauffmann Theilig & Partner is a partnership amongst Professor Andreas Theilig, Dieter Ben Kauffmann and Rainer Lenz which was founded in 1988. Situated in Stuttgart, the office collaborates with a variety of multidisciplinary engineers and experts to achieve integral design solutions. The office's international commissions range in a variety of scale from building construction to exhibition designs for a portfolio of clients, including adidas, Liebherr, seele, ADVA and Boehringer. / Photo by Wilfried Dechau

Landini Associates
landiniassociates.com

'Strategically driven but creatively led.' A former Conran creative director launched the Sydney's multidisciplinary design and brand consultancy in 1993. Today Landini Associates' team of 25 strategic planners, architects, interior, graphic and product designers focus on retail and hospitality projects and design every customer touchpoint to create a coherent, robust signature in buildings, interiors, identities, graphics, wayfinding, packaging, websites, uniforms and print. For Landini, trends aren't necessarily innovations, a belief that breathes longevity into the firm's projects.

Lautrefabrique Architects
lautrefabrique.com

Founded in 2001 by Jean-Pascal Crouzet, Lautrefabrique Architects work internationally, offering the full range of architectural services, on all scales. The office favours a pragmatic approach focusing on promoting straight forward, common sense solutions in both public and private markets. / Photo by Lautrefabrique Architects

Line-Inc.
line-inc.co.jp

Takao Katsuta founded Line-Inc. in 2002. Since then, the office has completed over 800 projects, including retail, bars, offices, restaurants, beauty salons and exhibition stands, with works worldwide in Shanghai, Hong Kong, Hawaii, London and New York as well as in Japan. Katsuta states that the office's strength is 'our experience and our ability to manipulate flexible ideas and inspirations'. / Photo by Kozo Takayama

Luchetti Krelle
luchettikrelle.com

Award winning Luchetti Krelle is a Sydney-based interior design and architecture practice founded in 2008 by directors Stuart Krelle and Rachel Luchetti. Although Luchetti Krelle have a diverse portfolio, their primary focus is in the hospitality sector. The studio endeavours to offer a total concept, including branding and identity design, and bespoke furniture and fittings. Their focus on developing a strong designer-client relationship allows for a dynamic and collaborative design process and a committed and personalised approach. / Photo by Toby Dixon

Marco Costanzi Architects
marcocostanzi.com

Bologna-born Marco Costanzi earned his architecture degree from Florence University with a thesis on architecture and the Japanese garden and launched his eponymous practice in 2006. Headquartered in Imola with an office in Rome, he takes on commissions in interior design, restoration and new builds. With high-profile projects like the much-lauded Fendi Hotel in Rome, Costanzi realises structures and spaces that demonstrate his skill in creating sumptuous environments, and his appreciation for the layered complexity of architectural space.

Mark't
getmarkt.com and marktheeuwes.nl

In 2012, creative director Mark Theeuwes launched Amsterdam-based Mark't. Theeuwes thinks fluidly across the creative and the commercial. He works on hospitality and residential and has studied retail deeply while working for 12 years in the fashion industry. Constantly asking himself how he can create the unexpected, Theeuwes pushes clients to take a '360-degree' view of retail and to succumb to the temptation of making 'disruptive choices'. / Photo by Miro Zwering

Maurice Mentjens
mauricementjens.com

Holtum, Netherlands-based Maurice Mentjens formed his interiors, furniture and product design studio in 1990. From initial design through the production or build-out of retail, office and restaurant or bar spaces, creativity and quality are the biggest priorities for Maurice Mentjens' dynamic, cherry-picked staff. The designer's richly layered environments are frequently influenced by the worlds of mythology, history, literature or the visual arts. / Photo by Veva van Sloun

Monki Store Concept
monki.com

The creative team of Stockholm-based international fashion retailer Monki have built more than 100 concept shops to date. Catharina Frankander directs concept designer Joel Degermark, store planner Sarah Otley and store developer Nick Scardigno, who have earned Monki a devoted clientele of young self-confident women through their eclectic, narrative, expressive interior concepts. Monki's imaginative worlds deepen the brand experience and make the shops, not just retail destinations but, destinations, in their own right.

Montalba Architects
montalbaarchitects.com

Architect David Montalba launched his eponymous practice in 2004. Today, his diverse team of 40 designers' work out of Santa Monica, California whilst maintaining a satellite office in Lausanne, Switzerland. The office's commissions include retail, residential and commercial projects in the United States, Europe, Asia, and the Middle East. Their human-centric, 'socially responsive' and aesthetically progressive design work focuses on context, but embraces the conceptual, as well. / Photo by Brin Morris

Moriyuki Ochiai Architects
moriyukiochiai.com

Tokyo-born Moriyuki Ochiai launched his practice in 2008 to do architecture, landscape architecture, interiors, industrial design and furniture with an emphasis on commercial environments, including retail and restaurants, even kindergartens and beauty salons. Ochiai finds inspiration in 'the vivacious beauty of nature,' especially that unique nature enshrined with care and discipline in Japanese temples and gardens. These qualities he interprets and applies to space with sophisticated naivete, in ways that are simultaneously straightforward and poetic.

Nomura/Ryutaro Matsuura
nomura-g.jp

Osaka-based Nomura may be one of the oldest continuously practicing design offices you'll see in the pages of avant-garde coffee table books: its history reaches back 120 years to 1892. Established by Taisuke Nomura, it originally designed displays of chrysanthemum dolls, which formed the basis of a popular pastime in late 19th-century Japan. Interior designer Ryutaro Matsuura is one of several Nomura creative directors taking on high-profile commissions for retail space, restaurants, hotels and shopping centres. / Photo by Nacása & Partners Inc.

Office AT
officeat.com

Headquartered in Bangkok, Thailand, Office AT came into being in 2002, founded by two partners Surachai Akekapobyotin and Juthathip Techachumreon. Having earned their early reputation from winning several competitions such as the first prize in an international competition sponsored by the Van Alen Institute of New York the firm now presents a wide range of expertise in architecture, interior design, master planning and research.

Open Air Studio
Openairstudio.com

Bangkok's Open Air Studio focuses on a materiality, structure, eloquent craftsmanship and the creation of 'sculptural experiences' that optimise the connection amongst objects, space and its users. Founder and designer Wit Chong earned a interior architecture degrees from Chulalongkorn University and the School of the Art Institute of Chicago, and on graduation, worked for Chicago-based Yabu Pushelberg and New York's AvroKO on hospitality projects, including hotels in Moscow and New Delhi and restaurants in New York, Las Vegas and Beijing.

Pablo Rodriguez
krop.com/pablo_rodriguez

Based in the Bavarian city of Herzogenaurach, renowned as the hometown of sportswear icons adidas and Puma, Pablo Rodriguez is a retail curator, who has designed global retail concepts, road maps and successful brand propositions for more than two decades. He has extensive experience creating retail design and development, retail marketing and communications and visual merchandising for a roster of big names, including adidas, Tommy Hilfiger, Samsonite and Levi's. Today he is Head of Global Retail Environments at Puma.
/ Photo by Adriano Biondo

Pinkeye
pinkeye.be

Antwerp-based Pinkeye is a design studio that values 'cross-inspirational' influences and the synergy inherent in multidisciplinary teams. Ruud Belmans and Thomas Vanden Abeele hung their shingle in the Belgian capital 10 years ago and now employ more than 20 graphic, interior and product designers whose boundary-hopping and collaborative process produce inventive solutions to projects ranging from logo, packaging and interior to product design. Pinkeye clients include Timberland, Coca-Cola, MAC Cosmetics and Douwe Egberts.

Prospace Asia
prospaceasia.com.cn/en

This retail insight and design agency in Xiamen also has offices in Sydney and Auckland. The creative teams' talents are focussed on the invention of fresh, relevant and engaging shopping experiences that give clients measurable results. The creative teams at Prospace Asia are made up of designers with diverse backgrounds and experience. Providing design, sourcing and project management, the firm has partnered with international brands in China, leading domestic retailers and clients hailing from around the globe.

Qwstion Studio
qwstion.com

In Switzerland, industrial designers Christian Paul Kaegi and Fabrice Aeberhard brought Qwstion to life together with Sebastian Kruit, Matthias Graf and Hannes Schoenegger in 2008 as a contemporary bag brand. Unable to find a backpack that could double as a functional and fashionable bag, they decided to make their own. Influenced by Swiss modernist design, they worked in Zurich's old industrial district, exploring their retail concept via four temporary spaces before opening the permanent shop and studio. / Photo by Sandra Kennel

Rafael de Cárdenas/ Architecture at Large
architectureatlarge.com

'We favour the strategic over the thematic, the cosmopolitan over the typological, and the atmospheric over the static,' says Rafael de Cárdenas, whose studio makes architecture, interiors, temporary spaces, furniture and integrated objects. Taking his earlier fashion career into design, Rafael de Cárdenas opened his own studio in 2006 in New York's Chinatown. The team – fashion designers to dancers and research scientists – is now 'day-dreaming the future' around the globe.

Rosie Lee
rosielee.co.uk

Rosie Lee are a hybrid design agency with offices in London and Amsterdam. Founded in 2000 with just two creatives, Rosie Lee has now grown to a team of over 25 talented individuals. Experts in retail design, branding and digital, their mission is to bring to life the innovative ideas brands need to flourish in today's cluttered marketplace. To keep concepts fresh, Rosie Lee have created a unique work environment where experimentation, collaboration and diversity are sown into the creative process. / Photo by Mark Whitfield

Savvy Studio
savvy-studio.net

Stories lie at the heart of Savvy Studio's design, architecture and branding. By collecting people's histories and emotions, Savvy weaves the concept for each project, thereby strengthening its client's relationship with the consumer. Savvy was established by Rafael Prieto and Eduardo Hernández in 2011. Today its three offices in Monterrey, Mexico City and New York City hum with the creativity of the 25 savvy graphic designers, architects, industrial and interior designers who put those tales to good use.
/ Photo by JuanPablo Celis

Schmidhuber
schmidhuber.com

Schmidhuber has designed expressions of brand through space for more than three decades. The firm's headquarters in Munich now consists of a multidisciplinary team of 70 creatives from the fields of architecture, design, and communications. This team provides a spectrum of solutions for representing a brand, and creating the experience of a brand, in three-dimensions. Repeat clients include companies in a variety of industries and various scales such as Grohe, Lamborghini, and Sony.

Sid Lee Architecture
sidleearchitecture.com
Formed in a 2009, merging with architecture firm Nomade, Sid Lee Architecture united architect and urban planner Jean Pelland and Martin Leblanc with a broad-spectrum creative agency. Working internationally from Montreal, the 35-person team comprises designers and artisans' expert in everything from urban studies and strategic development to brand integration and signage, who do cultural, residential, institutional, recreational and corporate projects. In 2015, Sid Lee joined kyu, a creative businesses collective and the second largest agency network in Asia.

Snarkitecture
Snarkitecture.com
Co-founded by Alex Mustonen and Daniel Arsham in 2008, Snarkitecture explores the disciplinary boundaries between art and architecture. The name is drawn from Lewis Carroll's *The Hunting of The Snark*, a poem describing an 'impossible voyage of an improbable crew to find an inconceivable creature.' From permanent architectural-scale projects to functional objects, the New York-based practice manipulates and reinterprets existing materials, structures and programs to make architecture perform the unexpected. / Photo by Noah Kalina

Square One
squareone.ro
Adrian Cancer-Zeana and Robert Marin launched Square One in 2001 as a multidisciplinary practice working across the fields of architecture, interior, product and graphic design. Today, the creative team, consisting of six architects and designers directed by Cancer-Zeana with partner Sabin Dumitriu, also do project management and delivers turnkey projects. Eager to explore new areas, they resolve every project –whether a building, environment, object, graphics or even scenography for film or theatre – using playfully sculptural forms.

Stefano Tordiglione Design
stdesign.it
Artist, art director, urban planner and architect Stefano Tordiglione was born in Napoli, but studied and worked in both New York and London for more than a decade. From 1991, he began to work for Italian studios that were doing retail, luxury hotel, restaurant and residential commissions. He finally established his own studio in Hong Kong – with collaborators in Rome, Milan, Florence and Bari – characterised by an 'East meets West' sensibility and research-driven process.

Studio Arthur Casas
arthurcasas.com
'From inside to outside, from object to landscape', the work of Studio Arthur Casas is contemporary, Brazilian, cosmopolitan and casually elegant, and relies on an intense dialogue between Arthur Casas and his creative team. Arthur Casas studied architecture and urban planning at São Paulo's Mackenzie University (1983). Today his São Paulo and New York offices take commissions – more than 200 in the last five years – that include residential and commercial architecture, interiors and product design. / Photo by Jhonatan Chicaroni

Studio David Thulstrup
StudioDavidThulstrup.com
Danish architect David Thulstrup launched Copenhagen-based Studio David Thulstrup in 2009. Today the 10-person practice provides architectural, interior and design services internationally for both private and commercial clients with a predilection for fashion retail projects and residential space. The studio is well-known for its preference for close collaboration with clients to craft inventive architectural solutions that respond to the individual's or business's functional needs while synthesizing and broadcasting their identity and essential values. / Photo by Peter Krasilnikoff

Studio Mokum
studiomokum.com
Amsterdam-based Studio Mokum provides comprehensive concept and design, inventing or reinventing brand identities, interiors, architecture and communications, including packaging. Architects Jasper Klinkhamer and Thijs de Ruiter, with brand designer Klas Bennergard, want to forge a deeper connection between building and brand design. Since 2015, they have been creating concepts, store formats, interior design, buildings, brand identity, graphic design, art direction and strategy for large multinational businesses, as well as ambitious smaller brands.

Studio Sklim
sklim.com
Singapore-born and based, Kevin Lim graduated from the Architectural Association in London and founded his own studio in 2010. Studio Sklim is an international agency, designing furniture, interiors, landscapes, and doing architecture and urban planning. Lim is interested in simplicity, material tactility and design's relationship with the environment. He also believes that 'banality breeds creativity': each project must put down roots in its own soil, in 'the pragmatics and constraints'. / Photo by Khoo Guo Jie

studiojosvandijk
studiojosvandijk.com
Amsterdam-based Jos van Dijk has been designing and creative directing for more than 15 years, working across several disciplines and teaching retail architecture at the Technical University of Delft in the Netherlands. Jos Van Dijk's eponymous studio has earned kudos for its dextrous development of strong architectural images through unexpectedly minimalist solutions. His creative process tends to flush away unnecessary details as it converts brand characters into robust spatial images and attractive architectural identities.

Suppose Design Office
suppose.jp

Since 2000, architects Makoto Tanijiri and Ai Yoshida have worked on local and international commissions from offices in Hiroshima and Tokyo. They have designed workspace, site frameworks, landscapes, products, art installations and more than 100 houses. Their interest in the problem-solving and creative challenges of architecture extends through all scales and budgets from 'dog houses to skyscrapers' and both the new and the familiar inform their search for fresh solutions to the issues of everyday life.

Triad China
triad.de/en

This Berlin-based creative agency specialises in spatial communication and has been designing and producing international exhibitions, museums, theme parks, trade fairs, brand environments, retail spaces and events since Professor Lutz Engelke founded the office in 1994. Today, Triad has offices handy in Berlin, Shanghai and Riyadh, where it draws on the expertise and imaginations of more than 200 managers, architects, designers, engineers and 'humanists', working on projects in more than 40 countries.

UXUS
uxus.com

The name of this Amsterdam-based global strategic design consultancy is an abbreviation of 'you times us'. The studio works to unite art and design and generate 'brand desire' in retail, hospitality, architecture, graphic, consumer experience and digital design for multinationals that include Selfridges, Sephora, H&M, Nike, InterContinental Hotels Group and the Tate Modern. As part of FutureBrand and IPG, the studio can also scale its services to any size or location. / Photo by Marc Haers

VIU
shopviu.com

Zurich-based VIU is a high-end eyewear label that puts particular emphasis on creativity and sustainability, wedding Swiss design to Italian manufacture and reasonable prices. VIU creative director Fabrice Aeberhard is responsible for designing both the brand's eyewear and its shop interiors. His simultaneously contemporary and classic frames come in subdued colours and are handmade in a traditional family-run manufactory in Italy through a meticulous 80-step process that makes them look as good as their optics are accurate. / Photo by Sandra Kennel

Wilson Brothers
wilsonbrothers.co.uk

The Wilson Brothers are London based siblings Oscar & Ben who teamed up to launch a creative partnership in 2006. Since then the two have worked internationally with global brands in various areas, often focusing on creating custom brand experiences within retail environments. The company also works on industrial design projects, and 2D graphics and illustration, alongside custom-made 3D furnishings and products / Photo by Sarah Wilson

shop addresses

adidas and Reebok Showroom (p.154)
by D'art Design Gruppe
Ostring 26
63533 Mainhausen
Germany
o1-mainhausen.de

Aesop Munich (p.056)
by einszu33
Maximiliansplatz 10
80333 Munich
Germany
aesop.com

Aesop Rundle Street (p.062)
by Genesin Studio
232 Rundle Street
5000 Adelaide
Australia
aesop.com.au

Air&Craft (p.312)
by Open Air Studio
7 Naradhiwas Soi 10
10120 Sathorn, Bangkok
Thailand
airandcraft.com

Amicis Women (p.158)
by Denis Košutić
Tuchlauben 11
1010 Vienna
Austria
amicis.at

Araldi 1930 (p.006)
by Grey Canopy
181 Orchard Road,
Orchard Central
238896 Singapore
Singapore
araldi.com

Audi Ultrastore (p.100)
(temporary store)
by Schmidhuber
Bikini Berlin
Budapester Straße 38-50
10787 Berlin
Germany

Avenue Coliseum (p.160)
by Claudio Pironi
& Partners
131 Neftchiliar Avenue
Baku
Azerbaijan

Bazar Noir (p.102)
by Hidden Fortress
Kreuzbergstraße 78
10965 Berlin
Germany
shop.bazar-noir.com

Bears & Friends (p.270)
by kplus konzept
Rathaus-Galerie
Mittelstraße 20
58095 Hagen
Germany
bears-friends.de

Birks (p.010)
by Sid Lee Architecture
9120 Leduc Blvd.
Quartier Dix30
Brossard, QC J4Y 0L3
Canada
maisonbirks.com

Bolon Eyewear (p.014)
by Ippolito Fleitz Group
1189 Nanjing West Road,
Jing'an District
Shanghai
China
boloneyewear.com

CA4LA (p.016)
by Line-Inc.
1F/2F Jinnanzaka Frame
1-18-2 Jinnan Shibuya-ku
150-0041 Tokyo
Japan
ca4la.com

Cardif Lab (p.374)
by Fabrice Ausset
Interior Design
8 Rue Du Port
92728 Nanterre Cedex
France
bnpparibascardif.com

Carturesti Carusel (p.078)
by Square One
Strada Lipscani 55,
Centrul istoric
030033 Bucharest
Romania
carturesticarusel.ro

Casa Bosques (p.084)
by Savvy Studio
Córdoba 25 Col. Roma Norte
06700 Mexico City
Mexico
casabosques.net

Casadei Flagship (p.352)
by Marco Costanzi Architects
Piazza S. Lorenzo
in Luchina 40
00186 Rome
Italy
casadei.com

Christian Louboutin (p.356)
by Household
Brentwood Country Mart
225 South 26th Street #35
Santa Monica, CA 90402
United States

COS (p.166)
by Snarkitecture
(temporary store)
912 South Hill Street
Los Angeles, CA 90015
United States
cosstores.com

**Crème de la Crème
Perfume Lab** (p.066)
by Inblum Architects
Viru Keskus Shoping center
Viru Valjak 4
10111 Tallinn
Estonia
virukeskus.com

De Balkonie (p.314)
by Studio Mokum
Jan Evertsenstraat 90
1056 EG Amsterdam
the Netherlands
debalkonie.nl

De Bijenkorf (p.136)
by Campaign Design
Piazza 1
5611 AE Eindhoven
the Netherlands
debijenkorf.nl

Delfina Delettrez (p.020)
by Rafael de Cardenas/
Architecture at Large
109 Mount Street, Mayfair
London W1K 2TR 5
United Kingdom
delfinadelettrez.it

Dinh Van (p.022)
by Stefano
Tordiglione Design
1008 1F, ifc Mall,
8 Finance Street
Hong Kong
China

Drubba Moments (p.024)
by Ippolito Fleitz Group
Seestraße 37-41
79822 Titisee-Neustadt
Germany
drubba.com

**Duke Street
Emporium** (p.108)
by Dalziel & Pow
55 Duke Street
London W1K 5NR
United Kingdom
dukestreetemporium.com

Elb (p.168)
by Corneille
Uedingslohmann
Architekten
Einkaufszentrum Gerber
Sophienstraße 21
70178 Stuttgart
Germany
guna.de

Elegant Prosper (p.170)
by Studio David Thulstrup
102 Fengqi Road
310006 Hangzhou
China
elegant-prosper.com

Engelhorn (p.140)
by Blocher Blocher Partners
O5.8
68161 Mannhein
Germany
engelhorn.de

Era Bank (p.378)
by IO Studio
ERA FC, Shopping
center Quadrio
Spálená 2121/22,
Nové Město
110 00 Prague
Czech Republic

Etq store (p.176)
by studiojosvandijk
Singel 465
1012 WP Amsterdam
the Netherlands
etqstore.com

Frame Store (p.110)
(temporary store)
by i29 Interior Architects
Keizersgracht 324
1016 EZ Amsterdam
the Netherlands

Frame Store (p.114)
(temporary store)
by i29 Interior Architects
Herengracht 178
1016 BR Amsterdam
the Netherlands

Galeries Lafayette (p.144)
by HMKM
110 Xidan N Street
Xidan, Beijing
China
galerieslafayette.cn

Georg Jensen (p.026)
by Studio David Thulstrup
Maffeistraße 4
80333 Munich
Germany
georgjensen.com

H. Stern (p.032)
by Studio Arthur Casas
649 5th Ave
New York, NY 10022
United States

**Hearts On Fire
Shanghai** (p.034)
by Christophe Carpente
CAPS Architecture
Interior Design
Nanjing Road
Shanghai
China

**Hearts On Fire
Taipei** (p.036)
by Christophe Carpente
CAPS Architecture
Interior Design
Eslite Dept Store
No.11 Songgao Road
Xinyi District, Taipei
Taiwan

**Henkel Global
Experience Center** (p.316)
by D'art Design Gruppe
Building A04, Factory Site
Dusseldorf
Germany
henkel.com

Home Park (p.272)
by Triad China
Yuanda Grand
Shopping Mall Level B1
Daoli District, Qunli Avenue
150070 Harbin, Heilongjiang
China

Honda Showroom (p.332)
by Office AT
99/8 Moo3 Srisathong sub-
district Nakornchaisri district
73120 Nakonpatom
Thailand

House of Smart (p.116)
by Maurice Mentjens
Willemstraat 29
5611 HB Eindhoven
the Netherlands
houseofsmart.nl

Hunter Gatherer (p.278)
by Triad China
Hubindao Mall B1-E04
150 Hubin Road
200021 Shanghai
China
behuntergatherer.com

Kindo (p.182)
by Anagrama
Río Volga No. 514
66220 San Pedro Garza
García, Nuevo León
Mexico
kindoshop.com

Klos (p.318)
by Nomura/Ryutaro Matsuura
Grand Front Osaka Tower A
12F, 4-20 Ofuka-cho
530-0011 Kita-ku, Osaka
Japan
koizumi-lt.co.jp/klos/

KPN (p.380)
by DoepelStrijkers
Barteljorisstraat 20
2011 RB Haarlem
the Netherlands

Krungsri Bank (p.382)
by Concept i
3F, Emquartier,
689 Sukhumvit,
Khlong Tan Nuea
10110 Vadhana, Bangkok
Thailand
krungsri.com

Kult (p.186)
by Corneille
Uedingslohmann
Architekten
Rathaus Galerie
Mittelstraße 22
58095 Hagen
Germany
guna.de

**Kurt Geiger
Harrods** (p.362)
by Campaign Design
Harrods
87-135 Brompton Road
London SW1X 7XL
United Kingdom
harrods.com

Lax (p.188)
by Genesin Studio
LG14 Adeliade Central Plaza
5000 Adelaide
Australia
laxfashion.com.au

Libreria Conarte (p.088)
by Anagrama
Abasolo, Barrio Antiguo
64000 Monterrey,
Nuevo León
Mexico
conarte.org.mx/lugares/libreria

Mackage Flagship (p.190)
by Burdifilek
CF Carrefour Laval,
3035 BLVD Le Carrefour,
Unit A-019A
Laval, QC H7T 1C8
Canada
mackage.com

Mark Lash Flagship (p.038)
by Burdifilek
480 Eglinton Avenue West
Toronto, ON M5N 1A5
Canada
marklash.com

**Matrix Pop-up Store
& Club** (p.336)
by KMS Blackspace
Westend Palais, Ludwig-
Erhard-Anlage 2-8
60327 Frankfurt
Germany

Max Mara (p.192)
By Duccio Grassi Architects
19-21 Old Bond Street
London W1S 4PU
United Kingdom
it.maxmara.com

Mazda Showroom (p.340)
by Suppose Design Office
5-14-22 Himonya, Meguro-ku
152-0003 Tokyo
Japan
kanto-mazda.com

Men at Work (p.196)
by Mark't
Magna Plaza
Nieuwezijds
Voorburgwal 182hs
1012 SJ Amsterdam
the Netherlands
menatwork.nl

Mercedes me Store (p.346)
by Kauffmann Theilig
& Partner and Atelier
Markgraph
Ballinndamm 17
20095 Hamburg
Germany
mercedes-benz.com

Momom Store (p.284)
by Moriyuki Ochiai Architects
Hino
Tokyo
Japan

R Hair Salon (p.068)
by Creneau International
Shopping 1
Rootenstraat 13, bus 13
3600 Genk
Belgium

Rattan Clouds (p.120)
by Studio Sklim
60 Somme Road,
Le Somme 01-03
207876 Singapore
Singapore
shop.eomm.co

Reiss (p.238)
by d-raw
220 Yonge Street
Toronto, ON M5B 2H1
Canada
cfshops.com

Run2Day (p.240)
by Brinkworth
Meent 75
3011 JE Rotterdam
the Netherlands

**Saraiva
Bookstore** (p.092)
by Studio Arthur Casas
Village Mall
Av. das Américas 3900,
Barra da Tijuca
22640-102 Rio de Janeiro
Brazil
saraiva.com.br

**Schüco
Showroom** (p.122)
by D'art Design Gruppe
Karolinenstraße 1-15
33609 Bielefeld
Germany
schueco.com

**Selfridges Denim
Studio** (p.242)
by HMKM
400 Oxford Street
London W1A 1AB
United Kingdom
selfridges.com

Septwolves Flagship (p.244)
by Prospace Asia
Wu Yi Industry &
Trading Area
189 Lian Yue Road
361000 Xiamen
China

Síminn (p.392)
by Haf Studio
Ármúli 25
Reykjavik
Iceland

Sleep Design (p.328)
by Creneau International
Hasseltweg 309
3600 Genk
Belgium
sleep-design.be

Stills (p.248)
by DoepelStrijkers
Steenhouwersvest 54
2000 Antwerp
Belgium
stills-atelier.com

Stone Fresh (p.302)
by Triad China
Plaza Mall 2F, Store 39B
196 Daduhe Road,
Putuo District
200062 Shanghai
China
stonefresh.com

Stride (p.250)
by Rosie Lee
Frunzenskaya
naberezhnaya 32
119146 Moscow
Russia
striderunning.ru

T2 (p.308)
by Landini Associates
48-52 Redchurch Street,
Shorditch
London E2 7DP
United Kingdom
t2tea.com

TCL Electronics (p.126)
by Coordination Asia
1F, TCL Tower,
Gao Xin South 1st Avenue
TCL Building, Science
and Technology Park
Shenzhen,
Guangdong Province
China
kuyumall.com

Telenet (p.396)
by Pinkeye
Zonnestraat 1
9000 Ghent
Belgium
telenet.be

**The Galleria Luxury
Hall West** (p.148)
by HMKM
110 Xidan N Street, Xicheng
Xidan, Beijing
China
galerieslafayette.cn

The Nike Studio (p.128)
by Coordination Asia
Beijing
China

**The Olive-Tree
Pharmacy Flagship** (p.070)
by dfrost
Neue Schoenhauser
Strasse 11
10178 Berlin
Germany

The Row (p.254)
by Montalba Architects
8440 Melrose Place
Los Angeles, CA 90069
United States
therow.com

The Secretcloset (p.260)
by Line-Inc.
1F Marunouchi Brick Square
2-6-1 Marunouchi Chiyoda-ku
100-6901 Tokyo
Japan
thesecretcloset-tokyo.com

The Tailor Shop (p.044)
by Ippolito Fleitz Group
Atrium Mall
ul. Zemlyanoy Val 33
Moscow
Russia

Tomorrowland
Boutique (p.132)
by Creneau International
Kammenstraat 43
2000 Antwerp
Belgium
boutique.tomorrowland.com

Toop (p.046)
by Pinkeye
Mechelstraat 41
3000 Leuven
Belgium
toopoptiek.com

Unilever Network (p.072)
by Open Air Studio
Unilever House 161
Rama 9 Road, Huay Kwang
10310 Bangkok
Thailand
unilevernetwork.com

VIU Flagship (p.050)
by VIU
Potsdamer Straße 77/79
10785 Berlin
Germany
shopviu.com

Vodafone Flagship (p.400)
by KMS Blackspace
Schildergasse 69
50667 Cologne
Germany
vodafone.de

Ware-mo-kou (p.262)
by Ito Masaru Design
Project/SEI
Jinnanzaka Frame Bldg. 1F,
1-18-2 Jinnan
150-0041 Shibuya-ku, Tokyo
Japan
waremo-kou.jp

POWERSHOP 5
New Retail Design

Publisher
Frame Publishers

Production
Melika Aghabeigi and
Sarah de Boer-Schultz

Author
Shonquis Moreno

Graphic Design
Studio Adriaan Mellegers

Prepress
Edward de Nijs

Cover Photography
Estudio Tampiquito and
Noah Kalina

Trade distribution USA and Canada
Consortium Book Sales
& Distribution, LLC.
34 Thirteenth Avenue NE, Suite 101
Minneapolis, MN 55413-1007
United States
T +1 612 746 2600
T +1 800 283 3572 (orders)
F +1 612 746 2606

Trade distribution rest of world
Thames & Hudson Ltd
181A High Holborn
London WC1V 7QX
United Kingdom
T +44 20 7845 5000
F +44 20 7845 5050

Trade distribution Benelux
Frame Publishers
Laan der Hesperiden 68
1076 DX Amsterdam
the Netherlands
distribution@frameweb.com
frameweb.com

ISBN: 978-94-91727-93-1

Whilst every effort has been made to ensure accuracy, Frame Publishers
does not under any circumstances accept responsibility for errors
or omissions. Any mistakes or inaccuracies will be corrected in case
of subsequent editions upon notification to the publisher.

Printed on acid-free paper produced from chlorine-free pulp.
TCF ∞

Printed in Turkey

987654321